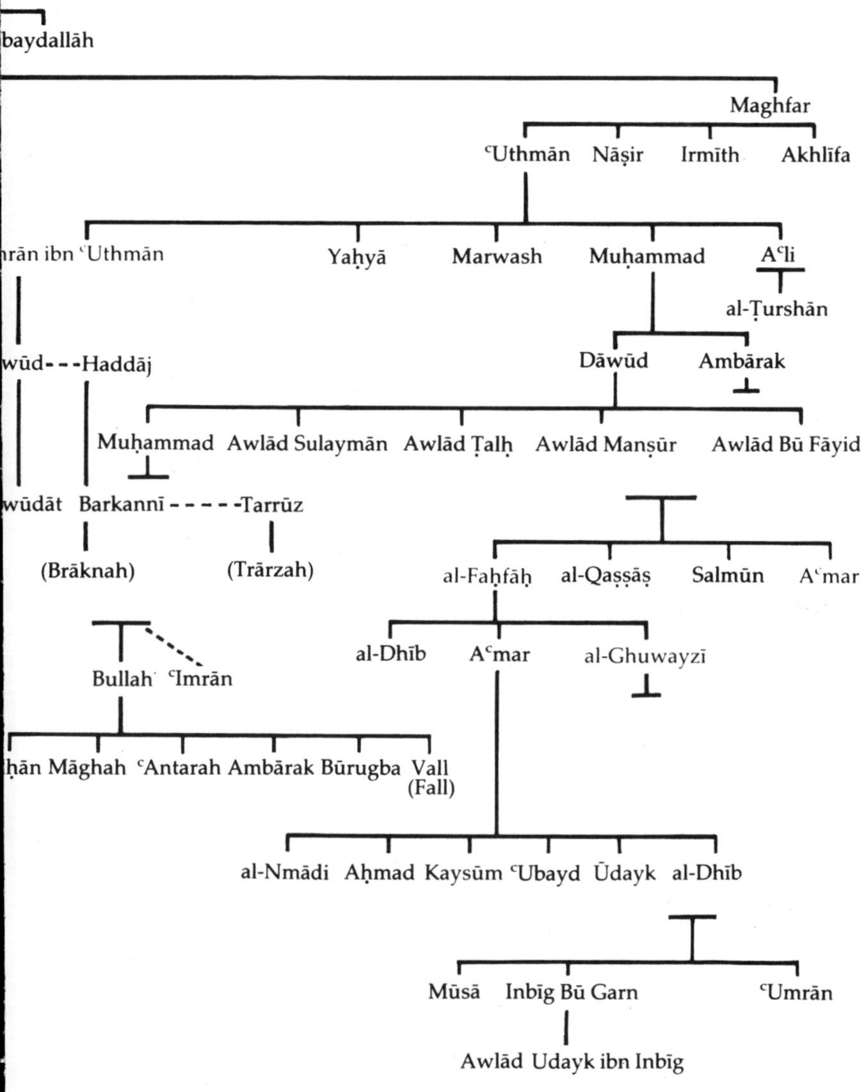

baydallāh

Maghfar

ʿUthmān Nāṣir Irmīth Akhlīfa

rān ibn ʿUthmān   Yaḥyā Marwash Muḥammad Aʿli

al-Ṭurshān

wūd- - -Haddāj   Dāwūd Ambārak

Muḥammad Awlād Sulaymān Awlād Ṭalḥ Awlād Manṣūr Awlād Bū Fāyid

wūdāt Barkannī - - - - -Tarrūz

(Brāknah)   (Trārzah)   al-Faḥfāḥ al-Qaṣṣāṣ Salmūn Aʿmar

al-Dhīb Aʿmar al-Ghuwayzī

Bullah ʿImrān

ḥān Māghah ʿAntarah Ambārak Būrugba Vall
(Fall)

al-Nmādi Aḥmad Kaysūm ʿUbayd Ūdayk al-Dhīb

Mūsā Inbīg Bū Garn   ʿUmrān

Awlād Udayk ibn Inbīg

Arab Background Series

Editor: N. A. Ziadeh, Emeritus Professor of History,
American University of Beirut

By the same author

Shinqīṭī Folk Literature and Song, 1968
Saharan Myth and Saga, 1972
The Tuaregs, 1975
The Pilgrimage of Aḥmad, Son of the Little Bird of Paradise, 1977
The Adventures of Antar, 1980
The Berbers in Arabic Literature, 1982

The Arab Conquest of the Western Sahara

Studies of the historical events, religious beliefs and social customs which made the remotest Sahara a part of the Arab World

H. T. Norris

Longman
Librairie du Liban

Longman Group Limited,
Longman House,
Burnt Mill,
Harlow, Essex, CM20 2JE

Librairie du Liban,
Beirut, Lebanon

First published 1986

British Library Cataloguing in Publication Data
Norris, H. T.
The Arab conquest of the Western Sahara : studies of the historical events, religious beliefs and social customs which made the remotest Sahara a part of the Arab world.—(Arab background series)
1. Arabs—Sahara—History
I. Title II. Series
964′.802 DT346.S7

ISBN 0-582-75643-X

Set in 11/12 Imprint
Produced by Longman Singapore Publishers (Pte) Ltd.
Printed in Singapore

Contents

Editor's Preface

The Arab world has, for some time, been attracting the attention of a growing public throughout the world. The strategic position of the Arab countries, the oil they produce, their sudden emancipation and emergence as independent states, their revolutions and *coups d'état*, have been the special concern of statesmen, politicians, businessmen, scholars and journalists and of equal interest to the general public.

An appreciation of the present-day problems of Arab countries and their immediate neighbours demands a certain knowledge of their geographical and social background; and a knowledge of the main trends of their history – political, cultural and religious – is essential for an understanding of current issues. Arabs had existed long before the advent of Islam in the seventh century AD, but it was with Islam that they became a world power. Arab civilisation, which resulted from the contacts the Arabs had with other peoples and cultures, especially after the creation of this world power, and which reached its height in the ninth, tenth and eleventh centuries, was, for a few centuries that followed, the guiding light of a large part of the world. Its rôle cannot, thus, be ignored.

The Arab Background series will provide the English-speaking, educated reader with a series of books which will clarify the historical past of the Arabs, and analyse their present-day problems. The contributors to the series, who come from many parts of the world, are all specialists in their respective fields. This variety of approach and attitude creates for the English-speaking reader a unique picture of the Arab world.

N. A. Ziadeh

Author's Preface

The aim of this book is to examine a number of themes which have appeared in my earlier publications written over a period of some twenty years.

New material, discovered in unpublished texts, and obtained through discussion with scholars in the Sahara, has made increasingly improbable my interpretations which seemed to afford an explanation, or to make sense, of the obscure past of the Western Saharan peoples. It became necessary to look afresh at the events and movements which made the Western Sahara, in its widest sense, a part of the Arabic-speaking world.

Some opinions expressed in previous works, more especially in *Saharan Myth and Saga*, 1972, and *The Tuaregs*, 1975, need to be completely restated and rephrased, and in several instances I would now favour a view which contradicts others I once held. I have to thank my Saharan and Sahelian friends, Shaykh Mukhtār wuld Ḥāmidun, Shaykh Muḥammad Ibrāhīm al-Aghlālī, Muḥammad al-Chennafi, Shaykh Muḥammad ag Nūḥ, Shaykh Muḥammad al-Imām ibn al-Shaykh Mā' al-ʿAynayn and M. Zoubeir. To the Centre Aḥmad Bābā, in Timbuctoo, to Dr S. Wood, to Dr J. Bynon and Paul Fox, both at the School of Oriental and African Studies, University of London, I am indebted for microfilms and illustrative material.

Some of the material which is to be found in the conclusion to this study was presented in a seminar held this March in the University of Exeter. I owe much to subsequent discussion and exchange of views.

Likewise, several topics which are introduced in the Epistle of Shaykh Muḥammad Ignan Wa-n-Fadasen al-Sūqī al-Gunahānī al-ʿArabī, Appendix II of this book, were discussed at the Paris Conference, *Les Agents Religieux Islamiques en Afrique Tropicale*, in December of this year, and I am grateful to its organisers for allowing me to make several quotations of, as yet, unpublished material.

I am most grateful to all the staff of the Arab World Division at Longman House for their help with this book. They have taken great pains to make it as accurate and as attractive as possible.

Newport, Essex, 1983

List of Plates

Plate 1

The Kel Intasar and the Iwillimmeden are usually included amongst the Tuareg peoples of the Central Sahara. They occupy the southern Sahara and the Sahel between the Niger Buckle in Mali and the Aïr Massif in the Niger Republic. The Iwillimmeden are sub-divided into the Kel Aṭarām (Western Iwillimmeden) and Kel Denneg (Eastern Iwillimmeden), in Mali and Niger respectively. All these Tuareg speak *Tamasheq* although they have their own dialects; nonetheless both the Kel Intasar and the Iwillimmeden have historical connections, social customs and material culture in common with the Moors of the Western Sahara. They are patrilineal in succession and the "maraboutic" class (whether Kel Es-Sūq *Ineslemen* or Kuntah *Zwāya*) amongst them is as clearly defined as it is amongst the Mauritanian Moors. The impact of Arab culture has grown amongst the Iwillimmeden since the seventeenth century. The Kel Intasar began to be Arabised at an earlier date. Many of them claim descent from the Anṣār, the Prophet's helpers, and they speak *Ḥassāniyyah*.

Johannes Nicolaisen wrote in his "Political Systems of Pastoral Tuareg in Aïr and Ahaggar", *Folk*, Vol 1, 1959, page 119:

"Arab pastoralists now living in Tuareg countries frequently use Tuareg mat-covered huts and skin tents. Of particular interest is the type of skin tent used by the Deremchaka Arabs living amongst the Eastern Ioullemmeden (the Kel Dinnik). To support the sheet of skin sewn together these Arabs use a very short crossbar resting on the tops of two oblique poles. A similar or related construction is found in black tents of the Brakna Arabs, and is common in black tents of Algeria including the northern parts of [the] Algerian Sahara. And according to tradition the Deremchaka Arabs have adopted a mode of construction typical of certain black tents [similar] to the Tuareg skin tent, and there may perhaps be another example of this among the Southern Tuareg:– The Tuareg known as Kel Antassar in the region of Timbuktu frequently use a very short crossbar resting on the tops of two central oblique posts to support their skin tents. The Kel Antassar Tuareg are of religious status; their presumed Arab origin gives rise to the supposition that they formerly had black tents."

Muḥammad al-Mukhtār (left) of the Kel Denneg, a friend of the author, is an Arabic teacher. He studied Classical Arabic in the Orient and he is acquainted with the poets of the Iwillemmeden who versify in Classical Arabic. There are many amongst the Kel Aghlāl, the Kel Es-Sūq and the Kel Intasar.

(Photo by H. T. Norris)

Plate 2

A Western Saharan Moor in the region of Āmugjār (Adrār of Mauritania). It is during his long solitary journeys that the Moor composes lyrics in *Ḥassāniyyah* in the manner of the poets of ancient Arabia. Many of the emotions, the vocabulary and the imagery are the same in their verse.

The following is a *Ḥassāniyyah* poem from Azawād (Mali) which expresses the sentiments of the Moor who is absent from his tribe and his beloved for long intervals.

Ghīd ghayrik
Women other than thou

Another than thou, O beauty of all beauties,
were I to say to her, I love her, it would be
to play deceitfully, or else to lie aloud, no less.

For thee my love is honest and sincere, it is –
be quite convinced of it – my truest feeling, it
is myself laid bare. Besides, thou hast already
seen it for thyself.

While I tarry in this neighbourhood, the tribal
homeland, no other maid will keep me company, nor be
seen to be the mistress of my heart. And even if I
have to take my leave, I shall depart. But note me
well. I shall not have another love where'er I go.

O flower of my heart, the proof that my heart loves
thee, that in thee can be found its deepest joy, is
that I can swear an oath before thee with my hand,

my right hand, a most solemn oath.
I also pledge, upon my honour, that amongst all
beauteous women, thou only art the antelope of beauty,
thou my *rīm*.

Cited by Hamid Ben Alhousseini
of Azawād, Mali.

(Photo by Dr Simon Wood)

Plate 3

The nomads of the Western Sahara and the adjacent Sahel have a number of underprivileged, oppressed and servile classes, not to mention a large number of slaves or ex-slaves. Some of these are represented by distinct ethnic groups – Negro or Berber – others are clearly distinct professions and "service industries", for example hunters, fisherfolk on the coast of the Río de Oro and Mauritania, smiths and artisans, and griots. Yet others are tillers in the oases and workers in date groves, the *Ḥarāṭīn*. Most of these folk are descendants of conquered peoples who dwelt in the Sahara in very ancient times.

It cannot be said that Arabic culture has affected them, save the smiths and the griots and the troubadours attached to the courts of the Ḥassānī and the Iwillimmeden princes. Arabic culture was a thin veneer in the bulk of Ḥassānī society. The accounts of Westerners such as George Glas, Thomas Pellow, Mungo Park and several Frenchmen whose accounts are given in Maurice Barbier's *Trois Français au Sahara Occidental en 1784–1786*, L'Harmattan, Paris, 1984, make this vividly clear.

Only recently has Mauritania seriously tackled the abolition of slavery within its borders. The Anti-Slavery Society and the United Nations have pressed hard for this to be carried out despite the frightful problems of the drought which has beset Mauritania and its neighbours and which affects all classes in the society.

It is usually overlooked that jurists amongst the Kel Es-Sūq and the Zwāya of Mauritania and Mali have, with the pen, for long castigated the practice of unlawful enslavement outside the rules of canonic law [the *Sharī'ah*]. Such enslavement is an example of property becoming so infected by illegal acquisition by purchase or seizure that this property is wholly "absorbed by illegality" [*Istighrāq al-Dhimmah*]. Only a direct ruling from a qualified jurist [*faqīh*] coupled with the imposition of the will of a truly Muslim prince, be he a Ḥassānī *Amīr* or a Tuareg *Amenukal* could, or can, cut the knot of this illegality. A scholar of the Kel Es-Sūq expressed his horror of this situation in his work, *Naṣīḥat al-Ummah*. In his view it had partly come about due to the taking of land tax [*kharāj*] from all and sundry despite its contravention of the *Sharīʿah*. He also blamed shortcomings in his profession, despite its Islamic education, "One reason for the confusion between free-men by birth [*aḥrār*] and others by manumission is due to inattentive *Qāḍīs* in time past, inattentive to the details of their profession; ignorance of lineages, history and local custom both good and bad".

(Photo by Dr Simon Wood)

Plate 4

The human caravan determined the siting of many of the towns in the Sahara. It was the trade in gold, the transport of slaves, the exchange of salt and the pursuit of learning which led to the founding of Sijilmāsah in Morocco, Awdaghust and the *quṣūr* of Wādān, Tīshīt and Walātah in Mauritania, Timbuctoo in Mali, and Ouargla (Wārjlān) and the *quṣūr* of Tuwāt in Algeria. All these towns were founded before the arrival of the Banū Maʿqil. Two that owed their very existence, in part, to the Ḥassānīs were Arawān and Bū Jbayha.

Arawān came into being on account of the opening of the salt mine at Taoudeni (Tawdannī) in Northern Mali. According to one tradition it was the dream of two scholars, Muḥammad Quṭb of the Kel Intasar and Sīdī Aḥmad ibn Āddah of the Kel Es-Sūq, who left Es-Sūq (ancient Tādamakkat) about 1575. He died around 1620. Arawān became an important holy place for the Ḥassānī Barābīsh. The foundation of Bū Jbayha was also due to the Kel Es-Sūq and it occurred towards the end of the eighteenth century. *Ṭālib* Sīdī Aḥmad ibn al-Bashīr ibn Muḥammad ibn Muḥammad Aḥmad ibn Mūsā ibn Būkum al-Sūqī, a highly respected scholar of Arawān, took with him *Shurafā*' of Mawlāy Aḥmad al-Sā'iḥ and several Īdaw ʿAlī, whose home town was Shinqīṭī in Mauritania, and they founded the settlement as a satellite of Arawān. They were supported by *Shaykh* Muḥammad ibn Raḥḥāl of the Awlād Sulaymān, one of the Barābīsh Awlād Ḥassān. Here is an example, and there are many, of cooperation between "Moor and Tuareg" in the region of Azawād. The common devotion to Arabic learning and Arabian lineages took preference to social customs which may have divided them. The Friday Prayer was said for the first time in Bū Jbayha on 3 *Ṣafar* 1212, 6 December 1797, though some sources dispute the lateness of this date.

Some caravans are seasonal, others small, when whole families move to new pastures and they take with them all that they possess, their families, their tents and their herds. The Moors have listed their possessions which they love the most in many of their poems. One of the most famous of *Ḥassānī gāfs* expresses it as follows:

> Here and now all that I wish for are five things.
> The man who possesses them can call himself truly happy.
> I desire a copy of the Mukhtaṣar of Khalīl [in *fiqh*],
> and to know by heart all the *Sūras* in the Koran.
> I wish to own a herd of camels, to have Khadījah as my wife,
> and, last of all, to gain my reward in the garden of Paradise.

(Photo by Dr Simon Wood)

Plate 5

The Marīnids were the dominant ruling dynasty in Morocco during the thirteenth and fourteenth centuries. Their forces are depicted in the *Cantigas* of King Alfonso El Sabio. They are familiar to English readers inasmuch as they are mentioned in the Prologue to Chaucer's *Canterbury Tales*. The Knight there is said to have raided them in the name of his faith, and to have jousted for the faith in Tilimsān (Tlemcen). It now seems likely that the Knight was a mercenary in his days, rather less a Christian knight. Some of the Banū Maʿqil were likewise mercenaries. One can, with justice, say that the conquest of the Western Sahara by the Maʿqil, the definitive "Arab" conquest, began in the days of the Marīnids.

The Maʿqil undertook errands of state for the Marīnids to the court of Mansā Mūsā, the king of Mali. Gifts were sent to the latter, so Ibn Khaldūn tells us, by the hand of ʿAlī ibn Ghānim, the *Amīr* of Maʿqil. The Maʿqil were masters of the oases of Tuwāt, key caravan centres, their territory "marches with that of the Sūdān".

The Moroccan Sūs was their sphere of influence and the Ṣanhājah nomads to the south were driven further into the Sahara in order to avoid them. Ibn Khaldūn says: "The Sūs is the territory of the Lamṭa and Gazūla; the Lamṭa [wander] towards the Daran mountains and Gazūla towards the desert and the sands. When the Maʿqil Arabs conquered and divided the plains of the Sūs the Shabānāt [division of Maʿqil] were nearest to Daran and so the Lamṭa clans became their confederates whereas the Gazūla became confederates of the Dhawī Ḥassān; and such is the situation to this day". (Ibn Khaldūn, *Kitāb al-ʿIbar*, as translated by N. Levtzion and J. F. P. Hopkins in their *Corpus of early Arabic Sources for West African history*, Cambridge University Press, 1981, page 337.)

This is amongst the earliest mentionings of the Awlād Ḥassān in the Western Sahara.

Plate 6

To the Arabs in the East, the Western Sahara was a remote region of sand on the route once followed by Dhū'l-Qarnayn, the "Two horned Alexander", or, alternatively, a ruler of the ancient Yemen, who marched to conquer the place where the sun set. It had to be crossed to arrive at Ghāna's gold mines. Those who dwelt in the oases there knew it better, because to visit Morocco, Cairo or Mecca they had to leave it or return to it. There was still the feeling that they lived on an island surrounded by a forbidding sea of sand and rock. A fourteenth-century Arabic poet of Ouargla, Abū Yaʿqūb Yūsuf al-Wārijlānī said:

> "May Allāh add further to the prosperity of Wārijlān, it is the paradise of the world, the open door to Mecca, and [southwards] to the mine of the gold dust of Ghāna. Legitimate riches will never be acquired, except by a man who is intrepid, who crosses the spaces which stretch towards Ghāna. He must have no fear of trackless deserts, nor of fatigue, nor the sun, nor the gloomy hurricanes of sand."

(Cited in Jean Lethielleux, *Ouargla Cité Saharienne, des origines au début du XX siècle*, Paul Geuthner S.A., Paris, 1983, page 104.)

The desert itself had no attraction, save in one respect. Long before the arrival of the Maʿqil, the remote Sūs, Darʿah and the Western Sahara were renowned in the Arab East and Moorish Spain for the great shields of oryx skin which were made there, the Lamṭī shields. The latter were made by the Lamṭah, the Massūfah and the Haskūrah in the town of Nūl, and also in Awdaghust and Kawkadam and in other small Saharan towns. These shields – examples of smaller size are to be seen in this picture of the siege of a city depicted in the *Cantigas* of Alfonso El Sabio – were highly prized and were stored in arsenals in Egypt. Ibn Khallikān wrote that the Almoravid, Yūsuf ibn Tāshufīn, gave these shields as a present to one of his scribes. Nūl Lamṭah, small though it might be, was famed in the whole Islamic world for these shields. The oryx were hunted in the Darʿah, in the deserts of Mali and Mauritania and nearer at hand in the region of the Sāqiyah al-Ḥamrā'. The oryx hunters and shield fabricators came under the rule of the Maʿqil by the fourteenth century. Ibn Khaldūn mentions that the *shaykhs* of the Dhawī Ḥassān dwelt in the land of Nūl and that they dominated the Sūs and its neighbouring regions. Since Leo Africanus makes considerable mention of these shields throughout the district of the Wādī Darʿah and beyond, their manufacture must have continued after the arrival of the Ḥassānīs and they were probably used in Mauritania as late as the War of Shurbubba, if not later. Tuareg shields are of this type.

Plate 7

The opening pages of the *Ta'rīkh Azawād fī akhbār al-Barābīsh* by an anonymous Sūqī? scholar, translated in part in Chapter 7. The opening of the work is an apology by the author for his limited knowledge of the subject. He then goes on to describe the pre-Ḥassānī dwellers in Timbuctoo district, then how Arawān came to be founded by *Shaykh* Sīdī Aḥmad agg (ibn) Āddah, variably spelt, and by the saint of the Ḥassānī Barābīsh, Abū Makhlūf, variably spelt, together with other clans of the Barābīsh whose Arabian ancestry is clearly set out in the text. This text may be compared with the so-called Arawān Chronicle used by Commandant Péfontan in his study of the town in *Bulletin du Comité d'Etudes Historiques et Scientifiques de l'Afrique Occidentale Française*, July–September, 1933, pages 411–43, and also, "Sur quelques textes arabes provenant du Soudan (région de Tombouctou)", by Vincent Monteil, *Bulletin du Comité d'Etudes Historiques et Scientifiques de l'Afrique Occidentale Francaise*, Vol 21, 1938, pages 499–517, especially pages 513–17. There are certain differences in dates and the names of personalities among the Barābīsh. Other chronicles are to be found in Tīshīt, Walātah and Niʿma (Néma) but these are not Ḥassānī year lists of the type known amongst the Barābīsh, the Awlād Nāṣir (in the *Ḥaswah*, see pages 72–6) and amongst certain tribes of the former, now disputed, Western Sahara (in its narrowest and currently political sense). See Julio Caro Baroja, *Estudios Saharianos*, Instituto de Estudios Africanos, Madrid, 1955, pages 339–90, 405–11 and Appendices.

(Photo by Aḥmad Bābā Centre, Timbuctoo, Mali)

Plates 8a and 8b

Ḥassāniyyah verse (*leghna*) is on the tongue of every Moor (*bīḍānī*). It is also sung by the griot class (*īggāwen*) in Mauritania, the disputed Western Sahara and Azawād. Both verse and music are of a marked individuality. The former is individual in its vocabulary, syllabic structure and rhyming patterns. The latter is individual in its sound, modal theory and musical instruments. Arabo-Berber and western Sudanic influences meet in this music. So individual is Mauritanian music (*azawān*) that a lengthy article by Michel Guignard, the leading authority, appears in Volume 11 of the *New Grove Dictionary of Music and Musicians*, edited by Stanley Sadie, pages 844–6. Guignard concludes his article by saying that "the music of the Moorish *īggīw* nevertheless remains one of the most interesting types of music in west Africa". He tentatively concludes that the vocal style is of Arabo-Berber origin whereas the instrumental techniques and the instruments themselves are western Sudanic. The classification of the modes is of Arabic origin. The caste of professional musicians is a Sudanic phenomenon and would seem to date from before the arrival of the Awlād Ḥassān. This is an art in which Almoravid Mauritania, the Ḥassānīs and the people south of the Senegal river, and eastward into Mali, have all made their contribution.

Many Moors will hotly maintain that their masterpieces in Classical Arabic are their richest cultural legacy. It is certainly true that this impressive corpus of works in verse, or about jurisprudence, mysticism and local history, is widely shared in the Sahara and Sahel and is even quoted in the Maghrib and the Middle East. Their colleagues, the *Ineslemen*, amongst the Tuareg, especially amongst the Kel Es-Sūq and the eastern Kuntah, admire these works and, in the past, corresponded in Arabic with their authors. Despite this, there is a very strong case for *Ḥassāniyyah* popular verse. In time, this may be seen to be the most deeply felt and most original contribution of the Western Saharans to Arabic culture, here defined in its widest sense. *Ḥassāniyyah* poetic art unites Moors who may be divided politically. It is adored by the Mauritanian Moors, it is employed and adapted by the Polisario guerillas.It is recited by royalist Tekna in the Moroccan Sūs. It is cherished by the Moorish minority in Malian Azawād. Though the Arabised Tuareg, in general, do not share thiṣ art, many of the Kel Intasar are an exception. Some of them who live as far east as Bourem and Gao in Mali speak *Ḥassāniyyah* and understand its verse. As modern Arabic literature in all its forms evolves in the Islamic Republic of Mauritania, this popular poetic legacy is bound to have a marked effect. The simplicity of its idiom and its succinct thought are not so far distant from poetic trends in the Middle East today, for example the verse of the Palestinian poet, Maḥmūd Darwīsh.

There are two traditional Mauritanian instruments used by the *īggāwen*: the *tidīnīt*, a plucked lute played by the men, and the *ardīn*, a harp played by the women. It is quite common to see men and women playing together in one orchestra. During many hours of the day the radio in Nouakchott plays programmes of this music and song.

Guignard writes, "the *tidīnīt* has four strings, two long ones on which the melody is played, and two short, which provide a fixed accompaniment. Certain musicians from eastern Mauritania, however, use three or four accompanying strings. The soundboard is made of skin, and the unfretted neck allows for abundant ornamentation. It is an instrument ideally suited to art music.

The number of strings on the *ardīn* varies from 10 to 14. They are tuned to the principal notes of the mode (usually pentatonic); other intervals cannot be played, nor can glissando ornaments. Consequently its music is more restricted than that of the *tidīnīt*, and it is less easy to distinguish between the black and white modes of the same modal complex. Musicians sometimes tap the soundboard of the *ardīn*, adding a percussive element to the melody."

(Photo 8a by Dr Simon Wood, Photo 8b by H. T. Norris)

Plate 9

Before the arrival of the Banū Maʿqil, much of the Ṣanhājah-controlled Western Sahara was known to Arab geographers as the "desert of Kākudam/Kawkadam", even Qūqadam (al-Idrīsī). It was the region of the hunting of the oryx, from whose skins the giant Lamṭī shields were made. The origin of this Saharan toponym is lost in the mists of antiquity. It is either the proper name of a tribe or chief, or else the name of a geographical feature in Zenāgah Berber or in an ancient pre-Arabic or pre-Berber language of the Western Sahara.

If it is the name of a chief, perhaps a tribe, then its root letters resemble those in the name Agdām, with variants. It is a Zenāgah Berber form of the Arabic "allusive" name Abū Bakr. This was the name of Abū Bakr ibn ʿUmar al-Lamtūnī, the leader of the southern Almoravids who was centred at Āzuqqī in the Mauritanian Adrār. Amongst the Haskūrah of the Darʿah region of Morocco, Ghujdāmah is to be found both as a tribal name and as a toponym. Another Haskūrah name, Zamrāwah/Īzamrāwan, resembles In-Zimrān, with variants, and this is a toponym in the Río de Oro, and, more significantly, the name of a key crossing point at the north-eastern limit of the Mauritanian Adrār where raiders from the desert of the Sūs used to waylay caravans. Yet another proper name, Bū Kqedma, "the father of Kqedma", was known among the Arab-Berber Shaʿānibah (Chaamba) who were in the desert of Ouargla (Wārijlān) in Algeria as far back as the twelfth century.

As a toponym, variant forms of Kākudam/Kawkadam are to be found spread throughout the Moorish and Tuareg Sahara. This often occurs at key crossing points along caravan routes and in isolated and waterless tracts, sometimes in the most formidable parts of the Sahara desert. Taken as a whole, from what little evidence we have, the centre point of Ibn Khaldūn's "desert of Kākudam" would seem to be that part of the Sahara which stretches southwards towards Ijjil in northern Mauritania – though al-Idrīsī may have understood that it included the Adrār as well – eastwards towards Taghāzā in Mali, commencing at the eastern end of the valley which is now known by its Arabic name of the Sāqiyah al-Ḥamrā', the "Red River Valley". The Berber name of this valley is quite unknown.

To this day, a pre-Arabic, probably Berber name is still to be found on some maps of the border region of the disputed Western Sahara, Mauritania and Algeria. The name resembles Kawkadam. The whole locality is in a commanding position overlooking the road from Morocco to Mauritania. This is Kreb Akouadim or Akwadem, in the territory of the Rgaybāt. Moors call it Agwātīm and it attains a height of over 1,640 feet.

The Saqiyah and Wād al-Ḥamrā' region is a necropolis of Muslim saints, both Berber and Arab. The following names selected from the 1/1 000 000 (2537) *Seguiet El Hamra* map, Institut Géographique National, Paris, 1962, lists the sites of the tombs of the following saints: Si Brahim el Aattami, Raudat el-Hach, Si Ahmed Rguebi, Raudat Hauwa, Raudat Sultana, Mohd Uld Brahim, Si Arabdalla Ben Musa, Si Ahmed Babo, Si Mohamed el Quenti (Kuntī), Rayem Ueld Aabeid Uallaher, Rayem el Buhi, Rayem Mohamed Embarac and Si bel Lal.

Ḍāyat al-ʿĀm indicates a seasonal lake or *mare* on a clay base. There are a number of wells nearby, the nearest shown being Hassi Hemra.

(Photo by Paul Fox)

Plate 10

Tract across the desert as followed by the caravans from Fas to Timbuctoo (by J. G. Jackson, 1809).

(Photo by Paul Fox)

The drawings on pages 23, 101 and 133 are by the Tuareg artist Ghassa Isa and show a young warrior with a Saharan sword and flowing locks – typical of young Moors and Tuaregs, though swords are rare in Mauritania – a camel, and a maiden of Niger or Mali.

Introduction

This book will examine some of the historical events and some of the Islamic social and legal sanctions which have determined and shaped the Arab character and destiny of the Western Saharans. I shall try to assess how these influenced or decisively defined the Arabisation of this whole region of North-West Africa. Much of this took place between the fourteenth century and the present day, but the story of the Arab extension of "Araby" into the southern Sahara is far from complete. As I write these words, the war in Chad, the war between the Polisario and Morocco, the dependence of the Sahelian states on financial assistance from Arab states in the Middle East, one and all, illustrate the interdependence of this region within Africa and the greater Arab World.

The Arab "Conquest" implies a detailed history of the sundry tribes of Arab nomads who entered the Western Sahara in the later Middle Ages. I mean, here, the Awlād Ḥassān and kindred groups of bedouin who claim descent from the Banū Maʿqil. This claim is common to the Arabs who dominate, to a large though not an exclusive degree, those vast territories which form the Western Sahara proper and which include some eastern marches in the Republic of Mali. However, to dwell exclusively on the saga of the Awlād Ḥassān, and to deem this to be the Arab "Conquest", would be false for several reasons. Among the most important are the following:

(1) By the time of Ibn Khaldūn (1332–1406), the Banū Maʿqil, including the Awlād Ḥassān, had already intermarried with the Saharan Berbers and with other Arab groups which had long preceded them. The distinction

between *Zenāgah* Berber and Arab may have had meaning in a local context, but it was, to a large extent, linguistic. These Berber speakers had been Islamised long before they were ever Arabised.

(2) The process of Arabisation had already begun in the Western Sahara long before the entry of the Banū Maʿqil and the Awlād Ḥassān. Its agents had been Arabian units in the *jaysh* or Arab merchants and traders who had followed them from the seventh century onwards, or who had formed part of the Almoravid movement in the eleventh century, or had been members of individual Arabian families, some exiled, together with descendants and clients, a few claiming to be *Sharīfs*, who had become "holy families" among the pre-Ḥassānī *Zenāgah* peoples of the desert.

(3) Many groups who claimed to be "Arab" in Western Saharan society did so on grounds of social status. Distinction on grounds of language was not always of primary importance. Thus, the Īdaw ʿĪsh Inbāṭ *Zenāgah* in Mauritania, who were Berber speakers until relatively recently, were deemed to be "Arab" alone because of their warrior status. Other Berber elements claimed to be warrior *Sharīfs*, for example the Rgaybāt, while the widely distributed, now Arabophone, sacerdotal people called the Kuntah were originally part of a Berber group, the Tājakānt. Certain half-Arab half-Berber groups among the Tuareg in the region of Timbuctoo, Kel Intasar and Imagsharen, have often been classed as "Arabs" because of their military power and custom in imposing tribute on sedentaries and clients among the nomads. Certain of them speak *Tamasheq* and are wholly Tuareg in their customs, yet they are referred to as "Arabs" in a number of the Arabic sources.

(4) Certain families of Arabian origin, which intermarried with the Berbers in the Western Sahara, were integrated into a class structure which was not that of the Awlād Ḥassān but one very similar to it among the Berbers, the Tuareg in particular. They were reduced to Marabouti c/*Zwāya*/*Ineslemen* status, henceforth devoting all their time to studying and teaching the Arabic religious and secular classics. Some groups called the Kel Es-Sūq among the Tuareg are deeply versed in Classical Arabic. They are part-Arab, part-Berber, in their ancestry. Some have Arab names, others

Tuareg, yet they regard themselves as quite distinct from the Tuareg amongst whom they dwell.

(5) The *lingua franca* of the Western Sahara today is the Arabic dialect of *Ḥassāniyyah* which is used as far east as the Niger buckle in Mali. Its diffusion cannot be explained solely by the distribution of the descendants of the Banū Maʿqil and Awlād Ḥassān. The role of "troubadours", some of mixed ethnic and social background, who excelled in verse in this dialect has been an important factor in the spread and dominance of this Arabic dialect.

(6) The Arabisation of the north-west of the Sahara, in the Darʿah (Draa) region of Morocco and in the Sāqiyah al-Ḥamrā', came about due to influences from the south-east in the Mauritanian Hodh as well as from the north. Factors which determined the history of the Hodh and of Azawād were of importance for the north-west between the fourteenth and the seventeenth centuries.

The sources

The following are the most important Arabic sources that I have used to make this study:

(a) The major works of two Mauritanian Berber scholars of the eighteenth century:
Ta'rīkh Amr al-Walī Nāṣir al-Dīn
Commentary to the ode Ṣalātu Rabbī
Urjūzat Ta'rīkh Mulūk al-Maghāfirah, by Shaykh Muḥammad al-Yadālī (d. 1166/1753)
Kitāb al-Ansāb
Kitāb Shiyam al-Zawāyā, by Shaykh Wālid ibn Khālunā, his pupil (d. 1212/1797).

(b) *Kitāb al-Ḥaswah al-Baysāniyyah fil-ansāb al-Ḥassāniyyah*, by the Ḥassānī scholar, Ṣāliḥ ibn ʿAbd al-Wahhāb ibn Aḥmad ibn al-Ḥājj ʿAbd al-Wahhāb al-Nāṣirī al-Walātī (d. 1256/1840?).

(c) *Ta'rīkh Azawād fī akhbār al-Barābīsh wa ḥurūbihim maʿ al-Rgaybāt wa Huggār wa Idnān wa Īfūghās wa dhikri baʿḍ akābirihim wa dukhūli'l-Naṣārā fī Tinbuktū wa ghayri dhālika*, by an anonymous Sūqī? scholar, *Institut Aḥmad Bābā* manuscript, 175, R.B.I.

(d) An abridgement of *Taysīr al-Fattāḥ fi'l-Dhabb ʿan Ahl al-Ṣalāḥ*, by Shaykh Muḥammad Ignan Wa-n-Fadasen al-Sūqī al-Gunahānī al-ʿArabī addressed to ʿAbd al-Kel Gefī, a scholar of the Kel Geres. The abridgement is by Muḥammad Ḥabba ibn Muḥammad Aḥmad al-Sharīf al-Idrīsī al-Sūqī.

Other Arabic texts will be introduced in part throughout this book.

An initial assessment of the causes of Arabisation

In my final chapter I shall discuss in some detail the profounder, and more ancient, causes of the Arab "Conquest" and reasons for the Arabisation of the Western Sahara. At the outset, however, it seems appropriate to summarise the main reasons which up to now Arab scholars or Western Orientalists have given for this phenomenon. They may be summarised as:

(1) The early Arabic expeditions of the seventh and eighth centuries, by ʿUqbah ibn Nāfiʿ, or, in some historical documents, by ʿUqbah ibn ʿĀmir, to the Moroccan Darʿah (Draa) and by Ḥabīb ibn Abī ʿUbaydah against the Massūfah. Important were the settlements of Ibāḍī merchants and the settlement of isolated endogamous "Arab" groups, for example the al-Hunayhīn, to the north of the Niger buckle.

(2) The military conquest of the Western Sahara by the Banū Maʿqil and the Awlād Ḥassān between the fourteenth and seventeenth centuries and their subjection of the Berbers to a subordinate status.

(3) The gradual spread of Classical Arabic and *Ḥassāniyyah* vernacular in towns such as Walātah, Wādān, Shinqīṭī, Timbuctoo and Arawān, and among the tents of the Awlād Ḥassān. Certain Berber groups such as the Īdaw ʿĪsh Inbāṭ *Zenāgah* abandon their Berber tongue, whilst other groups, such as the Kel Intasar speak *Ḥassāniyyah* as well as *Tamasheq*.

(4) Arab mastery of the oases of Tuwāt, certain caravan towns in Mauritania, and key Saharan routes. The wresting from the Berbers of three key salt deposits, Ijjil to the north of the Adrār in Mauritania, Awlīl in the south-west of Maurita-

nia, near the mouth of the Senegal, and lastly the salt mines of Taghāzā and Tawdannī in the desert of Azawād in Mali to the north of Timbuctoo.

(5) The establishment of Ḥassānī Amīrates in the Trārzah, Brāknah, Adrār and Hodh of Mauritania.

(6) The Muslim counter crusade against the Spanish fortresses on the Atlantic coast near the region of the Wād Nūn. During the course of the fifteenth and sixteenth centuries this led to important tribal upheavals and movements. Scholars who had been settled in the Sāqiyah al-Ḥamrā' left in order to find refuge in other parts of the Sahara.

(7) The journeys of the puritanical preacher, ʿAbd al-Karīm al-Maghīlī of Tilimsān (who died either in 1504 or 1532) in the Western and Central Sahara and his expulsion of the Jews from Tamanṭīṭ, one of the oases of Tuwāt.

(8) The Moroccan annexation of the oases of Tuwāt and Tigurārīn in 1583.

(9) The Moroccan expeditions into the Sūdān leading to the fall of the Songhai dynasty in 1591 and the establishment of the Pashalik at Timbuctoo (the *Armas*).

(10) The "War of Shurbubba" in Southern Mauritania. The defeat of the Berber Islamic reformer, Nāṣir al-Dīn, at the hands of the Awlād Ḥassān and the subjugation of the Berbers in that region at the end of the war in 1674/5.

(11) The growth in influence of the Arabo-Berber Kel Es-Sūq in Azawād and the Adrār-n-Īfōghās in Mali. Their influence was to be largely assumed by the Arabo-Berber Kuntah whose influence in this most easterly region coincided with, and was furthered by, the rise of the Iwillimmeden Tuareg confederation during the seventeenth and eighteenth centuries. Like the Kuntah, the Kel Es-Sūq undertook to teach Arabic and interpret the canonic *Sharīʿah* law among the Iwillimmeden.

(12) The establishment and wide imposition of a class system comprising "Arab" warriors, whether Ḥassānī or Tuareg, subdivided into Amīrates, each with its patrilineal chieftainship, served by a sacerdotal class of teachers, judges, scholars, rain-makers, miracle-workers, traders and mediators known as *Zwāya/Ineslemen* throughout the Western Sahara. Their activities were carried out in writing in Classical Arabic while the princely families were entertained

by bards who were artists in *Ḥassāniyyah*. Both classes were served by plebians and slaves. Equally characteristic of both the Ḥassānī and western Tuareg groups was the possession of large cattle herds.

Method of study

To my knowledge there has only been one study until now which has attempted to examine and to analyse on a wide and comparative scale many of the subjects stated above. This is by C. C. Stewart, "Southern Saharan Scholarship and the Bilād al-Sūdān", *Journal of African History*, XVII, 1, 1976, pp. 73–93.

In this book the subject will be approached on the basis of certain major tribal groups and an examination of certain key events and movements in their history. Each *sondage* will be carried out within the Arabic texts listed. The groups may be listed as:

(a) The Awlād Ḥassān of Mauritania and Azawād, more especially the Trārzah and Brāknah: the Awlād Ghuwayzī and Awlād Mubārak: the Barābīsh.

(b) The Kel Es-Sūq, to a lesser extent the Igellād and Kel Intasar, of Azawād and the Sahara of Mali. I have selected the Kel Es-Sūq to cover this region since they have been far less studied than the Kuntah.

(c) The Western Iwillimmeden and their relation to both the Awlād Ḥassān and the Arabic teachers in their midst from the Kel Es-Sūq and the Kuntah.

The "War of Shurbubba" will be reassessed and I have also included a short chapter on *Ḥassāniyyah* and Classical Arabic verse among the Awlād Ḥassān. One whole text which relates to the relationship between the protected scholars and their armed masters is translated and closely examined. It is to be hoped that at the end of the study a far clearer picture will emerge of the deeper factors which have brought about the Arabisation of the whole of the Western Sahara between the Atlantic and the Mali Adrār.

Note

It should be made clear at the outset what is meant by "Arab", and what is meant by "Berber" in this book.

By *Arab* is meant:

(a) A Saharan whose everyday language of discourse and communication is a dialect of spoken Arabic. This may be *Ḥassāniyyah*, although not necessarily so.
(b) One whose language for the purpose of reading and writing is Classical Arabic.
(c) One who claims patrilineal descent from an Arabian eponym.

Thus an Almoravid might qualify under (b) and (c), though he would not qualify under (a). This same criteria might exclude a member of the Kel Es-Sūq despite his claim to an Arabian pedigree.

By *Berber* is meant:

(a) A Saharan whose everyday language is a Berber dialect or language *as well as*, or, *to the exclusion of*, a dialect of spoken Arabic.
(b) One whose language for the purpose of reading and writing is Classical Arabic.
(c) One who claims patrilineal or matrilineal descent from *either* a Berber eponym, *or* an Arabian eponym.

In this way in Mauritania and in Mali certain peoples, for example the Īdaw ʿĪsh, have passed from one category to the other, either dramatically, imperceptibly, partially or incompletely.

Part I

The Tribal Tapestry

Chapter 1

The Historical Geography of the Western Sahara and its Peoples

It is possible to describe the borders of the Western Sahara in at least three different ways. In contemporary terminology, and in the narrowest sense, it includes all those territories which previously formed a part of the Spanish Sahara, a strip of territory along the Atlantic coast of Africa between Morocco and Mauritania. It is presently the bone of contention between the Kingdom of Morocco and the Sahrawi Polisario Front. John Damis has described this territory – which is subdivided into the northern Sāqiyah al-Ḥamrā' and the southern Río de Oro – as "a hot, arid terrain of either rocky or desert surface. Its area comprises 102,703 square miles. With only 75,000 inhabitants (1974), it is one of the world's least densely populated regions. Rainfall, except on the coast is negligible. The annual rainfall for most of the Sahara is less than two inches."[1]

Culturally, this whole region is a backwater if it is compared with its neighbours. Historically speaking, though, its barren territory, particularly the Sāqiyah al-Ḥamrā', is of importance in the story of Maghribī Islam and its movements. Part of the terrain, and the region of Ṭarfāyah to the north, was the battleground between Christendom and Islam during the Portuguese and Spanish incursions which spanned the years 1434–1638. Summing up this earlier period of the history of this coast John Mercer has remarked:

> "The coastal people were the indigenous Sanhaja Berbers and immigrant Hassaniya Arabs: the southern part of the territory, a Gadala preserve in Ibn Fatima's time, was by now becoming the domain of the Delim Arabs, probably by a mixture of fighting,

> treaty and absorption. As described, it was a time of change in the desert, though the Europeans were probably quite unaware of this. The Moslem religion was fervently practised – as it was then in all Islam – stimulating a strong feeling against 'infidels' appearing on the coast; the Saguiet-el-Hamra was a minor centre for scholars and mystics, growing parallel to the shrinkage of the Arab world, the fall of Granada in 1492 to be the last event said to have sent impulses into the desert. Another very active facet of nomadic life, noted by Ibn Khaldun, was the trade in negro slaves."[2]

The Sāqiyah al-Ḥamrā' was the resting place for several of the greatest Saharan saints, though it was more often the refuge of the devout from the Mauritanian Hodh or the springboard for Ṣūfī movements which became important far to the east of the Western Sahara. The valley shelters the tomb of Sīdī Aḥmad al-Rgībī, a *Sharīf* from whom the Rgaybāt claim descent, but towards its eastern end is located the scholastic and political centre of Smāra, founded by the warrior-scholar Shaykh Mā' al-'Aynayn al-Qalqamī at the turn of this century. The Kuntah maintain that this region was the centre of the activities of their ancestor, Sīdī Muḥammad al-Kuntī, and the birthplace of his son, Sīdī Aḥmad al-Bakkā'ī. The historical memories of the Kuntah tie the history of this valley with the activities of the Kuntah in the Hodh and the Azawād region of Mali. From there, their activities and influence spread into the Adrār-n-Īfōghās and the camps of the Iwillimmeden Tuareg.

Historically, then, this whole region cannot be studied and can hardly be understood without reference to the adjacent Islamic Republic of Mauritania, with over a million people, and occupying an area of over a million square miles.

The Western Saharans include the whole of Mauritania and the coast of the Río de Oro within the territory of Shinqīṭ or Shinjīṭ. The name is derived from Shinqīṭī (Chinguetti), a small town, founded in the Middle Ages, and sited in the Adrār province of Mauritania. Its name has become famous in the Arab World, and indeed the whole Muslim East, on account of its pilgrims, its merchants and its scholars of note who attained fame as poets, jurists and teachers in Cairo, the Sūdān, Jordan, Syria, Iraq and Arabia, and especially in the cities of Mecca and Medina.

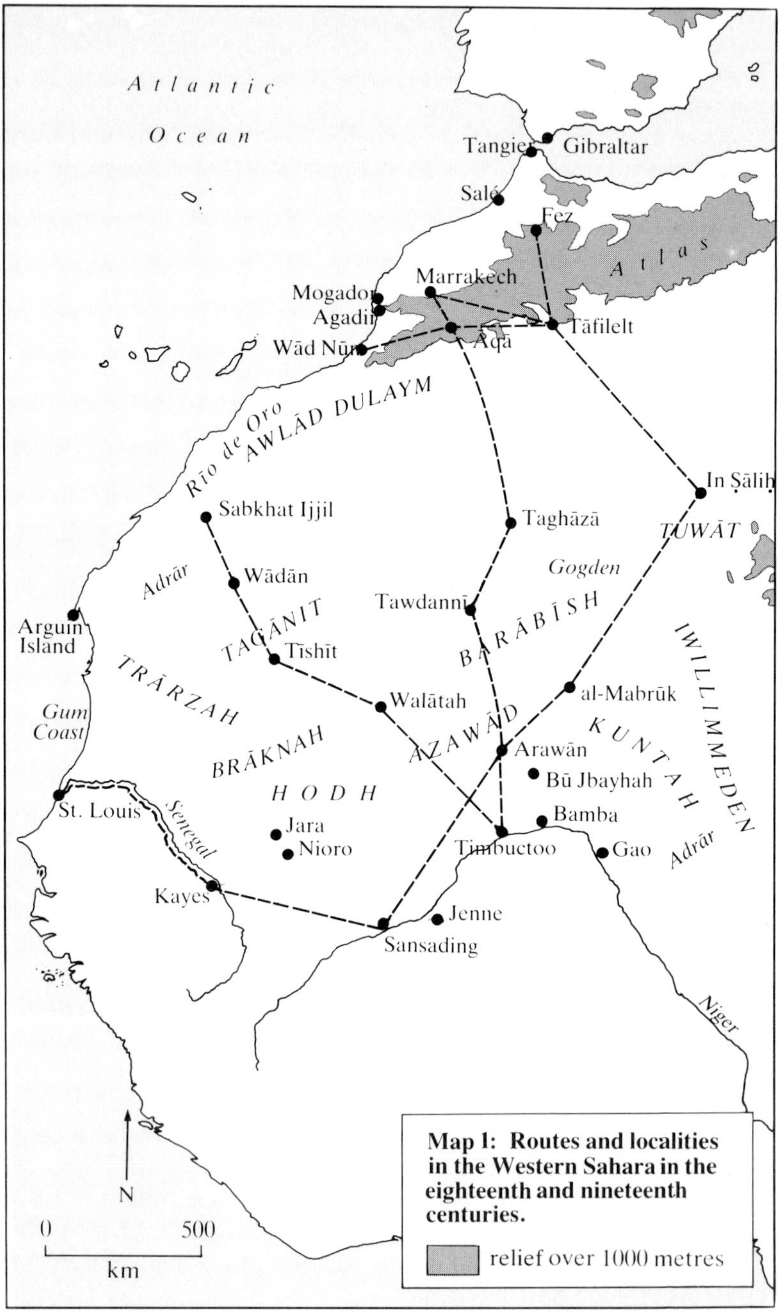

Map 1: Routes and localities in the Western Sahara in the eighteenth and nineteenth centuries.

The Adrār, a sandstone massif circular in shape, has numerous palm groves, and wheat and barley are grown annually. It contains other important historical sites and towns: Wādān, an important link between the salt mine at Ijjil and the region of Timbuctoo;[3] Tinīgī, the ruined village and aforetime capital of the Tājakānt, who are a major Berber, although Arabised, Western Saharan people; and Āzūgī (Āzuqqī), an Almoravid citadel, capital of the Lamtūnah in the Adrār in the eleventh century, described by al-Bakrī thus: "these mountains, easily defensible, abundant in water and pasturage, extend in length a distance of six days' travelling and in width a distance of one day. There is a fortress there called Āzuqqī surrounded by about 20,000 palms. This fortress was built by Yānnū ibn ʿUmar al-Ḥājj, a brother of Yaḥyā ibn ʿUmar."[4]

Tagānit, like the Adrār, and to the south-east of it, is stony and mountainous, rich in dates, and although Sahelian rather than Saharan in climate, flora and fauna, it was also a bastion of the Lamtūnah Berbers of the Western Sahara. The Īdaw ʿĪsh, who dominate it, claim to be their descendants, although this Arabised name has largely superseded their ancient name of Inbāṭ *Zenāgah*. East of Tagānit, sited on the Ẓhar Tīshīt, is the ruined caravan centre of Tīshīt with its splendid dry-stone architecture, mosques and houses, and, like Wādān, a town in which the Soninké language of Azayr was once spoken widely. Tīshīt was noted for its scholarship. Leo Africanus may have referred to it (though I have grave doubts) as an "ancient town built by the Numidians near unto the Libyan deserts. They paid tribute to the Arabians and many of its dwellers were of a black colour. The women were often the teachers and some of them obtained their living by spinning and carding wool."[5]

The Ẓhar of Tīshīt continues south-eastwards into the Ẓhar of Walātah, the ancient Massūfah cultural centre in the Hodh, and into the whole region of that name, a savannah region in many respects, with many ruined cities, including the probable site of Awdaghust, a former capital of the Lamtūnah, and much disputed between the Berbers of the

Map 1 Routes and localities in the Western Sahara in the eighteenth and nineteenth centuries (based on E. W. Bovill).

Western Sahara and the Kingdom of Ghānah which was centred in this same region near the present-day boundary with Mali. As for the other surviving and ruined mediaeval towns, with their Arabic inscriptions – towns such as Settah, and Tīzakht or Tīziggt, the town of the Anṣār, and at no great distance from Walātah itself – very little is known about them, and no systematic attempt has been made to date them, archaeologically. Such are their modern names. Only Īwalāten, wherever it may have been sited, is mentioned in early Arabic sources and this is the Berber name of the town and its region. When Leo Africanus described it between 1500 and 1600, it lay in the line of the Moroccan advance southwards into the heart of the Songhai empire. Like Tīshīt, at that time, it was probably already subject to the Ḥassānī Arabs. "The people of Vode [Ūday] enjoyeth that desert, which is situate between Guaden [Wādān?] and Gualata [Walātah]. They beare rule over the Guadenites, and of the Duke of Gualata they receive yeerley tribute, and their number is grown almost infinite."[6] As will be seen, Leo's statements are, on the whole, confirmed by other sources. In weighing up all the factors which brought about the growth and decline of the Songhai in the southern Sahara and the diffusion of the Kuntah to the eastward, the powerful presence of the Arabic-speaking nomads there – as opposed to the weak hegemony of the Dulaym or Dalīm in the coastal regions at that time, stressed by Leo in his writings – adds strength to the argument that the regions which were continuously open to the Arabs, to Islamic culture and to the closest ties with both the Maghrib and the East were mostly in the eastern marches of Mauritania as we know it today.

The whole of the "Western Sahara", in this second and wider sense, the "land of Shinqīṭ", was still in Leo's days "the dry and forlorne desert of Zanhaga", its borders the ocean, the salt mines of Taghāzā in Mali, the Darʿah (Draa) in southern Morocco, Walātah and Timbuctoo. It included Azawād.

The history of the Western Sahara is the history of its caravan routes and its caravans loaded with salt, crossing and re-crossing vast expanses of waste, often seasonal, and guided by Arab or Massūfah Berber *takshīfs* who were experienced navigators of these sandy seas. Routes changed during the centuries, though the major salt deposits, such as Taghāzā, later Tawdannī, remained the axis around which these routes revolved like spokes of a wheel. The Arab geographers, al-Bakrī, al-Idrīsī, Ibn Saʿīd, and others, describe these routes in detail. Yet so changed are the toponyms, so vague in direction, so clouded by legends and bizarre orthography, that today it is frequently impossible to tabulate these routes with confident precision. Only the journey of Ibn Baṭṭūṭah, in the fourteenth century, through Taghāzā to Walātah and later eastwards to the Hoggar, via Takeddā, convinces us, in any detail, about the distance in days from one stage to the next, the length of the halt in any one place; in short a first-hand description of one of the principal Saharan routes in the mediaeval period. Yet we must not be inclined to dismiss the value of all these early Arabic accounts, which are a unique source of reference, even though it is now almost impossible to trace the routes described, step by step and dune by dune.[7]

As late as 1800, the Maghribī caravans, the "*akkabaahs*", were still the subject of amazement, their diverse detours, their protracted delays and their adaption to a network of Ḥassānī tribes which, by then, were undisputed masters of almost all these routes. James Grey Jackson, in his *Account of the Empire of Marocco*, wrote:[8]

> "The akkabaahs perform the traverse of the Desert, including their sojournments at El-wahaht, or Oases, in about 130 days. Proceeding from the city of Fas, they go at the rate of $3\frac{1}{2}$ miles an hour, and travel seven hours a day; they reach Wedinoon, Tatta, or Akka in eighteen days, where they remain a month, as the grand accumulated akkabaah proceeds from the latter place.
>
> In going from Akka to Tagassa they employ sixteen days, here sojourning fifteen days more to replenish their camels; they then proceed to the well of Taudeny, which they reach in seven days; here again they remain fifteen days; their next route is to Arawan, another watering place, which they reach in seven days; here they sojourn fifteen days; and then proceed and reach Timbuctoo the sixth day, making a journey of fifty-four days actual travelling, and of seventy-five days repose, being altogether, from Fas to Timbuctoo, one hundred and twenty-nine days, or four lunar months and nine days.
>
> There is another akkabaah which sets out from Wedinoon and Sok Assa, and traversing the Desert between the black mountains of Cape Bojador and Gualata,[9] touches at Tagassa, El Garbie [both g's guttural, being the letter غ], or West Tagassa, and

staying there to collect salt, proceeds to Timbuctoo. The time occupied by this akkabaah is five or six months, as it goes as far as Jibbel-el-bied, or the White Mountains,[10] near Cape Blanco, through the desert of Mograffra[11] and Woled Abbusebah,[12] to a place called Agadeen[13] where it sojourns twenty days.

The akkabaahs which cross the Desert may be compared to our fleet of merchant vessels under convoy, the (stata) convoy of the Desert being two or more Arabs, belonging to the tribe through whose territory the caravan passes; thus, in passing the territory of Woled Abbusebah, they are accompanied by two Sebayhees, or people of that country, who on reaching the confines of the territory of the Woled Deleim, receive a remuneration, and return, delivering them to the protection of two chiefs of Woled Deleim; these again conducting them to the confines of the territory of the Mograffra Arabs, to whose care they deliver them, and so on, till they reach Timbuctoo; any assault made against the akkabaah during this journey is considered as an insult to the whole clan to which the (stata) convoy belongs, and for which they never fail to seek ample revenge."

If the whole territory of Shinqīṭ may, with justification, serve as a meaningful "Western Sahara", in order to study the history of its peoples, there remains a third definition of this region, containing within its borders the whole of the Sahara to the west of the Hoggar (Ahaggar), and, more especially the Adrār-n-Īfōghās and the Tanezrouft. The Adrār, more than Aïr, is historically a part of the Western Sahara. The Tuareg and Arab groups which inhabit it have historical links with the Moors of Shinqīṭ, just as its ancient ruined cities, above all Tādamakkat, were tied commercially, culturally and ethnically to Awdaghust, Ghānah, Walātah, and particularly with Arawān, which was founded by a scholar from the Adrār-n-Īfōghās.

Like the Adrār of Mauritania, the name signifies "mountain". But the Mali Adrār is a northward enclave of the Sahel in the Sahara, rising to between 1,600 and 2,600 feet. According to Maurice Cortier:

"L'Adŕaŕ est dans le désert, un pays non désertique. C'est au milieu du Tanezrouft une sorte de presque'île fertile, reliée aux contrées nigritiennes par la vallée du Tilemsi et qui forme, précisement sur la plus grande route de traversée du Sahara, comme un caravansérail avancé où le voyageur se repose et peut abreuver ses bêtes.

Autrefois déjà, l'Adŕaŕ était la principale étape et le noeud des routes qui, venues de Gao, la capitale de l'empire Sonrai, par Tachdaït et Kidal, aboutissaient à Taoudeni par Tessalit ou Guernen, au Touat par In-Ouzel; à Agadez par Aril, avec des ramifications sur le Maroc, le Ahaggar et la Tripolitaine."[14]

The Adrār-n-Īfōghās, as will be seen, was the ancient homeland of many Berber Saharan tribes who settled elsewhere but who, like the Lamtūnah, left behind a number of their kinsmen. It became an important centre for the Kuntah, and represents the easternmost marches of their activities. Henri Lhote has observed:

"Notons que l'Ădrar revient toujours dans les légendes comme étant le foyer original de dispersion des tribus touarègues, aussi bien chez les Ihăggaren que chez les Ioullimmiden.

L'Ădrar a dû jouer effectivement un rôle prépondérant dans le peuplement primitif. C'est là d'ailleurs que les historiens du moyen age fixent l'habitat ancien des Lemtouna et des Sanhadja."[15]

The Adrār-n-Īfōghās is a part of the Western Sahara. It is likewise linked, geographically and commercially, to the land of Shinqīṭ via the desert of Azawād and through Arawān and Taghāzā. Yet both Azawād and the Adrār-n-Īfōghās are distinctive and individual, and in earlier times they were viewed apart from the territory of "the Zanhaga", as described by Leo Africanus or as shown by the early cartographers of Africa. However, this distinction was only partial as far as the region of Arawān is concerned. It was there, in fact, that Leo himself was entertained with sumptuous hospitality by a Ṣanhājah prince in 1512, some time previous to the Ḥassānī domination. The banquet, to which he was invited, included roast meats, roast ostriches, spiced with herbs, eaten with bread made from millet and rape-seed and with dates, and receptacles of milk in plenty furnished the liquid refreshment for this feast. All conversation was in Znāga and Arabic through interpreters.[16]

But to Leo, and to those cartographers who followed him, the desert northwards of Azawād, and the Adrār-n-Īfōghās, to its eastward, was the specific territory of the Zuenziga:[17]

"This desert beginneth westward from Tegaza,[18] extending eastward to the desert of Hair which is inhabited by the people called Targa: northward it bordereth upon the deserts of Segelmesse, Tebelbelt, and Benigorai; and southward upon the desert of Ghir, which joineth unto the kingdome of Guber. It is a most barren and comfortless place: and yet merchants travel that way from Telensin to Tombuto: howbeit many are found lying dead upon the same way in regard of extreme thirst. Within this desert there is included another desert called Gogdem [*sic*][19] where for the space of nine days journey not one drop of water is to be found, unless perhaps some rain falleth: wherefore the merchants use to carry their water upon camel backs."[20]

On this forlorn note Leo concludes his description of a desert which, on the map of De Lisle (1792), was the terrain of the *Guanaseris*[21] whose mysterious name perhaps conceals the history of these remote marches. As I hope to show in my final chapter, it is the history of these routes, and the tribes and the guides which controlled them, the salt mines and the caravan commerce, which, in the last resort, determined the Arab mastery of the Western Sahara.

Chapter 2

The Yemenite Banū Maʿqil

Arabians entered the Western Sahara at different times and for different reasons: as mercenaries, teachers, scholars and traders. Few would dispute, however, that the Arabians who made the most lasting impression on the life of the non-Arab Saharans, and who most radically changed the cultural and linguistic character of this part of Africa, were the Banū Maʿqil. Who were these Arabians in reality? Do they truly represent an ancient Arabian tribal group with ties of blood kinship which relate to ancient peoples in a homeland in the south-western part of the Arabian peninsula? Or, on the contrary, are we concerned here with a lineage which came into existence relatively recently due to historical circumstances? Is it a lineage which, in fact, overlays a network of Berber pedigrees and lineal paradigms such as are now largely forgotten or else may be dimly detected through the heavily patrilineal lists of names which are deemed to be sacred by the Western Saharans of today? These lineages are memorised with the text of the Koran, the corpus of *Ḥadīth* and the events in the *Sīrah* of the Prophet. All abide by the saying that "men are to be believed in regard to what is said about their lineal stems".

One of the oldest Arabic authors who refers to the Maʿqil is the Yemenite, Hishām ibn Muḥammad al-Kalbī (d. 206/821/2) in his grand corpus of genealogies, *Jamharat al-Nasab*. His other works on the pagan religions of Arabia, and on the historical geography of the south-west part of Arabia are of unique value as source material.[1]

Nevertheless, a swift examination of the entry under "Maʿqil" in al-Kalbī's writings offers little in the way of evidence to prove the claims of the Western Saharans to an ancient Arabian ancestry. Over thirty Arabs who are called Maʿqil are listed in al-Kalbī's *Jamharat al-Nasab*. Some Mauritanian scholars of today will argue in support of the descent of the Moors of the Moroccan Sahara, Mauritania and Mali from that line which shows Rabīʿah, *who is Maʿqil*, as a direct descendant of Kaʿb, then al-Ḥārith, and, ultimately, to Madhḥij. The ties of the Maʿqil are with the Arabs of the Yemen rather than with those of the north. However, in earlier times, and the documents show this, it is the Maʿqilian lineage, which goes back to Jaʿfar and the Prophet's house, which has been the favoured line amongst the Western Saharans.

The historian, Ibn Khaldūn (732/1332–808/1406), in his *Kitāb al-ʿIbar*, his universal history, provides by far the most detailed survey and analysis of the Arabian clans of the Banū Maʿqil. Drawing attention to the fact that the Maʿqil entered the Maghrib with the Banū Hilāl, he emphasises that their number comprised only a few extended families; less than a couple of hundred souls, hardly more. It was only after their settlement in the remotest parts of the Maghrib that they became of any significance.

> "Their number, as we have said, was very few. Their number only grew to be a large total on account of those who joined with them from amongst those tribes who were not of their lineage. Amongst these latter were the largish camps and clans of the Fazārah, the Ashjaʿ and those elements which were present of the Shaẓẓah of the Karafah, and of the Mahāyah from ʿIyāḍ, of the Shuʿarā'[2] of Ḥaṣīn, and al-Ṣabbāḥ from al-Akhḍar, from the Banū Sulaym and from other groups besides . . .
>
> "As for the lineages among the mass of men these are wholly hidden and quite unknown. The genealogists who are amongst the Arabs of the Banū Hilāl count them among the Hilālī clans. But this is not so. They allege that their lineage comes within the household of the Prophet, going back to Jaʿfar ibn Abī Ṭālib.[3] Now that claim is likewise false. It is false because the offspring of Abū Ṭālib and the Hāshimites were not desert folk who wander in search of pasture. The sound explanation, and as to its correctness Allāh knows best, in regard to their claim in this matter, is that they are Arabs of the Yemen. Among the Yemenite Arabs there

are two specific clans. Each one of them is called Maʿqil. Ibn al-Kalbī and others have made mention of them. One of them is from Quḍāʿah ibn Mālik ibn Ḥimyar: Maʿqil ibn Kaʿb ibn Ghulaym ibn Khabbāb ibn Hubal ibn ʿAbdallāh ibn Kinānah ibn Bakr ibn ʿAwf ibn ʿAdhrah ibn Zayd ibn Al Lāt ibn Raqīdah ibn Thawr ibn Kaʿb ibn Wabrah ibn Thaʿlab ibn Ḥulwān ibn ʿImrān ibn al-Hāff ibn Quḍāʿah. The second lineage stems from the sons of al-Ḥārith ibn Kaʿb ibn ʿAmr ibn ʿUlah ibn Jald ibn Madhḥij. The latter was named Mālik ibn Udad ibn Zayd ibn Yashjub ibn ʿArīb ibn Zīr ibn Kahlān, who was Maʿqil [the eldest], and his name was Rabīʿah ibn Kaʿb ibn Rabīʿah ibn Kaʿb ibn al-Ḥārith.

"The most likely and probable lineage is that their descent stems from this latter clan, namely from Madhḥij, from Rabīʿah. Those who report historical happenings and who recount events and their stories reckoned Rabīʿah to be among the clans of the Banū Hilāl who entered Ifrīqiyah.[4] The homelands of the Banū'l-Ḥārith ibn Kaʿb were nigh unto Baḥrain where these Arabs were with the Carmathians[5] prior to their entry into Ifrīqiyah. Evidence supporting this is in the fact that Ibn Saʿīd,[6] when mention was made of Madhḥij, reported that they were in the sides looking towards the mountains of the Yemen, and amongst their clans he made mention of Zubayd and of Murād. Next, he said these words: 'In Ifrīqiyah there is found a group of them who are dwellers in woollen tents who migrate seasonally and who pitch camp there.' It was these bedouin whom he mentioned who were the sole true Maʿqil who are to be found in Ifrīqiyah. They are a group from amongst these who are in the furthest Maghrib."[7]

It is at this point in his text that Ibn Khaldūn outlines the main divisions of the Maʿqil, and their chiefs, in his century, the fourteenth. The divisions and the subdivisions which he tabulates, on the whole, square with those names which are listed nearly two hundred years later by Leo Africanus. Though it should be observed that by the time of Leo Africanus the southerly penetration into the desert had markedly increased.

Ibn Khaldūn's views are greatly respected by Western Saharan scholars although they may not share his views in a choice of lineage, and, even if they do so, any lineage chosen may be blurred and disjointed and many gaps need filling from one generation to the next. It is often impossible to know whether the names are of genuine people, or whether they serve the purpose of a social code, a genealogical cipher, an attractive mobile of Moorish names which catches the eye, or the ear, thereby giving the whole lineage a continuity and argument. The scholars, who have played a big part in working out these lineages, have selected names which stem directly from early Arabic books and histories and epics; names such as Ifrīqish or ʿAntarah, which would be highly suspect, as ancestors, to one such as Ibn Khaldūn. But whether they are true ancestral names or not they are often interesting in themselves as they shed light on the social status and the historical evolution of the group.

René Basset cites such an interesting example in his *Mission au Sénégal*:

> "The genealogists relate that Ḥassān ibn ʿAqīl [of the Maʿqilī Banū Maghfar] had two sons, Awday, or Addī, and Adlīm or Dalīm. According to others, Addī was the father of Dalīm and not his brother. The mother of the latter was a servant chattel of Addī who had relations with her in private without the knowledge of his wife. When she gave birth to a son, who was of small build and stature like herself and very like her, it was said that Dulaymah had given birth to Dalīm. He grew up, but his father renounced him on account of the jealousy of his wife who was one of the Banū Hilāl. When he was a full grown man his bravery was revealed. One day the fighting men departed. The Hilālī wife remained at the rear together with her children and Dalīm was with them. While she was arranging her camel litter, lo, some enemies descended in force upon them. Her children fled and only Dalīm remained. He fought until he had delivered the wife of his father and he had killed the enemy warriors. When they halted to eat, she, as usual, wished to give her sons priority and preference over Dalīm, but the latter exclaimed, 'By God, let none of them come before me, since all of them fled and it was I who was your deliverer!'"[8]

Basset adds that this whole tale appears to be based on an episode in the famous romance of ʿAntarah ibn Shaddād, the mulatto poet-warrior of ʿAbs in the pre-Islamic era. Weight is added to his argument by the fact that a certain ʿAntarah is named as a son of Maghfar ibn Ḥassān ibn Maʿqil in several of the Western Saharan genealogies, more especially those of the Awlād al-Nāṣir in the Mauritanian Hodh. A close look at the story, however, might also disclose parallels in the early life of

Abū Zayd in the saga of the Banū Hilāl. It is the theme of the story, rather than the detail, which suggests the ʿAntarah stories.[9] Unlike the appearance of Bū Qarn and Ifrīqish in some genealogies, at the behest of *littérateurs*, the story of Dalīm (Dulaym) owes much more to the story-teller and the popular bard.

The appearance of these exotic names in lineages which would introduce ancestors who, in theory, lived around 1500, or a little later, suggests that at about this time the Banū Maʿqil had many weak links in their growing genealogies, and that a major grafting of eponyms was, at that time, or later, actively undertaken.

An example from southern Morocco of this lineal reconstruction concerns the Barābīsh,[10] a branch of Maʿqil cognate to Dulaym, both of them descendants of Ḥassān ibn ʿAqīl through the line which commences in the household of the Prophet. This combined lineage relates to the Āqāwiyyah family, from Tāmdūlt Āqā in the remotest Sūs of south-west Morocco. This family came northwards from Timbuctoo.

According to Muḥammad al-Mukhtār al-Sūsī their genealogy is as follows: Muḥammad (Fataḥā) ibn Muḥammad ibn ʿAbd al-Raḥmān ibn Muḥammad ibn ʿAbd al-Raḥmān ibn Ibrāhīm ibn Muḥammad (Fataḥā) ibn Muḥammad (Fataḥā) ibn Aḥmad ibn Muḥammad ibn ʿAlī ibn al-Shaykh Muḥammad (Fataḥā), the famous, ibn Mubārak ibn ʿAlī ibn Zayyān ibn Mūsā ibn Muḥammad (Fataḥā) ibn Yaḥyā, the famous (buried in the cemetery of Timbuctoo), ibn ʿAbdallāh ibn Muḥammad ibn al-Shubkī (buried in the Ṣūfī retreat (*Zāwiyah*) of Asā in south-west Morocco where he was renowned), ibn ʿAlī ibn al-Shiblī ibn Yaʿlā ibn Muḥammad ibn *Barbūsh* ibn Waṣfī ibn Ẓafar ibn *Yaʿrub* ibn *Īlālen* ibn Ghafīr/Ghufayr ibn Ḥasan ibn Thābit, in whom, this latter, are joined the Banū'l-Ḥasan of the Jaʿfarīn (*Jaʿfariyyūn* who are descended from ʿAlī ibn Abī Ṭālib), namely Dulaym ibn al-Ḥasan/Ḥassān, Muḥammad ibn al-Ḥasan/Ḥassān, Raḥmān/Raḥmūn ibn al-Ḥasan/Ḥassān, and Barbūsh ibn al-Ḥasan/Ḥassān. This al-Ḥasan is the son of Thābit ibn ʿAbbās ibn ʿAbdallāh ibn Jaʿfar ibn Abī Ṭālib.

"Thus I found the lineage of this Āqāwiyyah family", writes the Sūsī scholar. He adds,

"They say that their ancestor, Yaḥyā ibn ʿAbdallāh, was buried in the city of Timbuctoo. From thence came some of his sons to the town of Tāmdūlt. Then, when it was ruined, they withdrew to Āqā where they are still to be found. They say that Muḥammad ibn Yaḥyā and ʿAlī ibn Zayyān both have their tombs in the cemetery of al-Qaṣabah at Āqā, and that al-Sayyid al-Shubkī has a sepulchre in the *Zāwiyah* at Asā. He was noted for the renown he enjoyed with Shaykh Yaʿzā Wihdā [W-Ihda], who died at the commencement of the eighth/fifteenth century. Those who claim this Jaʿfarī lineage are widespread in the Sūs and all of them say that they came from Tāmdūlt. I have seen the lineage of some of them in the tribe of Īgashān and Amalen and Īlālen. This shows that they are linked to these in their uppermost forbears. It is known that Ibn Khaldūn claimed that there was no entry of the Jaʿfarī [Maʿqil] into the Maghreb, however, the historian, Aḥmad ibn Khālid al-Nāṣirī, answered him in his book, *Ṭalʿat al-Mushtarī*,[11] so let him who so desires refer to it. Folk are to be believed in regard to their lineages."[12]

Here it may be seen that the Ḥassānī Maʿqilian name, Barbūsh, postdates the ancient textual Arabian name, Yaʿrub of the Yemen, which immediately follows the Berber name, Īlālen, eponym in fact of a Berber tribe in the Sūs. These juxtapositions seem to suggest the "snowballing" process of the Banū Maʿqil clans through clientage at that time where no clear line could be drawn between Maʿqil and Ṣanhājah, Maʿqil and Gazūlah, and Maʿqil and Iwillimmeden Tuareg in the north-western Sahara. It must have been either the lettered, the bards, or else some local genealogist who determined the shaping of this lineage, as indeed, in some way, every one of the others was shaped.

These men played a major part in shaping the history of the Banū Maʿqil in the Western Sahara. They betray the epic, the myth and indeed the true history of how the Maʿqil from their obscure homeland in Arabia Felix evolved into the Western Saharan people – the Banū Ḥassān – whose language, far more than their lineages, ultimately determined their Arabian identity.

Chapter 3

The Awlād Ḥassān and Their Branches

According to those Western Sahara scholars who are best informed regarding the coming of the Arabs to that region, the term "al-ʿArab" should be applied strictly, if not exclusively, to the aristocracy of the Maʿqil Arabs. Exceptions are few. This opinion does not exclude the view that those who were there at an earlier date were not in many respects Arabised, priding themselves on at least some Arab blood or affiliated in some way to major Arab tribes. Before the Banū Maʿqil reached the Western Sahara in the seventh/thirteenth century, some Arab settlement had already taken place, though on a very small scale. One such period of settlement had occurred at the time of the Almoravid, Abū Bakr ibn ʿUmar al-Lamtūnī, in the middle of the eleventh century. This came about when he, having divested himself of sovereignty to his cousin, Yūsuf ibn Tāshufīn, and on his way back to the Mauritanian Adrār, gathered to his company certain eminent Arab families, alleged offspring of ʿUqbah ibn Nāfiʿ and client tribes which were affiliated to them. These families were held to be "holy families" which were endowed with divine blessing or *barakah*.

Over a period these families grew in number. But they were incorporated into the Ṣanhājah Berber confederations, and the language and the culture of the Sahara was little changed by them except in certain desert towns. In the main, they themselves were absorbed, since they owed no allegiance to an Amīr of their own kith and kin. All that they retained was their geneaologies and some memory of their Arabian origins.

The Banū Maʿqil were very different, even though at first they were very few in number. When they entered Mauritania and its borderlands they were proud of their tribal loyalties and they were conscious of their goal, namely, the permanent conquest of the territories of the Muslim Ṣanhājah. In their camps they intermarried. They cherished their customs and their language, and those whom they conquered adopted, by degrees, their Arab habits and many of their customs.

In time the term al-ʿArab came to mean the upper class of the Maʿqil. By contrast the term Banū or Awlād Ḥassān came to mean both the upper and lower classes. This upper class monopolised the term "Arab", to the extent that it was enough for the lower classes and *clientèle* to say "our Arabs" when they meant "our lords". On the other hand, the *Zwāya*, those who were concerned with Arabic learning, with religion and the affairs of the mind and the spirit, some Arab in origin and others undisputedly of Berber descent, used the expression "our Arabs" somewhat differently despite their unarmed status and weakness and dependence. To them they were equals and not their superiors.

Although "the sons of Maʿqil" bespoke a unity and familial solidarity which set off these Arabs from those Saharans who were round about them, the *Zwāya*, who were schooled in the writings of Ibn Khaldūn and who, as we shall see, shaped the genealogies of the Maʿqilian clans, were not slow to point out that the Maʿqil stemmed not from one eponym but from three. According to Shaykh Muḥammad al-Imām ibn al-Shaykh Mā' al-ʿAynayn, who has researched profoundly into Ibn Khaldūn's writings and into other sources:[1]

> "In my view, it appears probable that the Jaʿfarī Maʿqil trace their genealogy to Jaʿfar ibn Abī Ṭālib, that the Quḍāʿī Maʿqil trace their genealogy to Maʿqil ibn Kaʿb ibn ʿAlīm ibn Janāb as far as Quḍāʿah, and the Kahlānī Maʿqil trace their genealogy back to Maʿqil ibn Kaʿb ibn Rabīʿah ibn al-Ḥārith ibn Kaʿb as far as Kahlān, who were the lords of Najrān.[2] From them stemmed the Banū ʿAbd al-Madān who were the kings of Najrān during the period of the Jāhiliyyah and of Islam, about whom the poet [unknown] said (in *wāfir*):
>
> > 'When we beheld, we used to say to him of sturdy bulk and eloquence, methinks, thou art, O one endowed with both these gifts, a kinsman of the Banū ʿAbd al-Madān . . .'

"Clans of these three Maʿqil, whom we have mentioned, joined the Banū Sulaym and the Banū Hilāl when they were in Upper Egypt, and the fact that they were all tent dwellers and had the same name joined them together so that they became known collectively as ʿArab Maʿqil. Most people do not distinguish clearly between these Maʿqil. They make them descendants of a certain Maʿqil and they relate all of them to him. Nowadays it is not easy to distinguish some from the others except for the Jaʿfarī Maʿqil. Even now they are distinguished by their name and their pedigree. Most of them are among those who are called Ḥassān, although some are reckoned to be *Zwāya*. The reason for their departure from their kinsmen in the Arabian peninsula was that the Jaʿfarīs were involved in a rift with their cousins, the descendants of al-Ḥasan ibn ʿAlī. The latter defeated them and expelled them, and it was for this reason that they moved to Upper Egypt. The history of the other two Maʿqils reveals that they moved as nomads from one pasturage to the next during the period when the Carmathians conquered the Arabian peninsula[3] when this schism rent Islam. Many of those who found it impossible to live beside them emigrated to the extremity of the country. They pursued their wanderings further and joined their tribal relatives in Upper Egypt. They were integrated into the Banū Hilāl. These three groups became distinguished from the rest and they were given the collective name of the Banū Maʿqil. Their number was extremely small and it only increased on account of those of other stock and clan who joined together with them. Amongst these were to be found Banū Fazārah and Ashjaʿ.[4] Both enjoyed esteem and were sizeable, and to them were added, following tribal fissions and feuds, elements from the Banū Hilāl and Banū Sulaym. Ibn Khaldūn has remarked – he being alive in the eighth/fifteenth century – that in his time the Banū Maʿqil were among the most amply provided of the nomad Arabian tribes. Their homeland lay in the deserts of the furthest Maghrib.[5] They were the neighbours of the Banū ʿĀmir ibn Zughbah (Hilālīs) in their tribal haunts to the south of Tilimsān and they extended as far as the Atlantic. They had three clans (*buṭūn*), Dhū ʿUbaydallāh, Dhū Manṣūr and Dhū Ḥassān.[6] The first of these was neighbour to the Banū ʿĀmir and their district lay between Tāwarīrt and the Tall and all the district lying to the south. The second group extended from Tāwarīrt to the Darʿah and to the Tall which faced it, whilst the third (Ḥassān) were in the territory between the Wādī Darʿah and the Atlantic. Their Shaykhs dwelt in the region of Nūl (the Wād Nūn), the capital of the Sūs. They were the overlords of the furthest Sūs and they pastured in the sandy regions as far as the terrain of the *mulaththamūn* – that is, the Gudālah, Massūfah and Lamtūnah.

"They entered the Maghrib in small numbers. It is said that they numbered barely two hundred. The Banū Sulaym stood in their way and weakened them. They were similarly subdued by the Banū Hilāl for a very long period. They settled at the limit of their terrain in the region of Malwīyah extending as far as the sand dunes of Tāfilalt. In the Sahara they were the neighbours of the Zanātah. They recovered their strength and they multiplied in number, moving into the deserts in the extreme Maghrib. They dwelt in the dunes and led their own nomad existence in the Sahara, remaining allies of the Zanātah while they still were powerful. In Ifrīqiyah (Tunisia) a small group of them still remained. They were eventually absorbed by the Banū Ka'b ibn Sulaym. They mixed and married with them and they were their ministers in the service of the Sulṭān and in courting the friendship of the bedouin Arabs. When the Zanātah ruled Morocco under the leadership of the Banū Marīn,[7] and they entered the provinces and the cities, these Banū Ma'qil remained behind in the Sahara. They were on their own there and they grew great, seemingly without a precedent, and they became rulers of the Saharan towns (*quṣūr*) which the Zanātah had founded, such as those of the Sūs and in Tuwāt, then others; Būdah, Tāmānṭīṭ, Wargalān (Ouargla), Tāsbīt, Tīgurarīn, in the east. Every one of these localities was a distinct country. It contained numerous *quṣūr* which possessed date groves and rivers. The majority of the people were Zanātah Berbers and there were wars and feuds amongst them about who should be the ruler. The Banū Ma'qil gained control of these territories and they imposed taxes and tributes. All taxes so gathered were theirs and it was in such that their sovereignty was assessed. During that period they used to pay alms taxes to the kings of the Zanātah.

"Ibn Khaldūn has reported that they paid blood money (if they had killed one of the Sulṭān's subjects) and they paid large sums which they called a right of transit tax.[8] Such was fixed at the whim of the Zanātah kings.

"Those Arabs did not scorn to treat as inviolate the remoter regions of the Maghrib and its uplands,[9] nor did they threaten to harm or rob along the route of Sijilmāsah, nor in any other Saharan route. This was due to the respect shown to religion in the Maghreb and firm border control during the days of the Almohads and the Zanātah (Marīnids) after them. In return, they enjoyed a fief from the ruling powers, but they had to stretch out their hand in humility to take it.[10] So few were they that it was only by the assimilation of tribes who were not of their lineage that they grew in number. Other men joined them after the lifetime of Ibn Khaldūn.

"Sīdī 'Abdallāh ibn al-Ḥājj Ibrāhīm remarked in his work, entitled "The facilitation of those who see his poem called 'the bower of the wild roses'":[11]

"The Banū Ḥassān were in the Sūs. They carried out mischief and did damage in the region so that wars took place betwixt them and the Banū Marīn. The latter expelled them from the Sūs to the border of the Sahara. When they reached the latter they extended their reach to its very borders, they wandered throughout its stretches of wilderness until they had overrun the whole of the utmost limits of Shinqīṭ. They had the power of authority there. There is no doubt that after they had come there numbers of Arabs joined their company. The causes of this were common and varied. There were a number of tribes represented in this whole, amongst them the *Shurafā'*, the descendants of Ḥasan and Ḥusayn, and many tribes from the clan of the Quraysh, some descended from Abū Bakr and others from 'Alī. Others were from Fihr. There were tribes of the *Anṣār* and from tribes other than them. Stocks were intermingled by marriage and the genealogies were fused by interrelationship and this took place among all the tribes in the whole country. Nonetheless, every class maintained its separate identity. They preserved their lineages and their honour to an extraordinary degree. They refused to marry outside their status and none was willing to forego the status of his forbears, whatever the hardship he might have to suffer. As for that one who was of a low standing, he had no desire to attain the highest rank even though he may have attained some status and possessed numerous kinsfolk. He did not withhold payment of his due to the highest class nor did he regard it as his loss. Thus they have preserved their honour and their lineage, handed down from father and son until this very day.

"The majority of names have been changed now. There are several reasons for this. There is, for example, the genius of a certain chief in a tribe, whose supporters grew and whose status reached such might and magnitude that the tribe rallied to him and they acknowledged him. Or it came about due to the combination of one tribe with another due to the greater strength of one, or on account of numbers. However, every tribe knows best to whom it is related from amongst those families who, without a doubt, came to the Maghrib. Those who are knowledgeable in such matters will be asked about every tribe. This is something essential in their eyes.

"The Ḥassānī tribes are subdivided. Each has its own territory and is ruled there by a princely house. The inheritance is transmitted in the family of the Amīr and is not coveted by the other groups. In regard to any overall sovereignty they recognise none, save the Sulṭān of Morocco.[12] One group [in the Adrār] is known as the Banū Yaḥyā ibn ʿUthmān. The headship rests in the family of Aḥmad ibn ʿAyyida. Another group (in the *Giblah*) are called the Trārzah, and the headship rests in the family of the Banū Muḥammad al-Ḥabīb ibn ʿUmar ibn al-Mukhtār. Another group [the inhabitants of Shamāmah and district] are called the Brāknah, and the headship rests in the family of the Awlād Āghrīsh from the Awlād al-Sayyid. Another group [in Tagānit] are called the Īdaw ʿĪsh, and the headship rests in the family of the Banū Bakkār ibn Aswayd Aḥmad ibn Muḥammad ibn Amhammad Shayn. They are peculiar, since they are all that remain of the Lamtūnah princes, of the family of Abū Bakr ibn ʿUmar. Another group [in the Hodh] are called the Awlād Mubārak, and the headship rests in the family of Ibn al-Faḥfāḥ. A group called the Awlād al-Nāṣir are also in the Hodh, and the headship rests in the family of the Ishbayshib. The overall leadership in the Hodh was held by the Awlād Mubārak until it was taken from them in the nineteenth century by the Mashḍūf. Since that time they have been the lords over all the Hodh. The Awlād al-Nāṣir were left with their leadership in their own special centre in the Hodh.

"As for the Awlād Mubārak, who had held the supreme leadership, only integration [with the Mashḍūf] was accepted from those who were their descendants. It is on account of this that the Mashḍūf [who were not originally Ḥassān] became qualified to be accounted among the major "Arab" tribes. It was they who unified the district and who established justice there after the Awlād Mubārak. The headship rests in the family of the Mḥaymīd.

"The group known as the Barābīsh are found in the district known as Azawād [with Timbuctoo as its capital] on the eastern border [of Shinqīṭ]. The headship rests in the Banū Sulaymān. Another group bears the name of the Banū'l-Ramaythiyyah of the tribes of the Dalīm and the sons of al-Labb, and their brothers who dwell to the west of the Adrār towards the sea and a low land there. No single Amīr embraces all of them, every sub-tribe amongst them has its own hereditary chief. As for the Arabs of the Wād Nūn, I have mentioned that this was where the Maʿqil Shaykhs settled in the seventh/fourteenth century until, at that time, the Banū Marīn expelled them to the borders of the Sahara.

It seems probable that the Tiknah tribe are among those who showed their obedience and who stayed behind in the country. In this context I shall make a few remarks about the Tiknah and the Wād Nūn, which lies outside the borders of Shinqīṭ. The term, Tiknah, is applied to tribes who are warlike, and who have strong tribal feeling of loyalty. They occupy the area from the Wād Nūn to the town of Asā, to the east, and the Sāqiyah al-Ḥamrā' to the south, this latter forming the northern border of Shinqīṭ, and, to the westward, the Atlantic. The Wād Nūn is their northern border. They hold in regard three noble qualities: generosity to the guest, the protection of the stranger and manly courage. They are subdivided into two groups: Ait al-Jamal and Ait Billa. The Ait Mūsā are among the chief tribes of the Ait al-Jamal, together with the Aʿli, the Ait al-Ḥasan and the Zarkiyyīn. Among the principal tribes of the Ait Billa are the Āzwāfīṭ and the Aytūs. There are sub-tribes and clans and chieftainships subordinate to all the tribes of Wād Nūn and Shinqīṭ which I have mentioned . . ."

Part II

The Arabian Locust

Chapter 4

The Awlād Ḥassān settle in Mauritania and Western Mali

Almost nothing is known about the distribution of the tribal remnants of the Almoravids in northern Mauritania and the Río de Oro towards the end of the fifteenth century. Western travellers who met these Saharan Berbers referred to them either as "Philistines", and confused them with the Tuareg, or else as Aznages. Here they distinguished between a hunter–fisher folk on the Western Saharan coast and other folk who lived in the interior of the desert, either in small towns on commercial routes or else in tented camps in the deserts of Mauritania and Mali.

Antoine Malfante wrote a letter from Tuwat in 1447, addressed to Giovanni Mariono in Genoa. He referred to the "Philistines" who ruled from the land of Gazola (Jazūlah/Gazūlah) on the Atlantic coast of Africa as far as Egypt. They were governed by kings "whose heirs are the sons of their sisters for such is their law". The Aznages, although men of the veil like the "Philistines", were located by the Europeans much further to the west, towards Cape Blanco, and in their most easterly wanderings were the neighbours of the "Arabs" who lived in the towns of the Western Sahara. The difference between the "Arabs" and the Aznages is demonstrated in the following passage from the Portuguese traveller Cadamosto, also writing in the late fifteenth century. He describes the contact between peoples at Arguin (Argin) on the coast of the Western Sahara:

> "You should know that the said Lord Infante of Portugal has leased this island of Argin to Christians [for ten years], so that no one can enter the bay to trade with the Arabs save those who hold the licence. These have dwellings on the island and factories where they buy and sell with the said Arabs who come to the coast

to trade for merchandize of various kinds, such as woollen cloths, cotton, silver, and 'alchezeli', that is, cloaks, carpets, and similar articles and above all, corn, for they are always short of food. They give in exchange slaves whom the Arabs bring from the land of the Blacks, and gold *tiber* [dust]. The Lord Infante therefore caused a castle to be built on the island to protect this trade for ever. For this reason Portuguese caravels are coming and going all the year to this island.

"These Arabs also have many Berber horses which they trade, and take to the Land of the Blacks, exchanging them with the ruler for slaves. Ten or fifteen slaves are given for one of these horses, according to their quality. The Arabs likewise take articles of Moorish silk, made in Granata and in Tunis of Barbary, silver, and other goods, obtaining in exchange any number of these slaves, and some gold. These slaves are brought to the market and town of Hoden (Wādān); there they are divided: some go to the mountains of Barcha (Cyrenaica), and thence to Sicily, (others to the said town of Tunis and to all coasts of Barbary), and others again to this place, Argin, and sold to the Portuguese leaseholders. As a result every year the Portuguese carry away from Argin a thousand slaves. Note that before this traffic was organised, the Portuguese caravels, sometimes four, sometimes more, were wont to come armed to the Golfo d'Argin, and descending on the land by night, would assail the fisher villages, and so ravage the land. Thus they took off these Arabs both men and women and carried them to Portugal for sale: behaving in a like manner along the rest of the coast, which stretches from Cauo Bianco to the Rio de Senega and even beyond. This is a great river, dividing a race which is called Azanaghi from the first Kingdom of the Blacks. These Azanaghi are brownish, rather dark brown than light, and live in places along this coast beyond Cauo Bianco, and many of them are spread over this desert inland. They are neighbours of the above mentioned Arabs of Hoden."[1]

The Arabic records of the age have no comparable passages which describe the *Zenāgah* and Arab life of this region. The tradition which is handed down among the Mauritanians is that within the interior of the desert, well inland from the battle areas between Christian and Moor between Ifni and the mouth of the Senegal river, due east of the Sāqiyah al-Ḥamrā', there was a confederation of Berber tribes who were descendants of the Almoravids of the eleventh century. They were called the Ibdúkalen, meaning "those who are banded together".

Dr T. Whitcomb has summed up almost all that is known about these Saharans in his study of the origins of the Kuntah who first appear in the history of the Western Sahara at that time. He writes:

> "What the Abdūkal, Lamtūna, and Murābiṭīn might have been in the ninth/fifteenth century is not certain. The Abdūkal were probably a tribe or a confederation of tribes which were not necessarily closely related. According to Mukhtār wuld Ḥāmidun, the leading Znāga-speaking Bīẓanī scholar (to whom I am indebted for most of the information in this article on Znāga names and words), the name Abdūkal is derived from the Znāga verbal root ḏ ḵ ḻ 'to assemble', and Abdūkal means 'those who have joined together'. They may have been part of the Lamtūna, but it would seem from the *Ghallāwiyya* that they did not include all who now claim Lamtūna origin, such as the Tajakānet, who were clearly a different group. The Lamtūna were the leading element in the fifth/eleventh-century Almoravid movement, but it is not known what the original nature of the group was. The name may have been applied to all who joined them or were conquered by them and became their tributaries, so that the name as it is used in the *Ghallāwiyya* could be considered to mean the Znāga of the western Sahara in general."[2]

Certainly Wālid ibn Khālunā, whose book on Saharan genealogies was written before 1797, described the Ibdúkalen/Abdūkal as "*Zwāya* Lamtūnah". They included the Banū Gujih, the Tāshidbīt, the Tākāt and Ijmalla. He adds that the Banū Gujih are from the Idnān (Tuareg),[3] the progeny of Magog the son of Japheth.[4] Such, then, is the local tradition as it has survived in the Western Sahara.

However, Ibn Khaldūn (d. 1406), in his description of this same region of the desert, knows nothing of these names. In his *History of the Berbers* he has recorded how the newly arrived Arabian tribes of the Banū Maʿqil paired and encountered, in peace and war, the enfeebled Berber groups which had dominated the desert since the eleventh century.

> "The tribes which wear the face muffler still exist in our days in the countries where they formerly devoted themselves to a nomadic existence. Their territory adjoins the countries of the Sūdān and separates them from the sandy region which touches the furthest and the middle Maghrib and Ifrīqiyā, where the Berbers dwell. One encounters the muffled folk from the Atlantic Ocean as far as the Nile in the East. The fraction of this race which

founded an empire in al-Andalus and in Africa, and which consisted of a paltry number of the Massūfah and the Lamtūnah, has perished in the manner whereof we have made mention, exhausted in the effort to maintain the domination, burnt out by long distance *sorties* and ruined by luxury. In the end they vanished having been slaughtered by the Almohads.

"As for those who still dwell in the desert, nothing has changed in their manner of living. At this very day they remain divided and disunited because of the diversity of their sentiments and their interests. Having submitted to the authority of the Sūdānese monarchy (*mālik al-Sūdān*) they pay the tax to him (*kharāj*) and they furnish contingents for his armies.

"They form, so to speak, a cordon on the frontier of the country of the negroes, a cordon which stretches eastward running parallel to that formed by the bedouin Arabs upon the frontier of the further and the central Maghrib and of the land of Ifrīqiyā. The Gudālah, one of their tribes, is face to face with the Dhawī Ḥassān, a branch of the tribe of the Maʿqil Arabs who inhabit the furthest Sūs. In front of the Lamtūnah and the Wanzīgah[5] are the Dhawī Manṣūr and the Dhawī ʿUbaydallāh who are Banū Maʿqil Arabs of the further Maghrib. The Massūfah face the Zughbah, who are an Arab tribe of the central Maghrib. The Lamṭah face the Banū Riyāḥ, an Arab tribe which occupies the Zāb, the rural districts of Bougie and Constantine. Lastly, the Tārgā [Tuareg?] are face to face with the Banū Sulaym, who are a bedouin Arab tribe in Ifrīqiyā.

"Camel breeding is the chief occupation of these (Berber) tribes. These animals furnish their subsistence and they also furnish mounts for them and their baggage. Only a few horses are to be seen amongst them. As favoured mounts they possess very nimble camels which are called by them, *nujub*,[6] and when a war breaks out among these folk they fight mounted on the backs of these. The pace of these *nujub* is between an amble and a gallop.

"The Arabs of the waterless desert, more especially the Banū Saʿīd, who are a clan of nomads who are part of the Banū Riyāḥ, make raids from time to time on the territories wherein dwell the tribes which wear the face muffler, though they depart from them as speedily as they can having despoiled all whom they have encountered on their way. Then the alarm is sounded and spreads in the camps, the [Berbers] mount their camels and they hasten to occupy and hold those points where the raiders must needs halt in order to draw their water. Nearly always they are overtaken before they can escape homewards. A fierce battle then takes place and the Arabs only carry off their booty after having suffered grevious affliction and the loss of not a few of their comrades."[7]

Ibn Khaldūn introduces the names of the Saharan nomads who had made their name in world history many centuries before. Were they still known by these names when he wrote? In all probability they were and therefore any other names like the Ibdúkalen and their branches cannot be confirmed as historical at that time. Furthermore, maps of the post-mediaeval period drawn in Europe show certain tribes, which are mentioned by Ibn Khaldūn, as being in a very different homeland from the area which is covered in his passage cited above. Certain tribes are not in the places where the earlier Arabic geographers place them, either, and one must allow for considerable shifting of tribes over a period within the Western Sahara and outside it. Thus, the Lamtūnah, who are located in the Adrār of Mauritania and to the north and east of it, are placed in Elwe's map of 1792, *Carte de la Barbarie de la Nigritie et de la Guinée* as far east as Kawar in north-east Niger. The *Desert des Lumptunes*, who are called "*une nation superbe et brutale*", may in fact refer to the Lamṭah, or the Iwillimmeden, while the Arabs of the west are mixed with the *Zanhaga*. They are *Ludayes*, that is Ūday Banū Ḥassān, while the region of the Ibdúkalen is the land of the *Derveches*. No mediaeval map or later, Arab or European, aims at a tribal precision *in situ*. Since none of the Mauritanian *Zenāgah* names for the Ibdúkalen appears in the mediaeval Arab geographers we cannot be sure that they are not simply later tribal traditions which have been projected backwards into a far earlier era. At most, they can be accepted as sub-tribes which have evolved from the major Ṣanhājah divisions at some stage. This is likely to have happened in the far west. All sources support a wandering westward of the Ṣanhājah

Map 2 The expansion of the Awlād Ḥassān into Mauritania during the fifteenth and sixteenth centuries (based on Julio Caro Baroja).

Map based on that of Antonio Rumeu de Armas (*España en el Africa Atlantica*), showing the strategic and commercial importance of the North-Western Sahara for Spain and the World of Islam during the fifteenth and early sixteenth centuries. This age marks the rise of the Kuntah in the region of the Sāqiyah al-Ḥamrā' and Zammūr, the southern drive of the Maʿqil into Mauritania and Azawād and the digging of wells by the ancestors of the Barābīsh and Kel Intasar to the north of Timbuctoo.

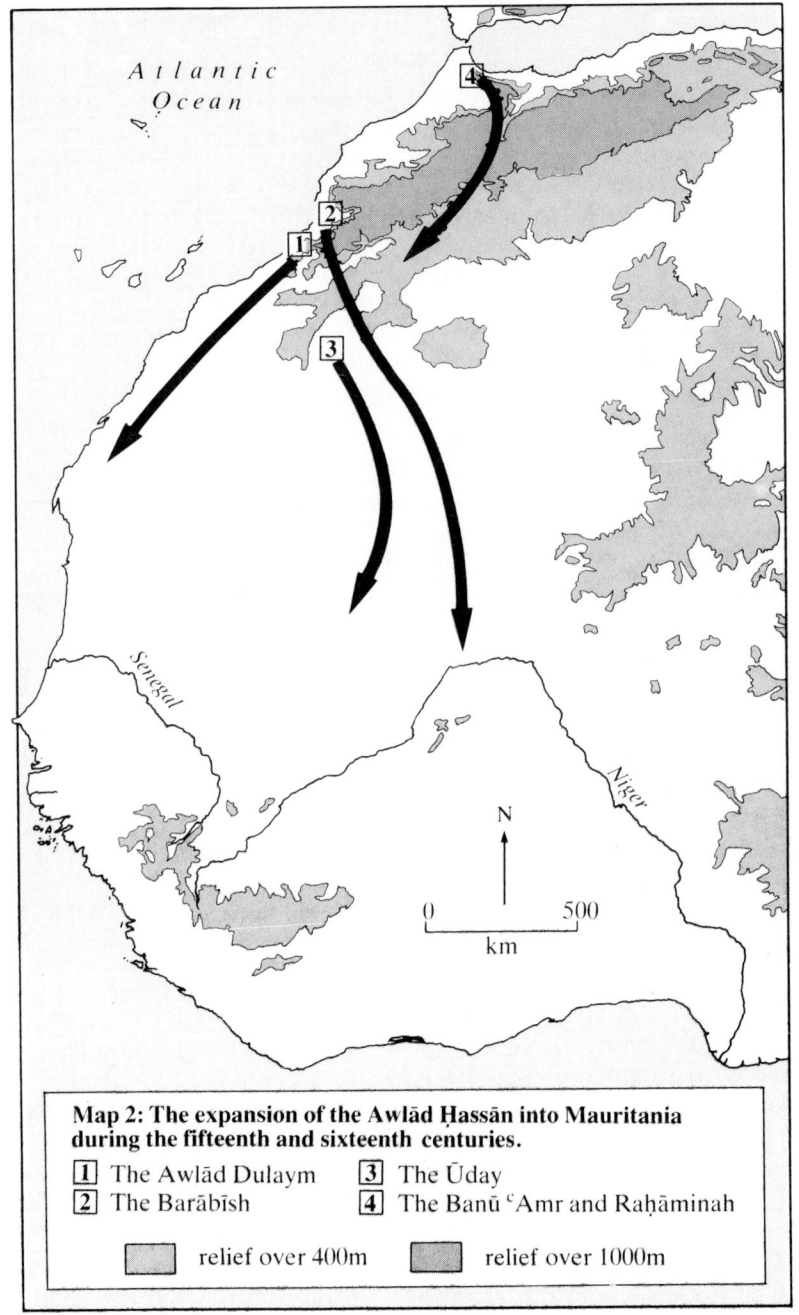

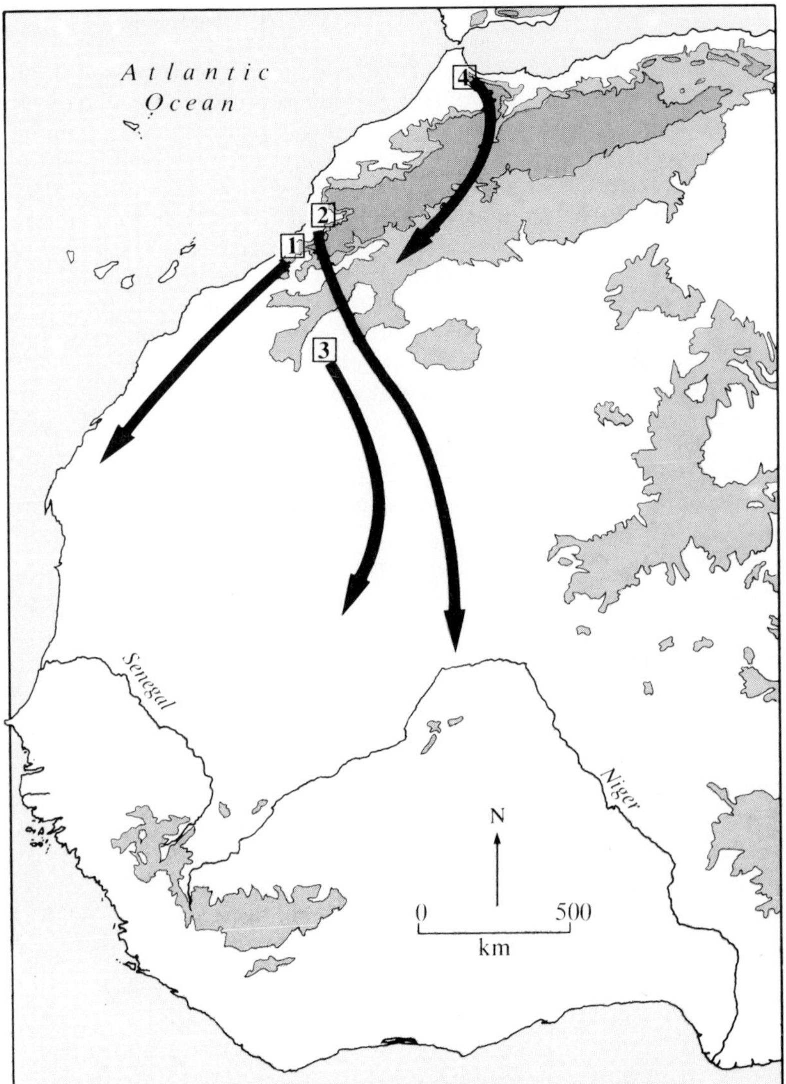

Map 2: The expansion of the Awlād Ḥassān into Mauritania during the fifteenth and sixteenth centuries.

1 The Awlād Dulaym
2 The Barābīsh
3 The Ūday
4 The Banū ʿAmr and Raḥāminah

relief over 400m
relief over 1000m

groups. A text from Aïr region makes this clear:

> "The Ṣanāhjah[8] are a host of tribes which have dispersed in all directions from the land of Aïr. Among them are those who dwelt to the east, and they were the allies of the princes of Aïr. Among them are those who dwelt to the west and they were allies of the *Ṭubūl* [Sulṭāns] of the Iwillimmeden. Notwithstanding, they chose one from those who were most learned and superior among them and, on their own account, they assigned to him the power to impose penalties in their affairs. Him they call the *Imām*. They have inherited that from father and son since they came forth and ever afterwards. Such then is proof enough for anyone who has the least ability to perceive what befell some of the princes of Aïr and Ḥadāḥadā and Ḥamidtu and what took place between them and the jurists and *Shaykhs* in correspondence."[9]

Several of the tribes of the Western Sahara who are mentioned by the Arab geographers seem also to have been known in the Central Sahara. Some still survive. The evidence, scanty as it is, supports the supposition that these tribes moved westwards. As they did so their names were altered, though not to the extent of being unrecognisable. Such names as appear in mediaeval documents – Anbiyah, Gudālah, Lamtūnah and Lamṭah, Massūfah and Watrīkah/Watzīlah, arguably Wanzīgah (so possibly the Zuenziga of Leo Africanus), all tribal names from the Western Sahara – can be matched by tribal names, which seem to be related, far to the east in the Central Sahara: possibly the Inemba among the Hoggar, the Igdalen, the Ilemteen and Dag Elemtei of Ghat and the Mali Adrār, the Inessufen of Aïr and Azawagh. Where these names differ from the former is in their 'I' prefix. Sir Rennell Rodd has shown, in his studies,[10] that this is a characteristic of the most ancient Ṣanhājah and Tuareg in the Sahara. Where these names appear in the west their form has an Arabic stamp. It shows the effort of someone shaping the names into patterns which the Arabic speakers found acceptable to pronounce, or seemed to derive from other names they knew.[11]

As ancient Berber tribes moved west, the Āzgār Tuareg were as far west as Sijilmāsah, Morocco, by the twelfth century,[12] so they were followed or hard pressed by incoming Arab nomads, the Banū Maʿqil amongst them. As has been seen, it was the region of Tuwāt and Gourara, then the Sūs, which bore the brunt of the Arab bedouin and suffered their ultimate control. It was a long process. The face-to-face encounter, which Ibn Khaldūn describes, may be illustrated by the fact that when Ibn Baṭṭuṭah crossed the Sahara with a Massūfah Berber *takshīf* guide in 1352, the Marīnid Sulṭān, Abū'l-Ḥasan in 1337, after his capture of Tlemcen (Tilimsān), had previously arranged that a Malian emissary mission of negroes and Ṣanhājah should be escorted homeward by Ma'qil Arabs, headed by 'Alī ibn Ghānim, Amīr of the Awlād Jār Allāh.[13]

The capture of Zammūr and Tīris

According to Saharan traditions two major engagements, different in date, determined that the Awlād Ḥassān should gain a mastery of the region between the Dar'ah (Draa) in southern Morocco and the Senegal basin. Further to the east in Azawād, as we shall see, there were other factors which determined the conquest. The first engagement allegedly occurred near the massif of Zammūr in the Río de Oro. About the year 1450, Sīdī Muḥammad al-Kuntī, the eponym of the great Kuntah confederation of the Western and Central Sahara, who had grown up amongst the Ṣanhājah Tājakānt, bestowed his blessing upon the Awlād al-Nāṣir, a branch of the Banū Ma'qil who had been harassed by the descendants of the Almoravids in that region, namely the Ibdúkalen/Abdūkal.[14] In the fighting which followed the Awlād al-Nāṣir, and the Awlad Ḥassān in general, were the victors, aided, it is alleged, by the miraculous intercession and sanctity of the Kuntah saint. The Berbers submitted and became clients of the Banū Ma'qil, their confederates, on the lines reported by Ibn Khaldūn as having taken place over half a century before in the Moroccan Sūs to the north:

> "The Sūs is the territory of the Lamṭa and Gazūla; the Lamṭa [wander] towards the Daran mountains and the Gazūla towards the desert and the sands. When the Ma'qil Arabs conquered and divided the plains of the Sūs, the Shabbānāt [division of Ma'qil] were nearest to Daran and so the Lamṭa clans became their confederates whereas the Gazūla become confederates of the Dhawī Ḥassān; and such is the situation to this day."[15]

The way was now open for the conquest of the Mauritanian Adrār.

The above account, which has been considerably summarised, is accepted as historical by the leading historians of Mauritania. It must be stressed, however, that there is no external historical source either to confirm it or deny it.

Shaykh Mukhtār wuld Ḥāmidun, in his great history, has written as follows:

"In the eighth and ninth centuries of the *hijrah* [the fourteenth and fifteenth centuries of the Christian era], the Banū Ḥassān entered Mauritania. They swept away the rule of the Abdūkal in the Sahara and the Anbāṭ in Tagānit and the ʿAṣābah and the Īdayshalli in the Mauritanian Adrār and the In'irzīk in the south-west (*al-Giblah*) and they imposed tributes and *Danegeld* (*maghārim*) upon all the Ṣanhājah and they exclusively applied the name of *al-Zenāgah* to those who paid the tributes and the name of *al-Zawāyā* and *al-Murābiṭīn* was confined to those others who were men of religion and of culture. Hitherto, all the Ṣanhājah were named *al-Murābiṭīn* and *Ahl al-Zāwiyah* by association with the *Ribāṭ* of (the Almoravid) ʿAbdallāh ibn Yāsīn, and the retreat (*zāwiyah*) where he devoted himself to pious devotion.[16]

"At the outset the Banū Ḥassān descended and settled upon the region of Igīdī in the province [ʿamālah] of Tīris Zammūr. To quote the [*Risālat*] (*al-Ghallāwiyyah*) of the Kuntah, 'Shaykh Sīdī Muḥammad al-Kuntī al-Kabīr grew up among his maternal uncles, from the Abdūkal Ṣanhājah, who, at that time, dominated the Sahara and those who were within it to the borders of the Sūdān. He rode away from them, angry with them, and he was visited by raiders of the Awlād al-Nāṣir. They had received news of his displeasure at the conduct of his maternal uncles. They asked him to give them the dominion [*dawlah*] of the Lamtūnah [*an yadʿuwa Allāha lahum bi mulki Lamtūnata*]. He said, 'I have given the *dawlah* to you on the condition that you, when you have attained the lawful bound whereby you are safe from their military power, you will raise the sword aloft from them and will spare their lives for the sake of the life of my sons and your sons, for verily, I have called upon Allāh's wrath to descend on them by taking away their *dawlah* and to render feeble their military power. He has answered my prayer in regard to them'.

"So they returned to their families. The Banū Ḥassān rallied those who were their confederates, and one morning they surprised the Lamtūnah when they were naked and unequipped. Those tribes which were close by them were appointed the task of fighting the Banū Ḥassān, while the others carried on their vassal activities, so contemptuous were the Lamtūnah of these Banū

Ḥassān, and little their regard for their power to attack. The Banū Ḥassān defeated those who were close allies and clients of the Lamtūnah in their very first attack. The latter were pressed to flee on their mounts together with those who were beyond them, those who had lent them no assistance to wage war against their foe. Thus the Banū Ḥassān defeated them so decisively that no community of them survived. The Banū Ḥassān spared the remnants, who are called the tributaries [*laḥmah*], while those who were men of religion and Arabic studies [*zawāyā*] were left to their religious pursuits."[17]

This story has all the charm of a folk-tale. It is not a record of a war, rather it is an account of a miracle of a saint of the Kuntah. Even so, it discloses some contact, intermarriage even, between Ṣanhājah and Ḥassānīs in the area of the Río de Oro at that time. The war may be based on some historical engagements and there are a few who, with serious reservations, are prepared to accept some historical value in such accounts.[18] If it occurred, however, there is no contemporary record to indicate its magnitude or its precise location. According to Valentim Fernandes (1506/7), the mountain of Kedyet Ijjel, near Tīris and close to a salt mine which was later controlled by the Kuntah, was a bastion of the Saharan Lamtūnah. "The kings of this mountain, as all the population, are Aznages. They are great enemies of the Arabs. While they dare not leave the mountain, the Arabs dare not penetrate therein."[19] Here "Arabs" must denote the Awlād Ḥassān, though not necessarily the Awlād al-Nāṣir. Possibly, these events in Kuntah tradition refer to a major assault on the massif called Jabal Ḥassān. Its loss left the Lamtūnah little choice but to go south or to make peace with the Ḥassānīs.

The War of Shurbubba, its causes and its consequences

The second major engagement between the Awlād Ḥassān and the Mauritanian Berbers took place about 1674/5. This is often called the War of Shurbubba, the latter being the name of a tributary of the Tāshidbīt Lamtūnah whose advice to his chief led to the interference of the Ḥassānī Banū Maghfar prince of the Trārzah, Haddi ibn Aḥmad ibn Dāmān, in a dispute which had hitherto only involved the Berbers of south-west Mauritania. Others, however, see this as a mere coincidence or a folk-tale. For them "Shurbubba" was a war cry, a war cry of the subjugated Berbers of the region to the north of the Senegal river against the Awlād Ḥassān who then oppressed them.

It is now apparent that the story of this war, and the martyrdom of its leaders, more especially of the *Imām* of the Lamtūnah and the Tashumsha Berbers, Nāṣir al-Dīn al-Daymānī, is a record of several events which have been woven together into a hagiographical narrative, diversified into a series of Chronicles whose author was the saint, Muḥammad al-Yadālī, or his pupil, Wālid al-Daymānī. Both were Berbers, yet both were laudatory of the Ḥassānī princes whose fathers had been responsible for the death of their patron saint, who had died when still a youth yet had the audacity to call himself Commander of the Faithful (*Amīr al-Mu'minīn*) and to wage a *jihād* against the Wolof, the Awlād Ḥassān and their Berber allies for a period, so it is alleged, of a generation.[20]

Shaykh al-*Qāḍī* Muḥammadh ibn Muḥunḍ Bābā has reported in one of his poems that the war began in the year *Shanah* (1055/1645) and that it ended in the year *Shafah* (1085/1675), but it is now the view that this extended period refers to the whole lifetime of Nāṣir al-Dīn's religious movement in southern Mauritania and Senegal and that it marks the period when the Ḥassānī Banū Maghfar effectively imposed their domination over other groups in the south-west of Mauritania. The Walātah Chronicle from eastern Mauritania corroborates evidence for the actual brevity of the war. It states tersely that a battle between the Banū Maghfar and the *Zwāya*, referred to as *waqʿat Ashrābība*, took place in 1084/1674. This no doubt refers to the battle of Tin Yifḍāḍ, where the Berbers were decisively defeated by the Ḥassānīs and where the *Imām* al-Mukhtār Agd ʿAbdallāh, the sixth successor to Nāṣir al-Dīn (who had been slain in the earlier battle of Tirtillās) fell from his horse. He had no successor to carry on the struggle which had seemed doomed from its very beginning. Although both sides fought effectively on horseback and the Berber *Zwāya* were inspired by a religious visionary and a strong feeling of injustice, they had lost the war against the Banū Maghfar because they had an inadequate knowledge and experience of military tactics, and because they failed to take advantage from their initial victories.

Leaving aside the war and its battles, and leaving aside Nāṣir al-Dīn himself, whose life and miracles belong to the history of the Mauritanian Berbers rather than the history of the Arab domination of this district, it is now possible to summarise the main reasons why the Awlād Ḥassān were able slowly, but surely, to establish their control as far as the Senegal basin during the course of the seventeenth century:

(1) Between 1600 and 1638 the Lamtūnah remnants in the Trārzah of Mauritania were nominally subject to the Peul who, we now know, had established an empire over large tracts of the northern bank of the Senegal river as far east as the Mauritanian Hodh.

(2) Many of the Berbers of the Trārzah had been compelled to pay *maghram* and *ḥurmah* (a payment to Ḥassānī protectors, on demand, of an annual sheep, or two calves, or a piece of *guinée* cloth) to tribes of the Awlād Ḥassān which had entered Mauritania prior to the Banū Maghfar (Trārzah and Brāknah). They included the Awlād Rizq, who were later supplanted by the Banū Maghfar, the Awlād al-Nāṣir and the Awlād Mubārak, who later moved into the Hodh, but, worst of all, to the Awlād Bū ʿAli, the chief of whom, Gaddūl ibn Bū Mūsā, committed unspeakable atrocities against the Berbers.[21] In time this led to military resistance on the part of the pacific Berbers and a switch of foe on the part of those Berbers who had been engaged in a *jihād* against the negro populations to the south of the Senegal river.

(3) The movement of Nāṣir al-Dīn, which was called the movement of repentance (*tawbah*), the Toubenan, was a religious movement aimed at converting the negroes of Senegal and inciting them to depose their impious rulers. Its aim was not directed initially against the Amīrs of the Awlād Ḥassān, whose influence in the south was such that they had an entrepôt for gum and slaves at Portendick where they traded with the Europeans, especially the French. Many of the Banū Maghfar were prepared initially to recognise the religious authority of Nāṣir al-Dīn. The conflict deteriorated into a Berber *Zwāya* versus Ḥassānī conflict only in the later stages of the Toubenan movement. Several of the *Zwāya* leaders had married into Ḥassānī families and even when the

conflict was at its most bitter, when the Berbers regarded the Ḥassānīs as little better than infidels, certain tribes remained aloof from the war. The following passage, which appears in al-Yadālī's commentary to his ode *Ṣalātu Rabbī* and his *Ghazawāt Shurbubbah* and his *Amr al-Walī Nāṣir al-Dīn*, furnishes a picture of relations between the two combatants, indicating how deeply inter-related Berbers and Awlād Ḥassān had already become in the Mauritanian south-west by the middle of the seventeenth century:

> "I [*al-Faqīh* ibn al-Muṣṭafā] accompanied Shaykh al-Amīn ibn al-Fāḍil and Muḥammad ibn Aḥmad, on their way to the [Ḥassānī] Maghāfirah seeking their favour and peace (*ʿāfiyah*) so that both of them could take out their families from the camp of the [Berber] *Zwāya*. We came to the Trārzah and we asked them for peace. They responded to our request until Maḥmūd ibn ʿAballa of the Maghāfirah reached them. He invalidated it all. They became dissimulators, intent upon making a raid on our soldiers. So we came to the Trārzah and said to them, 'What is the meaning of this?' They made the excuse that they wished to journey with their comrades there. I said to them, 'Allow us to live the *Sunnah* and to establish Allāh's law. We shall serve the cause of learning and teaching and will adore the Lord. We shall make the country prosperous for you and we shall act justly within it. We shall not stand in your way, nor in the way of your *Zenāgah* tributaries, nor in the path of your herds and flocks, nor in any other way. We have committed no act which merits a retribution. All we have done is to swear allegiance to an *Imām* who will govern us in the matter of our religion and our worldly affairs.' They answered 'In that case we answer No, by Allāh, we shall never forswear to you.' I said to them, 'If you deceive us then how evil it is if you break your oath to us; how evil a broken promise will be. So do not go forth on any raiding until we have separated from you and do not make for our military camp.' They agreed and they fulfilled their promise. Then I rode as a warner to the army of the *Zwāya* and I left my companions behind with them. I rode quickly and I came to the camp at nightfall. I had hardly spent any time with my family when Munīr al-Dīn, the brother of Nāṣir al-Dīn, came to me mounted upon a grey mare. He told me to report to our *Imām*. I accompanied him until we drew nigh the high seat where he was. The first thing which he said to me was, 'What did al-Majmūr son of ʿAballa – that is "him burnt by a fiery ember" – say to you? I mean the one who is the son of the one who will enter into Hell fire, bound in fetters. All the people of Hell will enter it

in fetters.' I then knew that no man had told him that. It had been a revelation disclosed to him since I had informed none about that episode and none had gone ahead of me to tell him nor had I accompanied another who could have in any way informed him about it."[22]

(4) The Moroccans became actively involved at this time, in supporting the Amīrates of the southern part of Mauritania. This point is made by Michel Abitbol in his history of the *Armas* of Timbuctoo.[23] Abitbol has pointed out that active Moroccan interference in the affairs of southern Mauritania commenced during the War of Shurbubba. The Ḥassānīs appealed to the Sulṭān for help and many Ma'qil bedouin were incorporated into the Sharifian army. The alliance was sealed, at the end of the war, in 1678/9, by the marriage between Mawlāy Ḥasan and the daughter of the Amīr of the Brāknah. In that same year, Mawlāy Ḥasan received the submission of many of the tribes of the Awlād Ḥassān in the entire Western Sahara. According to al-Wafrānī, this, in effect, extended his domain to the Senegal river and beyond.[24] This said, one suspects that this hegemony was in name rather than in the exercising of any effective control. However, it marked an important opening of communication between Mauritania and the north.

In a later passage Abitbol adds further to his statement.[25] He points to the links which developed between the Sulṭān and Sharifian families amongst the *Zwāya*. Closer links with Tagānit and the Hodh were also established. There was a strong influence from the Dar'ah region, especially the influence of the Ṣūfī brotherhoods. This was combined with increased caravan commerce, safer routes for travellers and exchange of visits by noted scholars.[26]

Both the "rediscovery" of the tomb of the Almoravid *Qāḍī*, the *Imām* al-Ḥaḍramī, at Āzuqqī, by the Āṭār *Imām*, al-Majdhūb, and the mission of Nāṣir al-Dīn (a "neo-Almoravid" revivalism of a marked Ṣūfī character rather than an obvious tradition handed down from the days of the historical Almoravids) occurred at around the same time. Their mid-seventeenth century date formed a watershed in the history of Islamic revivalism amongst the non-Ḥassānī *Zwāya*. A similar revivalism was afoot amongst the Kel Aghlāl (who claimed descent from the Mauritanian, Muḥammad

Ghilli, or Ghulli, the founder of Shinqīṭī) in Niger. There were a number of such *jihāds* at that time. The claim made for the authenticity of the *Qāḍī's* tomb, and Nāṣir al-Dīn's Mahdist claims, were bitterly opposed by certain Western Saharan scholars, as well as by the Ḥassānīs. The coeval *Zwāya* activity around Āṭār and the Shurbubba war in the southlands is not easy to explain in the light of the meagre evidence which we have. ʿAbd al-Wadūd wuld *Shaykh* has very tentatively suggested that the situation between *Zwāya* and Ḥassānī may have been exacerbated by the latter's interruption of the *Zwāya* caravan trade across the Sahara, northwards, while the Awlād Ḥassān may have been frightened by Islamic revivalism as a possible threat to their trading posts along the Senegal river and on the Trārzah coast.

The following passage about Nāṣir al-Dīn, and about the tomb of al-Ḥaḍramī, citing near contemporary sources, is from a work by Jīli wuld Intahāh (ibn ʿAbd al-Wadūd):

ظهر في الرابع والثمانين بعد الألف رجل من طلبة البادية قريباً من منتهى الاسلام بالمغرب الأقصى يسمّى أوبك ([اكد]؟) امْ فادّعى أنّه يتلاقى مع الخضر عليه السلام وأنّه يأمره بأشياء وينهاه عن أخر وأظهر أمره في الناس وأشاعه وكثر قاصدوه لما يخبرهم به من المغيّبات وأنّ فلاناً عُمره كذا وموته محلّ كذا بسبب كذا وأنه شقيّ أو سعيد وأنّه يسلم في الآخرة من هول الصّراط ويقع في هول المـيزان وأنّه يأخذ كتابه بيمينه أو بشماله وادّعى أنّه سيملك الأرض ويقال بمسمع منه أنّه المهديّ المنتظر ولا ينكر بل ربّما أشار إلى أنّه هو ويخبر الناس بقدر مكثهم في النار فيزعم أنّ مكث هذا أشهر وهذا أكثر وهذا دون وربّما أخبر أحدهم بما يزعم أنّه حدث به نفسه ويوافقه ويفرق بين الأزواج ويقول كوشف لي بأنّكما غير متزوجيْن إلى غير ذلك ولم يزل أمره إلى أن بويع له ممّن كان هناك من الزواية وهو خلق كثير ألوفاً وقام يحارب العرب من المغافرة فوقع بينهما حروب وهلكت فيها الناس والمواشي وقتل ذلك الرجل فتلاشى أمر أصحابه حتى هلك جلّهم وخلت البلاد وسفكت الدماء وضاع العيال وانطلقت أيدي العرب بالفساد فإنّا للّه وإنّا إليه راجعون ...

Most of the work consists of *Nawāzil* or juridical rulings, but the specific passages are attributed by a copyist to Muḥammad ibn Abī Bakr ibn al-Hāshim al-Ghallāwī of Walātah, who died on Friday 16 *Dhū'l-Ḥijjah*, 1098/1686. The text is therefore close in date to the events. This scholar took up the views of his master, Well Billa'mash, and formulated a severe judgement against the "Mahdism" of Nāṣir al-Dīn and the *Imām* al-Majdhūb.

Nāṣir al-Dīn.

"There appeared in the year 1084/1674 a man of the *Ṭulbah* (*Zwāya* of the Tashumsha) of the desert, nigh unto the very limit of Islam in the furthest Maghrib. He was called Awbek (agd?) Am (Abū Bakr). He claimed that he was one who met (the holy being) al-Khiḍr, peace be upon him, face to face, and that he commanded him to do certain things and forbade him from doing others. He made manifest his authority amongst men and he made it known abroad. Many there were who sought him on account of what he told them of the divine secrets. To a certain man he would foretell his age to be such and such, and that his death would be in such and such a place for such and such a cause. He would predict his wretchedness and his happiness and that in the world to come he would be safe from the horror of the heavenly path (*ṣirāṭ*) and that he would fall into the terror of the scales (*mīzān*). He said that he would take his book in his right hand or his left. He claimed that he would possess the earth. It was said, within his hearing distance, that he was the awaited *Mahdī* and he made no denial, nay, rather, sometimes he drew attention to his person in respect of this claim. He would inform men as to the degree of their sojourn in Hell's inferno. He would allege that the stay of this man would be months, and this man more, and this man less. Sometimes he told one of them about what he alleged he had deliberated about inwardly with his soul and how they had concurred. He would sever the ties of matrimony and say 'It has been disclosed to me that you are not truly man and wife'. This, and other matters like it, were characteristic of him.

"Thus continued his affair until homage was sworn to him by those of the *Zwāya* in his country. Several thousand they were in their number. He engaged in battle with the Arabs of the Banū Maghfar and a number of combats took place between the two participants. Both men and cattle perished. That man was slain and the power of his companions was destroyed until the bulk of them were wiped out and the land was a void and much blood was spilt and the kinsfolk and descendants were lost. The hands of the Arabs were set free to commit mischief and to despoil. Verily we are from Allāh and verily to Him we are returning."

وانظر أيضاً صاحب أهل آطار الّذي يقول إنّ العلوم تقع في قلبه من غير تعلّم ولا احتياج إلى مراجعة كتب فانّه من هذا القبيل لأنّه.زعم أنّ صاحب قبر هناك يخبره بالعلوم وعيّنه وعيّن قبره وبنى على قبره فهو بدأ (؟) يزوره وزعم أنّه يوقع العلوم تارة بقول في قلبه وتارة يجري بها يديْه بالكتابة هذا وقد قيل لابن عبد السّلام ان بعض الفقراء يزعم أنّه يعرف موضع قبور الصحابة بتونس فقال لو عرفناهم لسجنتم لأنّهم أخبروا بأمر غير معلوم يوقع تشويشًا (انتهى) وما أخلقه أعنى صاحب آطار بما همّ به ابن عبد السّلام فلقد أوقع فيما خاف منه ابن عبد السّلام (انتهى) وكان أنكر عليهم ذلك شيخنا الحافظ أبو عبد اللّه محمّد بن المختار ابن الأعْمش العلويّ وسمّع حتى يكفّر من شايعه علي ذلك ولعمري إنّه لخليقه بأن ينكر عليه لتعرّضه للغيب الّذى استأثر اللّه به وللطّراح (؟) (لاطّراحه ؟) مراجعة كتب اللّه وسنّة نبيّه صلّى اللّه عليه وسلّم وكلام السلف واستغنائه في الأحكام بما زعم أنّه تلقّاه من الخضر عليه السلام ولتعرّضه للفتن بين المسلمين عافانا اللّه من شرّ فتنته ومن شرّ جميع الفتن بمنّه وكرمه ....

The tomb of the Imām al-Ḥaḍramī (colloquial, Ḥaḍrāmī, Abū Bakr Muḥammad ibn al-Ḥasan al-Murādī, died 489/1096).
"See, also, the lord of the people of Āṭār, who says that the sciences (of the divine secrets) descend into his heart without bookish learning and without the need to refer to books. He is like this because he has alleged that the occupant of the tomb there (at Āzuqqī) informs him of these sciences. He has singled him out, and so too his tomb, and has raised a structure over his tomb. Now he has begun to visit it and its incumbent. He has alleged that he (the *Imām*) sends down the sciences. At times he does so by a word in his heart, at another he causes his hands to write them down. Ibn ʿAbd al-Salām was told that some of the poor (*Ṣūfis*?) allege that he knows the place of the

tombs of the Companions (of the Prophet) in Tunis. He said, 'Were we to know them then you would be shut up (made mute?), because they have revealed an unknown ordinance which inflicts a derangement'. How fit is he, I mean the lord of Āṭār, (to match) what Ibn ʿAbd al-Salām had anxieties about! For he has fallen into the snare so feared by Ibn ʿAbd al-Salām.

"That was held against them, refuted and disapproved of, by our Shaykh, al-Ḥāfiẓ Abū ʿAbdallāh Muḥammad ibn al-Mukhtār ibn al-Aʿmash al-ʿAlawī (d. circa 1107/1695/6) and he gave utterance to his revilings to the extent that he deemed one who was one of his sect, on account of that, to be guilty of unbelief. By Allāh, he is one fitted to refute him on account of his venturing in person into the world of the divine secrets, which is the monopoly of Allāh alone, and on account of the discarding (by this lord of Āṭār) of the study of Allāh's books and the *Sunnah* of His Prophet, His blessing be upon him, and of what was said by the forefathers, and his dispensing with the statutes and the precepts, whereby, he alleged, (he did so) by what he had received from al-Khiḍr, peace be upon him, and (likewise) for his daring to cause feuds and dissensions betwixt Muslims. May Allāh spare us from the evil of his impiety and from the evil of all dissensions by His grace and by His munificence . . "

European sources and the Awlād Ḥassān

European accounts which refer to the Awlād Ḥassān may be sketchy but, as we have already seen, were significant. They suggest that Arab elements were everywhere, both to the north and to the south of the Senegal river. They indicate that Ḥassānī hegemony or influence in some regions had been established possibly two hundred years before the "War of Shurbubba". It was deep and strategically predominant before major battles were fought in Tīris and Zammūr. The Portuguese had a base at Arguin and a "factory" at Wādān in the Adrār. Something was known about the interior as well as the coast. Pacheco Pereira,[27] who wrote between 1506 and 1508, is quite specific about who was then the master of the Mauritanian Adrār: "All these nations are vassals of a nation of Arabs called Ludea", that is to say, the Ūday of the Awlād Ḥassān.

Leo Africanus, likewise, in 1514/15, confirms that the "Arabs" were the Awlād Ḥassān: the Dulaym, the Barābīsh and the Ūday. The Barābīsh dominated the town of Tīshīt (in the Darʿah or in Mauritania), while the Ūday were the lords of the deserts between Wādān and Walātah. They received an annual tribute from the "Duke" of the latter. The "Arabs" were wealthy and powerful warriors, though with little cavalry. They travelled much to Tīshīt (Tissint perhaps) and to the Wād Nūn. Leo states that "those which we call Makil came first forth from Arabia Felix and derive their pedigree from Saba".[28]

It is clear from these accounts that the Awlād Ḥassān were established throughout the Western Sahara by the early sixteenth century. They controlled its commercial and strategic routes which had formerly been the exclusive territory of the descendants of the Almoravids, especially the Massūfah. Wādān, Tīshīt, Walātah and the whole Tuwāt probably paid them tribute. What did it matter, one might ask, that pockets of Berber resistance still defied these Arabs in the mountain of Ijjil, or in Tīris and Zammūr? The mastery of the south-east already belonged to the Dulaym, Ūday and Barābīsh.

These three Ḥassānī groups had expanded into *Zenāgah* districts which were tribally defined in the Almoravid age. The Gudālah may be paired with Dulaym, the Lamtūnah with Ūday and the Massūfah with the Barābīsh and, in many respects, the new Saharan tribal map bore a resemblance to the Sahara of the eleventh and twelfth centuries as it is described by al-Bakrī and al-Idrīsī.

The similarity of the tribal distribution may be explained by the geography of the Sahara. The human beings who dwelt in certain districts of it may have moved elsewhere or have been absorbed by more powerful or by more numerous groups. If one excludes major tribes such as the Tājakānt, who were widely spread over the whole Western Sahara, one may suggest that between 1400 and 1500 many of the Western Saharan peoples redesigned their lineages and genealogies. This may well have taken place with a marked switch from semi-matrilineal kinship nomenclature to that of patrilineal eponyms, many of them alleged descendants of the Prophet himself or one of his Companions, or else family trees which illustrated lateral ties with eponyms of the Maʿqil bedouin.

On the other hand the fifteenth and early sixteenth centuries may seem to be far too premature a date for this to have happened. There is an alternative, and this alternative has been examined closer in an earlier chapter, namely, that, at a date later than this, the scholarly fraternity, amongst both Berbers and Arabs in the Western Sahara, perfected a formula which they had discovered in the masterpieces of the Arabic mediaeval historians and genealogists, whose works were now in their hands to be studied, copied and imitated, and that they projected backwards into an earlier age the social metastasis which was taking place before their eyes between the Atlantic and the Tuareg Massifs of the Central Sahara, between the foothills of the southern Atlas and the banks of the Senegal and the Niger.

The preface to *The book of the notification of reports* by Muḥammad ibn Aḥmad Yūra al-Daymānī

Muḥammad ibn Aḥmad Yūra ibn Muḥammad ibn Aḥmad ibn Muḥammad al-ʿĀqil al-Daymānī has said:

> "There is no disagreement among our scholars and those who were experts in lineages from amongst our men of former times, such as Sayyid Muḥammad Wālid, the authority on the genealogies of the Saharans, and his Shaykh, Muḥammad al-Yadālī, that the Banū Ḥassān were Arab in origin. Muḥammad Wālid said, in a poem in *rajaz* metre, regarding the kings of the Banū Maghfar;
>
> > 'They have inherited from the Quraysh the quality to advance boldly towards the army, and generosity, and a courageous succour.'
>
> "Sīdī Muḥammad al-Yadālī said, in an ode in praise of the Amīr, Aḥmad ibn Hayba al-Barkannī [d. 1175/1761], wherein he enumerated their forebears, he traced them back to Jaʿfar ibn Abī Ṭālib al-Hāshimī al-Qurashī. This lineage became widely divulged on the tongues of the vulgar and the élite, and both young and old have become obsessed by it. Their [Ḥassānī] bard (*zaffān*), Aʿli ibn Mānu, said, praising Aʿmar ibn Aʿli Dayya ibn Aḥmad-Dayya ibn Haddi ibn Aḥmad ibn Dāmān at the start of a *Ḥassāniyyah* ode (*gāf*);
>
> > 'The name of Allāh, the Merciful, be upon you, the Compassionate, the Lofty and the Great.

> O Thou great Sulṭān of Sulṭāns whose ancestry is from ʿAbd-allāh ibn Jaʿfar [ibn Abī Ṭālib]'.

"His son, Al-Khu ibn Aʿli ibn Mānu, said, praising Aḥmad ibn Aʿmar ibn al-Mukhtār;

> 'The one who is nicknamed Ibn al-Laygāṭ, a *Qā'id* from a *Qā'id*, from heads and chiefs.
> He who does not disdain to be in the line of ʿAbd al-Muṭṭalib and ʿAbbās. Their esteem is his esteem!'

This is from a *Ḥassāniyyah* ode. They spell ʿAbdallāh as ʿAbdalla ibn Jaʿfar. Know, that the derivation of the Banū Ḥassān from the Quraysh is not unanimously agreed upon. Sīdī Muḥammad al-Yadālī traced it back to Ibn Khaldūn. As for them being Arabs, there is no disagreement at all about this. Some trace back their descent to Hawāzin, some to the Quraysh. Allāh knows best the truth of the circumstances, and what is the truth amongst those words which have been said. Refer to the *Kitāb al-Istiqṣā'*[29] in regard to the history of the furthest Maghrib. In it you will discover all you need to satisfy your desire. The case is strengthened by the fact that they have never spoken any other language but the Arabic tongue. I have heard from more than one source that the language of the first of them was pure Classical Arabic. There was no mixture of Berber within it, although it was an Arabic which was not inflected. Amongst the famous Banū Ḥassān who are mentioned here are Udday (Ūday) and Dulaym (Dalīm). As for Dulaym, his sons were Dirʿun and Sinān, Shwaykhu and the Awlād Mawlāt. As for Ūday, his offspring were the Wadāyā who lived between Marrakech and Fez. I do not know their forebear's name. As for Maghfar ibn Ūday, then his offspring were ʿUthmān ibn Maghfar, the ancestor of the Maghāfirah who are with us. Well known amongst us are Yaḥyā ibn ʿUthmān, the ancestor of the Awlād Yaḥyā ibn ʿUthmān who reside in the Adrār, and ʿUmrān ibn ʿUthmān. The descendants of the latter are Dāwūd ibn ʿUmrān, the ancestor of the Awlād Billa, the Awlād ʿAllūsh who reside in Tīshīt and Walātah, the Awlād al-Nāṣir and al-Faḥfāḥ ibn ʿUmrān the ancestor of the Awlād Ghuwayz/Lighwayz, the Awlād Inbārik (Mubārak) and Haddāj ibn ʿUmrān, the father of Tarrūz and Barkannī.

"This is what I have received in regard to their lineage. All knowledge is from Allāh. They entered this country and they conquered it together with those Sūdānese round about it in the year 1040/1632/3, when the Awlād Rizq fought one another, they having preceded the Banū Ḥassān. Their word did not accord and they grew weak as is always the case. The affair is in the authority of Allāh, beforehand and afterwards [Koran *sūrah* xxx.3]. The ode of al-Yadālī, referred to already, commences;

> 'The wisdom of the Almighty determined and decreed, with might and with victory, [in favour] of the offspring of "the mother of might and of renown".'
>
> "This ode is a long one and I have a copy of it written by al-Yadālī's own pen, praising therein Aḥmad ibn Hayba al-Barkannī and the sons of Umm al-ʿIzz ('the mother of might and of renown') from the Brāknah. It is a name given to the Awlād Nughmāsh and the Awlād al-Siyyid [*sic*] and the Awlād al-Mukhtār and the Awlād Ibbaysh because their mother's name was *Umm al-ʿIzz* al-Faḥfāḥiyyah. Their father was ʿAbdalla ibn Karrūm al-Barkannī."[30]

The views of Muḥammad al-Yadālī's pupil, Wālid ibn Khālunā, regarding the Ḥassānī princes were very similar to his own. While the Banū Maghfar are fiercely condemned for the martyrdom of Nāṣir al-Dīn, and for the suffering and loss endured by the *Zwāya* during the "War of Shurbubba", those princes who ruled the south in the eighteenth century and who resisted European encroachment are singled out for individual praise. A poem in *rajaz*, published with the Arabic text and the French translation in René Basset's *Mission au Sénégal*,[31] describes ʿAlī Shanẓūrah (d. 22 May 1727) as a "*just Imām*", *imām muqsiṭ*, a brave and a courageous lion. As for his brother, Shaykh ʿAmar, (d. 26 February 1757) he is described as the "*Imām* of the whole Maghrib", who, during his time, never attacked a Muslim; on the contrary, he was the servant of the scholars, *khādim al-ṭalabah*, and due to this he attained the highest status. He helped the poor, the needy, the widows and orphans, "the refuge of the *Zwāya* and the sheltering cave of every Muslim", *ma'wā 'l-zawāyā wa kahf kull muslim*. Such sentiments in praise of the protectors of Islam amongst the scholars are similar to those expressed by the Kel Es-Sūq towards certain princes of the Iwillimmeden (see the remarks made by al-Gunahānī in his manuscript on page 214).

Chapter 5

The Arabic Culture of the Awlād Ḥassān

The *Ḥassāniyyah*-speaking Moors of the Western Sahara have enjoyed a reputation for their ability, even genius, to improvise poems on every conceivable topic. Some of these poems, *thaydīna* or *kerza*, have an epic quality. They are laudatory, addressed to great men or chiefs, and some of them are closely modelled on Classical Arabic masterpieces. Others are amatory and flippant and expressed in a way which shows little debt to Classical Arabic. They are the perfect expression of the vernacular language of the Western Sahara, the *Klām Ḥassān* or the language of the Awlād Ḥassān.

Marmol Carvajal, who drew upon Leo Africanus, in his description of Africa, 1573, described the bedouin who lived between Numidia and Libya as "very witted and conceited in the penning of verses; wherein each man will decipher his love, his hunting, his combats and other his worthy acts and this is done for the most part in ryme after the Italians manner".[1] Verse and music went together, and at the beginning of the seventeenth century, le Père Labat remarked (according to the statement of Brue) that the Moors had a taste for verse and that likewise,

> "amongst them they have a type of music and some instruments which are very similar to our guitares. They love poetry and early compose verses which those who understand Arabic hold in high esteem for their liveliness, the difference of expressions, the majesty of the style and a certain lightness which reveals the brilliance of their wit and the variety of their thoughts."[2]

This talent of theirs has never once deserted them, whether they inhabit the most barren terrain of the Río de Oro, the ancient caravan towns of Walātah or Timbuctoo, or in a modern capital such as Nouakchott where the Radio Station has promoted their talents far and wide in the Sahara and African Sahel. There is a certain aggressiveness in this genius. Robert Adams, a seaman who was a captive among the Awlād Dulaym in the Río de Oro in the eighteenth century, described their behaviour as "haughty and insolent, they spoke with fluency and energy, appeared to have great powers of rhetoric and I was told that many of them possessed the talent of making extempore compositions in verse, on any object that attracted their notice".[3]

At about this time Jackson remarked, likewise,

> "The Arabic language as spoken by the camel drivers, is particularly sweet and soft, the gutteral and harsh letters are softened, and with all its energy and perspicacity, when pronounced by them is as soft and more sonorous than the Italian: it approaches the ancient Koranic language and has suffered but littler alteration these twelve hundred years. The Arabs of the Morffra (Maghāfirah) and those of the Woled Abbusebah [Awlād Bū Sbāʿ] frequently held an extempore conversation in poetry, at which the women are adepts, and never fail to show attention to those young Arabs who excel in this intellectual and refined amusement."[4]

From these, and other accounts, the following facts emerge, facts which are confirmed by all expert Mauritanians who have studied the poetry of the Banū Ḥassān and who have some inkling of the historical evolution of this poetry, meagre as it is: the poetry in *Ḥassāniyyah* Arabic or a form of *Ḥassāniyyah* Arabic has been a marked feature of the Arabs of the Western Sahara since the sixteenth century at least, probably earlier, and that it shows an affinity with the literary language of Classical Arabic even if some concessions are allowable in the composition of verse; that poetic language is not the monopoly of any one class in Western Saharan society and that its delights are shared by the women as well as the men; lastly, and most importantly, there is a close connection between the poetry of the Ḥassāniyyaphones and the music of the Western Sahara, known as *Azawān*, which has become the private art of the musician, the *Īggāwen*, who have no parallel in Tuareg society though they are known in the Western Sūdān.

Shaykh Muḥammad al-Imām ibn al-Shaykh Mā' al-ʿAynayn has written in regard to these people:

> "The Banū Ḥassān have a great love of listening to verse and musical instruments and they have countless modes of singing and a class of men who are skilled in them and who excel in them and who have an expert knowledge which they hand down to their descendants. This class is peculiar to the chiefs. The latter lavish precious wealth upon it and take pride in being associated with it. They desire that this class should praise them in sung verses (*ashʿāruhu al-malḥūnah*) and they reward the class with the rewards which are bestowed upon the poets, excellent rewards."

Ḥassāniyyah, the language of Arabic in which the poetry is composed, has all but replaced the languages of the Western Sahara which preceded it, *Zenāgah* Berber which is now only spoken by a small community in the Trārzah of Mauritania, and *Azayr*, a language related to *Sarakollé*, which was a language of the ancient caravan towns of the Adrār, Tagānit and the Hodh. In the east there is a linguistic overlap. In the Malian regions of Timbuctoo, Azawād and Aribinda, the *Songhai* and *Tamasheq* speakers have successfully resisted *Ḥassāniyyah*, although in some groups, among the Igellād of the Kel Intasar, for example, there is some bilingualism. In the past the *Zenāgah* speakers showed some resistance to the spread of *Ḥassāniyyah*. This was in part due to the strength of Classical Arabic among the lettered, many of them of *Zwāya* or Berber origin and background. They cherished and prided themselves on an expert knowledge of the Koran and the *dīwāns* of Classical Arabic verse. This led to some resistance to the adoption of *Ḥassāniyyah* as a vernacular tongue. *Ḥassāniyyah* has borrowed a large vocabulary from *Zenāgah*. It is particularly noticeable in toponyms, names of plants, terms connected with cattle herding and some material culture. It is also very marked in the music, a fact which leads one to suspect that this art must have existed in the Western Sahara in some form prior to the domination of *Ḥassāniyyah* in the poetry itself.

Along the coast, at least, Arabic in any form was spoken by very few. Ibn Saʿīd al-Maghribī, who died about 1286/7, and who wrote his *Book of Geography* about 1270, cites the account of a voyage by a certain Ibn Fāṭimah whose ship came to grief off a "gleaming mountain" which may have been located near Cap Blanco or within the hills of the Adrār Sutuf to the east of the bay. The Gudālah Berbers who befriended them and who took them to their capital, Taghīrā, somewhere in the Río de Oro, could not understand their Arabic. Matters were made simple when "someone came who understood both languages and asked them how they went astray."[5]

It is certain that in the fifteenth century a large part of the Río de Oro, at least the coastal region, was still little affected by the culture of the incoming Ḥassānīs. Gomes Eannes de Azurara draws attention to this in his *Chronicle of the Discovery and Conquest of Guinea*. Recounting the voyage and military operations of Nuno Tristam on that coast he has recorded:

> "Then those captains returned to the ships and bade that Arab whom Nuno Tristam had brought with him, to speak with those Moors but they were not able to understand him, because the language of these people was not Moorish, but Azaneguy of Sahara, for so they name that land. But the noble, in that he was of better breeding than the other captives, so had he seen more things and better than they; and had been to other lands where he had learnt the Moorish tongue; forasmuch as he understood that Arab and answered to whatever matter was asked of him by the same."[6]

However, the situation in the interior, especially in the area of Old Ghana and the Mauritanian Hodh, was certainly different. Here there had been considerable Arabisation before the entry of *Ḥassāniyyah*-speaking Maʿqilian groups in any number. The fourteenth-century Arab traveller, Ibn Baṭṭūṭah, had little difficulty in conversing in detailed conversation in Arabic in the town of Walātah, among the mixed population there whom he described as mostly belonging to the Massūfah. The cosmopolitan character of the citizens and their knowledge of Arabic, other than in a religious context, and the manners of the Maghribīs, is to be observed in one of his anecdotes.

> "One day I went into the presence of Abū Muḥammad Yandakān al-Massūfī in whose company we had come and found him sitting on a carpet. In the courtyard of his house there was a canopied couch with a woman on it conversing with a man seated. I said to

him; 'Who is this woman?' He said: 'She is my wife.' I said: 'What connection has this man with her?' He replied: 'He is her friend.' I said to him: 'Do you acquiesce in this when you have lived in our country and become acquainted with the precepts of the *Sharʿ*? He replied: 'The association of women with men is agreeable to us and a part of good conduct, to which no suspicion attaches. They are not like the women of your country.' I was astonished at his laxity. I left him, and did not return thereafter. He invited me several times but I did not accept."[7]

I would suggest that here there is evidence which indicates a very marked difference indeed between the scrappy Arabic known among the Western Saharan Berbers on the Atlantic coast and in the remotest desert, and the Arabic of the Berbers who were partly urbanised in parts of the Hodh and the Mauritanian Adrār. Here the contact with Arabic speakers had been continuous since the age of the Almoravids, contact with scholars, pilgrims, traders and slave merchants. Loan words from Sūdānic languages had been Berberised before their acceptance into *Ḥassāniyyah* or into the form of vernacular Arabic which must once have preceded it.

Ḥassāniyyah, if compared with the Arabic of Maghribī sedentaries, is a conservative dialect; sharing much of its vocabulary and syntax with other bedouin dialects, common to the dialects of the Algerian Sahara in regions where the Maʿqilian Arabs are known to have settled during the course of their migrations into north-west Africa, retaining a few features of the Arabic spoken in the more southerly parts of the Arabian peninsula. Individual to *Ḥassāniyyah* is its syllable structure. *Ḥassāniyyah* prosody has taken advantage of this in order to vary metre patterns. These syllabic forms show little change within the last two centuries.[8]

Ḥassāniyyah verse and its relationship with Maghribī *malḥūn*

It is a view commonly held among Mauritanian scholars that *Ḥassāniyyah* poetry has evolved from a type of verse which has been somewhat loosely called "Hilālī poetry". Some scholars also maintain that an element of Maghribī and Andalusian strophic poetry had been fashionable and influential in the Western Sahara during the period between the collapse of the Almoravids in the twelfth century and the coming of the Ḥassānīs in the fourteenth and fifteenth centuries. This type of poetry may have helped shape the characteristic verse of the Awlād Ḥassān.

Others deny any influence of Andalusian *muwashshaḥ* and *zajal*.[9] Muḥammad wuld Mawlūd wuld Dāddāh goes back to the *Muqaddimah* of Ibn Khaldūn to find the sources of *Ḥassāniyyah* verse. There, and in the *Kitāb al-ʿIbar* as a whole, are to be found short poems in colloquial Arabic spoken by the Hilālī and Sulaymī bedouins. Such, in his view, offer the truest examples of Saharan bedouin verse, although one must allow for the fact that the Maʿqil, who were companions of the Hilālīs, were also independent from them in certain respects. The Ḥassānīs stem from the Maʿqil and not from the Hilālīs. Over a period of centuries *Ḥassāniyyah* poetry grew apart from the Hilālī forms. These latter, based on the examples given by Ibn Khaldūn, showed clearly that not only did the Banū Hilāl adhere to the subject matter of ancient Arabian verse, that is warlike boasting (*mufākharah*), love poetry, eulogy and satire, but that they also preserved much of the ancient metre and the unity of rhyme to be found there. The major change occurred with the loss of vocalisation of desinential inflection. Having accomplished the latter, *Ḥassāniyyah* proceeded to create and invent its own individual metres, discarded unity of rhyme or reasserted a new unity, and departed further and further away from the Classical poetic forms. Muḥammad wuld Mawlūd wuld Dāddāh insists, however, that nothing is known of the poetry of the Banū Maʿqil during the period when they first advanced south and west into the Western Sahara.

It is not easy to obtain a true picture of the evolution of this poetic genre. Firstly, it is known from Ibn Khaldūn's examples and comments that the unity of rhyme must have been markedly modified in popular Arabic verse prior to his day and certainly prior to the major intrusions of the Awlād Ḥassān into the Western Sahara.

Ibn Khaldūn wrote:

"The Arabs have another kind of poetry which is widely in use among them. It employs four lines (*a a*?/b b b a/c c c a/d d d a etc.), wherein the fourth has a rhyme different from the first three. The

> fourth rhyme is then continued in each stanza throughout the whole poem similar to the quatrains and the stanzas of five lines which were originated by recent poets of mixed Arab and non-Arab parentage."[10]

As will be seen, this rhyme scheme, known as a *ṭalʿah* in the poetry of the Awlād Ḥassān, was to dominate among the various patterns of rhyme which they employed, and still employ, in their folk poetry.

Muḥammad al-Marzūqī, who was a leading authority on the popular poetry of the Tunisian bedouin and a student of Hilālī poetry, was of the opinion that the examples which he had seen of Hilālī verse manifested a Classical form in general although with some concession and relaxation in the use of desinential inflection, and some mixture with Berber and Byzantine elements which had entered Hilālī poetry. In his view, this poetry showed little departure from Classical Arabic poetry, although the isolation of many of the bedouin groups must have led to changes in the form of this poetry after a period of time. Some of the poetry kept very close to the Classical. This was the case where Hilālī Shaykhs were required to address governmental officials or the cultured intelligensia. An example is the *qaṣīdah* by ʿInān ibn Jābir, Shaykh of the tribe of Mirdās of the Banū Sulaym, addressed to Abū ʿAbdallāh Muḥammad ibn Ḥusayn, the chamberlain of Zakariyyā' the Ḥafṣid, in the fourteenth century. A link was preserved between the Classical and Neo-Classical metric poetry (*mawzūn*) and the popular (*kalām*) rhythmic (*malḥūn*) verse which was measured numerically in the verses according to a syllable count. This was in keeping with the pronunciation, stress, vowel pattern and sonority of the dialect. Classical again is the poem of Khālid ibn Ḥamzah, Shaykh of the Kuʿūb of the Awlād Abī'l-Layl among the Banū Sulaym, composed in the fifteenth century. This contrasts with another, approaching the Colloquial *Qasīm*, composed by the Sharīf, Shākir ibn Hishām, on the subject of a dispute which arose between him and Mādī ibn Muqrib, the Shaykh of the Banū Hilāl.[11] An impact on Hilālī verse from al-Andalus cannot be discounted. Examples of *muwashshaḥāt* and of *zajal* are likely to have been known to them prior to the expulsion of Moors on a large scale to North Africa.

When the Awlād Ḥassān entered the Western Sahara from southern Morocco they had already been under the cultural influences which were the fashion at court in Morocco and the fashion outside it. Popular Moroccan poetry was also sung poetry. According to Muḥammad al-Fāsī:

> "the essential difference between Moroccan *malḥūn* and Arab Classical poetry is that the former is primarily composed to be sung. It is the 'science which is bestowed' (*ʿilm mawhūb*) and according to the tradition its earliest example was the poem of Ibn ʿAbbūd of Fez, composed in the sixteenth century. Every conceivable subject might be introduced and employed; epic, parody and religion."[12]

Under the Moroccan Marīnids, poems were composed in the vernacular about the birth of the Prophet (*mawlid*), though these cannot be separated from the poems in Spanish-Arabic dialect which served as words to be sung in the performance of the Classical music of al-Andalus. At this time most of the latter were poems based on the quantity, that is short or long, of the syllables which appeared in each verse. However, after the Saʿdians (1511–1659) there was a marked change. The metre in vernacular poetry was chiefly based on the number of syllables, regardless of length, in each verse. This was combined with the use of a special *koiné* (*malḥūn*) which was derived from popular Moroccan Arabic although markedly influenced by the bedouin dialects. This "bedouin" verse flourished under the Saʿdians and the ʿAlawites. Whole odes were composed in *malḥūn*. One of the earliest was composed in the sixteenth century by Abū Fāris ʿAbd al-ʿAzīz al-Maghrāwī, who was one of the bards of the Saʿdian Sulṭān, al-Manṣūr al-Dhahabī (1578–1602). Much of this poetry was religious. An example is that of the poet and saint, ʿAbd al-Raḥmān al-Majdhūb al-Dukkālī (d. 1569), who composed mystical verses in this genre. A number of the great poets in *malḥūn* came from the region of Sijilmāsah, on the edge of the Western Sahara. The movement came to be known as the *Grīḥa* in Morocco of the Saʿdian era and it became the established and most prevalent form of the popular singers. Their verses married the tradition of the long pre-Islamic ode and the vernacular, and they were now written in *malḥūn*, based on popular Moroccan Arabic though markedly influenced by the bedouin dialects. Case endings and forms essential in Classical Arabic grammar were discarded. The versification ignored the quantity; now it was based solely on the total number of the syllables. Accentuation was quite external to the poetry itself. It was subordinate to the function of the song for which it was composed. *Malḥūn* had a dual meaning; "faulty" and "sung".[13]

If now one turns to examine what is known, or conjectured, regarding the history and form of Ḥassānī verse the following factors have to be taken into account:

(1) In much of the Western Sahara, although not in the towns of the Hodh, the cultural level of the *Zenāgah* was pre-Islamic. It would have been limited to the literature of a pre-Islamic society, comparable with certain Berber tribes in Morocco today, superficially arabised, where there is a rich oral literature, that is in verse, folk-tales and legends. Any *Zenāgah* poetry was oral and almost none of it has survived.

(2) That in the opinion of Mukhtār wuld Ḥāmidun, himself a *Zenāgah* speaker, some *Ḥassāniyyah* verse is unquestionably older than *Zenāgah* poetry and the latter has derived many of its terms for verse and hemistich, for prosody and rhyme, from the former.

(3) That *Ḥassāniyyah* poetry (*leghna*), seems to possess some features which derive from Andalusian forms but that Classical Arabic verse in the Western Sahara has eschewed *muwashshaḥ*.[14]

(4) That following from (3) this Andalusian influence was either present in the mediaeval cultural centres, such as Walātah, prior to the Ḥassānī entry into the Western Sahara, but was almost totally absent from the rest of the desert, more especially the coastal districts, or else it arrived with the Ḥassānīs.

(5) That, in the view of Mukhtār wuld Ḥāmidun, the Sa'dians in Timbuctoo, and their *Armas*, had a marked influence, culturally speaking, on the Ḥassānī nomads throughout the whole of the Western Sahara. It is therefore not unreasonable to expect some connection between the *malḥūn* which was in vogue under the Sa'dians and the *leghna* and *Azawān* of the troubadours of the Ḥassānī princes, more especially as most of the earliest and the greatest of them attained their fame in the Amīrates of the Hodh and in regions adjacent to Timbuctoo.

(6) That *Ḥassāniyyah* Arabic poetry (*leghna*) is so closely connected with the art of the Īggāwen and with *Azawān*, sung poetry set within musical modes or styles of singing,[15] showing markedly *Zenāgah* and "Black African" influence, even dominance, that these two must have been a united art form at an early stage in the evolution of the vernacular poetry of the Western Saharans.

(7) That the most evolved, complex, and least popular, forms of *Ḥassāniyyah* verse, the *rasm* and *thaydīna*, for example,[16] are heavily influenced by Classical Arabic poetry in *recherché* expressions which reveal the influence of the pre-Ḥassānī and post-Ḥassānī *Zwāya* scholars. In fact, it is not always possible to make a distinction between poets in the two poetic forms: (a) *Ḥassāniyyah* improvised verse and *Ḥassāniyyah* sung poetry (both called *tawshīḥ*, in the *Kitāb al-Wasīṭ*) and (b) Classical Arabic poetry and Classical Arabic sung poetry.

The examples of two Mauritanian poets may serve to illustrate this interconnection.[17] The first of the poets is Muḥammad ibn Haddār, who was also renowned as a singer. He was a member of the tribe of the Liḥrakāt, which had a reputation for skill in composing in *Ḥassāniyyah*. Some of the poems of Wuld Haddār are in Classical Arabic, introducing *Ḥassāniyyah* proverbs, whilst others are long odes in the vernacular addressed to the Amīr of the Trārzah, Sīdī wuld Muḥammad al-Ḥabīb (d. 1871). The latter gave Wuld Haddār the task of copying out the great commentary on the grammarian, Khalīl, *al-Muyassar al-Kabīr*, written by the scholar Maḥanḍ Bābā (d. 1860). Upon completing the task the poet wished to keep the paper which he had not used for the copy but the Amīr insisted that he should return the paper. Wuld Haddār's first reaction was to compose a satire against the Amīr. However, realising that it might cost him his tongue, he composed a poem in *Ḥassāniyyah* in praise of the Amīr and in it he makes a continuous allusion, interspersed with profuse praise, to the proverb that "the surplus belongs by right to the artisan". This poem enhanced his reputation and brought him a reward. Noteworthy is the fact that Wuld Haddār, an admired poet in Classical Arabic and a copyist of no mean talent, should have selected *Ḥassāniyyah* as the proper vehicle to express his sentiments which were a combination of some genuine pique at the miserly conduct shown towards him by his prince and at the same time genuine fear of him, knowing that he depended upon him for his livelihood as a poet laureate.

In one of his *Ḥassāniyyah* poems Wuld Haddār praised the neo-Jāhilī poet, Muḥammad ibn al-Mukhtār al-Yaʿqūbī, known as Wuld Ṭulba. Wuld Haddār described him as "the pole (*quṭb*) of the *Zwāya* of Tīris and their *Imām*". Wuld Ṭulba was not a *Ḥassāniyyah* poet, on the contrary he was something of *un poete sayyid de la gentilité*,[18] and he considered himself to be the equal of the pre-Islamic poets themselves. According to the author of the *Kitāb al-Wasīṭ* he had an insatiable passion for Classical Arabic which he wrote elegantly and employed every poetic epithet he could find in the lexicons.

> "It is said that when he travelled and halted at a *Zawāyā* camp by day the first thing which he asked them for was the lexicon, and if they had it he asked them to bring it to him so that he could spend the day looking at it. If they were without it he went on his way and did not waste his time. He used to make arrows and to hunt game with them because of his passion for imitating the pre-Islamic Arabs and he had a great love for the land of Tīris. You can hardly find a place in it that he does not introduce somewhere into his verses. One day, after he had composed his poem which rhymes in the letter *jīm* and he had divulged it to the people, he said, 'I beg the Almighty that I may sit together with al-Shammākh ibn Ḍirār (and Ḥumayd ibn Thawr) in a gathering of the people of Paradise so that we may recite our odes before them so that we may know which of the two odes is the best'."[19]

Whatever the heavenly company may or may not have thought of the poems in question, there is no doubt that this derivative, though sometimes majestic, poetry, as graphic as a photograph in its imagery although very static in style and feeling, has not been unanimously praised by the Moors of the Western Sahara, partly because it had no appeal to those outside the *Zwāya* fraternity – even if its content was intelligible – partly because, however close the environment of the Western Sahara and pre-Islamic Arabia might be, it lacked the more forceful impact of such verse in the vernacular.

René Basset has compared a poem of the pre-Islamic poet, Imru'ul-Qays, with that of a nameless poet of Tagānit (in *libtayt al-tāmm* metre, c c c b, c b, c b, c b, a b, a b), and the similarity between the Arabic and *Ḥassāniyyah* is readily apparent. The former begins:

"Help me on account of a flashing fork which I behold ablaze,
lighting up an approaching cloud among the lofty cumulus.
Sometimes its lightning is stilled, at another time it rises up,
despite its heaviness, like the slow gait of a three-legged camel.
Glinting flashes come forth from the cloud, methinks they portray
the winning hands of him who wagers with the gaming arrows.
I and my comrades sat there, betwixt Ḍārij, the brooks of Yathlath,
and al-ʿArīḍ.
The sand dunes which twist in Qaṭātayn were struck and ran in flood,
likewise the valley of Badī. It turned its course toward Arīḍ.
It is a broad land and a soft land and torrents of rain poured in a vast expanse. Hour by hour it poured forth water from every store held in the clouds, gathering lizards in the level desert."[20]

The *Ḥassāniyyah* poem is a *ṭalʿah*, followed by a *gāf*, (a b, a b) and it reveals the poet as one versed in the poetic masterpieces of early Arabic verse.

"A far-off memory has been stirred within my heart. It has
been released from its preoccupation with the loss of a
new loved one,
by the sight of a lightning flash which I beheld far to the
north. I spent my night watching it with my gaze,
trying to discern the locality over which it flashed, I
was seated on the sand-dunes, there, on the northern side
of Umm Maghrīd,
and then I noticed that it was above the abandoned camps
in al-ʿAyn, in Antar, in Nawāshīd, in Ijrān of the dates
and in Nfār. The swathes of herbage in that spot are cut
and severed by the flood beds, and then their combes continue
the blue traces left by the water from the rocks."[21]

This published poem, and there are many others unpublished like it, demonstrates that there is no clear line of distinction in subject between Western Saharan verse in the vernacular and the verse in Classical Arabic. Both reflect the life of the desert and a pastoral society, both portray a similar landscape and both display the depth of Classical Arabic learning among the Moors from the seventeenth century onwards, among the *Zwāya* in particular. According to Mohamd Moktâr ould Bah:[22]

> "between the eighth and the sixteenth century the Arabic culture of the Western Sahara is wholly religious. It is only after the arrival of the Banū Ḥassān that a second change came about: the integration, within the *ensemble* of Arabo-Islamic literature, of the culture the vehicle of which we shall very briefly examine: the *Ḥassāniyyah* language and its poetic and musical expression."[23]

Elsewhere Muḥammad wuld Mawlūd wuld Dāddāh al-Chennafi has observed: "The arrival of the Banū Ḥassān brought about the arabisation of the country and after the introduction of grammatical and lexicographical studies Mauritanian poetry was born towards the middle of the seventeenth century."[24]

The repertoire of this poetry reveals the puritanical religious taste of the *Zwāya*. There is laudatory praise of patrons, and there are many poems in praise of the Prophet. Boasting and tribal patriotism (*fakhr*) is also to be found, moving elegies and satirical and sarcastic verse. Many poems describe Saharan scenery and customs, plants and trees. Throughout there is a severe, inhibited sentiment, didactic and predicatory, little that is bacchic, nothing that is sodomite or of the chase, and, apart from the form of *Ḥassāniyyah* verse, no marked influence in any way from Andalusian *muwashshaḥāt*. The *Zwāya* poets have at times viewed with disfavour the profession of the Īggāwen musicians who sing to the accompaniment of the *tīdinīt* guitar or to the Mauritanian harp, the *ardīn*. Their distaste is in part aesthetic, in part moral, eschewing the avarice and permissiveness which on occasions has characterised the lives of the professional entertainers whose class in society is among the debased. Nor is it possible to separate the *Zwāya* of Berber origin from those who are unashamedly Ḥassānī in their birth. One of them is mentioned in the text, *Fatḥ al-Shakūr*-Sīdī Muḥammad ibn Aḥmad ibn Yaḥyā ibn Ibrāhīm ibn ʿUmar al-Maʿqilī al-Ḥassānī al-Dulaymī who lived between 1600 and 1650. The

Awlād Dulaym are one of the tribes of the Río de Oro although it is probable that this scholar was one of their number who were settled in the Hodh. He wrote a commentary on the *Ṣughrā* of al-Sanūsī. Kinsfolk of the Awlād Ḥassān were members of the Saharan and Sahelian scholastic college.

In the main, however, it would be truer to say that the greatest of the poets seem to have come from the great tribes of the Berber *Zwāya* although deriving much from their patrons who were Awlād Ḥassān, or who had reason to show favour to the Awlād Ḥassān. In Moroccan history the power of the "pretorian" cavalry of the Maʿqil Ūdayah, who were quartered in new Fez, was of significance in the reign of Mawlay Ismāʿīl in the seventeenth century. Their communal benefice was the tax-farm of the city's agricultural environs. They were relations of the "Reyna Negra" of Tuwāt, the principal wife of Mawlay Ismāʿīl, and it should not be overlooked that this same ruler later married into the Ḥassānī Brāknah, these alliances showing the favourable policy towards the Awlād Ḥassān in Mauritania. Perhaps the greatest of all the Mauritanian poets of that age was Sīdī ʿAbdallāh ibn Muḥammad ibn al-Qāḍī, known as Ibn Rāzgah. According to Mohamd Moktâr ould Bah:

> "Muḥammad al-ʿĀlim, fils du sultan Mūlāy Ismāʿīl, lui dit: 'Cesse de parler de Ḥarrāq et de Min Naḥna, toi seul, tu vaux l'ensemble!' . . . . On sait qu'il a été plusieurs fois à la cour du sultan Mūlāy Ismāʿīl, ou il lia amitié avec son fils Muḥammad al-ʿĀlim. Ce dernier lui donna une bibliothèque très importante dont quelques ouvrages sont encore dans la tribu. Muḥammad al-ʿĀlim soutint son ami W. Rāzga et l'emir ʿAlī Šandūra en leur accordant un contingent armé [*mḥalla*], ce que assura le triomphe des Trārza dans le Gebla."[25]

A great contemporary, Muḥammad al-Yadālī, was in favour at the court of the Amīr of the Brāknah, Aḥmad wuld Hayba, who died in *Rajab* 1762.[26] He angered the Amīr because he chose the metre of a long *Ḥassāniyyah* ode (*kerza*) composed by an *īggīw* in praise of this prince to be the "loom" (*minwāl*) upon which he composed a lengthy ode, *tarbīʿ* in form, each verse containing four hemistichs according to the scheme a a a b, c c c b, d d d b, etc., to compose the most famous Western Saharan poem of all in praise of the Prophet. The vocabulary is largely a string of pious epithets, yet these are arranged in such a manner as to produce a hypnotic effect when they are recited. The ode is one of the best examples which show the exchange of ideas and form between *Ḥassāniyyah* rhyme and prosody and Classical Arabic verse in the desert at that time. Apart from the praise of the Prophet and gratitude for his miracles, the intention of al-Yadālī was also didactic. He makes this clear in his commentary:[27]

> "In these successive verses there are various kinds of *badīʿ*, such as *insijām* which is among the finest arts in rhetoric and in choice and eloquent expression. The expression used should be free from discordance, just like the flowing of water going down a slope. Due to the ease of its arrangement and the sweetness of its words it is almost a soft and gentle flow. Such is found in this ode, Allāh be praised, through the *barakah* of the one who is praised in it, Allāh's blessing be upon him. Therein too are to be found examples of *tansīq* whereby the Prophet is mentioned by epithets which are consecutive and which cohere soundly and eloquently in their own right, so that each verse stands independently. *Taʿdīd* is also to be found, whereby specific nouns are patterned in a thread. This kind is common in this ode. Another kind is *tardīd* whereby nouns are repeated and ajoined to one another so that the ideas and meanings intended are diversified. Another form of *insijām* to be found is where the two last words in the rhyme agree in one letter, for example *kamāl* and *jamāl*. As for *jamāl* and *jalāl*, they are examples of *jinās lāḥiq*: a difference in one letter which is not closely related in its pronunciation . . . *ḍāfī* and *ṣāfī* and *dalāl* and *zalāl* and *zulāl* are *tajnīs muḍāriʿ* since the difference of one letter applies to one which is closely related in its pronunciation."

It is not surprising that *Ḥassāniyyah* poetry is equally open to similar analysis.

Leaving aside the explanations given by al-Yadālī for its composition, the form of his poem suggests two main influences: some influence from Andalusian *muwashshaḥ* and *zajal*, and much from the distinctive prosody and verse form of *Ḥassāniyyah leghna*. In Mauritania this poem of al-Yadālī is sung to the "mode" of *Kar* which is used by the *Īggāwen* musicians for praise and eulogy, particularly praise of the Prophet. It is often referred to as Ibn Wahīb. In his commentary, however, al-Yadālī sought to stress the Classical Arabic features in his poem. He excuses his admiration for any *Ḥassāniyyah* original on the grounds that music and song may stimulate devotion to the Prophet and love of him in heart and mind, but he also adds:

> "The metre of this ode is not one of the Classical metres together with the *Mutadārik*. It most closely resembles *mashṭūr*, whereby each hemistich forms, as it were, an independent verse and rhymes with the preceding verse, in *mukhalla'*, that is dislocated or luxated *Basīṭ*."

The prince of the Brāknah rewarded al-Yadālī with clothes or a camel and made it an obligation on himself and on his offspring.[28]

Ḥassāniyah leghna and *Azawān*

The flourishing of the poetic art in the Western Sahara between the end of the seventeenth and the middle of the nineteenth centuries should be viewed against the background of another flourishing, and not unrelated, art: the poetry, sung verse and musical art of the *Īggāwen* singers and musicians whose talent took them into the camps of the Ḥassāni princes between the Sāqiyah al-Ḥamrā' in the north and Timbuctoo in the south-east. Their eulogies were composed in long odes which were called variously, *thaydīna* or *kerza* or *rasm*, each with its distinct measure or manner of singing.[29] The names of several of the most famous *Ḥassāniyyah* poets have survived. The art of both poet and musician was particularly in fashion in the Hodh among the Awlād Mubārak, and several of their chiefs were noteworthy poets in *Ḥassāniyyah*. From the east it spread to the Īdaw 'Ish in Tagānit. It was also popular among the Brāknah and in the Trārzah. From there it spread into all parts of the Adrār and the Río de Oro.

Muḥammad wuld Mawlūd wuld Dāddāh al-Chennafi has made a special study of the history of this bardic age and has outlined its history as follows:

> "In the year 1040/1630/1, the Maghāfirah [Awlād Ḥassān] put an end to the rule of the Awlād Rizq over the south-west of Mauritania. Only a short while after this the *Zwāya* and the Maghāfirah were involved in a war which lasted thirty years, the War of Shurbubba. The war ended in the year 1085/1674/5 with the *Zwāya* defeated and with their acknowledgement of the

overlordship of the Maghāfirah. In the Mauritanian Adrār as well the Maghāfirah extended their influence at this time. As for the east and the south-east, Tagānit, the Rgayba and the Hodh, the rule of the Awlād Mubārak continued, likewise that of their brethren, the Awlād Ghuwayzī, throughout the whole of this century and into some of the next. Tradition has it that the termination of the authority of the Awlād Mubārak over these districts was the result of their failure to bring about the submission of the Īdaw ʿĪsh in the battle of Ḥunaykāt Bughdād round about the year 1192/1778/9. The unfolding of these events led to the Mauritanian community taking its final shape. Little change has occurred since then. It has remained static since the eighteenth century and tribes occupied the pasturages where they have remained ever since. They submitted to the form of authority which manifested itself in those Amīrates and Shaykhdoms which some families continue to inherit. This was an agent which encouraged the unification of the Zenāgah dialects and it assisted likewise in unifying the language of the land and fixing it to some degree by the diffusion of verse and the recitation of the poetry composed in all districts of it. Unfortunately, this poetry has been, and still is, exposed to loss because no heed has been paid to the recording of it. It has been left to the memory to preserve it or else to forget it. For that reason we now see that the oldest which has been memorised, that is poetry which can be traced back to a specific date, is not more than two hundred years old. On account of this, we are unable to follow the stages of its development and evolution to its present form, nor how its constituents evolved, that is, its metres and subject matter. What we are aware of is that *Ḥassāniyyah* poetry, from the moment when it appears to us in the middle of the twelfth/eighteenth century, had attained a mature form and style. This indicates a long past about which we know absolutely nothing. We see that *Ḥassāniyyah* poetry, after it had passed through obscure stages, started to flourish from the middle of the twelfth/eighteenth century until the middle of the thirteenth/nineteenth century.

"The honour for all this goes back to poets of genius who blazed a trail and who guided the verse to its perfection until their poetry became an example which was to be followed and imitated by their successors. We should never forget that this bloom would have been impossible had it not been a consequence of the art of the *Īggāwen* class. This word is taken from one of the languages of Senegal though the form of the word shows a Zenāgah stamp, perhaps then it was adopted before the spread of *Ḥassāniyyah* and reveals the existence of a class of people who handed down the custom of singing and versifying, living among the princes and the Shaykhs, borrowing also from the Sudanic community since we see nothing similar to it in the other Saharan societies. The presence of these people in Mauritanian society shows the strong link between poetry and song, and this is underlined by the fact that the same word is applied to both in *Ḥassāniyyah*. The poet is not only a boon companion who praises his master, he is also a singer. He guards the pride and honour of his master. The oldest mention made of these people is that reference to them in one of the compositions of Muḥammad al-Yadālī, who died in 1757. With his ode in praise of the Prophet he opposed a poem composed by one of the ancestors of the sub-tribe of Manūfī who had lauded the Prince of the Brāknah, Aḥmad ibn Haybah, who died in *Rajab* 1762.

"At this time, or very shortly after it, the renown of Saddūm ibn Injartu began to spread among the Īdaw ʿĪsh and the Awlād Mubārak, and the narrators inform us that he became attached to the Prince of the Īdaw ʿĪsh, Bakkār ibn ʿUmar, who was alive in the year 1171/1757/8.[30] After his death Saddūm ibn Injartu became attached to his son, Muḥammad Shayn, who died in 1202/1787. Saddūm lived until after 1797, and one of his *qaṣīdahs* shows that it was composed after the battle of Ḥunaykāt Bughdād in 1192/1778/9, since there is an echo of these events in his poem. Also, the reciters quote poems which date back to the epoch of the Amīr ʿAlī Shanẓūrah who died in 1139/1727, though we do not know how authentic this poetry really is. It was during this golden age of *Ḥassāniyyah* verse that an intellectual movement was crystallised in the minds of Sīdī al-Mukhtār al-Kuntī who died in 1226/1811 and his contemporary, al-Mukhtār ibn Būna,[31] of the Tājakānt. Famous men, about whom maxims were coined, lived in the south and in the Hodh, and amongst them I shall mention Hannūna al-Mubahdhil, the *Shaykh* of the Awlād Mubārak, who died before 1163/1749. Here is to be seen the influence of the Awlād Mubārak and their neighbours, also the Brāknah, in the flowering of this type of *Ḥassāniyah* verse and its encouragement. *Ḥassāniyyah* poetry continued to thrive until a certain tepidness affected it after the end of the thirteenth/nineteenth century, reflecting the anarchy which afflicted the land in general. A decline in the quantity of output did not follow as its consequence. Poets appeared beyond number and we still find them in all classes though some kinds of verse are special to the *Īggāwen*."[32]

Special mention should be made of Shaykh Muḥammad ibn al-Bukhārī ibn Ḥabīb Allāh ibn Bārikalla ibn Bā Zayd (d. 1282/1865), known as Shaykh Muḥammad al-Māmi of the Ahl Bārikalla of Tīris in the Río de Oro. Many of the works of this scholar are in Classical Arabic. He was a brilliant poet in Classical verse and his knowledge of Arabic learning extended beyond theology and law, including tribal law (*'urf*), to mathematics and occult sciences which were disclosed to him by the *jinn*. He was also a brilliant poet in *Ḥassāniyyah* verse. His extensive *Dīwān* contains many deeply religious quatrains and extended odes in the colloquial dialect of the Western Sahara which are rich in imagery and which are not heavily indebted to Classical prototypes. Some of these poems survive, although they are read in the vernacular, rather than recited, since they do not fit into the musical context of much *Ḥassāniyyah* verse. They are didactical, although this is in itself a paradox, since those Moors who can understand their content are equally at home in Classical Arabic. Even so, Shaykh Muḥammad al-Māmi seems to have succeeded to an astonishing degree in turning an Arabic dialect into a literary language in its own right to an extent unparalleled elsewhere in the Arabic-speaking world. To cite *Dhāt Alwāḥ wa Dusur*:

> "He put into [*Ḥassāniyyah*] verse all the sciences: *fiqh*, grammar, theology, logic and elocution, the *Sīrah* of the Prophet, lineages and genealogies and astronomy in flowing *Ḥassāniyyah* verse. The ear is not tired by it, despite its length, nay, rather, the oral telling of it enhances the beauty of it to those who hear it. It is a wonder of wonders, and a *dīwān* of all the sciences."

These sciences extend to mathematics and surveying. One poem is an exposition of how the stones of the ground may theoretically be measured. This is worked out in detail, mathematically, by means of squaring roots and by elaborate mathematical formulae based on the measure of the size of barley seeds and the hair of a hackney horse. An involved and detailed commentary, with simple diagrams, explained in Classical Arabic, is required to grasp the system behind this academic exercise. In these poems *Ḥassāniyyah* poetry has traversed a long distance from the spontaneous improvisations of the camel-drivers of the Western Sahara.

Chapter 6

The Amīrates of the Mauritanian Hodh

It was mentioned in my last chapter that the Awlād Mubārak had played some part in the history of south-western Mauritania in the years prior to the War of Shurbubba in the seventeenth century. Under their chief, Ūdayka al-Aqraʿ, they drove out the Ḥassānī Awlād Rizq who had preceded them and they imposed a *gharāmah*, a protection money, on the largely Berber inhabitants of that district. This imposition, which was also known as *ḥurmah*, as has been mentioned, ensured protection of the subjected peoples by the warriors of the Awlād Ḥassān but at the same time it entailed much hardship for these subjected peoples.

The historian of the Banū Daymān, Wālid ibn Khālunā, gives a detailed account of the event: "After the victory over the Awlād Rizq, Ūdayka al-Aqraʿ, known as the 'bald', came to the Tashumsha and asked them who they were. 'We are free men', they replied. He gave them his lance as a sign of his protection."[1]

Shortly afterwards the Tashumsha were visited by another chief of the Awlād Ḥassān called Aḥmad ibn Dāmān. He put the same question to them and they gave him the same answer. He conceded that if their status had been acknowledged as free by the Awlād Rizq then he, likewise, would deem them to be free. Nevertheless, he warned them to avoid contact with Ūdayka al-Aqraʿ. They accepted his counsel and they moved their tents and their herds towards the coast.

Wālid ibn Khālunā continues:

> "Then they [the Tashumsha] journeyed towards the coast. We have reported, on the authority of Muḥammad ibn Ḥabīb ibn Khayr, quoting the *faqīh*, Muṣṭafā ibn Ḥabīb ibn Khayr, that

Ūdayka came afterwards to the Īdaygub at Tinimjaw seeking for *maghram* [*gharāmah*]. He had with him a quantity of millet, some items of clothing and some tobacco which he had collected from the [Berber] *Zwāya*. Aḥmad Dawlah came to him and informed him that the *maghram* was unacceptable. Ūdayka replied that either the *maghram* be paid or else his people would suffer a Ḥassānī raid. Muṣṭafā, the *faqīh*, the aforementioned, and Ḥamaḍḍa al-Yaʿqūbī, he being a skilful guide, passed the night gathering among the outlying tribesmen of the Īdaygub. In the morning they came to the camp [of the *Zwāya*]. Aḥmad Dawlah said to the *faqīh*, Ḥabīballāh ibn Yaʿqūb, 'My tongue availeth nought in regard to this tyrant. It is through you that we beseech mercy from our Lord.' It so happened that a warner came to Ūdayka from his own household saying to him that the Awlād al-Zenāgiyyah[2] were harassing and were hostile against them. Ūdayka mounted and rode forth that very hour, leaving his baggage behind him with the *faqīh*, Ḥabīballāh ibn Yaʿqūb. He caught up with the army of his people. The battle which followed took place at Agayart. He was struck down by the hand of al-Uqayraʿ ibn al-ʿAfan. Thus, Allāh requited equitably for the tyranny of Ūdayka towards the Tashumsha and towards others among the holy men up to this day. In truth, all those who seek to do them a hurt are punished by Him for their iniquity. The Tashumsha dwelt in the land with the [Berber] Inbāṭ *Zenāgah* and they likewise oppressed them. Allāh drove them away and the Tashumsha inherited their land. Then they were followed by the Awlād Rizq, then the Awlād ʿUgba, then the Awlād Dāwūd ibn ʿUmrān. Now it is the turn of the Banū Maghfar. Allāh is the One from whom help is sought. Then the *faqīh*, Ḥabīballāh, sent the baggage left behind by Ūdayka to his people. When the tidings of the death of Ūdayka were carried to his wife called Karṭūfa she climbed a tree which is called in Berber *tishitayit* at Insāghayān for the Awlād Mubārak at that time where there. She wept for him and she mourned. Henceforth that tree was known as *tishitayit* Karṭūfa."[3]

The Awlād Mubārak were only wayfarers in south-west Mauritania, having been pushed southwards by other Ḥassānī groups. Once masters of Tīris they had been pushed into the Mauritanian Adrār during the sixteenth century by the advancing Trārzah and Brāknah. Their wanderings did not terminate in the north. Some moved south into the south-west, but the greater part of them, the Awlād Muḥammad, their relatives with them, moved into the south-east of

Mauritania into the Hodh and its western borderlands. This seems to have taken place late in the seventeenth century, a little after the time of the episode described by Wālid ibn Khālunā in his history reported above.

Despite the unhappy portrait of the chief called Ūdayka, the Awlād Mubārak and the Awlād Ghuwayzī who branched forth from them at a later date[4] were in time to attain a high esteem among the lettered in the whole of Mauritania, even amongst the scholars of the Tashumsha in the south-west. Poems in praise of them were composed despite their reputation for uncouth manners and indignity towards others. Aḥmad ibn al-Amīn al-Shinqīṭī in his *Kitāb al-Wasīṭ* has defined their qualities and defects in a series of epithets, portraying them as men of honour and bounty (*karam*), men of justice (*ʿadl*), men of military power and bravery (*shawkah*), yet also men of contemptuous challenge and scorn (*ubbahah*). These finer qualities appear to have become attached to them on account of their fame in the Hodh.[5]

Paul Marty has summarised the facts as far as they are known.[6] The descent of the Awlād Mubārak into the Hodh, at the beginning of the eighteenth century, appears to have been led by the sons of Mubārak, whose posterity were later to disperse on the borders of Mauritania and the Sahel: Muḥammad Zenāgī, ancestor of the Awlād Mubārak (of the Hodh), Ghuwayz the ancestor of the Awlād Ghuwayzī, ʿUmar al-ʿAbaydī (Laʿbaydī) the ancestor of the Aʿbaydāt, Lūdayka and the Awlād ibn ʿUmar.

Muḥammad Zenāgī left five sons: Bū Sayf who is the ancestor of the princely encampments, such being the case of the fractions of Ballé as of Nioro: Hannūn al-ʿAbaydī who succeeded Bū Sayf and who would have received from the Sulṭān the investiture of Bakhounou which he conquered from the Peuls. This tradition, reported by M. A. Le Châtelier, in his masterly work *L'Islam en Afrique Occidentale Française*, gives the name of the Sulṭān as Mawlay Ismāʿīl. Without doubt this is correct, but he fixes the date of the investiture as 1672 which is quite clearly too early. It is only towards the end of the reign of Mawlay Ismāʿīl (1725) that Hannūn was able to receive this authority: Mūmu, the ancestor of the Ahl Mūmu (Ballé): Ḥammu, the ancestor of the Ahl Ḥammu: Buhdal, the ancestor of the Awlād Buhdal.

At this date for the first time one sees the name of the Awlād Mubārak appearing in local chronicles. The old *Ta'rīkh* of Walātah tells that in 1736–7 Ibn Dukhnān, ʿAlī Baybah and al-Baykam died in a war between the Awlād Mubārak and the Awlād al-Zenāgī, sons and brothers of Muḥammad Zenāgī.[7]

Hannūn al-ʿAbaydī was succeeded as chief of the Awlād Mubārak towards 1755 by his son, ʿUmar, who retained authority until 1762. He was succeeded by his son, ʿAlī.

It was during the reign of the latter, a very long reign lasting from between 1762 and 1808 or thereabouts, during which the authority seemed to be definitively fixed in his tent, or, to follow the expression of the Moors, in that of ʿUmar his father, that one adopted the habit of describing the princely house under his name. The Europeans of this time (Houghton and Mungo Park) have made from Wuld ʿUmar the name Ludamar and by this name they have designated the sovereignty, the "kingdom", if one wishes so, of the Awlād Mubārak.

King ʿAlī was to be the harsh and fanatical host of the Scottish explorer, Mungo Park, who attempted to cross this Moorish realm in 1795.

> "The usual place of rendezvous for the indolent is the king's tent, where great liberty of speech seems to be exercised by the company towards each other, while in speaking of their chief they express but one opinion. In praise of their sovereign they are unanimous. Songs are composed in his honour, which the company frequently sing in concert; but they are so loaded with gross adulation that no man but a Moorish despot could hear them without blushing. The king is distinguished by the fineness of his dress, which is composed of blue cotton cloth, brought from Timbuctoo, or white linen or muslin from Morocco. He has likewise a larger tent than any other person, with a white cloth over it; but in his usual intercourse with his subjects, all distinctions of rank are frequently forgotten. He sometimes eats out of the same bowl with his camel driver, and reposes himself during the heat of the day on the same bed."[8]

Mungo Park points out that the kingdom of Ludamar was essentially Sahelian in its heartland. The Awlād Mubārak by the eighteenth century had largely forsaken the Sahara itself. Their use of horse reveals this: "The military strength of Ludamar consists in cavalry. They are well mounted, and appear to be very expert in skirmishing and attacking by surprise."[9] Furthermore,

> "Ludamar has for its northern boundary the Great Desert of Sahara. From the best inquiries I could make, this vast ocean of sand, which occupies so large a space in Northern Africa, may be pronounced almost destitute of inhabitants, except where the scanty vegetation which appears in certain spots affords pasturage for the flocks of a few miserable Arabs, who wander from one well to another."[10]

They possessed large cattle herds.

> "The Moors, indeed, subsist chiefly on the flesh of their cattle, and are always in the extreme of either gluttony or abstinence. In consequence of the frequent and severe fasts which their religion enjoins, and the toilsome journeys which they sometimes undertake across the Desert, they are enabled to bear both hunger and thirst with surprising fortitude; but whenever opportunities occur of satisfying their appetite, they generally devour more at one meal than would serve a European for three."[11]

Despite their lack of education, certain of the Moorish women impressed Mungo Park by their forceful character and opulent life. Queen Fāṭima and her sisters among the Awlād Mubārak aristocracy reminded him of "the great ladies in some parts of Europe". Particularly interesting are his observations on the quality of Islamic learning among the Ludamar. He writes:

> "The Moors are rigid Mahomedans and possess, with the bigotry and superstition, all the intolerance of their sect. They have no mosques at Benowm, but perform their devotions in a sort of open shed, or enclosure made of mats. The priest is at the same time schoolmaster to the juniors. His pupils assemble every evening before his tent, where, by the light of a large fire made of brushwood and cow's dung, they are taught a few sentences from the Koran, and are initiated into the principles of their creed. Their alphabet differs little from Richardson's Arabic Grammar. They always write with the vowel points. Their priests even effect to know something of foreign literature. The priest of Benowm assured me that he could read the writings of the Christians. He showed me a number of barbarous characters, which he asserted were the Roman alphabet; and he produced another specimen, equally unintelligible, which he declared to be the *Kallam il Indi*, or Persian. His library consisted of nine volumes in quarto; most

of them, I believe, were books of religion, for the name of Mahomet appeared in red letters in almost every page of each. His scholars wrote their lessons upon thin boards, paper being too expensive for general use. The boys were diligent enough, and appeared to possess a considerable share of emulation, carrying their boards slung over their shoulders when about their common employments. When a boy has committed to memory a few of their prayers, and can read and write certain parts of the Koran, he is reckoned sufficiently instructed, and with this slender stock of learning, commences his career of life."[12]

The stay of Mungo Park with these Awlād Mubārak was most uncongenial, nor was it of a kind which would recommend Saharan culture to a Christian in that age. However, it would seem that the greater days of the Awlād Mubārak were at that time a thing of the past. It has to be recalled that the Moors of the Hodh were to a considerable extent an Oriental people lost on the borders of the Sahara and the Western Sudan. Though influenced by adjacent Black Africa they were also to some degree aliens to it. They were often cut off from centres of culture and of letters. Even the neighbouring towns of Walātah, and Timbuctoo at a further distance, passed through phases when the lamp of learning burnt with little more than a glow. Nonetheless, those coloured letters on the folios which Mungo Park had been permitted to see suggest an era when Saharan scholarship was well established in these camps and when Ḥassānī princes of the Awlād Mubārak were, as the Berber scholars of south-western Mauritania believed, patrons of scholars, poets and bards.

The *Ḥaswah*

Evidence for this is afforded by a Saharan chronicle which records the series of events which befell the Awlād Ḥassān along the present-day border between Mauritania and Mali. The period covered is between 1600 and 1800. This chronicle was written by a noted scholar poet of Walātah who was himself of the Awlād Ḥassān. He was to become the *Qāḍī*, the judge in canonic law, of sections of the Awlād Nāṣir of the Hodh and he was called Shaykh Muḥammad Ṣāliḥ ibn ʿAbd al-Wahhāb ibn Aḥmad ibn al-Ḥājj ʿAbd al-Wahhāb al-Nāṣirī. He died in the middle of the last century. The most important of his works is probably his history of the clans of the Awlād Ḥassān, their genealogies, their chiefs, their battles and their poems: *al-Ḥaswah al-Baysāniyyah fi'l-Ansāb al-Ḥassāniyyah.*[13] Here is a valuable historical document patterned on mediaeval Arabic masterpieces such as the chronicles of al-Ṭabarī and al-Balādhurī, *al-ʿIqd al-Farīd* of Ibn ʿAbd Rabbihi and similar works. It furnishes a corpus of dated material on the wars, migrations and leading personalities of the Arab tribes of the Hodh during the seventeenth, eighteenth and nineteenth centuries. Attention is paid to details, and names are often spelt with full vocalisation. The book is less dry than an annual chronicle, omitting the legendary tales which pass muster as historical facts in so many local histories.

The text begins with a statement of the genealogy of the Awlād Ḥassān who stem from the Banū Maʿqil, and delineates their branches.[14] This introduction is followed by an account of the entry of the Awlād Ḥassān into the Hodh to the west of Timbuctoo. In the main the genealogies conform with the accepted lineage of the Awlād Ḥassān known elsewhere in the Western Sahara and among the Berber scholars of south-west Mauritania. The author states that the work was written for Muḥammad al-Mukhtār, a son of the famous Mauritanian scholar, Sīdī ʿAbdallāh ibn al-Ḥājj Ibrāhīm (d. 1815). The genealogy of the Awlād Ḥassān which opens the work was derived from a gloss in a venerable Saharan copy of the *History of the Berbers*, by the fourteenth-century historian Ibn Khaldūn. This text confirms that between 1650 and 1800, the Awlād Mubārak and the Awlād Ghuwayzī, who were collateral relations of the former, patronised Islamic scholars in the Hodh, and they promoted the artistry of the *Ḥassāniyyah* bards.

Amongst the Awlād Mubārak the most important leadership was to reside in the house of Hannūn al-ʿAbaydī and his descendants, the Ludamar of Mungo Park. A battle in which they fought has inspired the oldest surviving couplet (*gāf*) in *Ḥassāniyyah*. Here is the poem in its context in the *Ḥaswah*:

> "Hannūn Laʿbaydī had several sons: Bū Sayf, Ḥamma, Mamma and Sīd Aḥmad, all of them sons of al-ʿĀliya [?], and ʿUthmān and Aḥmad and Bakkār, who were the sons of ʿĀyisha bint Muḥammad Khūna Aznāgiyyah,[15] and al-Labb ibn Hannūn who had no blood brother. His mother, Dayda, was one of the Bū Fāyid and

he was killed by his maternal uncles, the Awlād Bū Fāyid. His death was the cause of the battle of Kasāri. His mother deeply lamented and urged war against her people in revenge for his blood, saying,

raaḥu larmaag ahzaali-min tivgaad el-faraaḥi
(u)kayv elli ma ja walli-waktan Dayda ma raaḥi[16]
'I have breathed my last breath and my happy days are spent,
On account of this my loss, no other joy I'll know,
Dayda has no friend in tribal tent whom she can seek,
She knows not how she came, nor where she ought to go.'

"She slaughtered a young unweaned [*ḥuwār*] camel and she spent the night in isolation until the following morning.

"Then Hannūn La'baydī arose, he and his cousin 'Alī ibn al-Mukhtār ibn Ūdayka. They rallied the Aznāg [Berber Ṣanhājah Īdaw Īsh] led by A'mar ibn Muḥammad ibn Khūna, the Awlād al-Nāṣir led by Buhdil ibn Muḥammad ibn Ashbīshab, and Buhdil ibn Muḥammad ibn Ḥammād of the Awlād 'Abd al-Karīm. They raided as far as Inwal, pronounced with a thickened letter l [*lām*], the famous water-hole [*manhal*] in the Hodh. Then they decided to return since they were ignorant of the territory which lay before Inwal, until they were met by Hartūm al-Zaydī and his kinsmen. He guided them to a locality called Kasāri where the Awlād Bū Fāyid were with their brethren, the Awlād Manṣūr and their companions, the Īyddās, and their scholars the men of letters, the Ījummān and others. The battle went against the Awlād Bū Fāyid and their allies. It is said that the Īyddas had six hundred horsemen. The battle of Kasāri was fought in the year 1124/1712 and it lasted for seven days. The Awlād Bū Fāyid were only defeated after their foes had been helped by the negroes. It was in that battle that Buhdil ibn Muḥammad took the drum of authority of the Āl 'Abd al-Karīm and it is still in their hands. 'Abd al-Raḥmān ibn Sayyid al-Mukhtār al-'Alawī al-Arawānī [of Arawān] said, regarding the date of Kasāri, that it was in the year Dkfsh, in the month of *Shawwāl* in that year."

A similar chronicle of warfare, settlement, poetry, scholastic pursuit and close relationship with the non-Arab inhabitants of the Hodh is recorded about the Awlād Ghuwayzī, who although descended from the same stock as the Awlād Mubārak were sometimes their opponents on the battlefield. They had a reputation for piety and scholarship.

According to a passage in the *Ḥaswah*:

"As for the Ahl al-Labb ibn Bū Sayf, pronounced with a thickened letter l [*lām*], they were the first of the kings of the Banū Maghfar amongst the cattle herders and in the land of the negroes. They possessed Āskur because they had inherited the kingdom of the [*Ḥassānī*] Awlād ʿUgba. The pasture land [*Grārah*?] of Ibn Dahmūsh became theirs. They seized all he possessed, likewise in the possession of the Awlād Bū Kār and others among the Awlād ʿUgba whether 'white' or 'black'. The first of them was their ancestor al-Labb ibn Bū Sayf ibn Ūdayka ibn Inbīg [al-Nābighah?] Bū Garn, then his son, Hannūn al-Kawrī ibn al-Labb. He was killed by the Awlād Inbīg in a war between them and the Awlād Ūdayka ibn Inbīg, then his son, Bū Bakr ibn Hannūn al-Kawrī ibn al-Labb. He was among the best of the Banū Maghfar. He was slain by the Awlād Mubārak in the battle of Jagum [*circa* 1161/1748]. About him it is said,

> *Ya'ssaayel ʿan akhyaar laʿrab-wuzyanhum diin wunzalhum imlayka Buu Bakr wuld Hannuun wuld al-Labb wuld Buu Sayf wuld Uudayka*[17]
> 'O you who ask about the best of the Arabs,[18] the most pious in religion and the most angelic bearer of compassion, [he is] Bū Bakr ibn Hannūn ibn al-Labb ibn Bū Sayf ibn Ūdayka'.

"After he died the throne vanished from the family of Hannūn al-Kawrī ibn al-Labb and it became the possession of the Ahl Aḥmad ibn al-Labb. The first of them was Sīdī Aḥmad ibn Muḥammad ibn Aḥmad ibn al-Labb. He became king after Bū Bakr ibn Hannūn al-Kawrī. He was one of the lords of the Banū Maghfar and their knights. He was a man of justice and religion. He was slain by the Litām."

The *Ḥaswah* mentions a number of famous poets among the chiefs of the Awlād Mubārak and what is of unusual interest are the peculiar names of certain of these kings. There was a close relationship between the Awlād Ḥassān, the Berber *Zenāgah*, more especially the Inbāṭ *Zenāgah*, certain Tuareg groups and the Sūdānic communities on the southern fringes of the eastern Hodh. The names of a few of these kings are common to the Awlād Ḥassān and the lineage of the western Iwillimmeden Tuareg, for example Buhdil and Buhdhil among the Awlād Mubārak, Buḍal among the Tuareg, Inbīg among the Awlād Ghuwayzī and Ănnabigh among the Tuareg, al-Labb among the Awlād Ḥassān and, possibly, Laba among the Tuareg. The Awlād Mubārak division called the Mzāzga are probably a pre-Ḥassānī Tuareg people.

Other names are borrowed from Classical Arabic literature or appear in the tales of pre-Islamic Arabia. A number of these are not names which are to be found in Maghribī bedouin groups but appear to have been adopted for some social or historical or literary reason. Names such as Bū Garn (Bū Qarn), Bū Sayf and Ifrīkish [*sic*], which occur here and there in the *Ḥaswah*, are Yemenite names, or rather names which occur in Yemenite romances of the very early mediaeval period. These cannot be everyday family names among the Banū Ḥassān, since, with the exception of ʿAntarah among the Awlād Nāṣir, they are not typical of other Ḥassānī groups. They could only have become a fashion due to the influence of the lettered among the Awlād Mubārak at a period in the late seventeenth and the early eighteenth century. They markedly contrast with other names which are pure Berber. Many of the princes had Berber mothers. Muḥammad Aznāgī ibn Banyūg is an essentially Berber name. Ties were also close with the Inbāṭ *Zenāgah* Īdaw ʿĪsh. The Īyddās are in all likelihood the same as the Maddāsah or Indasen, spelt Maddūsah by the geographer al-ʿUmarī (1301–49).

Chapter 7

The Awlād Ḥassān and the Kel Es-Sūq of Azawād

The desert of Azawād, now in the Mali Republic, is a region of unusual interest for the study of the history of a progressive Arab settlement in the Western Sahara, whether in war or in peace. It was an important meeting place of the Arab and Berber worlds. It was an important point of contact between the Awlād Ḥassān, the Tuareg, the Kel Es-Sūq and the negro peoples of the Niger Buckle. Azawād is situated to the north of Timbuctoo astride a desert route which links that city and the river region to the salt mines of Taghāzā and Tawdannī. It has a tiny capital at Arawān and its satellite Bū Jbayha. This district has been one which has seen constant battles, constant raiding and seasonal caravan trading. It has also witnessed the digging of wells combined with vigorous scholastic pursuits which have been influential far beyond Azawād.

Several of the most distinguished scholars of the Western Sahara, among them Shaykh Sīdī 'l-Mukhtār al-Kuntī, were either born in Azawād, or made it their permanent residence. It was strategically placed, yet at the same time it was sufficiently remote to afford sanctuary and tranquility provided that the Ḥassānī Barābīsh and Awlād ʿAllūsh were there as protectors or as respectful followers of the saintly men who, to a large extent, controlled the resources which made it possible to live in such an inhospitable environment.

Wherever the cultural divide between the world of the Moor and that of the Tuareg is delineated by language, custom or territory, the lettered among the Saharans regard the region of Azawād as part of that Arabic-speaking region which they call Shinqīṭ. Aḥmad ibn al-Amīn al-Shinqīṭī makes this quite clear in his *Kitāb al-Wasīṭ*. He writes:

"*Azawād*: This name is pronounced with a thickened *z*. It lies between a *ẓā'* and a *zāy*. The territory is a large tract beyond Arawān. In it are to be found many of the Kuntah tribe. It was there that the pious scholar, Shaykh Sīdī al-Mukhtār, the aforementioned, resided.[1] His offspring, I mean his grandsons, continue to dwell there.[2] Among the most noted of them is Bāy, a famous and pious scholar who is still alive today although I have no knowledge of where his domicile is located.[3]

"*Arawān*: It is a famous town. It is situated at a distance of ten days march from Timbuctoo. It is sited in the sand dunes without plant and without herbage and there are neither trees there nor crops, not even date palms. Its houses are simply built of mud. The inhabitants say that the rain does not fall on the houses due to the prayers of a saint. He prays for them in that matter. Were rain to fall then their buildings would be destroyed. I enjoyed the company of a man from among them in the year 1317/1899/1900. It was in the city of Medina and we travelled together until we had completed the pilgrimage. Then we travelled to Turkey and there we parted. I had no criticism to make of his religion. I once asked him about what was said as an explanation of that phenomenon. He said, 'The rain only rarely falls in that country. When it does so it does not strike that town save for a piffling amount. Sometimes the people have gazed towards the sand hills around them. They have seen rain falling there but nothing reaches the houses, save for a tiny amount.' Glory be to the Almighty decreer on account of what He wills."[4]

Arawān and Azawād are, by repute, very dry and barren and very holy. But what they lack in moisture they make up for in the presence of salt mines and direct access to them in the north. The history of Azawād, in as far as that history can be reconstructed, is the history of the control of this salt and the history of the route of this salt and of its annual Azelay caravans bearing salt to the negrolands of the south. It is also the story of how an important and ancient branch of the Banū Ḥassān, the Barābīsh, became the permanent masters of this land, yet who were beneath the spiritual guidance of a Muslim saint of the Kel Es-Sūq who had hitherto lived in the Tuareg lands to the east of Timbuctoo in the Adrār-n-Īfōghās.

The early Azawād

The earliest masters of Azawād were Berbers. They were Massūfah who once possessed the salt mine at Taghāzā, but who were later reduced to the status of serfs or slaves. They had been masters of this Saharan route for many centuries, as camel guides for caravans, at least since the days of the Almoravids and they had been subject to the empires of Mali and the Songhai. Shaykh Ṣāliḥ ibn ʿAbd al-Wahhāb in his *Ḥaswah* makes a specific reference to this tradition. "Every *Zwāya* town in the Sahara of Takrūr, such as Arawān, Abū Jbayha, Walātah, Tīshīt, Wādān, Shinjīṭī, Tījikja, Tugba and Taranni – their people are of the Massūfah."[5] That this is certainly true of Arawān, however improbable it may be of certain others, is confirmed by the presence of the Massūfah family of the great scholar Aḥmad Bābā in Arawān, the Aqītūn, whose links and ties elsewhere in the desert point to an origin in the Mauritanian town of Wādān. In about 1500 this Berber character dominated the region. The wells of Arawān, the name of which is derived from the quantity of rope needed to use buckets in these wells, were much visited by the Imagsharen who camped in the summer on the banks of the Niger but who in autumn stayed in the vicinity of Arawān.

There was also an important Songhai presence. The locality was of sufficient importance to need both an *Imām* and a *Qāḍī* in 1481. Certainly the impression left by Leo Africanus, about 1512, when he described what happened during his reception by a *Zenāgah* chief in the plain of Arawān, was that the Berber tribes which had long inhabited it were still its masters. The hospitality which he received, roast meats, soups, roast ostriches, negro spices, millet bread and rape grains finely ground, dates and bowls of milk, was at the hands of a sheep-rearing Berber ruler.[6]

Yet, there was undoubtedly an Arab element as well in the district and the nature of this element has presented a problem of identity which is still unresolved. These are the Barbūsh or Barābīsh. Both Leo and Marmol describe the Barbūsh as a branch of the Dawī Ḥassān. They are described as camel owners to be found in the Wād Nūn in the north and the region of Tīshīt in the south. There are also references to elements of the Barābīsh further to the south within the city of Timbuctoo during the days of Askiyā Muḥammad.

Contemporary, or near contemporary, references, to the presence of both *Zenāgah* and Ḥassānī groups in Azawād, prompted Paul Marty to suggest that a first Arab "invasion" by the Ḥassānī Banū Ḥamma ibn Barbūsh in the fifteenth century had successfully absorbed Berber elements to form the Barābīsh of the earliest records in the histories of Timbuctoo and the Sūdān. They were the first "agents of the Arabisation of the Imagsharen". It was, however, a second "invasion" of Banū Ḥassān, that of the Raḥāminah, the descendants of Raḥmūn ibn Rizq ibn Ūday, towards the end of the sixteenth century, which had a far more radical impact on the history of Azawād, coinciding as it did with the occupation of the Niger Buckle by the Moroccans in 1591. The invasion of the Raḥāminah

> "was part of a movement in a south and south-easterly direction, more especially at the commencement of the reign of Mawlāy Aḥmad al-Dhahabī [*circa* 1578] although the Raḥāminah appear to have been preceded by the Barābīsh who were sons of Ḥamma. They became the salt carriers, first of all at Taghāzā and later at Tawdannī".[7]

More recently, Abitbol has mentioned that

> "Les Berabich, dont un premier noyau vivait déjà dans la région de Tombouctou, à l'époque du Grand Askya, furent renforcés, dans le courant du XVIe siècle, par deux vagues de migrations Hassane du Sud-Marocain, suivant l'axe Maroc-Touat-Taghaza-Niger.
>
> "L'une de leurs fractions, celle des *Awlad ʿAbd al-Rahman*, est signalée successivement 'derrière Taghaza' en 1594, sur la route de Arawan au Touat, en 1631, et a 'peu de distance' de Tombouctou en 1632."[8]

If this, indeed, is the historical truth in regard to the first settlements of the Banū Ḥassān in Azawād, then it would appear to parallel the penetration of elements of the Awlād Rizq and Awlād Mubārak into south-western Mauritania, who were followed later, and replaced by, the Trārzah and the Brāknah. As was seen, this was complicated by the movement of Nāṣir al-Dīn and the "War of Shurbubba". In Azawād the history of the Barābīsh is complicated by the Moroccan invasion and by the settlement of scholars of the Kel Es-Sūq and Kel Intasar.

Aḥmad agg Āddah

Paul Marty has explained the circumstances as to how the Barābīsh and a holy man who had wandered from Tādamakkat (al-Sūq)[9] came to combine their activities. He based his information on the so-called "History (*Ta'rīkh*) of the Barābīsh".[10]

> "It was some thirty or forty years after the first migration took place, at the end of the reign of Mawlay Aḥmad al-Dhahabī [hence towards 1603], when a holy man of the Raḥāminah, Abū Makhlūf, came to seek his fortune in the country where his compatriots had been so successful for the period of a generation. He established himself in Arawān beside Shaykh Sīdī Aḥmad agg Āddah, called 'Laggada', the ancestor of the Ahl Arawān of today, and he gained a reputation for his Islamic virtues and his commercial abilities and acumen. Several of his relations came to see him and they also devoted themselves to commerce. One day, four camps of the Raḥāminah, grouped under the name of Awlād ʿĀmir, began to move in their turn from the Maghrib, and arrived to settle in Igīdī. They were the Awlād Sulaymān, the Awlād Aḥmad, the Daluwāt who are certainly Awlād ʿĀmir, the Awlād Yaʿīsh, who are also the same, though somewhat less surely, unless they are Awlād Ḥamma ibn Ḥassān. Sulaymān, the elder of the first camp and the chief of the migration, was the eldest son of Abū Makhlūf. The Arab kernel of the Barābīsh tribe was from that time constituted. It was going to increase its own numbers naturally and also by the addition of numberless tents and clients from outside the tribe. The new arrivals established an important commercial flow of activity, in all probability with salt, between Igīdī and Azawād."

Later, he remarks: "Towards 1575, then, a holy man of the Kel Es-Sūq, Aḥmad agg Āddah, abandoned al-Sūq, at that time ruined for good, and after sundry wanderings in Tuwāt and Faguibine established himself in Arawān."

The *Tārīkh al-Sūdān* says that the Sherifian contingents of Jawdar Pasha did not pass through Arawān itself, but to the east of this town (1591). They did not hesitate to requisition the camels which they needed. Local tradition completes the information provided by the *Tārīkh* in adding that Aḥmad agg Āddah, who was then living at Telik, was arrested by Jawdar, and then set free.

Aḥmad agg Āddah built himself a house; others did likewise around it. Then he constructed the mosque which bears his name to this day. In a few years, and for the same reasons as those which drew the wondering crowds of Upper Egypt around the column of the monk Paphnuce of "Thais", a city was built in the shade of the *barakah* of the Islamic saint. A tradition of the Kel Intasar says that their ancestors, the Igellād,[11] participated with Aḥmad agg Āddah in the renewal of the *Qṣar*. This was the second Arawān and it is the sole one which has been preserved in the memory as disclosed by oral tradition.

It was there that Aḥmad agg Āddah gave asylum to the harbinger of the second "invasion" of the Raḥāminah, Abū Makhlūf, who, at the beginning of the seventeenth century, came to seek for calm to study and to reflect silently in prayer beside this great *murābiṭ*. Aḥmad agg Āddah died a little after 1620 and was buried in the town. Today his tomb is the object of general veneration.[12]

The Kel Es-Sūq of Arawān confirm this tradition in their own records.[13]

> "Among the saints of the Kel Es-Sūq was the *faqīh*, Sulaymān, and his nephew, Aḥmad ibn Āddah, and al-Ṣāliḥ ibn Abī Muḥammad ibn Aḥmad ibn ʿAbdallāh. Al-Sūq was ruined. It was ruined by the Askiyā in the age prior to Jawdar. The people abandoned it and they became nomads. The dug wells and they settled. Then at a later date Aḥmad ibn Āddah and Abī Muḥammad, two of Allāh's saints and both seeking to adore him, came to the well of Arawān, known also as Inshakgā. Men lived close to the well. They were hunters, a breed of Tuareg known as Idnān. Both men stayed at the well and adored Allāh, Almighty. This was before the time of Jawdar. They built a few buildings, living with a few who dwelt there for purposes of divine adoration. They became famous for jurisprudence and for their sanctity and faith. They enjoyed a status of inviolability [*ḥurmah*] throughout all the land. People began to bestow alms upon them and to seek their *barakah*, from them and from their descendants until today. The town became an inhabited place on account of them. Authority was fixed there and Jawdar ruled there. The salt mines of Taghāzā were discovered[14] and the people began to carry salt from it and to sell it in Timbuctoo until a new authority was in power at Taghāzā. The entire country became governed and well settled, Allāh be praised. They built a mosque in Arawān. Then

Aḥmad ibn Āddah went on the pilgrimage. He returned, Allāh be praised, and he remained resident until his decease. He was buried in his aforementioned mosque in Arawān."

This development of the region of Arawān was not the exclusive achievement of a saintly family from the Mali Adrār and family members from the incoming Raḥāminah of the Barābīsh Arabs. The Kel Intasar Igellād were also directly involved. An early eighteenth-century text of theirs recounts a similar movement westwards to the Arawān district, this time from as far east as Aïr.

"Al-Muẓaffar settled among a tribe of the Berbers of the Aïr mountains in the district of Agades. He married a wife from among them and she bore him Muḥammad Aḥmad, nicknamed Agg Ayr. When al-Muẓaffar died he left offspring, and he was succeeded by Agg Ayr. Agg Ayr, when he died left two sons, al-Muzammil, who bred descendants through al-Muṣṭafā, and, secondly, Aḥmad. Both are in Tārika Tarakta [Mali Adrār?]. The tribes of Tahabannat [near Gao] are descended from Aḥmad, while from al-Muṣṭafā are descended those who lived opposite the village of Amawwel in Agades district. Before his death, Agg Ayr counselled his son, al-Muzammil, to follow the family tradition of ascetic retreat and the way of the itinerant mystic. Then al-Muzammil died during a journey to the city of Timbuctoo.[15] He was buried at Kerchouel [Igashshawel near Gao]. He left a number of offspring but two of them succeeded him, Muḥammad al-Muṣṭafā and al-Bukhārī. Their mother was from the Idnān Tuareg. When Muḥammad al-Muṣṭafā ibn al-Muzammil died he counselled his son, Infa, to follow the ascetic path of his forebears. He married a wife named Fāṭimah bint Aḥmad ibn Firdaws. *She was also the mother of the ancestor of the Kel Arawān, Aḥmad ibn Āddah*, and she bore him a son called Muḥammad. When Infa was old he appointed Muḥammad to be his successor. Muḥammad went to the city of Timbuctoo during the ninth century of the *hijrah* [fifteenth century AD]. At Ibnayb he stayed with a *Sharīf* called al-Hāshim. He had two men living with him, Sanaduh the ancestor of the Kel Aghzāf, and Shagsan the ancestor of the Kel Intashghīn. He married a daughter of Hāshim ibn al-Mukhtār ibn [Iw . . ?] Allāh gave him a *barakah* which far surpassed that of others among the lettered.

"It was Muḥammad who, in the deserts of Timbuctoo, dug the well of In Talak [Telek], then the wells of Aghzāf [near Bū Jbayhah], Halūl, In Afas and Arawān. *The latter locality at that time was a desert waste devoid of habitation.* Muḥammad was followed by his sons in the digging of new wells as far as Agg Aghisen. When he died he left four sons, Ummāmah, Bullah, Aḥmad and Muḥammad Quṭb. He enjoined on the last of these to follow the tradition of asceticism and retreat."[16]

Allowing for exaggerated piety and error in local traditions, the following facts in regard to the rapid development of Arawān seem clear. The *Quṭb* of the *Qādiriyyah* Ṣūfī order, Aḥmad ibn / agg Āddah, left Tādamakkat in Mali about 1575. He travelled to Arawān, married into the Kel Intasar and died there in about 1630. His religious circle included the saint of the Barābīsh, Abū Makhlūf, whose relatives among the Raḥāminah were drawn to the region of Azawād by the salt route, by the increased number of wells being dug at the time, by the Moroccan expeditions southwards along that route, and by the increasing convergence of Saharans, some Tuareg, some Arabs of the Central Sahara, and some of them Banū Ḥassān, towards the districts immediately adjacent to Timbuctoo and to Walātah. The power in the desert was largely in the hands of the Barābīsh. In 1593 an embassy sent by the *Qāḍī* ʿUmar of Timbuctoo to Mawlāy Aḥmad, on its return from Morocco placed itself under the protection of ʿĪsa ibn Sulaymān al-Barbūshī the chief of the Raḥāminah in the vicinity of Taghāzā.

Scholars of Arawān in the eighteenth century

The literary activities, legal services and mediatory role of the Arawān scholars, who were of varied tribal origin, were to characterise the whole region of Azawād well into the eighteenth century. Several of the leading figures were descendants of Sīdī Aḥmad ibn Āddah. Others were Kel Es-Sūq who had left the Mali Adrār and who had studied in Arawān with the scholars who had lived there for a long time and made it their home. Some of the latter were scholars who had come there from the Mauritanian Adrār, from Shinqīṭī and Wādān. Their services were required by the chiefs of the Barābīsh and at least one of them intermarried into the family of the chiefs of the Maḥāfīẓ, an important Arab group.

One of the most important of these scholars was Sīdī'l-Wāfī ibn Ṭālibinā ibn Sīdī Aḥmad ibn Āddah. He was appointed

Qāḍī of Arawān in 1713 by the Moroccan Pasha of Timbuctoo, 'Abdallāh ibn al-Ḥājj ibn Sa'īd. His *nisbah* al-Galládī seems to indicate a connection with the Kel Intasar in that town.

According to a passage in the work entitled *Fatḥ al-Shakūr fī Ma'rifat A'yān 'Ulamā' al-Takrūr*, written in 1799/1800 by Muḥammad al-Bartīlī of Walātah, Sīdī'l-Wāfī was a jurist, a recounter of the tradition of the Prophet and was both *Muftī* and *Qāḍī* in Arawān. He taught the *Saḥīḥs* of al-Bukhārī and Muslim, the *Shifā' of the Qāḍī* 'Iyāḍ, the *Muwaṭṭa'* of *Mālik* and the *Khaṣā'iṣ* of al-Suyūṭī.

His son, Ṭālibunā, nicknamed Ṣanbir, was a jurist and grammarian and he held the post of *Qāḍī* after the retirement of his father. He wrote a number of books and was noteworthy for his academic zeal.

The *Fatḥ al-Shakūr* recounts how:

> "It is told that he was sitting one day in the house looking at his books when his wife's sister came to him, and she said to him, 'Your wife is in child-birth, come out and we will bring some millet to make a gruel (*leḥsa*) for her.' But he did not go out, so she came back to him again, but still he did not leave. She said to him, 'As for books, *leḥsa* cannot be made out of them.' So he went to the door of the house. A Barbūshī passed him, and he brought him some twenty *mithqāls*. He paid it to his sister-in-law and said to her, 'Take this, here it is, make a gruel for my wife out of it. As for the books, no *leḥsa* is to be made from them.' He died, may the Almighty have mercy on him, in the last night of *Ramaḍān*, 1180/1767."

Other scholars were a major factor in the foundation of the satellite town of Bū Jbayah which lies some hundred kilometres to the south-east of Arawān. It was founded during the time of the chieftainship of Muḥammad ibn Raḥḥāl of the Barābīsh. The scholars were led by al-Ṭālib Sīdī Aḥmad ibn al-Bashīr of the Kel Es-Sūq who had married a wife among the nobles of the Barābīsh, Khadījah bint 'Abdallāh al-Maḥfūẓiyyah. His divorce of her may have prompted his departure from Arawān. He originally came from the Mali Adrār, studied with a scholar of the Hoggar near Ra's al-Mā', and came to Arawān when he was twenty-five years old. According to *Fatḥ al-Shakūr*:

> "He betook himself to Arawān, and he stayed with the Moroccan governor of the town. He studied the litany [*wird*] of the Qādiriyyah and learnt it from Sīdī Aḥmad ibn ʿAbd al-Qādir ibn Aḥmad ibn Aḥmad al-Raqqādī, and one of the seven Koranic readings from Shaykh Sīdī'l-Amīn ibn Ḥabīb al-Jakānī [of the Tājakānt], and from Sīdī Ibrāhīm ibn al-Imām al-ʿAlawī [of the Īdaw ʿAlī]. They gave him their licence to quote and to teach [*ijāzah*]. He studied the readings in Prophetic *ḥadīth* from al-Bukhārī and Muslim, and the *Shifā'* of the *Qāḍī* ʿIyāḍ and the *Khaṣā'iṣ* of al-Suyūṭī, and also other works, all on the authority of the *Qāḍī*, Sīdī'l-Wāfī ibn Ṭālibinā al-Arawānī. He also studied exegesis in Arawān."

This scholar died in Bū Jbayha, "the father of the small brow, the saintly brow", named after him, about 1770/1. He was eighty-four and his cries in praise of God were to be heard in his tomb.

Equally important was his son, Sīdī Muḥammad al-Amīn, who was born in Bū Jbayha. Besides his expert knowledge in *Ḥadīth* and jurisprudence, which he studied in Arawān, he was also an authority on Arabic grammar.

Bū Jbayha remained a satellite of Arawān. This is shown by the content of an Arabic manuscript in Niamey (folio in the Centre Nigérien de Recherche en Sciences Humaines, No. 2501), called "The answers of the *Qāḍīs* of Arawān to Shaykh Zayn ibn ʿAbd al-ʿAzīz of Bū Jbayha regarding the legal question relating to the performance of the Friday prayer in the town of Bū Jbayha" (*Ajwibat quḍāt Arawān lil-Shaykh ʿAbd al-ʿAzīz al- Bū-Jbayhī fī qaḍiyyat iqāmat ṣalāt al-jumʿah fī qaryat Abī Jbayha*).

The example of all these Sūqī scholars of Azawād indicates the indefinite line of distinction between Ḥassānī Moors and scholars born in the Tuareg world during the seventeenth and eighteenth centuries. The history of the Barābīsh in Azawād region should be seen as part of the complex movement and settlement of the Maʿqilian tribes and the resettlement of families from Tādamakkat in the Mali Adrār along the key route for commerce and salt between Morocco, Taghāzā and Timbuctoo.

The early part of the history of Azawād in the reports of the Barābīsh and their wars with the Rgaybāt and Hoggār and Idnān and Īfoghās, the mention of some of their notable men and the entry of the Christians into Timbuctoo and other matters, written by an anonymous scholar of the Kel Es-Sūq. Timbuctoo manuscript, 175, R.B.I.[17]

Although bereft of Arabic verse, which is found elsewhere in Western Saharan Arabic works – *al-Wasīṭ* is a good example – both this text, and the biographical *Amr al-Walī Nāṣir al-Dīn*, by Muḥammad al-Yadālī, illustrate a fusion of simple year lists (*ḥawliyyāt*) which are characteristic of the oral traditions of the Banū Ḥassān and the Tuareg, be they in *Ḥassāniyyah* or in Berber, with a more literary tradition which reflects the writings of such masters as Ibn ʿAbd Rabbihi (860–940) in his *ʿIqd al-Farīd*, with lists of Saharan battles such as Jīwa, Tirtillās, Tin Yifḍāḍ, and here, Gīr, Zīr ibn (*sic*) Zimrān (In-Zimrān), and Kadām, strung in a series like a list of battles of al-Nihā, Dhanā'ib, Wāridāt and Qiḍḍah (Taḥlīq al-Limam) during the War of al-Basūs in pre-Islamic Arabia. All of this *genre* of Western Saharan literature drew extensively upon the *Ayyām al-ʿArab* literature as much as it did on the religiously coloured and didactical *Maghāzī* literature. The pre-Islamic verse, which fills the masterpieces of early Arabic literature, was replaced by *Ḥassāniyyah* war verse which was sung by the *Īggāwen* griots to the princes in the "mode" of *Fāghū*, which is the "mode" of courage and prowess in Western Saharan music.

"One of the wise, whose wishes I could not oppose, asked me to write a book, concise and readable in its wording, about the history of those who dwelt in Azawād, from Arawān and its neighbourhood as far as Timbuctoo and its neighbourhood, to the east and to the west, from among the Imaghsharen, the Awlād al-Raḥmān and the Barābīsh, from their origins until their decline and the departure of the deceased who lived amongst them. It will likewise tell of other matters, about their feuds and the wars which were fought between themselves. I responded to this request, as far as my ability allowed me to, though my knowledge of it all was deficient – and I openly acknowledge my inability – since I have been greatly busied with the subsidiary branches of jurisprudence and not with history. Jurisprudence is of greater import.

"Therefore, when I saw that there was no way of avoiding my

answering his request I responded to his call and I assisted him in what he had demanded. I endeavoured to fulfil his wishes. I began to collect together all the ancient books which I could find, information out of learned histories, both scattered and tattered, and from those things which I had heard from the lips of men whose words were to be trusted in the matter of histories. I also gathered together those learned sayings which had been told me by my Shaykhs of the past, men who were accurate, sound and precise. Perchance, I may make mention of rare anecdotes from all this information. I shall mention the disagreement there is in the matter, honest disagreement, no less. Perhaps I shall mention that statement over which no expression of disagreement exists. If Allāh wills I shall make it explicit and clear. I ask Him for His help. There is no power nor might save in Him the All Powerful. His blessing and His peace be upon our Lord Muḥammad, the Lord of the Messengers who has been sent, also on his household and on his Companions one and all.

"I declare that with Allāh is my success in being accurate in making statements and in repeating them. Verily, I have heard and verified and beheld, written and recorded, from my elders, and from their histories, from what I have learnt from them, from the genealogists, and what I have gleaned from ancient leaves and folios, namely, that the Imaghsharen,[18] and those who were with them, dwelt in Azawād, and its neighbourhood after Islam, at the end of 500/1106/7 or a little before. They were a tribe, major in size and number, and they inhabited the region from Taghāzā as far as the neighbourhood of Timbuctoo. Their settlement was so great that it was said that a woman went forth in search of her stray calf and she walked from Timbuctoo, or from quite near it, until she reached Taghāzā. She carried no water with her, nor did she spend her nights in an empty wilderness.

"It is said that the Imaghsharen originally stemmed from the Ḥimyarite Lamtūnah whose maternal uncles were the Berbers. They derived their mother tongue from the latter and the tongue is spoken by the Tuareg [Iwillimmeden] who are a remnant of part of them. However, it is also said that this was not so and that various tribes mixed with them. Some of them were Arabs even, and it was on account of this that they were given the name, the *Ṭawāriq*, which in Arabic means 'the tribes'.[19] Allāh is best acquainted with this fact.

"They continued to prosper, to multiply in their number, to increase in their strength in their settlements until the pious saint who is my ancestor, Shaykh Sīdī Aḥmad ibn Āddah, came to them. I shall refer to this again when I report the age when he came, that is if Allāh so wills it.

"Azawād district was blessed with rivers and watery expanses and with trees and groves, as we have heard. The Imaghsharen, and the offspring of their father Idnān, continued in that land after their settlement in a state of perfect prosperity and powerful rule, that is after the year 500/1106/7 as I have mentioned, and I have heard that this was the age when the city of Timbuctoo was founded and when its buildings were constructed. It was said that Timbuctoo was the name of one of the women clients of the Imaghsharen, or one of their slave women, who was in her tent near that spot. When the town was built it was named after that woman who dwelt in the place where it was sited. Such is reported in one of the histories of the Sūdān. It was rumoured that she was a slave woman of the Kel Anakundur who are a people among the *Zwāyā*.[20] In their lineages it is said that they are descended from the Anṣār, the Companions of the Prophet. It is also said that this is not the case. Allāh knows best. The Imaghsharen and their brethren and those who were with them remained in this country, being great in number and in power and in inviolability. Centuries passed. It was at the very commencement of the century, around the year 920/1514, that the Awlād ʿAbd al-Raḥmān camped amongst them. They were a band of the Raḥāminah, people from the Ḥawz of Marrakech. This came about due to the wars which took place between them. The people whom they fought drove them from their land of the Ḥawz. They left it and wandered with their tents into this country. They too were a great number. They camped among the Imagsharen and those who were with them. They arrived in their midst when they still possessed the power and owned the localities. They dwelt side by side with them for some eighty years as they approached the limit of their strength.[21]

"Towards the end of the tenth/sixteenth century, the armies of Jawdar arrived. The reason why he came during the days of power of the Sulṭān Mawlāy Aḥmad al-Dhahabī was that the latter had sent word to the pilgrim, Muḥammad Askiyā, the Songhai Sulṭān with the demand that the latter should surrender the salt mine of Taghāzā to him. He replied to the effect that the 'Aḥmad' to whom one should listen was not Aḥmad al-Dhahabī, and that the 'Isḥāq' to whom one should listen was not him, the latter, either, and that his mother had yet to bear him in her womb.[22] Then he, the ruler of Mali [and the Songhai] despatched two thousand Tuareg raiders. He ordered them to attack the fringe of the Darʿah (Draa) region towards Marrakech. None should be slaughtered and they should return again by the same route.

"They raided the market of Ibnay [two sons?] Aṣbīḥ, while it was in progress. They consumed all that they found in the market, whether it be in goods or properties, and they returned as they had been commanded to do, having killed nobody. This was only to show the Sulṭān of Morocco how powerful he was. The Sulṭān had corresponded with him before this occasion and had sent to him two *ḥarīsh*[23] and two iron horse-shoes, symbolic of his might and power. In the year 998/1590 the Askiyā was wrathful against Ibn Karnfarma [Kirinfil], who was one of the servants of the Songhai *Amīrs*.[24] He sent him to Taghāzā with a decree that he should be imprisoned there. The locality was at that time under his authority. But it was Allāh's decree that he should escape from prison and that he should flee to Marrakech. In the following year the Sulṭān Mawlāy Aḥmad al-Dhahabī equipped his army and appointed Jawdar to be its commander. A poet has mentioned that this took place in the year 999/1591 and that Jawdar made the year momentous although he was a eunuch and very short in stature.

"He came to Taghāzā but was reluctant to enter it. He destroyed its fortress, left it, and went to Telek and dug the wells there.[25] He departed and reached Timbuctoo. Upon his arrival he held a great feast out of delight at his safe-coming to the river bank. After this he left for Gao having stationed his soldiers there.

"In the year 1011/1602 Shaykh Sīdī Aḥmad agg Āddah came to Arawān and found it to be a well where the Imaghsharen drew their water and where they, in the bliss of those days,[26] sited their habitations. He built a flimsy shelter and the people from every tribe began to visit him there. After twelve years he had finished building a castle. Among those who came to study with him was Ab[ū] Makhlūf who had four sons. The oldest of them was ʿĪsā, the second was Muḥammad, the third was Aḥmad and the youngest of them was Sulaymān. They were accompanied to Azawād by Muḥammad ibn Aḥmad ibn ʿĀmir ibn Sulaymān ibn Masʿūd ibn Sulṭān ibn Zammām ibn al-Dhuwādī ibn Dhuwād ibn Mirdās ibn Riyāḥ ibn Abī Rabīʿah ibn Nahīk ibn Hilāl ibn ʿĀmir ibn Ṣaʿṣaʿah ibn Muʿāwiyah ibn Bakr ibn Hawāzin ibn Manṣūr ibn ʿIkrimah ibn Khaṣfa ibn Qays ʿAylān ibn Muḍar.

"Sulaymān, mentioned above, was the son of Saʿīd ibn Ḥāfiẓ ibn ʿUqayl ibn ʿAskar ibn Zayd ibn ʿĪsā ibn Ḥumyān ibn ʿUqbah ibn ʿAbbās ibn Thādī ibn Shibl ibn Yad Zayd ibn Ṣāliḥ ibn Muḥammad ibn ʿAbd al-Raḥmān ibn al-Imām Abī Bakr al-Ṣiddīq ibn ʿUthmān ibn ʿĀmir ibn ʿUmar ibn Kaʿb ibn Luwayy ibn Fihr. I here conclude my quotation of the book called *Zahrat al-Akhbār fī Nasab al-Nabī al-Mukhtār*. Shaykh Aḥmad agg Āddah died in the year 1044/1635. Abū Makhlūf lived with him during his lifetime until he also departed this life and he was buried beside him. His sons used to come to visit him from the bank of the river Niger and to pursue their commerce and their trade. They were accompanied by their paternal cousins from the Banū ʿĀmir and from Arabs who inhabited Azawād. At that time they were the Awlād ʿAbd al-Raḥmān, the Awlād Saʿīd, the Awlād Jalūl, the Akhzūrāt, the Ahl Ghaylān and the Nahārāt. Afterwards they behaved oppressively. They were unruly and aggressive to an excessive degree. They committed acts of injustice which were intolerable to the extent that their Shaykh allowed none to possess a camel which had a grey coat of hair [*zāʾilah zarqāʾ*]. He alone possessed them. He alleged that this was the mark of his camels. Aʿysh ibn al-ʿAṭshān was among the group who came from the river bank for trade and for commerce. He had a *zāʾilah zarqāʾ* with him so the Shaykh of the Awlād ʿAbd al-Raḥmān demanded it from him. He refused to give it to him so the Shaykh punished him by shaving off his beard. The latter began to wear a face-muffler out of shame for what he had experienced. Aʿysh was among a party including his sons.[27] After the seizure of his camel he left his sons who were in that party in order to go in search of his camel and to recover it from him who had taken it. When he returned to them he was muffled. The company assembled and agreed that they would fight the Awlād ʿAbd Raḥmān. The chief of their party was ʿĪsā ibn Abī Makhlūf. He took his younger brother who lived with their father Abū Makhlūf. He was called Sulaymān. The son of Sulaymān ibn Abī Makhlūf was al-Ḥājj Muḥammad. He had seven sons: Masʿūd, Daḥmān, Aʿysh, Manṣūr, Yūsuf, Bū Bakr and Bayd. This al-Ḥājj Muḥammad had two blood brothers, Sulaymān the Shaykh and Muḥammad.

"They journeyed to the bank of the Niger, although the family tents of Sulaymān, and his son, al-Ḥājj Muḥammad, remained pitched in Azawād, because his wife was one of the Awlād ʿAbd al-Raḥmān. They were joined by sixty Tuareg who were intent on gain. They welcomed them and made them happy, but then, after they had afforded them their protection they behaved with treachery against them and they slew them all. They dug a grave for them and they buried them in it, they and their camels, their weapons and their goods. This event was named *Tādrīs*. It took place in the year 1092/1681/2. It was the year when Shaykh Sīdī Aḥmad al-Khalīf al-Raqqādi died.[28]

"When the party marched from Arawān they reached al-Wayd where Amjabūr went back from amongst their number. Then they raided the camels of the Awlād ʿAbd al-Raḥmān. The latter tribe were in some fear of pursuing them. However, they engaged in battle in the land of Inān, because at that time there was no well there. During the course of this combat between them the family of ʿĪsā ibn Abī Makhlūf were defeated. ʿĪsā himself was killed by them. They joined their party and they reached their tribe, the Raḥāminah.

"Qays, the son of ʿĪsā, rose up [revengeful] and sent forth his clan of the Raḥāminah. They were eight hundred mounted men led by Qays ibn ʿĪsā ibn Abī Makhlūf. They raided the Awlād ʿAbd al-Raḥmān at Tintahūn,[29] where they found their company dispersed. The majority of them were treating the animals of their Shaykh for an epidemic of the mange. They arrived among their tents and they left them scattered to the four winds. They pursued some of them to the land of Bamba and they kept the spoils which fell into their hands. One hundred and fifty of them stayed in Azawād whilst the remainder returned to the bank of the river taking their booty with them.

"At the end of 1093/1682 the Barābīsh encamped at Arawān with four hundred of the Ṣā'imīn. They joined their brethren whom they had left there,[30] in the land of Azawād. They came with the tents of their people who were centred in Azawād before them. As for the rest, they were men who were returning from Igīdī to their land. These were the Awlād ʿĀmir, the sons of Sulaymān, and the Awlād Akhmad. The tribes which came with them were the Awlād Bū Khaṣīb, the Awlād Aʿysh, the Awlād ʿUmrān, the Awlād Ghannām, the Awlād Idrīs and the Maḥāfīẓ. They all settled in Azawād. *The whole group began to call themselves the Barābīsh.* Their first Shaykh was Anas ibn ʿĪsā, the Saḥḥār Sulṭān,[31] then his cousin, al-Ḥājj Muḥammad ibn Sulaymān, then after him ʿAlī ibn Daḥmān. In the year 1141/1729 the army of ʿAlī ibn Daḥmān attacked the Awlād Bū Fāyid in the *Gibla*.[32] But they were defeated and ʿAlī was taken captive. Wuld Aʿbīd Umm al-Ghallāwī gave one hundred she-camels for his release. In 1142/1730 the power of the Banū Maghfar was discomforted at Ra's al-Mā'. Then in the year 1149/1737 the battle of al-Zalāyib took place between the Barābīsh and the Nabkah . . . The Awlād ʿUmrān and the Maḥāfīẓ and the Awlād Aʿysh became one group. Their Shaykh was Ḥām wuld Budal[33] and this was due to the battle with the Awlād ʿĀmir. The second group were under Aʿli wuld Muḥammad wuld Budal. The third group was led by Sulaymān wuld Aʿli wuld Manṣūr Laʿīsh. The Amīrate reverted to one of the family of Budal after him. After the death of Aʿli, and in the time of Aʿli ibn Daḥmān, Muhammad al-Amḥad, the ancestor of the Rgaybāt,[34] came to marry the daughter of the Shaykh of the Awlād Saʿīd. He begat two sons by her, Muḥammad al-Mukhtār and ʿAbdallāh. Muḥammad al-Mukhtār was the ancestor of the Awlād al-Ṣāliḥ and ʿAbdallāh was the ancestor of the Ahl al-Gaḥla, that is, the Awlād Shuwayikh, the descendants of Ḥassān. In his time the Turmuz of Azawād settled there. They swore allegiance to him, Ibn Daḥmān, the Shaykh of the Awlād ʿĀmir and Awlād Sulayman and Awlād Aḥmad, [and then] his cousin, Ḥāfiẓ wuld Aʿysh wuld al-Ḥājj Muḥammad took the office of Amīr. Then he was succeeded by [his son] ʿAlī wuld Ḥāfiẓ. Due to this, fighting and conflict ended among the Barābīsh. Then one of the Awlād Ḥāfiẓ, named Muḥammad, assumed the office of Amīr, but it was taken by force from him by his cousin, Muḥammad ibn Yūsuf. He became the Shaykh of all the Barābīsh and he took the tribute from all those who came to Azawād. The first group who, at times, were to dispute the authority of the Awlād ʿĀmir were called ʿArab al-Giblah.[35] They were the Muḥāfaẓat Awlād ʿUmrān. The Awlād Aʿysh began to serve the Awlād ʿĀmir when Muḥammad ibn Yūsuf became the Amīr. When they commenced their service they formed a union with the Awlād Aḥmad of the Abnāʾ ʿĀmir and with the Maʿātīg, the sons of Muḥammad ibn Abī Makhlūf. They appointed Bīd to be their Shaykh. He was one of the Maʿātīg. They were keen to create an opposition between him and his cousin, Muḥammad ibn Yūsuf. The beginning of this dissent involved the leading men of the Niger buckle where merchant *Sharīfs* were to be found. A major battle took place between the two parties. This was the second slaughter known as Arāk in the year 1165/1752. Muḥammad ibn Yūsuf died in the year 1168/1755 after the truce. The Awlād Aḥmad betrayed him, together with the sons of Bīd in the town of Arawān. The two men in question were Muḥammad ibn al-Amīn ibn Bū Rās and Muḥammad ibn Aʿmar ibn al-Amīn.[36]

"Muḥammad ibn Raḥḥāl ibn Daḥmān, who has been mentioned, became the Amīr. The feuding continued amongst themselves after they came to Ambarāk al-Shaykh[37] in regard to their dispute as to who should command the tax on those who came to Azawād. Muḥammad ibn Raḥḥāl drew closer to Wuld Abī Rās in his disappointment. The feuding continued. Among their battles was the day of Khasīn. It was in the year 1170/1757. In the same year the battle of the white pit took place. In the year 1172/1759 the battle of al-Ghashwah was fought between the parties. In the same year 1179/1766 was fought the battle of the stockade [*zarībah*] and in 1183/1770 the battle of al-Ṭuwayrāt. A further feud occurred between them called the battle of Tahakīmat. This was in the year 1204/1789. Another war then took place between them. I shall not expand on it in detail since my aim is to shorten and abridge.

"Then the situation recovered amongst them. They made peace with Ibn Kanī and with others. In his succeeding year Muḥammad ibn Raḥḥāl sent a man to murder him. After his murder, the Awlād Aʿysh departed from the Giblah. In the year 1204/1790, Shaykh Sīdī Aḥmad ibn Sīdī Ṣāliḥ rode to meet them.[38] He made peace between them. It was on condition that not one of the Barābīsh would do them an injury. He sent them away to Azawād. Abthīt al-Tārig died in the year 1205/1791. He was killed by the negroes. The Tuareg beseiged Timbuctoo for a long while. Then Shaykh Sīdī Muḥammad [al-Amīn] ibn al-Shaykh Sīdī Aḥmad ibn Ṣāliḥ rode forth to them and he made peace with them. [I recall to you] that it was reported to [his father] Ṭālib Sīdī Aḥmad [long before this] that a man from the Kel Es-Sūq heard the report that Sīdī Aḥmad al-Hoggarī was in Ra's al-Mā'. Ṭālib Sīdī Aḥmad set out to visit him and to study with him, but when he came to him, he said, 'You will find that thing which you desire of me in Arawān.' Shaykh Sīdī Aḥmad and his son, Muḥammad al-Amīn, came to Arawān and they studied with the *Qāḍī*, Sīdī'l-Wāfī, and with the perfect *Quṭb*, Sīdī Aḥmad, and from him learnt the true *wird*. Muḥammad al-Amīn became wealthy and Muḥammad Raḥḥāl brought him to Bū Jbayha, which was then only a well. He built a house and a mosque for him there. He built a fortress and he stationed eighty slaves there during the period of his wars with the Awlād Aḥmad.[39]

"After the death of Muḥammad Raḥḥāl, his son Aʿli became the Amīr. He gathered together those who were scattered among the Barābīsh. Among them were Ahl al-Shayn from Turmuz who were with the Āl al-Shaykh al-Kabīr.[40] Their disagreement amongst themselves was very great. When he died the Amīrate was invested in his brother, Imhammad. He began a feud with the Awlād ʿAllūsh. Among their battles was the day of Tukarmīn and the day of Tinfāt in which his son, Bū Bakr died. After this they were asked by the Ahl al-Kawr that they should advance against the Baṭn al-Jamal,[41] with force, although Imhammad disregarded this until his death. Before that occurred the Kel Intasar killed forty men of the Ahl al-Kawr, but Imhammad ignored this due to their injustice and their tyranny. They killed sixteen of the Qamīrāt when they refused to obey them. After the death of Imhammad, his nephew, Aḥmad ibn ʿUbayd became the Amīr. The Awlād Sulaymān and Ahl al-Kawr were in disagreement. The Awlād Sulaymān attacked the Baṭn al-Jamal in the battle of Ifrabnīn. They rode in pursuit of them and attacked the Awlād Idrīs by mistake. Because of this attack the Awlād Idrīs joined with the Awlād Sulaymān. In the year 1217/1802 the Baṭn al-

Jamal left in a large body. Among them were the Awlād al-Mawlāt and there were others. They intended to raid Ḥamd ibn ʿUbayd who was in Bū Jbayha. He had three hundred men with him and they fought. The Baṭn al-Jamal were defeated. In the year 1232/1817, the Baṭn al-Jamal raided Aḥmad ibn ʿUbayd for a second time. He had eighty tents with him at Am-Munlaḥ. They attacked him and they fought. The Baṭn al-Jamal were defeated and they showed no ardour of war since that time. The year 1255/1839 was called the year of *al-Aḥmā*. It was followed by the year called *Gīr*, then *Lkhn*, then *Bdq*, then *Zīr ibn* [sic] *Zimrān*. In that year people from the Sahel attacked the Barābīsh and raided their camels. They were met by Muḥammad ibn Aḥmad ibn Aʿbayd. He surrounded them until they killed him, he, together with a group of his people. The enemy defeated the rest and they led away the camels. After that, Aḥmad ibn Aʿbayd, whose father, Muḥammad, had been slain, attacked them with his army in order to obtain his revenge. He did so in the locality called *Zīr ibn* [sic] *Zimrā* [n]. He fought them fiercely and they were defeated before him, after he had slaughtered many of their men and he had seized and carried off their herds and possessions. Then came the year of the death of Ibn Lazgham, then the year called *al-thānī*, 'the second'. The Barābīsh arose and carried out a raid on the people of the Sahel at al-Khaṭṭ. There they fought them. The people of the Sahel were defeated after both sides had sustained loss and damage. Maḥmūd ibn al-Ḥājj Muḥammad was wounded. He was the head of the army and the Barābīsh took away what camels they possessed. This year was followed by the year of *Tīhat al-Ẓahr*. Its circumstance was as follows. The people of the Sahel made an attack on the Barābīsh in a place known as al-Ẓahr. The people of the Sahel were defeated and they returned downcast. Then followed the year of the Azelay[42] of the Horses. It was on account of the defeat; the enemy were defeated after having slain the one who was called *By him who sleeps not* (*alladhī lā yanāmu*).[43] Then came the year of the Death of Sidagīn, then the year *Atasawhil*, of the family of Mawlāy al-Ṭāyiʿ. That was because the Ahl Arawān expelled them from Arawān, so they journeyed towards the Sahel,[44] they and the sons of Bahand, until they passed through Tawdannī.[45] The Hoggar Tuareg came up with them and slew them. Not one was left, perhaps one or two; they, a tiny remnant, returned to Arawān. Then came the year of the 'Pilgrims', then the year of the Date Crop, then the year of the Abundant Rains [*ahālīb*]. In that year the people of the Giblah made a raid on the Kuntah and they stole their herds. Muḥammad ibn ʿUluwāt, the chief of the Hammāl rode his camel and made it kneel upon his arrival before Aḥmad ibn Aʿbīd. He asked him for his help. The Barābīsh mounted their beasts and they engaged the Awlād ʿAllūsh[46] and fought them and chased them away from the camels. Not one camel was unaccounted for. When the Barābīsh returned, the chief of the Hammāl turned to them and said to them, 'Take one third of the camels.' They refused and said, 'We shall not take any of them.' The owner of the camels swore that each one of them should take a camel and they did so. Then in the year of Arawān, the Dāwūd raided the Barābīsh. They numbered eight hundred men, among them eighty horsemen. When they reached Tagānit Kayn they suffered from a terrible thirst and they made for Arawān in search of water. The Barābīsh heard of them while they were in the territory of Bū Jbayha. They rode towards them and came upon them in the town of Arawān. The Dāwūd encountered them and a fierce combat took place between them. The Dāwūd were defeated after seventy-two men had died among them. Then followed the year, *Aghreyga 'l-Nabga*, then the year of the Death of al-Ghaylānī, then the year of *Tagūrārt*, then the year of *Aʿjan*. In that year the Awlād ʿAllūsh raided Azawād and attacked the camels of Mahammad ibn Aḥmad [ibn] Aʿbīd. He was, at that time, separated from the rest of the people, except for two tents of the Gwānīn and two of the people of Sīdī ʿAlī. They killed one of the men of the Sīdī ʿAlī and one of the Gwānīn. It happened that Mahammad was in Timbuctoo at that time. The Gwānīn who survived rode to him by horse and told the news to him in the city. Mahammad then mounted himself in order to show himself to them. He was amidst an army of the people of the river region, that is to say those Arabs who lived on the river bank. He met them but he got nowhere with them. On the contrary, they defeated him and his people and they went away with their spoil in the direction of their own people. Then they returned again and they raided camel herds in one of the localities in Azawād. The Barābīsh rode in pursuit of them and found Mahammad was pursuing them. They caught up with them at a place called Tākhmart and a sharp battle took place between them. The Awlād ʿAllūsh were defeated after a large number had been killed and the camels had been recovered.

"In the year of *ʿIlb amal* the Awlād ʿAllūsh launched a raid on the Barābīsh. The latter defeated them. Then came the year of the Cold. Then came the year of *Aẓrāẓ*, then the year of *Ṭabl al-ʿAkl*. Then came the year of *Lḥsīn*, then the year of *al-Naʿam*, then the year of *Aghwīs*, then the year of *Fūta*, then the year *Kaʿwān*, the year of the Violent Red Wind, [*al-rīḥ al-ḥamrā'*], then the year of *Awzāg*, then the year of *Dagāg*, then the year of *Tin Mazūrāt*. In that year the people of the Sahel attacked the Barābīsh and took their camels away from them. I have no firm knowledge of the circumstances of the battle. Then came the year of *ʿIrg Azūzāl*. The Dāwūd raided the Barābīsh but they fought them until the former were defeated. Then came the year of *Kadām*. In that year the people of the Sahel raided the camel herds of the people of Arawān. The Barābīsh caught up with them at a place called *Kadām*.[47] The Barābīsh were defeated after their leader, al-Bakkāy ibn Aḥmad ibn Aʿbīd, and his brother Muḥammad, nicknamed Būb, had been slain. Then came the year of *Gīr*.[48] Then the year of *Gānb*. In that year Mahammad raided the enemy who had killed his two brothers. The enemy were herders (*ruʿyān*) and he attacked them in a place called Gānb. In the year of *al-Aʿlāb*,[49] the herders made an attack on the Barābīsh in this locality. They were defeated by the Barābīsh. Then came the year *Ajdar*, then the year of *al-Rigg*. In that year the people of Bard came to Tawdannī in order to carry salt. They did so without the permission of the Barābīsh. The latter prevented them and a battle took place between them. The Awlād Bard were defeated and the camels which they possessed were taken from them. The leader of the Barābīsh was Sīdī Muḥammad ibn Mahammad. Then came the year of the death of Wuld Sayyid ʿUlūwāt. It came about that the Kel Intasar killed one of the Ahl *al-Shaykh*.[50] Due to that a major conflict broke out between the Kuntah and the Kel Intasar. Then came the year of the Death of Mahammad ibn Aḥmad wuld Aʿbīd. This was the year called *Aʿrīk wuld Ahman*. Then the year of *Asradūn*. Then the year of the *Azelay ʿashara*, then the year of the Customer (*al-zabūn*), Wuld ʿAysh, then the year of *Ittiniḥiyya*. In that year the people of the Sahel raided the Barābīsh and they drove away the camels. The Barābīsh caught them up at a place called by this name and they pursued them after they had taken the camels from them. Then came the year of *al-Amghīṭ*, and then the year of the Star called Umm Asbīb, which heralded the commencement of a new century.

That year was famous for a well-known event. A tribe from the people of the Sahel raided the Awlād Ghannām at the well known as Gīr. The Barābīsh pursued them, led by Daḥmān and his nephew, Sayyid Muḥammad ibn Mahammad. They caught up with them and took what they possessed after having killed a number of them. The remainder fled and one died among the Barābīsh. They suffered a number of injuries and wounded men. After that the Azelay commenced its journey and it reached Tawdannī. The Barābīsh departed, they travelled to Tawdannī on account of the Azelay. When they reached Tawdannī a party of the Rgaybāt attacked the camel herds of the people of Arawān there. Daḥmān ibn Aḥmad Aʿbīd rode forth in the midst of a company of a squadron of the Barābīsh. He caught up with them in the Sahel at a place called al-Ḥank.[51] He attacked them and a great battle was fought between them. The Barābīsh speedily defeated them and they recovered their possessions of the camels of the Ahl Arawān. They firmly took hold of the enemy and left them in a state of humiliation and wretchedness. The Rgaybāt split up in parts of their territory. Tribes from those territories gathered around them and they rode in pursuit of the Barābīsh. The latter had been safe from the enemy until they caught them up. A bloody conflict took place. Among the Barābīsh there died many men. I have no knowledge as to their numbers. Among the most notable was the brother of Daḥmān, the leader of the army, and his nephew. Then came the year called Leaving off the Raiding [*tark al-ghazw*]. The year was given this name because the Barābīsh had been determined to raid the Rgaybāt but in the end they forsook the raid. Then came the year which was known as *al-Nafga*. It was a grevious year due to a shortage of food. So grave was it that the *nafga* – that is, the pay of the [salt mine?] workers was reduced to a loaf of salt.[52] Then the year came known as the Expedition (*zawgat*) of the Awlād Ghaylān and the Awlād Aʿysh to the Adrār [n-Īfōghās]. The reason for that was that they were angry with the chief in Azawād, Sayyid Muḥammad ibn Mahammad. The latter sent his cousins, and Sayyid al-Ḥabīb, one of the saints, after them [the men of the Īfōghās], in order to be kindly and lenient with them so as to restrain them. They had a meeting and an agreement was made between them. Then they all returned.

"Then came the year 'during which fighting occurred between the Tuareg and the Barābīsh'. The cause of this was that a group of people from the Awlād Sbāʿ came [to Azawād] but they were prevented by Tuareg from [meeting with] the Barābīsh. Now the situation was that none comes from a foreign country to Azawād but he [first] obtains a safe conduct [*amān*] from the Barābīsh. Having done so, he can afterwards proceed to wherever he likes. These men in question supported the action and the claim of these Tuareg. Hence, a dispute arose.[53] The Sudanese joined with the Tuareg and a battle took place between the two parties. The Tuareg were defeated. Then peace was made between the Barābīsh and the Tuareg and this affair was resolved.

"Then came the year of the Seven Companions. It was named thus because the rain continued to fall for seven days, by day and by night. Then came the year called *Tinkuṭṭāy*. In that year a people from the herders [*ruʿyān*],[54] raided Azawād but they did not arrive there before they had suffered many deaths due to the intensity of their thirst. The Barābīsh seized them, but then they pardoned them and did all they could for them in giving them provisions. So they returned to their people in safety. Then came the year called *Tādaraysa*. This was a very evil year on account of paucity of food, so that the people started to subsist on the grain of a plant known as *Tādaraysa* wherever it might be found growing in hollow spots in the hard ground.[55] Then came the year called *Arūsh al-Khayl*, so called because this is a malady which afflicts the horses. Many horses died in that same year due to the prevalance of it. In that year the Hoggar raided part of Azawād, when the people were inattentive, and they obtained control of it.[56]

"Then came the year called the Year the Cattle Died. In that year, the Turmuz of the Maghrib, the people of 'the veracious one' [al-Ṣiddīq?], went their way and they camped among [the enemy], the Awlād ʿAllūsh. They became their allies and they joined with them in their intent to go up into Azawād. They did so, and they attacked the camel herds of the people of Azawād at a place called Tartarīragh[?]. It is a place which is situated between Bū Jbayha and Inlāḥi.[57] They killed a man of the Awlād Sulaymān. The Barābīsh pursued them. They were led by Daḥmān and his nephew, Sayyid Muḥammad ibn Mahammad. They caught up with them at their tents at a locality with a well called Bū Zarība. The army separated. The Awlād Sulaymān went in one direction, while all the Barābīsh went in another. The enemy met them and there was a pitched battle. The enemy were defeated, those, that is, who were towards the Awlād Sulaymān. The latter entered their tents and they took their drum [of chieftainship], their *ṭabl*. They began to play a game of *hība*.[58] They did not know that their people had become engaged in a fierce conflict with a second group. When they heard the sound of fire-arms they realized what had happened and they hurried to assist them against the enemy. They left Daḥmān in the camp where the tents were pitched and they did not catch up with them until the Barābīsh had already been defeated and the enemy had overcome them. The defeat hurt both sides in the engagement, though Daḥmān and those with him knew nought of it. They were a small group. The enemy returned to them and slew them all because they refused to flee.

"Then came the year *Mṣṣgīl*. In that year the Barābīsh rode forth. They were led by the Amīr Sayyid Muḥammad ibn Mahammad and Maḥmūd ibn Daḥmān was amongst them. This was the first ride he undertook. He was a lad of tender years at that time. They had ridden, carrying their tents with them, to Ra's al-Mā'. They left their families there. The men rode further and arrived in the territory of the Awlād ʿAllūsh. They heard that they were coming and they fled through the desert and they entered their camps. The Barābīsh went back to one of their camps among the camel herds and they raided it. They killed the men and seized what they possessed.

"Then came the year called *the year of Māmūr*. The Awlād ʿAllūsh rode forth accompanied by the Ahl Sayyid Mashẓūf.[59] They raided the region of Timbuctoo. They found nothing although they killed one man from the Banū Sulaymān after he had killed one of their number. They returned downcast. The Barābīsh pursued them. In fact the Barābīsh were unaware that they were two tribes. They went on pursuing them until they arrived among their tents. The enemy went forth against them, fighting very hard, but the Barābīsh defeated them. They only stayed there about one hour. By this time the Ahl Sayyid together with the [enemy] people had assembled together as one body against them. The Barābīsh were defeated when seventy-two of their number had been killed. The enemy lost some forty men. When the Barābīsh came back they concurred that they should journey to Ra's al-Mā', or before it to the locality called Iglayb al-Aghnām.[60] They left the women and children there. A raiding party of the Barābīsh attacked some of the Awlād ʿAllūsh called ʿAllūsh al-Baqar. They slew some of them and they seized their cattle and live-stock. Then they returned in safety with their spoils to their families. Then they agreed to make a second raid. All of them were mounted, ready for their march, when they heard that the Christians had landed at Kabara.[61]

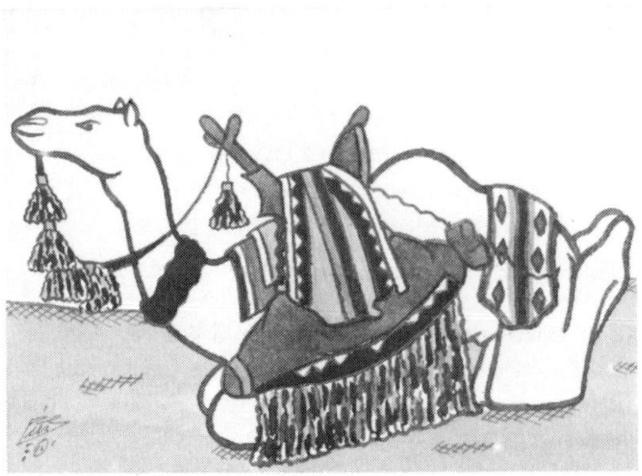

Part III

The Conquest by the Pen and the Amulet

Plate 1

Plate 2

Plate 3

Plate 4

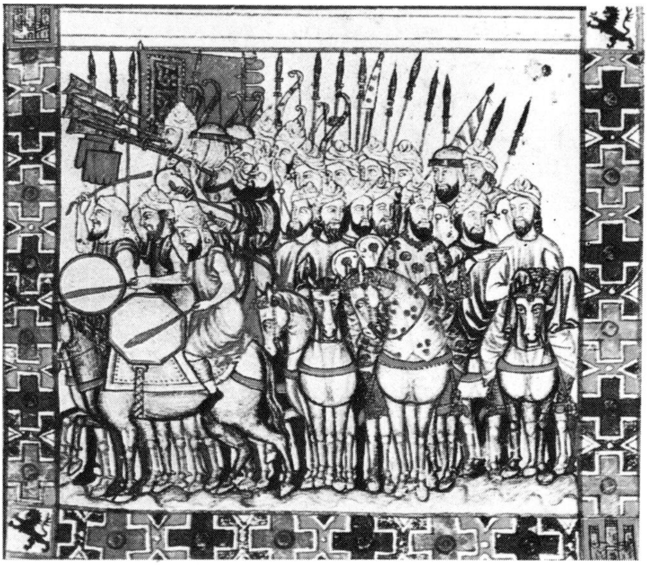

Plate 5

Plate 6

Chapter 8

Social, Cultural and Juridical Metastasis within Saharan Societies

Warrior and *Zwāya/Ineslemen*

In previous chapters I introduced examples which illustrate the domination of the anciently fixed Western Saharan Berber nomads, and Berber and negro sedentaries, by Arab military conquest. This entailed the imposition of an Arab segmental lineal system comprising patrilineal genealogies, and a dominant Arab dialect, upon a group or groups which before that period had only been partially Arabised. These people had passed through a phase, prior to the period between the fourteenth and the sixteenth centuries, where foreign Arab intruders, who had been few in number, had been incorporated as clients into long-established Saharan and Sahelian groups, some of them Berber and some of them Fulani. I had suggested that the imposition of a tribute system, a *gharāmah* or *ḥurmah*, often unlawful according to the *Sharīʿah*, had become a widely prevailing measure whereby the recent Arabic-speaking intruders into the southern Sahara and its southern borderlands had maintained a permanent mastery. They had organised much of the region which they controlled into Amīrates. Each had its princely house the members of which had either sworn homage (*bayʿah*) to the ruler of Morocco, or to another influential regional authority, or else it had retained its independence due to geographical isolation or to special historical factors and circumstances.

In my last chapter I examined the case of the borderland region of Azawād which broadly divides the world of the Arabic speakers, "the Moors", from that of the Tuareg. The process whereby an allegedly Arab group, the Barābīsh, attained mastery of a region and how it was eventually able to control one of the key salt deposits at Taoudenni (Tawdannī) was revealed as a process which was far less military and less Moroccan-controlled than was the case even in parts of southern Mauritania. In Azawād the process of cultural Arabisation commenced, it would seem, by the presence in the area of a neutral "mediatory" figure. He was a holy man from the Kel Es-Sūq of Tādamakkat aided by another holy man of the Arab Awlād Ḥassān. The foundation of the town of Arawān, and the exploitation of the salt of Azawād, provided a spur for the establishment of the Barābīsh in the region. They came to regard the tombs of these saints as tribal shrines, a place of pilgrimage, and the descendants of the saints became holy families within a predominantly Arab group. This presence of a non-Arab or only part-Arab ancestry in the group superficially seems to offer the converse of the prevalent situation elsewhere, where an "Arab" holy family or holy families was, or were, central to the social adhesion of the group. The contrast is not as marked as it first appears. These *Tamasheq* or Arabic-speaking Kel Es-Sūq claimed *Sharīfian* descent or descent from ʿAlī the son-in-law of the Prophet. They represent a layer of human history which is part of the little known story of the pre-seventeenth-century Arab penetration of the Western Sahara.

These families of the Īfōghās and the Daghūghiyyīn, some of whom claimed to be descended from the Sharīfian families settled at Sijilmāsah in Morocco, established their chief influence in groups in the southern Sahara, more especially among the Tuareg who were centred to the west of the Adrār-n-Īfōghās and along the Niger buckle to the east of Timbuctoo. This influence was especially marked in the eighteenth century. There were two important reasons for this. One was the close link which the Kel Es-Sūq established with the Kuntah, to whom some of them were related; the other reason was the presence of a number of Kel Es-Sūq scholars in the camp of Shaykh Sīdī'l-Mukhtār al-Kuntī (1729–1811), and among his successors. There was an ancestral link in common. Both claimed descent from the Arab conqueror of North Africa, ʿUqbah, either Ibn Nāfiʿor Ibn ʿĀmir, and both were involved in offering their religious services to the Iwillimmeden Tuareg. In the sixteenth and seventeenth centuries this latter confederation, *Tamasheq* in language and Tuareg in character in most respects, took on, over a period of time, many of the essential features of the Amīrates of the Awlād Ḥassān of the Hodh and southern Mauritania. At an early date, the Kel Es-Sūq and the Kuntah were able to monopolise the religious-cum-political "chaplaincy" of the Iwillimmeden. They taught Arabic, they judged, they mediated and they moulded the character of their Tuareg flock into an Arab-Berber community.

The case of the *Iwillimmeden*

The Iwillimmeden Tuareg, who live in the Sahelian states of Mali and Niger, once controlled almost the whole of the Niger buckle and they offer a special case for study. Between the seventeenth and the nineteenth centuries they extended their riparian domain from Timbuctoo in the west almost to the foot-hills of Aïr in the east. Their society, nominally ruled by a Tuareg monarchy (*tamenukala*), was, in reality, composed of a variety of nomadic tribes some of whom were Arabs, others sedentary peoples, several interdependent social classes and innumerable negro slaves.

Western Saharan and Sahelian geography reveals two massifs which border upon Iwillimmeden country to the north, the Adrār-n-Īfōghās in Mali and the Aïr Massif in Niger. The heartland of the Iwillimmeden domain is centred at Menaka on the Mali–Niger border and it now extends further to the east in the district between Tahoua and Agades. But, during the earliest period of these people's history, their heartland lay to the west and was far closer to the Western Saharan bank of the Niger river. It was bounded by the Niger valley from Timbuctoo to Gao, but it also extended to the southern bank of this river, westwards to the Hombori range, and southwards to the borders of present-day Burkina Faso. The cultivated land along the river Niger became the economic and geographical heart of this empire.

It has been explained that the Ṣanhājah, that is the Berber-speaking or Arabised Tuareg and Moorish peoples of the Western and Central Sahara, have throughout their Islamic history claimed genealogies which attached them to pre-Islamic Arabia or to the *Anṣār*, the Medinan helpers of the

Prophet Muḥammad. Opponents and men of letters, sometimes with good cause, have challenged and sometimes dismissed these claims, yet the social motives which inspired them were a powerful force in the moulding of the social mores of these people and in their gradual Arabisation.

As amongst the Moors, more especially in the Hodh, the Islamised Tuareg groups accepted "Arabian royalty" as the ideal of the secular Tuareg chief. Appointed within the patrilineal or the semi-matrilineal succession (*eṭṭebel*) of his extended family, he was elected to summon his armies by his royal drum and to signal the annual march (*tábu*), a veritable camp on the march like the vortex of a dust storm. It was a display of force and a tax-gathering expedition combined. Such ritual and precedent maintained some semblance of cohesion among these nobles. The ideal of Muḥammad's followers inspired the king's religious counsellors, called *Ineslemen* by the Tuareg, and they formulated his laws in Arabic, mediated, studied, wrote devotional works, healed the sick and evoked the rain. They, more especially the Kel Es-Sūq and Esh-Sherifen, unashamedly claimed descent from the Prophet's family or from Yaʿqūb al-Anṣārī or others among the Prophet's Companions.

In the earlier Middle Ages these Saharans clearly distinguished between the secular and the religious offices (*al-ṭabl/eṭṭebel* as opposed to *Imāmah*). This dichotomy has marked the Saharan social systems to such an extent that outsiders have sometimes been mystified by what appears to be the presence of scholars in Arabic, preachers and teachers of purist Islam, amidst laymen whose beliefs are of a benighted animism. Among some groups the offices were occasionally combined, the secular king or Sulṭān (*Amenukal* in Tuareg) was also the religious leader or *Imām*. At other times two brothers shared the burden of these offices. This is known among the Kel Intasar and also, as we have seen, among the Ḥassānī Barābīsh. The ruling hierarchy of the Iwillimmeden confederation was founded on the clear-cut distinction between a secular king in a patrilineal line among the nobles (*Imajaghen*) and an advisory college of religious counsellors who depended upon him for their protection. Granted the exceptional energy, military skill or charisma of the former, and the sanctity, political tact and wisdom of the latter, these

Saharans were capable of establishing control over large areas of the desert and the river. But in doing so they gave up something of their desert Berber culture.

The eponym of the Iwillimmeden was called Muḥammad, either Wa-n-Ara "of the generation", or the latter's son, War-llemmed "the nameless one". His successors, who split into two distinctive branches, were given the name of *War-(L)lemmeden*, the descendants of Muḥammad "who bore the title of *Ilemmed* or *Illemmed*". As centuries passed subtle nuances became attached to the name. They were called "non-conformers to the Tuareg rule of the succession of the *tegehe/tegeze*, a sister's eldest son". Another explanation, under Arab influence, was the sense of "the learners and pupils", from *elmed*, which, in *Tamasheq*, the Tuareg language, means "to learn". The title is somewhat similar to the Arabic *talāmīdh* meaning "novices" of a Ṣūfī Shaykh. Historically, the most romantic of these Arab-Tuareg identifications and *jeux de mots* is that this name could have some relationship to the mediaeval Almoravid tribal name, Lamṭah or Lamtūnah.

It is unfortunate that among the Iwillimmeden of today the historical records of past events are either lacking or are legendary. Their history prior to the seventeenth century is common Tuareg legend and epic. Nevertheless, it is significant that Muḥammad Wa-n-Ara has been personified as a Moorish prince of the Arab Awlād Ḥassān, born in southern Mauritania in the middle of the sixteenth century. As we have seen, this age was the one when all the branches of the Banū Maʿqil had extended their hegemony over large areas of the formerly Almoravid Sahara, a fact which is confirmed by contemporary European sources. The Iwillimmeden may be regarded as the last and most easterly example of a high tide of Arabisation which spread eastwards over the Western Sahara during the sixteenth and seventeenth centuries.

Muḥammad Wa-n-Ara went to the Adrār-n-Īfōghās and offered his military services to Alad, the chief of the Tuareg of Tādamakkat. He married the daughter of the latter as a reward for his services. Some Tuareg maintain that Muḥammad War-Ilemmed, who was his son, was not the son of this Arab adventurer, but was the child of Alad's daughter when married to Afagag, the *Amenukal* of the Izewwaren.

These claims can be neither proved nor disproved. Even if it is part legend, the alleged Ḥassānī ancestry is not impossible. It may well have some truth in it. At this time the region near the Niger buckle was full of wandering scholars and mercenary Arab princes. As has been explained, the Awlād Mubārak and Barābīsh Moors had built up their princedoms in the region of the Mauritanian Hodh and to the north of Timbuctoo between 1600 and 1750. They were patrons of *Ḥassāniyyah* bards and troubadours and protected Arab and Berber scholars. Some of them mixed with, and acted as, clergy and teachers of the adjacent Tuareg peoples. Some of them also fought in their wars.

When Alad died about 1600, the Tādamakkat tribe split. Karidenna, who was the youngest son of Muḥammad War-Ilemmed, was favoured by some although he was initially unsuccessful; others favoured the claims of the descendant of a daughter of Attafrīj, who was another kinsman. A substantial number of the tribe maintained that according to the Tuareg custom the succession should be determined by the bestowal of the chieftainship on male offspring born of a sister of the deceased chief. This practice was *de rigueur* among the little-Arabised Kel Ahaggaren, the Kel Aïr and other Tuareg who considered a measure of matrilineal succession to the *eṭṭebel* to be desirable. In this particular case the issue was disputed. Three factions competed in the choice. One faction supported Karidenna, another supported a co-lateral claimant. The latter group, who were also heirs of War-Ilemmed, broke with their brethren and moved east. They were to form the eastern or autonomous central division of the Iwillimmeden, later to be known as the Kel Denneg or Tagaraygaray. The third faction, the Kel Imeglalen, did not favour any kinsman of Alad, through Muḥammad, as an eligible candidate for the chieftainship of the Tādamakkat.

In a war which followed, Karidenna was to emerge triumphant. In the Western Sahara he retired to Tasselit and to the district of the nominally Moroccan salt mine at Taoudenni (Tawdannī). There he assembled a fighting force of Hoggar Tuareg and Īfōghās, who, under Rayyak, had established a powerful presence in Adrār region of Mali.

According to the explorer, Henry Barth, the original group of the Iwillimmeden,

> "dwelt formerly in Igídi near the Welád Delém, a Moorish tribe which has received a great many Berber elements, till they emigrated to A'derár, the country N.E. of Gógó, from whence . . . under the command of Karidénne, son of Shwásh, or rather Abék, they drove out the Tademékket, at that period the ruling tribe of this whole region."[1]

We also know that among the Ḥassānī groups established among the heart of the Tuareg there were also to be found the Erátafán or Ghaṭafān, a noted Arabian people, from whom some of the Awlād Ḥassān claim their descent. They were settled as a subordinate group on the middle course of the Niger quite early on at the time of the rise of the Iwillimmeden. Tuareg accounts tell of the formation of a number of groups as a result of Karidenna's battles and marches. Such were the Kel Nan, Kel Aghlāl, the Tellemedes, Kherkheren, Zeryaden Teggermat and Rawelan.

Karidenna repeatedly raided the Adrār. He also defeated the Kel Imeglalen and those eastern brethren who were later to form the Kel Denneg. He expelled many of the Tādamakkat who opposed him to the region of Timbuctoo, and he welded sundry groups of Tuareg and negroid sedentaries into a recognisably "Mauritanian" segmentary class structure to be known as the Iwillimmeden. At his side were the Īfōghās from whom came his warriors and some of the *Ineslemen*, the Islamic clerical fraternity who were to advise on matters which related to canonic law (*al-Sharī'ah*).

Karidenna (d. prior to 1700) became a folk hero. His adventurous life was embellished by *märchen*, but there is at least some documentary evidence, for example in al-Sa'dī's *Ta'rīkh al-Sūdān*, and *Tadhkirat al-Nisyān*, which tells us a little about him.[2] The Sahara's southern borders suffered a long period of drought during the reign of Karidenna and his immediate successors. This may partly explain why he was increasingly drawn towards the granaries of the Niger. About 1650 he occupied Gao and held it for eight years until he was expelled from it by Manṣūr, the Moroccan *Qā'id* of Timbuctoo. Karidenna learnt from this rebuff. He thought it advantageous to establish a *modus vivendi* with the Moroccan Pashas.

In 1690 he sought investiture from them and they bestowed it upon him in Timbuctoo. This ritual continued during the reign of Karidenna's successors; Agg Esh-Shīkh was invested in 1715 by the Pasha ʿAlī ibn Raḥmūn or by ʿAbdallāh ibn al-Ḥājj al-ʿImrānī, and his son, Ḥāmma in 1741.

The now close association of the Iwillimmeden with the agricultural sedentaries of the river, and as allies of the Moroccans, however nominal and tenuous relations with the latter may have been, furthered a steady Arabisation of the more lettered elements among the Iwillimmeden. It also influenced some of the non-lettered. There were a large number of Tuaregs in the army of the *Armas* side-by-side with Fulani, Ḥassānīs and Oudalen. Economically this interdependence helped to ensure the survival of the giant herds of cattle which the Iwillimmeden had acquired by this time, and it offered them some protection from the worst effects of the years of drought. After 1700, Karidenna's successors were thwarted in their activities by the Timbuctoo Tādamakkat chief ʿUghmar agg Alad, who reigned for fifty-five years and who twice defeated the Iwillimmeden, at Bamba in 1726 and at Tagahia in 1737. During all this period the Iwillimmeden monarchy built up its cohesion, continuing the process of Islamisation which had begun with Karidenna.

The association with the Moroccan Pashas was counterbalanced by closer, and perhaps more fundamental, Islamic links with the Tuareg Sultanate of Aïr, which was located much further east in the city of Agades. Among the *Ineslemen* of the Kel Es-Sūq there is a written record that the power of appointing *Qāḍīs*, the Islamic judges among the Iwillimmeden, the power to take oaths of Islamic allegiance (*bayʿah*) and other honours and offices were bestowed upon Karidenna by the Sulṭān of Agades, whose predecessors at an earlier date had received this privilege and authority in Cairo from the ʿAbbāsid Caliph or from one of his Ottoman successors.

According to Ḥammād ibn Muḥammad ibn Muḥammad al-Sūqī:

> "Our forebears and descendants have concurred that the Tuareg Amīr, Karidenna, journeyed from our land to Agades at the time when the *Imām* there was al-Ghudālā, and he returned with the crown of the deputyship from the *Imām* in those countries and his

administration of the *Qaḍā'* was firmly fixed in his hand. When he reached his homeland and people he was warmly welcomed and he endowed our uncle, Taballa, with the office of *Qāḍī*, telling him to be heedful and attentive, nay, he did do rather in a general gathering of the nobility, after Taballa had made certain to bring him seven riding camels. These almost surpassed all standards of beauty, because they were from the mounts of the Banū Akkār, camels still noted for their breeding and their liberty, and he also brought him a date gathered from a date palm. When Taballa loosened his turban in the fulfilment of this office, held in great awe and esteem by most men, he relinquished it to his brother and close colleague, the famous saint, Muḥammad, and this he did without any shame nor in disgrace, he did so simply to show his affection . . .".[3]

The presence and influence of Arabic scholars, who were often independent yet were protected by the *Imajaghen* Tuareg aristocracy throughout the area controlled by the Iwillimmeden and in the peripheral areas of the Agades Sultanate of Aïr, were of importance in the Islamisation of the Tuareg of the south-west. Some of the Iwillimmeden were under the control of the lettered of Timbuctoo, who called them their "Arabs", their warriors. Others were under the control of the Barābīsh chiefs of the Banū Raḥḥāl and were employed to gather taxes. The scholarly pursuits of the lettered were to be followed by some of the members of the class of artisans and smiths (*ineden*) who were very influential in the Iwillimmeden camps. There was also some involvement of the Barābīsh in administration of the Iwillimmeden camps. There are references to Barābīsh scholars in the anonymous text, *Kitāb Muṭarrib al-ʿIbād*. The lettered Ilemtien (Lamtūnah) of the Īfōghās, and the Kel Es-Sūq Sharīfs, enjoyed particular favour and influence in the entourage of these Tuareg princes. Some of the scholars were wholly unattached. They had cultural ties with scholars in Agades, in Sijilmāsah and in the *Zāwiyahs* in the Atlas. Some claimed descent from the Caliph ʿAlī through Ibrāhīm al-Daghūghī, the eponym of the Kel Es-Sūq Esh-Sherifen. They were mostly adherents of the Ṣūfī order of the *Qādiriyyah*. They had lodges in remote valleys of Aïr and the Mali Adrār, in Azawād and also in the Iwillimmeden camps on the banks of the Niger.

The names of several of these scholars (*ettali/eṭṭalaba*) are known from Arabic documents, although the dates of their lives appear to span several of the reigns of Karidenna's successors. One mystic of Agades, Aḥmad al-Targī al-Lamtūnī (d. *circa* 1679–80) lived during the reign of Karidenna. Although normally resident in the city of Agades, he had familial links with kinsmen in the *Zāwiyah* at Dilā' in Morocco. The routes in the Western Sahara between Morocco and Agades passed through the territory of Karidenna. The Sharīf, Agag al-Ghazālī, one of the holiest saints of the Īfōghās, married a daughter of Karidenna. Al-Bakrī ibn Agg Ayyay, another scholar called Intakluṣut of the Kel Tekerrenat, Muḥammad his son, and the *Qāḍī*, Ḥanna agg Immattāl, a jurist and mystic who was a strong opponent of divorce, were all Kel Sūqī scholars who lived during the reigns of the early and late *Amenukals* of the Iwillimmeden.

Like the *Zwāya* in Mauritania, the Kel Es-Sūq and their colleagues played the major role of settling feuds between the *Imajaghen* nobles, the resolving of complex problems regarding the status of slaves and tributaries – Songhai, Jerma and Fulani – and the combating of pagan ways among the Iwillimmeden Tuareg by Islamic law, mystic initiation and thaumaturgy inspired from Morocco and from Mamlūk and Ottoman Egypt. Far above these Tuareg scholars must be placed the supreme scholar and counsellor of them all, the Shaykh of the Arabophone Kuntah, Sidi'l-Mukhtār al-Kuntī al-Kabīr.

At about the same time as the emergence of the Iwillimmeden, the Kuntah confederation had been born amongst the holy families and the allied clans of the Tājakānt in Mauritania.[4] After 1700, one of their branches had settled to the east of Timbuctoo, and Sīdī'l-Mukhtār, the greatest of their scholars, was born in Azawād in 1730.[5] His home country was to be the haunt of the Kel Es-Sūq at al-Mabrūk and al-Ma'mūn. His influence was especially marked among the Barābīsh of Bū Jbayha and it was respected in Arawān itself. The Tuareg, the Iwillimmeden in particular, were to be a very fertile field for his religious teachings and his political pretensions. However, he had no illusions regarding their capacity to create a social order of lasting stability which to some degree matched his Islamic ideals. The Shaykh was pragmatic. He decided that the Iwillimmeden were to be preferred to their rivals, the Tadamakkat and the Fulani, so he used them to further his interests.

The patronising view which he took was akin to that which he showed towards his own groups of *talāmīdh*, his novices who enjoyed his protection and rendered him service. In his writings he remarked, "Truly they are named Iwillimmeden, for they are the latest or the last to hold the reins of power in this country." This quotation is to be found in a different form in Tuareg oral tradition: "*Inn-esen alfeqqi ayyet tan, a-di beraren-n-iwillimedan*", "The holy man said to them, 'Leave them, they are my children, they are my novices and I am teaching them'."

In the south-west, Shaykh Sīdī' l-Mukhtār was succeeded by his novice and admirer, Shaykh Sīdiyya al-Kabīr of the Intishait of Mauritania,[6] and also in the east by the Kel Es-Sūq Esh-Sherifen to whom he was related, whom he flattered and who greatly admired his erudition. Arabic texts survive which show how varied were the academic discussions between them on points of Islamic law. This exchange of ideas continued between the Kel Es-Sūq and the successors of Shaykh Sīdī'l-Mukhtār. During the reigns of the greatest of the Iwillimmeden *Amenukals* it was the constant adjustment of Kuntah policy and the harmonious dialogue with the Kel Es-Sūq, who also advised the Iwillimmeden, which furnished a basis for tribal stability, agreed facility of commerce and communication and long-term policies for this loose Arabo-Tuareg confederation. The process of Kuntah involvement in Iwillimmeden affairs was expedited after 1755, due to the death of 'Ughmar agg Alad of the Tādamakkat. The latter was succeeded by his son Mukhtār, then by Babati, his grandson, who was killed by the *Armas* of Timbuctoo in 1770. In that same year, the Iwillimmeden captured Gao. The Tādamakkat besieged Timbuctoo. Only the intervention of Shaykh Sīdī'l-Mukhtār saved the city from starvation. He made peace with the Tādamakkat but their new chief, Khumayka agg 'Ughmar, renewed the siege of that city after a brief respite.

But the Kuntah Shaykh had him unseated and he appointed Basha to the *eṭṭebel*. Once more his wishes were flouted, so, in despair, he enlisted the help of the Iwillimmeden to aid him.

Ḥāmma agg al-Shaykh, who was the acknowledged and invested chief of the Western Iwillimmeden, entered the conflict. He reinstated Khumayka in order to please Shaykh Sīdī'l-Mukhtār. Khumayka, though, enjoyed little popular support. Attacked by his relatives, he appealed to the Iwillimmeden for help. Initially they suffered a defeat, but gradually they gained the upper hand. Shaykh Sīdī'l-Mukhtār by now held the reigning Iwillimmeden *Amenukal* in personal contempt although he hardly dared to oppose him.

For a short while Mukhemmad and Kedidu, both of them descendants of Ḥāmma agg al-Shaykh, held the office of *Amenukal* of the Iwillimmeden. Then in 1787 the Iwillimmeden captured Timbuctoo. They imposed a *gharāmah*, or tax in horses, seven thousand *mithqāls* of gold, cloth, millet, rice, honey and other riches. This marked the final humiliation of the Moroccan Pachalik. A mayor was appointed. It was his duty to invest the chiefs of the Iwillimmeden and to raise the annual taxes. The Iwillimmeden now controlled both banks of the river Niger from Timbuctoo to Gao. Since 1780, at least, they had been ruled by the greatest of their leaders, Kawa ag Kedidu. He was to establish the maximum borders of the territory of the Iwillimmeden.

Much obscurity surrounds the early years of the reign of Kawa and the precise date when he became the *Amenukal* of the Iwillimmeden. It is sometimes held that he was invested in 1770, the year of the capture of Gao, yet this seems to be too early if short reigns for both Mukhemmed and Kedidu, the father of Kawa, are to be fitted into the Saharan chronologies. According to the Kel Es-Sūq, the mother of Kawa was named Tadhanit. She was a princess, holding the office of the *Imārah*; and this, in itself, indicates the powerful status of noble women in Iwillimmeden society. There is also some evidence to support the view that Kawa shared the office of *Amenukal* with his brother, Muḥammad, and that duties were divided on a family basis. After 1780 the Iwillimmeden enjoyed a period of almost unbroken successes and victories on the Niger river and beyond it. The control of its sources was complete.

The Iwillimmeden owned large herds of oxen, goats, horses and camels. These were tended by slaves who also collected gum and nenuphar seeds and they sometimes helped in the transport of merchandise by camel to Timbuctoo.

Most of the western Tuareg, and certain Arab groups, became subjects of the Iwillimmeden. The Igoudaren, who were formerly vassals of the Tādamakkat, submitted in 1780 and settled in the region of Bamba. In that same year the Tādamakkat paid tribute and were driven towards Goundam westward of Timbuctoo. In 1800 they disintegrated and split into three factions, the Tenguereguifs, the Irregnaten and Kel Temoulait. In 1803 and 1804 they made a last attempt to free themselves from the Iwillimmeden but they were crushed on the banks of the river. Other groups, the Immededren, the Udalen, the once powerful Arab Ighatafan near Say, and the Ansongo Fulani submitted. The Kuntah families became ever more dependent on Kawa's support. In 1810 the Ḥassānī Barābīsh paid tribute. The mounted army of Kawa (the *tábu*) was likened to a *simoom* which blew before a tornado. The Tuareg king travelled westwards in great pomp and ceremony. His visits to Timbuctoo to receive taxes and gifts lasted for months and the burden of entertaining his court and restraining the looting of his militia was a severe strain on a city which was then in decline.

Kawa was at the peak of his success at this time. Along the Niger buckle and to its south he was the master. However, if he was triumphant in the west and the south, he was less successful in the east. Saharan history has numerous examples of the division of a once single tribal group into two or more divisions after a span of time. Such a disaster bedevilled the Iwillimmeden during Kawa's reign. In fact, this division harks back to the earlier split when the Kel Denneg, the Iwillimmeden of the east, under Attafrīj, had broken away from Karidenna's son, Muḥammad agg al-Shaykh, and from the other descendants of Muḥammad War-Ilemmed, in order to seek pasture, to preserve their liberty and to enjoy the protection of other Ṣanhājah groups in the east among the fanatical Muslim Ibarkurayen and within the Sultanate of Aïr. These "Iwillimmeden Wa-n-Buḍal", named after Buḍal ag Katami ag Muda ag Karoza agg Attafrīj, have a history of their own chiefs setting them apart from Karidenna, Kawa and their descendants. Their clans comprised the Kel Nan, Teggermet, Kherkheran, Rawalan and Tellemedes.

In 1795 one of the Kel Nan, Katami ag Muda, took up arms against Kawa. He rallied the Rawalen, the Teggermet, the Kherkheran and Tellemedes whose pasturage was then centred to the east of Menaka in Azawagh, on the eastern marches of Iwillimmeden country. In 1800 fighting commenced and it ended in a decisive battle on the banks of the Niger to the south of Ansongo near Gao at the foot of two mountains, Ayola and Tikamaziten, opposite the island of Bourra. Kawa retained his mastery of the terrain, and he pursued these dissidents as far as Menaka. There they scattered in the valleys of Azawagh and they sought refuge with their kinsfolk among the Kel Denneg and their allies, the Ibarkurayen. Apart from Katami, Kawa's own brother, Khettutu ag Muda, who was *Amenukal* of the Kel Denneg, was also increasingly estranged from him. He resisted him where he could and eventually became dependent on the Ibarkurayen for their help.

In 1807 Khettutu was dethroned, and his place as *Amenukal* was quickly taken by the warrior fanatic of the Ibarkurayen, Muḥammad Ibrāhīm ag Muḥammad Iskakkaghan al-Jaylānī, who was born about 1777.[7] Al-Jaylānī was a believer in Holy War (*jihād*), he was a zealous puritan, an Arabic scholar of ability, a poet in *Tamasheq* and Arabic, and an ally of the Sokoto *jihādist*, Muḥammad Bello. He was a foe of Kawa and the Sulṭān of Agades. At first he shared power with Khettutu; the latter was the secular *Amenukal*, while al-Jaylānī filled the office of *Qāḍī*. But this arrangement did not last, and after al-Jaylānī had defeated the Kel Geres in 1813 he ruled the Kel Denneg as both their *Imām* and *Amenukal*. By this date Khettutu was on tolerable terms again with Kawa. His callous dethronement and the excessive demands of al-Jaylānī had helped to resolve the past differences which had arisen between him and Kawa because of the slaughter of their respective sons in a combat.

Kawa, despite his successes in the west near Timbuctoo, was uneasy about al-Jaylānī's thrust along his eastern borders. His anxieties where shared by his religious advisors. Kawa depended heavily on the Kuntah for counsel, although this was less effective under Sīdī Muḥammad al-Kuntī and his successors than under Sīdī'l-Mukhtār al-Kabīr. Opinions between Kel Es-Sūq and Kuntah occasionally diverged in regard to law and policy. Kawa's chief counsellors among the Kel Es-Sūq at this time were Muḥammad al-Sūqī, the *Qāḍī* Immattāl and the *Qāḍī* and saint, Salahu al-Sūqī. The latter was important as a go-between in contacts which involved Kawa and the Kuntah. As will be seen, shortly, this Sūqī family played a role in the Arabisation of the Tuareg. Salahu wrote several scholarly Arabic works. He was described by one of the Kel Es-Sūq as the *Qāḍī* who combined "the stage of divine unity which embraces all realities", mystical insight (*al-ḥaqīqah*), with the canonic law (*sharī'ah*) and Ṣūfism of the Qādiriyyah (*ṭarīqah*). He was also described as "the protector of mystical insight, the generating power of the hot rain cloud and the driver of the camel caravan, (*ḥāmī'l-ḥaqīqah wa nāsil al-wadīqah wa sā'iq al-wasīqah*)." His son, Hammahamma was, likewise, a lettered divine, and his grandson, Muḥammad al-Amīn ibn Hammahamma ibn Salahu was, again, an honoured Arabic scholar. He corresponded, in Arabic, with Mūsā ibn Buḍāl (Buḍal/Balla) (1819–1840), the *Amenukāl* of the Kel Nan. As will also be seen, it was the latter's son, Măkhămmad ag Ghăbdessălam El-Kumati (1875–1905) who was advised by the Sūqī scholar, Muḥammad Ignan Wa-n-Fadasen al-Gunahānī (see pp. 214–15). All these scholars exemplify the increasing spread of Classical Arabic amongst the Tuareg, the Iwillimmeden in particular, in the latter half of the nineteenth century. It owed much to the influence of the Kuntah, something to the Sokoto *jihād*, and a little to contact with wandering Mauritanian *Zwāya* scholars and with the lettered who were resident in Azawād and in Timbuctoo.

The Kuntah were anxious to counter the charismatic movement of al-Jaylānī. Some of the Kuntah believed that he had declared himself to be the *Mahdī*, or eschatological Messiah of Islam, or at least a "renewer" (*mujaddid*) who would herald the *Mahdī's* advent. Both claims were unacceptable to the Kuntah. They therefore urged Kawa to campaign against him. According to a passage in *Kashf al-Ghummah*, written by Sīdī 'Umar ibn 'Alī al-Kuntī:[8]

> "Then al-Jaylānī continued and prolonged his evil conduct. He impelled Salahu and Kawa to resist him, and wars were set ablaze between him and Kawa . . . The latter sent a letter to Shaykh Sīdī

> Muḥammad al-Kuntī seeking his help and his counsel. The Shaykh wrote an epistle refuting the claims of al-Jaylānī to be the *Mahdī*. He encouraged Kawa and those with him to resist him if he did not refrain from intrusion into their country and to rebuff him if he kept to his land."

The year 1816 was an important one in Iwillimmeden history. During the rainy season the Kel Denneg left for Aïr. They stopped at Shin-Wezazel, a locality lying to the east of In Gall, now in the Niger Republic. It seems that a *cure salée* for camel herds in the saline area of Taguidda-n-Tesemt was partly the reason for their expedition. Khettutu was now no longer an ally of al-Jaylānī who had ousted him and who despised him and those Kel Denneg who had made conciliatory gestures towards Kawa and the western Iwillimmeden (the Kel Aṭarām). Kawa himself had been persuaded to go into battle. He set out for In Gall among a body of mounted men. The move was unwise. Kawa's continued success depended upon his control of the Niger river valley between Ansongo and Timbuctoo. This was always the heartland of the Iwillimmeden empire. To venture east of the town of Menaka was to tempt fate, particularly as he was personally involved in the expedition. Although an *Amenukal* was the Commander-in-Chief (*amaway-n-egehen*) it was common practice for a Tuareg *Amenukal* to refrain from direct involvement in battles remote from home. Kawa rashly advanced to Shin-Wezazel and passed the night there. The following morning a sharp engagement took place, and by the midday prayer his Kel Aṭarām had been beaten. Those Kel Denneg who were the allies of al-Jaylānī pursued and harassed them and slaughtered them beyond In Gall. Kawa fled but he never reached In Gall. He sought refuge among the hills of Tawraren. Two Ibarkurayen, mounted on horseback, met him. They stopped him, killed him and carried away his body together with his valuables including a gold amulet. Shin Wezazel and the year 1816 ended his reign. Khettutu fled from In Gall after he had heard the news of the disaster. Kawa's foes boasted of their victory, but their own successes were short-lived. It would be a mistake to see in his death the end of the Iwillimmeden as a major confederation in Western Sahara history. Several of the *Amenukals* who succeeded him were men of strong personality.

The Tuareg were never again to rule the river Niger as Kawa had done, nor for so long. Travellers, foremost among them René Caillié and Henry Barth, who traversed these lands after Kawa's death, had little good to say of the "Sorgoos", then the nickname of the Iwillimmeden Tuareg. They give little evidence that an organised system of government and any sort of economic stability had prevailed during the years which predated their journeys.

Kawa of the Kel Talatayt lived at a time when the Moroccan Pashas, or *Armas*, of Timbuctoo were in the ultimate stage of their decline. It is possible that Kawa himself gave their rule in the Sudan the delayed *coup de grâce*. He was particularly fortunate in having the counsel of two Shaykhs, Sīdī'l-Mukhtār and Sīdī Muḥammad of the Kuntah. The first of these was certainly among the greatest of scholar-saints to have been born in the Moorish Sahara. Among his part-Tuareg, part-Arab advisors, Kawa had a counsel of Kel Es-Sūq to advise him. They were colleagues or students of the Kuntah and they were their equals in many aspects of Islamic learning and practice.

Among the last of the *Amenukals* of the Iwillimmeden, whether western or eastern, whose successes were in some respects worthy of Karidenna and Kawa, one should count Măkhămmăd ăg Ghăbdessălam "El-Kumati" of the Kel Nan, who ruled the Kel Denneg, the eastern Iwillimmeden, between 1875 and 1905, when he died unexpectedly during the annual *cure salée* of the camels in the rainy season.

When Măkhămmăd "El-Kumati" came to power, the Kel Denneg had been enfeebled by war, more especially against their bitter foes, the Kel Geres, who had repeatedly pillaged them. With the help of Arabs from Tuwāt, who had been offered asylum in the Kel Denneg, "El-Kumati" raided Agades in 1878. Two years later, the year of Kefi, the Kel Denneg under his command, allied to Wagheyya, the unsuccessful contender for the vacant office of the *Amenukal* of the Kel Geres, punished his enemies. In 1881, the Kel Geres attempted a retaliatory raid against the *Ineslemen* groups, the Kel Es-Sūq Esh-Sherifen amongst them, at In Jakaran. They were worsted there by these clerical tribes who had turned warriors. Between 1892 and 1897, Măkhămmăd "El-Kumati" was engaged in fighting the Ahaggar Tuareg who were pushing southward. In 1901, four years prior to his death, he made peace with the French and offered them his allegiance. Expediency determined his decision no doubt. Nevertheless, one can also see the counsel of his *Ineslemen* in his decision, a silent and often aloof company of Muslim counsellors, some Arab and some Berber, who, from the days of the earliest kings of the Iwillimmeden in the seventeenth century, had unobtrusively Arabised and Islamised and shaped the social, legal and political life of the Tuareg "sons of the nameless one".

If one is to select one aspect of their life and social customs most obviously influenced and changed by this process, most clearly owed to the Arab influences then entering this region, then I would choose the rules which governed the succession to the chieftainship among the Iwillimmeden. J. Nicolaisen has written:[9]

> "In regard to Tuareg rules of succession there can be no doubt that the matrilineal principle was originally recognized in all groups, but the patrilineal principle has been introduced into certain groups owing to Arab influence. The Tuareg who have adopted patrilineal succession are notably the two groups of *Iwllemmeden*, the *Kel Adṛaṛ*, and Tuareg of the Ineslemen class in various groups. In fact we know that the *Iwllemmeden* adopted patrilineal succession as early as in the 17th century and patrilineal succession is undoubtedly also of great age among the *Kel Adṛaṛ*, where the dominant tribes belong to the *Ineslemen* class. As to the two important groups of southern Tuareg, the *Kel Ayr* and the *Kel Geres*, Nicolas states that succession among them is matrilineal, as it is in Ahaggar and matrilineal succession is also mentioned as traditional to the Ayr Tuareg by Rodd. I have not been able to confirm these statements during my investigations among the *Kel Ayr* and the *Kel Geres*. All people questioned in these two groups claimed that the proper successor to chieftainship would be the deceased chief's son, though it was admitted among the Ayr Tuareg that a sister's son might be elected chief if considered better fitted for this position than a son. It would be correct to say that both the *Kel Ayr* and the *Kel Geres* today acknowledge the patrilineal principle of succession, but it is not quite certain when they adopted this rule. There can be little doubt that it was introduced among them owing to contact with other people, perhaps with the *Ineslemen* Tuareg. The *Kel Ayr* and the *Kel Geres*, like other Tuareg, once in the past followed

matrilineal rules of succession, for this is proved by history and tradition."[10]

Hence, the history of the Iwillimmeden cannot be ignored when considering the evolution of Tuareg institutions and the process of Islamisation of their culture. Nor can it be ignored that the origin of the rise of this confederation is intimately tied into the history of those groups of the Awlād Ḥassān who bordered their territory to the west. The evolution of the Ḥassānī Amīrates and the Iwillimmeden have many common features, and the role played by the lettered in Arabic, whether Kuntah or Kel Es-Sūq, is remarkably similar. The difference lies in the fact that the Iwillimmeden retained their Berber language, while such groups as the Īdaw ʿĪsh in Mauritania, under Ḥassānī pressure, relinquished it.

The teachings of al-Maghīlī regarding the status of nomad raiders

It was an important task amongst the many which confronted the Islamic scholars of the Arab and Tuareg groups in the Sahara to clarify the legal status of the Awlād Ḥassān or the Massūfah and others if and when they carried out unlawful raiding. Were they infidels or were they not? Besides, what was the status of those groups, *Zwāya* or *Ineslemen, Zenāgah* or *Imghād*, who were protected clients of these nomads but who, in normal circumstances, did not participate in the seizing of booty or in the shedding of blood? A certain number of Saharan documents have survived specifically concerned with this question. There are a few in Mauritania; for example, the "Book of the Beduin" (*Kitāb al-Bādiyah*) by Shaykh Muḥammad al-Māmi of the Ahl Bārikalla of Tīris who, as has been mentioned in Chapter 5, cautions and lectures to the Ḥassānīs on this and other points. However, it is unfortunate that the vast bulk of the documentation is late; it is in fact almost entirely from the eighteenth century or later, and we have few clues which enable us to be certain about earlier rulings by scholars concerning this perennial raiding and how it might be curbed.

An exception, however, is to be seen in the rulings given by the formidable scholar of Tlemcen (Tilimsān), Muḥammad ibn ʿAbd al-Karīm al-Maghīlī (d. 1504), in the answers to the questions which were put to him by the Songhai ruler, Muḥammad Askiyā (1493–1528). Al-Maghīlī was a figure of paramount importance in the definition of Islamic belief and law among the Arabs of Tuwāt, the Kuntah in the Western Sahara, the Tuareg *Ineslemen*, the Songhai and in Hausaland. He taught in Tageddā, the commercial centre of Agades in the south of Aïr, Gao, the capital of the Songhai empire, in Kano and Katsina, and by tradition he met and influenced the religious leaders of the early Kuntah, although this is far from certain.

In the main, al-Maghīlī was an advocate of fundamentalist and legalistic Muslim orthodoxy. In his view, the canonic law had to be applied strictly. The faith demanded a renewer (*mujaddid*) who would prepare the way for the *Mahdī*. The faith eschewed the venal scholars (*ʿulamāʾ al-sūʾ*) and required a clear statement of belief. There was to be no "mixing" in doctrine, no concessions in social customs or in the status of the sexes and the classes in the *ummah* of the Western Sahel and the Sahara. This view of al-Maghīlī was not shared by his great contemporary, al-Suyūṭī (d. 1505) in Egypt. The latter never visited the Maghrib and West Africa, but he guided and taught not a few of its scholars and rulers. Unlike al-Maghīlī, he was flexible and liberal in his concession to local custom. He was a participant in the mystical quests of the Mamlūk age. Astrology and thaumaturgy found a place in his definition of Islam, which, like the world, included all men and embraced almost everything. Whereas al-Maghīlī was exclusive, al-Suyūṭī was inclusive. The latter issued legal rulings (*al-fatāwī*). He wrote letters to African Muslim rulers and he eased their investiture (*taqlīd*) at the hands of the Cairene Caliph should they choose to pass through it on their way to the holy places.

These two men, al-Maghīlī and al-Suyūṭī, typified the range of options and the choice of texts which enabled the Shaykh, king, Sulṭān or chief in the Sahara or Sahel to determine the welfare of or rule his Muslim subjects. Contradiction was accepted together with conformity. Scholars had to be consulted in order to iron out differences or to establish peculiar circumstances which presented special cases. The problems which they faced were immense. They applied to towns, villages and nomadic settlements alike. The latter were often unsuited to the adoption or the adaption of the five pillars of Islam. How was the Islamic ethic to be enforced in private and public life? There were numerous slaves as well as the enfranchised. Their numbers were large, so were the herds. The spread of Islam compounded and did not resolve this ancient problem which was born from the conflict of races, the fickle climate and the interdependence of the desert and the sown. Local rulers, kings and chiefs had certain rights which they enjoyed. Were these rights hereditary or did they rest on the ability to use a sharp sword or upon the whim of predatory Arab, Berber or Sudanic groups? Islam needed to be taught, but how? Was it to be in Arabic, and was this Arabic to be the inflected parlance of Fez, Cairo and Medina or some form of the vernacular, either *Ḥassāniyyah* or Berber, be it *Zenāgah* or *Tamasheq*? How could doctrine be transmitted? How was the application of Islamic injunctions to be effected without the self-destruction of pastoralism and those communities which were wedded to it, whether by choice or of necessity?

The attempt made by the Islamic scholars to resolve such dilemmas was tenacious and resolute, but it hardly succeeded, except among a few of the Mauritanian *Zwāya* and the Kel Es-Sūq and the Kuntah. Throughout the Western Sahara and Sahel there was a thin veneer of Islamic confession and practice, or, alternatively, a deep but narrow adherence to orthodox Islam, cherished by the lettered few. Life amidst the pastoral societies where they lived and were protected was determined by other forces. Many of these forces were regarded as supernatural, though they were also explicable by the milieu, the climate and the ancient social fabric of Saharan and Sahelian society. The commercial routes which first brought Islam to Mauritania, Mali and Niger, also brought trade, slavery and salt and an ever-increasing number of wells and small towns and communities. There was drought or abundant rain from one year to the next. There was overgrazing, raiding and disease. While Islam adapted itself, the structure of Ḥassānī, Tuareg and Fulani society remained fixed if adaptable. It differed little from the ancient and unknown societies which had preceded it. Occasionally, very occasionally, the pattern might be reshaped but, if it were, then Islam *per se* was sometimes only of marginal importance in the outcome. Islam adapted itself. At the end of the process a familiar pattern, echoed in a well-known hymn, reasserted itself: "The rich man in his castle, the poor man at his gate . . .".

The castle may have been a tent of camel hair, but the dependant, or *jār*, was always without and within. A Shaykh could interpret the canonic law, but there were other customary laws, which differed quite markedly, and often none in supreme authority could interpret them.

Despite the occasional pedantry and unreality of the questions, one can sympathise with those devout men who asked for guidance amid the confusion and social chaos of the desert or semi-desert communities. At certain times, during the rise of an empire or with the appearance of a charismatic leader, this guidance was particularly demanded. The hour did not lack the man who offered counsel and solace. One such age was in the closing years of the fifteenth century. Al-Maghīlī answered the searching questions of the Songhai ruler, Muḥammad Askiyā. The pastoralists and their problems were included in those questions.

The Askiyā asked:

> "Among the Fulani or others who fight us there are the [Berber] Massūfah. These latter claim to be Muslims although they live with the [former], follow them in their transhumance and mix with them in all circumstances and affairs. It is with their mounts that they attack, such being the common practice. Yet, there are also among them those who wage no war unless it be on account of their closeness to them. When we attacked the latter during a battle our army encircled them and they were brought to us. 'We are Muslims', they said. 'Why then do you join company with those who fight us?', we enquired. They answered, 'We cannot free ourselves from them. If we free ourselves, we fear lest they take us into captivity, and, even if we achieve our liberty, another group will take us captive, for we are feeble men [*masākīn*] who are in need of protection, and we cannot defend ourselves alone.'"

The Askiyā had treated them leniently but he had realised the dilemma this presented to him, particularly if these subject tribes chose their liberty. Should he attack with the full knowledge that Muslims who refused to leave their protectors might be harmed? Troubled by his jurists the Askiyā appealed to al-Maghīlī for a ruling.

His reply was comprehensive. Not only did his answer cover this specific point, it also roundly condemned the wicked customs of these Massūfah. Inheritance by the sister's son, a common practice among the nomads but, as we have seen, to be abandoned under Muslim pressure by the Iwillimmeden, was the habit of the infidels, or, if they admitted that it was illicit (*ḥarām*) in the eyes of canonic law, then they were "grave sinners" who needed to repent and change their customs. Were they to refuse, then the Sulṭān had every right to seize their herds and their other possessions. As for the slaves, who were many among the nomads, their specific status needed to be defined. They were to be classed as mortmain (*ḥubus*), consecrated to the service of their Sulṭān, a ruling which in effect changed their status from slave to villein (*Zenāgah/Imghād*). This status would remain. A Muslim prince should not take them and place them in the "public treasury" (*bayt al-māl*), save those whom he was certain had been forcibly taken (*ghaṣb*), in some way or another. As for the rest, then they were mortmain for whosoever possessed them in accordance with their customs.

Regarding those client Massūfah who had fought, they should be attacked. No responsibility for making any distinction rested on the Askiyā, unless he had the foreknowledge of some mischief. Then his actions should be circumspect and restrained. He should do his utmost to forestall that mischief so that the entire blame fell on the mischief-makers. *Dependent Muslims should be unharmed, though the Askiyā should make sure that these dependent Muslims had not resided with his enemies of their own free will, that they had not raided his lands, nor acted as collaborators. If this was the situation then they should be left in peace and their property should be respected.* As for the rest, they should be killed and their goods should be seized. The repentance of one from amongst them should not be accepted if he were put within the Askiyā's power by the Almighty's decree.

Arbitrary and legalistic though some of the counsel may seem, it at least had the merit of trying to bring some order to the Muslim *Ummah* in the turbulent southern Sahara. Local custom was so strong that only a man whose authority was supremely respected could resolve the countless intractabilities among the tribes. The answers of al-Maghīlī established a preçedent. The example of the Massūfah was applied to the Awlād Ḥassān and the Tuareg by the scholars of the Kuntah and Kel Es-Sūq.

The epistle of al-Gunahānī, the Arab

An impressive example of a statement which clearly sets forth the standards, loyalties, teachings and principles of the Islamic scholars of the south-western Sahara and its borders may be seen in an epistle written by one of the lettered of the Kel Es-Sūq, Muḥammad Ignan Wa-n-Fadasen, from the branch of this Arab-Berber people called the Kel Gunahān or Ġuñhăn.[11] They derive their name from a locality which is marked on the maps of Henry Barth as a "ruin"; the camping ground of Yúnhan or Gúnhan, by tradition the site of a flourishing town in the Middle Ages, lying south of the site of the great Islamic town of Tādamakkat (Es-Sūq). The Kel Es-Sūq take their name from this latter town. The scholar also has the tribal *nisbah* of "the Arab", *al-'Arabī*. This either refers to his assertion of Arabian descent, or else to some relationship with the *Sharīfs* who are known as Kel-Arábbo, this name itself indicating, it would seem, an Arab origin or affiliation.

At some date in the last century, between 1875 – when Măkhămmăd ăgg al-Kumayt ("El-Kumati") became *Amenukal* of the Kel Denneg – and 1881, when the Kel Geres Tuareg made their raid on In Jakaran, a group of the Kel Es-Sūq, amongst whom this scholar al-Gunahānī was residing, were raided by the troops of the Kel Geres. Their possessions were seized, amongst them some precious Arabic books. This outrageous act led to an Arabic correspondence between al-Gunahānī and a certain 'Abd al-Kel Kefī or Gefī, a lettered man among the Kel Geres. Al-Gunahānī demanded the return of the looted property including the books. No copy of this initial letter has yet been found. Nor do we know 'Abd al-Kel Gefī's reply, although it is clear that he flatly rejected the request. He argued that the Kel Es-Sūq, who had been raided, *resided with infidels and were protected by the infidels.* They therefore came within the category of those "Massūfah nomads" who were condemned outright by al-Maghīlī in his epistle and its answers to the Askiyā. Al-Gunahānī rejected this charge in his lengthy reply which was composed in elegant Classical Arabic. It is a masterpiece of Arabic prose from the region of the southern Sahara. He answers his opponent, charge by charge, and he explains the authority upon which the Kel Es-Sūq rest their case. In his view they are among the earliest of all the Muslim peoples in the south-western Sahara, predating the Awlād Ḥassān, the Kuntah and most of the Tuareg, more especially the Iwillimmeden, and claiming descent from the Prophet's Companions. Since the sixteenth century they had been "chaplains" and religious advisors of the nomad princes in the company of the Kuntah. None had surpassed them in their task of proclaiming the true teachings of Islam or in teaching the Arabic language in the south-western Sahara and the Sahel.

The Kuntah warrior and mystic in the Western Sahara
(based on a shortened version of the *Kitāb al-Ṭarā'if wa'l-Talā'id* from Walātah)

The Kuntah transcend the political borders of the twentieth-century Sahara. Tribal elements of this grand Saharan confederation are to be found within the disputed territory of the Western Sahara, in Igīdī around Algerian Tindouf, around the tombs of the holy founders in the Sāqiyah al-Ḥamrā', in the Islamic Republic of Mauritania, and in Mali, more especially in Azawād and the Adrār-n-Īfōghās. Small groups of Kuntah are to be met in Morocco, in Niger and in Hausaland. There are also Kuntah deep within Algeria itself. This is especially true of the region of Saoura (Sāwirah), Tuwāt and the Hoggar. The Kuntah descend from ʿUqbah ibn Nāfiʿ al-Mustajāb, and they may sometimes be seen visiting his tomb at Sīdī ʿUqbah. Another of their centres is Zāwiyat Kuntah, which keeps their name, in the Algerian Adrār.

The Kuntah are a confederation of saintly families all of which held, or hold, great spiritual and academic prestige, with the rare ability finely to balance the duties towards the interpretation of the *Sharīʿah* canonic law on the one hand,

and, on the other, the austere and ascetic path of Ṣūfism, especially the Qādiriyyah *Ṭarīqah*. All the greatest Shaykhs of the Kuntah tradition, Sīdī Aḥmad al-Bakkāy, Sīdī ʿUmar al-Shaykh, Sīdī'l-Mukhtār al-Kuntī al-Kabīr, and Shaykh Bāy, to name only four, enjoyed a great respect as mediators in tribal disputes, not only amongst the Arabs – the Chaamba (Shaʿānibah) in Algeria and the Banū Ḥassān – but also amongst the Berbers of Tuwāt and the Tuareg.

The Kuntah represent an eclectic cultural element, both culturally and spiritually, and they are eclectic in the sense that their literary works, *Kitāb al-Ṭarā'if wa'l-Talā'id, al-Risālah al-Ghallāwiyyah* and *Tawārīkh Kuntah*, although composed in Classical Arabic, resorted to borrowing folk tales, legends, myths and anecdotes from the surrounding Berbers and Sūdānese who dwelt deep in the Sahara. Such material was inserted into a matrix of literary archetypes, essentially Arabic, of two kinds: *epic* (based on the *Siyar* of the companions of the Prophet, the *Ayyām al-ʿArab*, and *Maghāzī*) and *homiletic* (based on the *Manāqib al-Awliyā'* and *Karāmāt al-Mutaṣawwifīn*). Introduced into this genre are major historical figures who are geographically and ethnically external to the principal participants in the Saharan stories.

As will be seen, one such figure in particular fulfils this function. He is none other than Shaykh ʿAbd al-Karīm al-Maghīlī al-Tilimsānī who died in 1503/4. It is made explicit in all Kuntah texts that it was the friendship between al-Maghīlī and Sīdī ʿUmar al-Shaykh al-Kuntī, their pilgrimage to Mecca and their meeting with the great Egyptian scholar al-Suyūṭī, that gave to the Kuntah a new spiritual motivation in the early sixteenth century: legal, mystical and commercial. The Kuntah became trans-Saharan traders. It happened at the very period when an axis of trade – formerly handled by the Jews before al-Maghīlī expelled them from Tuwāt – was being developed by the Kuntah and by others. The axis went south to Katsina and Kano, joining Tuwāt in Algeria to Hausaland, and it offered a grave threat to the Songhai rulers who were then centred at Gao on the Niger.

In a subsequent century, the Kuntah, based at al-Mabrūk in Azawād, and elsewhere in Mali, gradually extended their hegemony in peace and war over all the Sahara, especially its caravan commerce and its salt (by tradition the Kuntah owned

Sabkhat Ijjil, Afdayrak in Mauritania). In fact nearly all the Western Sahara, from the Atlantic to the Hoggar and from the northern Algerian oases to the Niger, was nominally Kuntah spiritual domain.

The Kuntah also represented a socio-political force in the Sahara, including the Algerian Sahara, and popular literature serves to illustrate this force. Directed by great spiritual leaders, popular literature was integrated into the legendary curriculum vitae of these leaders. They were the magnets, so to speak, for popular literary motifs and themes. At the same time they, themselves, served to reinterpret, refashion and revivify and export elsewhere, throughout the Sahara, all of this popular literary material.

Turning to the examples in the text which follows one should bear in mind the following points when interpreting, analysing and assessing such literature.

(1) That the spiritual goals, the inner meaning, the miraculous deeds of the Kuntah Shaykhs, as revealed in popular literature, were primarily homiletic and hagiographic. Their function was to provide an ideal example to the devout believer.

(2) Within this homiletic content there was borrowed folkloric material which was primarily secular.

(3) The function of the personality of al-Maghīlī was twofold:

   (a) To portray an historical scholar. He was the *mujaddid*, the revivifier of Islam in that age. Where he appears in this role, then a basically factual biography of al-Maghīlī, derived from the work called *Nayl al-Ibtihāj* by the Timbuctoo scholar, Aḥmad Bābā, is cited.

   (b) This historical personality as then transformed into another al-Maghīlī, who is a "metamorphosised al-Maghīlī" = Aḥmad Bābā, and others, plus the legendary exploits.

   Thus an historical personality may be embodied in a legend to express, poetically, some lateral historical fact.

(4) An illustration of 3(b) in the text which follows, may be illustrated by the comical episodes involving al-Maghīlī and al-Suyūṭī (who is likewise metamorphosised), the

latter outclassed academically and outwitted even by al-Maghīlī and Sīdī ʿUmar al-Shaykh. There is nothing factual in this story. The statement that the Egyptian city of Assiut is on the Mediterranean sea discloses a fable immediately. The basic truth in the story, however, is:

(a) That al-Maghīlī communicated with al-Suyūṭī in letters.
(b) That both were in a sense rivals for the favours of the rulers of the Sahara and Sahel.
(c) That on many issues both men were opposed.

An example of the latter is information which is supplied in the biographical work called *al-Tarjamah*, by al-Dāwūdī. The latter cites a letter in verse from al-Maghīlī who criticised al-Suyūṭī for his attitude towards logic, and al-Suyūṭī's answer is cited also in verse.

Another illustration of some disguised historical truth is the long account in the story of a thirty-year-old friendship between Sīdī ʿUmar al-Shaykh and al-Maghīlī. This is a Kuntah story, and it is not confirmed elsewhere.

The two earliest references to the Kuntah (and even they are suspect) are, first, a letter sent by the ruler of Bornu to all the Kuntah of Tuwāt. It is dated either 1440 or 1478. It mentions "all the *Murābiṭūn* and the descendants of Shaykh al-Mukhtār and Sīdī ʿUmar al-Shaykh and to all their brothers of the Dirimshāka in Tuwāt". On chronological grounds this Sīdī ʿUmar can hardly be a young novice of al-Maghīlī.

Secondly, another document of the Tuwāt Kuntah says that "in 1460 our uncle Sīdī Muḥammad al-Wāfī, came to settle at Zāwiyat Kuntah, and the following year *Murābiṭūn* from our master and ancestor, Shaykh al-Mukhtār, came to inhabit Zaglū". Nowhere does Sīdī ʿUmar appear in the text. One, therefore, suspects the total historicity of Sīdī ʿUmar, at least in his relationship with al-Maghīlī.

How then, could such a story have arisen? There is another possible interpretation, namely, that both Aḥmad al-Bakkāy and Sīdī ʿUmar became confused, or rather fused, with a scholar who *was* a pupil of al-Maghīlī, namely Ayd Aḥmad al-Tāzikhtī, Tāzikht or Tīzikht being "old Walātah".

According to Elias Saad in his *Social History of Timbuctoo*, Cambridge, 1983, p. 67:

> "Ayd Aḥmad had travelled from Timbuctoo to Tagedda, where he studied under al-Maghīlī, and in the east he was certified by al-Qalqashandī, al-Sunbāṭī, and others of equal stature. We do not know how long he remained in Timbuctoo on his return to the Sudan; he subsequently travelled to Hausaland and settled in Katsina where he became judge. But his *sanads* left a lasting influence in the Sahel where they were eventually passed on to numerous scholars from Walāta, Shinqīṭ and Tīshīt."

If confusion of fact, of date, of lineage one and all, have to be accepted as endemic in such texts, Kuntah or non-Kuntah, then the following hypothesis, a lineal transplant of an early date has to be faced as a possible explanation. That is that Ayd Aḥmad was possibly the prototype figure upon whom the Kuntah story-tellers fashioned their story. Unlike these others, Ayd Aḥmad was a figure with several historical documents to substantiate his life and attainments.

Father	Son	Ayd (Aydah) Aḥmad (of Walātah/ Tīzikht)
Sīdī Aḥmad al-Bakkāy (of Walātah)	Sīdī ʿUmar	Pupil of al-Maghīlī
Teaches and dies in Walātah *circa* 1502	Pupil of al-Maghīlī	Meets Egyptian scholars
	Meets Egyptian scholars	Goes to Katsina with al-Maghīlī
	Goes to Katsina with al-Maghīlī	Qāḍī of Katsina and dies there *circa* 1551
	Dies in Morocco *circa* 1552	

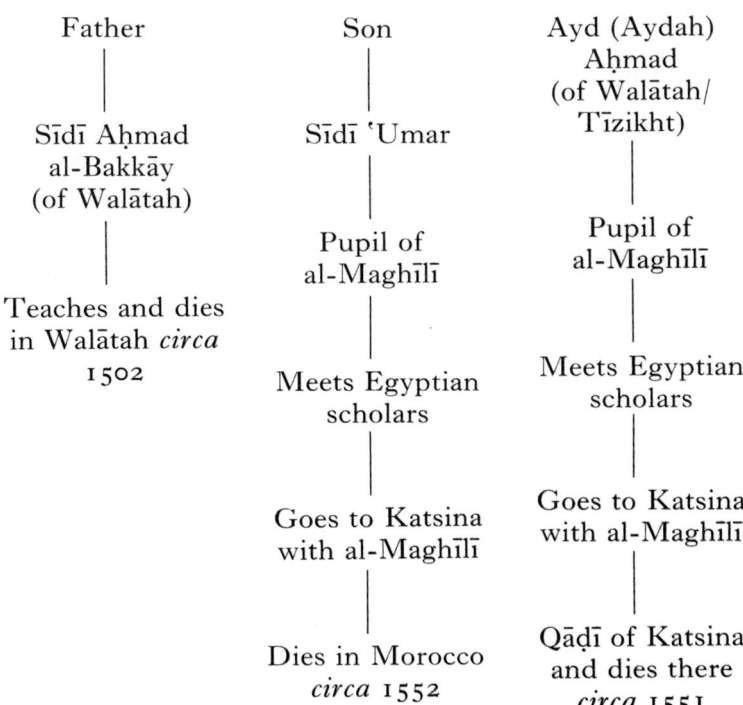

There are two other stories in this document which merit special attention.

(1) The transformation of Sīdī ʿAbd al-Qādir into a dog. This act was accomplished in order to defeat the Hoggar Tuareg. It is reported in the complete *Kitāb al-Ṭarā'if wa'l-Talā'id.* It is basically a Berber story and it is recounted in Tuareg tales from the Hoggar region. Stories of a pagan city of dogs (*Madīnat al-Kilāb*) are found in recent Mauritanian folk tale, and *jinn* in the form of dogs is a common theme in stories in Morocco.

(2) The petrification of Aḥmad al-Fayram and the caravan would appear to contain elements from Berber folklore, Arab tales which are about the Sahara and its peoples, Arab tales of a type which are found in the *1001 Nights* and reference to *Sūrat al-Baqarah*, where the Koranic verse, *Allāh will suffice you against them* (*fa-sayakfīkahum*) is transposed as a talismanic formula of protection. Interestingly, this formula is widely used in painted inscriptions in the Algerian Sahara grotto of Timmissao, a grotto frequented in the past by the more pacific spiritual colleagues of the Kuntah, the Kel Es-Sūq.

This text, then, is a patchwork of folk literature from family archives, historical documents, Berber stories and hagiographical homilies. It can be matched by many other such documents in the Western Sahara which furnish the folklorist and the student of popular Arabic literature with a vast corpus of source material.

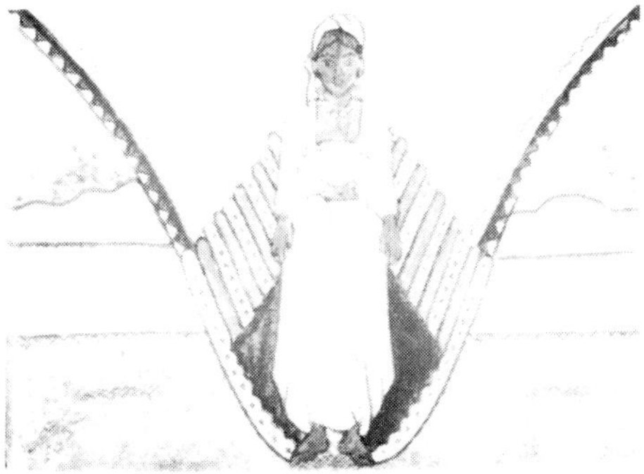

Part IV

The Arabisation of the Western Sahara

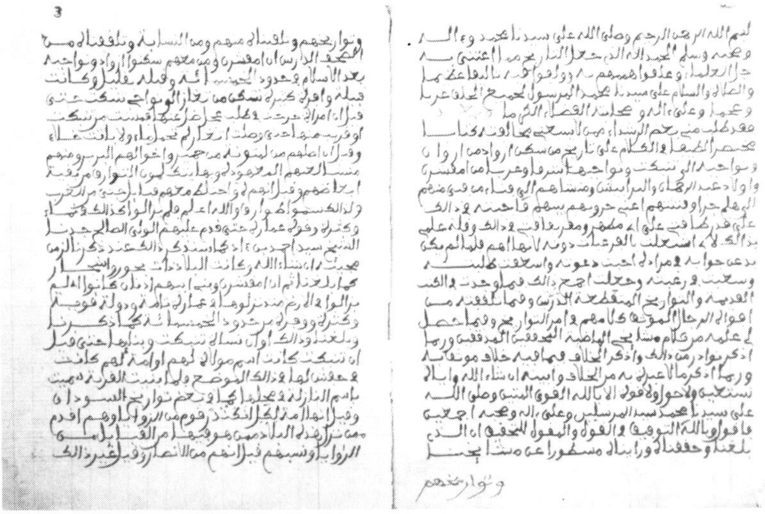

Plate 7a

Plate 7b

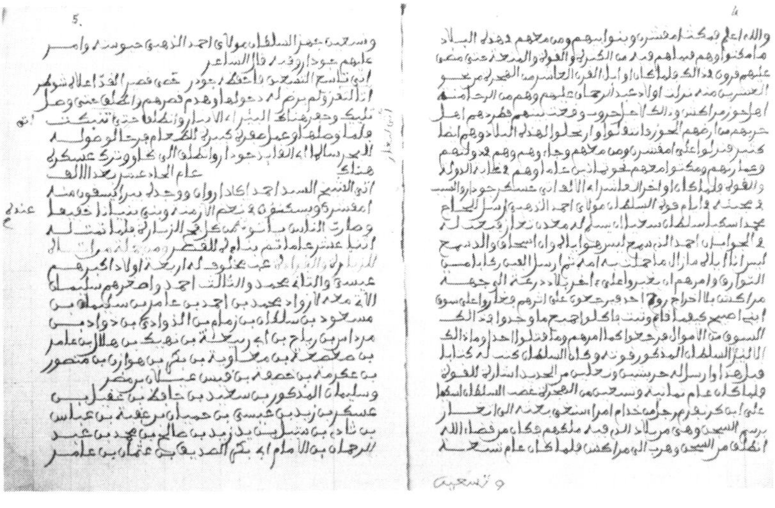

Plate 8a

Plate 8b

Plate 9

Map
shewing the
TRACT across the DESERT,
as followed by the Caravans
from
FAS to TIMBUCTOO;
By
Jas. G. Jackson.
1809.
ALGIERS
Algiers
Tunis
Melilla
Tafilelt
Bled el Jereede
Maroc
SUSE
Station for the accumulated Caravans to Soudan.
Tatta
Dikna u Mjot plundering Arabs
Tuat Arabs
Mograffra Arabs
Ludaya Arabs
East Tarassa
Hahr or Stoney Desert
Tuat Encampment
Tuat Arabs
Sahara Yeseer or deep loose Sandy Desert
Woled Abbusebah
Tejakant Arabs
Taudeny
Arawan
Gum Forest
West Tarassa Arabs
Brabeesh Arabs
Timbuctoo
White People
Nile of Slaves
Nile el Abeede
Jinnee
Gold Mines
BAMBARA
Ialoffe
Gambia R.
Sego
Gold Mines
Guago
Cannibals
Woled ben Musie
Gold Mines
Mountains of the Moon
Jibbel Kumra or
Mountains of Kong
GENOWA or GUINEA
DAHOMY
ASHANTEE
Gold Coast
BENIN
WAREE

Plate 10

Chapter 9

The Arabisation of the Western Sahara, the Wādī Dar'ah and the Sūs

The Sahara's links with the north

Some recent studies about the Islamic past of the Western Sahara have possibly underestimated the fact that the ties of its peoples with the north, with Morocco and Algeria in particular, were of far greater historical and social importance than those with the adjacent regions of West Africa.

This point has been stressed by Dr Sabah I. al-Sheikhly, an Iraqi historian.[1] In her study of the "Arab military and commercial penetration of the Maghrib and its Sahara, the Western Sūdān and Southern Europe during the 5th/11th Century", she observed, "The Almoravid movement is of importance for its having transferred the Saharan Ṣanhāja to the North", and again:

> "The economic motive was not less important than the others in the expansion of the Almoravids northwards. The occupying of the Maghrib, especially Sijilmāsa, which was under the control of their rivals the Zanātas, was of strategic importance for the Ṣanhājas, because it was the northern gate of the Saharan trade-routes, and its control meant their commercial ascendancy there.
>
> "The Almoravid drive to the North would also seem to have been inspired by tribal motives. As the northern tracts of the Maghrib, particularly Sijilmāsa and al-Sūs, were subject to Zanātas, the Ṣanhājas seem to have directed their attacks against these [Zanātas], the Berber enemies of the Ṣanhāja. It may also be inferred that the Saharan Ṣanhāja probably entertained a desire to join their Ṣanhāja relatives who were already settled in the north under the control of their rivals, the Zanātas."[2]

My research leads me to a similar conclusion. The Almoravid movement had three major centres, not two; Marrakesh and the north, Āzuqqī and Awdaghust, and *perhaps* Ghānah, in the south, and a third centre, lying between the north and the south, namely the southern Sūs and Darʿah as far east as Sijilmāsah, the border region between the southern Atlas and the Saharan Igīdī, with its own centres of commerce, its oasis cultivators, the *Ḥarāṭīn*, its mines of copper and silver and its local industries which engaged the Gazūlah, the Lamṭah, the Haskūrah, the Lamtūnah and the Massūfah. Among the most important of its centres were the great salt workings at Taghāzā. There was also the local hunting of the Lamṭ oryx, from whose hides the manufactured shields, the Lamṭī shields, became the prized possession of many an Arab and Berber prince.

This intermediate, north-westerly, region is the key to the mastery of the entire western desert. It was the spring-board for the conquest of the Maghrib, of Mauritania and the western Sūdān. It could be argued that whoever wishes to create a Saharan empire must effectively control this northern region in the Western Sahara. The Banū Maʿqil achieved this control. Their next advance was the conquest of southern Mauritania, either as princely chiefs or else as agents of the rulers in Morocco. At the same time they established control south-eastwards over the oases of Tuwāt. The Sāqiyah al-Ḥamrā' was the first stage of the remarkable Sahelian religious mission of the Kuntah; it was, by repute, the region which offered sanctuary to Karidenna before he moved south-eastwards to found the Iwillimmeden empire. At the turn of this century, Smāra, the religious sanctuary in the east of the Sāqiyah al-Ḥamrā', was the selected base from which Mā' al-ʿAynayn made his bid to save the Maghrib from the domination of the West.

Within the world history which Muslims have conceived there is a special destiny apportioned for these sandy tracts

Map 3 The Saharan commercial routes, based on the routes furnished by al-Bakrī (eleventh century) in his *Kitāb al-Masālik wa'l-Mamālik*. (Based on D. and S. Robert and J. Devisse, *Tegdaoust I*, Paris, 1970.)

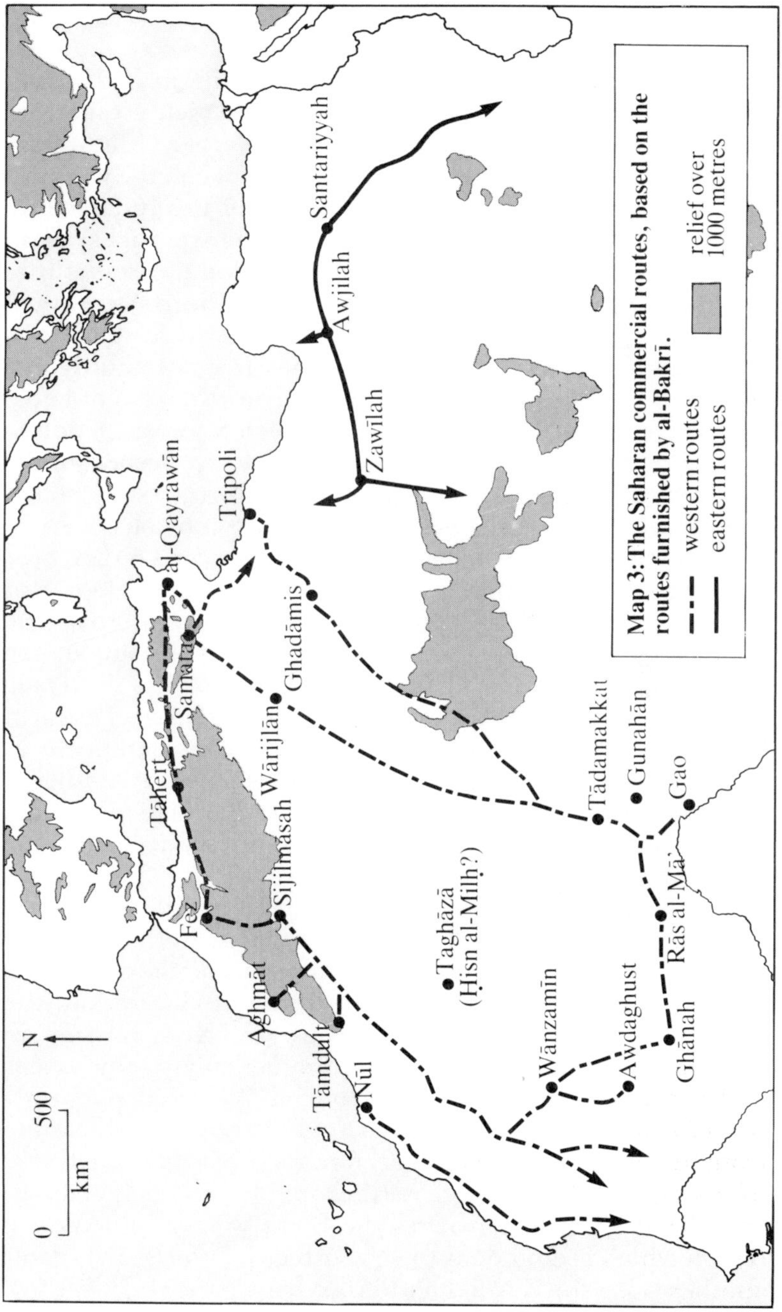

Map 3: The Saharan commercial routes, based on the routes furnished by al-Bakrī.

around the Sāqiyah al-Ḥamrā', since, as we shall see, a *Mahdī* to come, a descendant of Fāṭimah, will one day unite its tribesmen and lead them to victory; in Spain, in Byzantium and in the Holy Land, the liberation of which awaits that leader who will summon these Arab and Berber "blue-men" to rescue Islam and to herald the great day when the whole of humanity will be summoned to the seat of the Judgement.

Some of the Western Saharans, whether in tribes, or in clans, or in families, have felt equally at home at certain times and at certain seasons in those regions which lie to the south of the Atlas range as much as they do deep within the desert itself. It is as if both these *milieux*, the desert and the cultivated valleys of the Sūs and the Darʿah to the north, were of equal importance in the history of the Western Saharan peoples.

Andrzej Dziubinski has pointed out that the Berbers of the Western Sahara had numerous branches which resided in the Moroccan mountains. The *Zenāgah* – the Ṣanhājah – were to be found to the north of Tissint in the Moroccan Darʿah, near the water sources of the Asif Ait Douchchene in the region of Tazenakht. The traveller, Marmól, reported that the Ṣanhājah Ait Atta camped in the region of Tissint in the fifteenth century. He calls it the "province of Ytata". Dada Atta, the ancestor of the Ait Atta, was buried at Takkat n Ilektaout in the Darʿah region. These Ṣanhājah were of importance there in the fifteenth and sixteenth centuries. Their importance was to grow greater, rather than to decline, as the whole district became more and more influenced by the Arab nomads who came to settle there.[3]

Two examples from the eleventh century illustrate how early this dual settlement was by the tribes, in this case one tribe, the origins of which are very obscure, and the other tribe amongst the most famous of all: the Banū Wārith and the Lamtūnah. Both, it would seem, were Arabised, in name, in system of descent, the right to chiefly office and to some extent in language. Al-Bakrī, citing from al-Warrāq's *Kitāb al-Masālik wa'l-mamālik*, perhaps, and describing the route from the city of Aghmāt to Fez *before the Almoravid conquest of Morocco*, writes: "From there [the long and vast *faḥṣ* plain of] Imlellū, the traveller reaches the Banū Wārith. Theirs is a region which is abundant in euphorbias [*al- furbiyūn*]. After another stage the Zuwāghah Berber tribe is reached." A few pages later, when describing the route from the Wādī Dar'ah to the Western Sūdān, al-Bakrī further writes: "There is also to be found a tribe of negroes to the west of the town of Bānklābīn. The latter is inhabited by the Muslim Banū Wārith of the tribe of the Ṣanhājah."[4] Here we have one Ṣanhājah group who found the Moroccan plains and the south-west Sahara equally acceptable as places in which to live.

The Lamtūnah had their own tribal homelands. Al-Bakrī reported that their territory extended southwards from Īzāl (probably the Kidyat Ijjil in northern Mauritania) over a distance of "two months", in breadth and in length, between the lands of Islam and the countries of the Sūdān. At one point they were near the latter – there were only ten stages between them. At the same time, al-Bakrī also says that the Lamtūnah spent their summers between Āmaṭlūs and Tāliwīn, possible alternatives, although the fortress of Āzuqqī and its palms was the chief Lamtūnah centre in the Mauritanian Adrār. Āmaṭlūs is almost certainly the region of Āmaṭlīsh to the south of the Adrār. On the other hand, Tāliwīn could well be far distant in the south-west of Morocco. One place like this name [Tiliwīn] is to be found due west of Goulimine in the extreme Sūs, while another far more important district, of a similar name, is important enough to be shown on many large-scale maps of Morocco, east of Taroudant and to the west of Jabal Siroua. Such uplands in Morocco are well-known grazing districts for the Saharan nomads today.

That the Lamtūnah – even after the fall of the Almoravid empire – were not only in the Adrār but were also to be found in the region of Goulimine and the area of the Nūn, side-by-side with the Lamṭah of the district, is specifically mentioned by al-Idrīsī. He writes, "Nūl is a large town, well populated, on a river which comes to it from the east. Tribes of the Lamtūnah and the Lamṭah live along this river and in this town the Lamṭī shields are made."[5] This same way of life is characteristic of the Tiknah, the Rgaybāt, the Tājakānt and the Banū Ḥassān until recent times. The cultural overlap between the southern slopes of the Atlas, the Anti Atlas, Jabal Banī, Wādī Dar'ah and the vast Sahara of Mauritania and Mali, has been a great feature of this region since prehistoric times.

The arrival of the Arabs in the Wādī Darʿah

It is a mistake to attach too much importance to the Lamtūnah alone in the long history of the Western Saharan peoples. The fame they attained as the paramount power amongst the Almoravids is indisputable. Yet after the eleventh century their hegemony waned, and before that century, where the Arabic accounts tell of the earliest Arabisation of the region, these same Lamtūnah are nowhere mentioned. It is the Ṣanhājah Massūfah of the Anti Atlas and Darʿah and the Ṣanhājah Haskūrah of the same region who were then the most significant peoples in the north-west Sahara.

There is a passage in the *Kitāb al-Ansāb* by Abū Ṣāliḥ ibn Abī Ṣaliḥ ibn ʿAbd al-Ḥalīm, admittedly a late work, which makes this clear. He describes the expeditions attributed to ʿUqbah ibn Nāfiʿ in the nearest and furthest Sūs;

> "When ʿUqbah had finished with the Middle Maghrib he entered the Furthest Maghrib. He did so in 681. He was the first of the Muslim governors to enter it. He reached Tangier and he found its governor who surrendered to him. ʿUqbah continued his advance until he reached Wulīlah. There he faced the Berber hosts and he did battle with them. He defeated them and pursued them to Darʿah and from thence he descended into the country of Īghirān [Īfrān?] Yaṭṭūf. It is said that he returned from the nearer Sūs to the country of Darʿah. He brought the Ṣanhājah into submission, likewise the Haskūrah."[6]

Ibn Khaldūn reports that these Ṣanhājah were specifically Massūfah *Mulaththamūn*.

The next important event in this district, and here the evidence is far stronger, was the foundation of the town of Tāmdūlt (Āqā) by ʿAbdallāh ibn Idrīs, in the ninth century, and al-Balādhurī also reports that the Wādī Darʿah, centred upon Tīyumatīn, was ruled by ʿAlī ibn Aḥmad ibn Idrīs ibn Yaḥya ibn Idrīs. Nevertheless, it is the geographer, al-Yaʿqūbī (d. 891), who gives the most complete description of this whole region at that time. He makes it clear that:

(a) The Darʿah settlements were dependencies of Sijilmāsah. Amongst them Tāmdūlt was guarded by a fort and possessed gold and silver deposits. It belonged to Yaḥyā ibn Idrīs, the ʿAlid.

(b) The Tarjā were the most important Berber group in that district.
(c) The Ṣanhājah of the desert were called the Anbiyah. No distinction was then made between the Gudālah, Lamtūnah and Massūfah.
(d) Ghust (Awdaghust), far to the south, was still a pagan city.[7]

How the Lamtūnah came to dominate the entire Saharan confederation through their kings is far from clear. The record is a late one and gaps are many. One can only suggest that this domination, if it be real, prior to the Almoravids, was centred in the more southerly regions of the Western Sahara, in the Mauritanian Adrār, the Hodh and Azawād.

The desert routes according to al-Bakrī

The eleventh-century account of al-Bakrī mentions three major routes in the Western Sahara: Tāmdūlt to Awdaghust, the latter city to Sijilmāsah and the route from the Wādī Darʿah to the Sūdān. In his day, it is no doubt the first which had the greatest topical importance. He wrote on the eve of the Almoravid triumph in Morocco. The route to Awdaghust was the principal axis along which the Lamtunah-led *daʿwah* of ʿAbdallāh ibn Yāsīn pushed into the Sūs and ravaged Awdaghust. It linked Āzuqqī in the Mauritanian Adrār with the north, although it should be noted that nowhere does al-Bakrī mention that this route was deflected into the Adrār to pass through Āzuqqī.

Some of the wells on this route were named after Arab commanders who led the first expeditions southwards in the desert. One of them was attributed to ʿAbd al-Raḥmān ibn Ḥabīb, who was the governor of Ifrīqiyā in 745.[8] Another marked feature of this *Routier* is that, notwithstanding the extreme remoteness and wildness of the terrain, the general accuracy of al-Bakrī's account is at times almost amazing.

Perhaps the key point on the entire route is the watering point called Wānzamīn. He writes:

> "Four days' journeying from here brings you to the place called Wānzamīn, where there are wells of small depth, some with sweet water and some with brackish water. Above this place rises a long steep mountain inhabited by many wild animals.[9] All the roads

> leading to the land of the Sūdān meet at this watering place. It is a dangerous spot, for the Lamṭa and the Gazūla attack caravans here, having selected this site for their ambushes because they know that all roads lead here, and that travellers must come here for their water supply.[10]

This reference to the Gazūlah, the tribe of Ibn Yāsīn himself, as long-distance raiders from the north may imply some historical decision on the part of Ibn Yāsīn to concentrate the Almoravid operations northwards.

Nowadays, the term "Gazūla" has a dual character. Vincent Monteil has pointed out (in his *Notes sur les Tekna*, Paris, 1948, pp. 13 and 14) that the great *leff*, or tribal confederation of the "Gazūla", betwixt the Wād Nūn and the Atlas, embraces both mountain Berbers and desert or semi-desert warriors.

It is hardly likely that the Gazūlah/Jazūlah, who are described in this passage of al-Bakrī, refer to all these people. It must refer to desert folk, distant ancestors of those people whom we now call Tiknah, although they were not known by this name in the eleventh century. Their two *leffs*, which are to a point fluid in regard to their membership, are together given the name *igizūln*, which is a Berber name. However, the "Berber" *leff* is called Ait ʿAtman. They claim descent from

Map 4a The eleventh-century Western Saharan 'route of the Lamtūnah', following al-Bakrī's toponyms (based on D. and S. Robert and J. Devisse).

It should be emphasised that the identification of Tn-Dfas with Tindouf is extremely doubtful. According to Professor Muḥammad al-Fāsī, the toponym Tindouf is Ti-n-Ḍūf, meaning 'centre for the guard', or 'look out post'. It was given this name because it guarded the route from Morocco to Mauritania. The heart of the word is *Aḍūf* which also has the meaning of 'look out post'. Other Berber words in Morocco and its borders which denote this sense of 'watch' are Tamkhīḍat, Ṭāwaz and Akdīm (compare Ouagoudim), the latter conveying the notion of *ḥirāsah* in Arabic. If Tn-Dfas is not Tindouf then al-Bakrī's route across the Ḥamādah of Darʿah cannot be shown with any proximity to modern toponyms. My identification of Wīn Haylūn with Wuín el Wán of Barth's map is very tentative, although there is a good case for the route following a curve which skirts the western edge of Erg Īgīdi. The identification of Wānzamīn with Inzimrān is virtually certain.

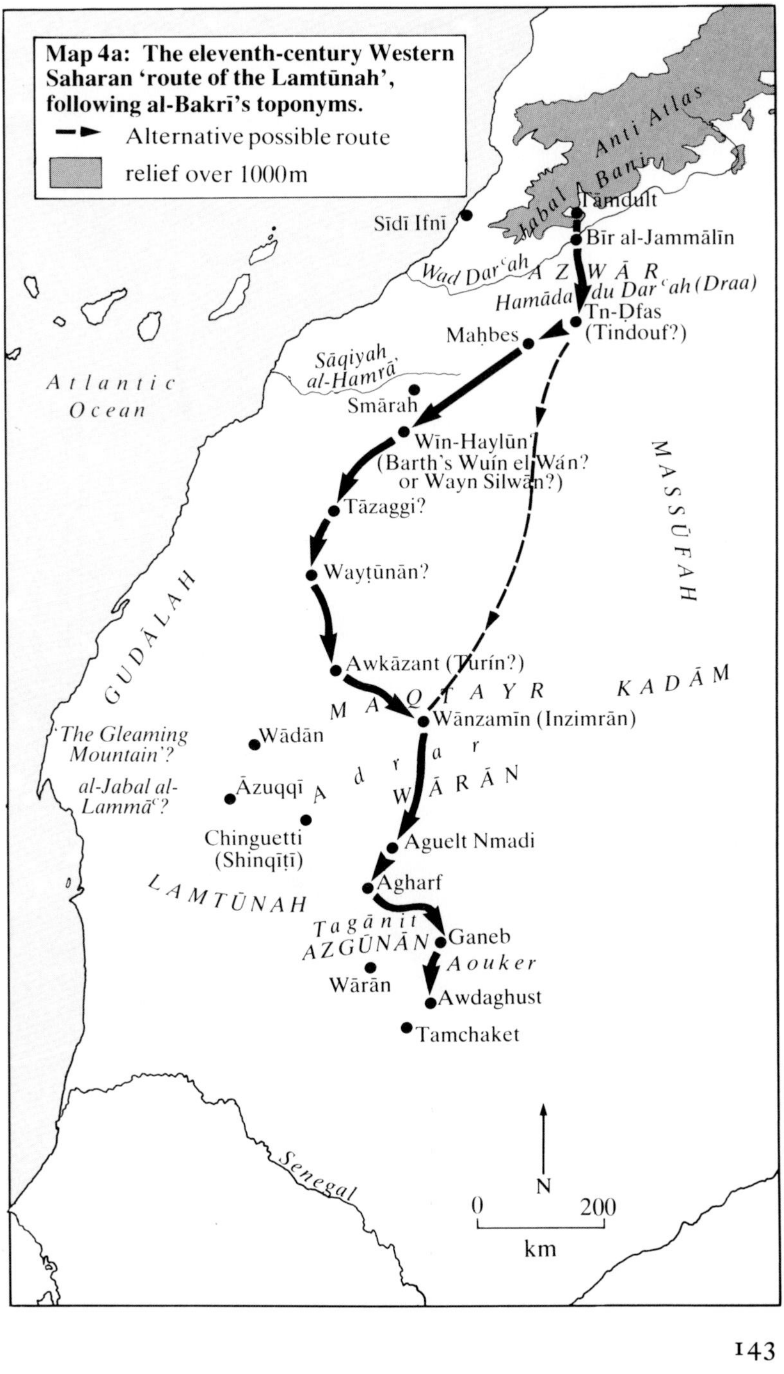

Map 4a: The eleventh-century Western Saharan 'route of the Lamtūnah', following al-Bakrī's toponyms.
Alternative possible route
relief over 1000m
Anti Atlas
Jabal A Bani
Tāmdult
Bīr al-Jammālīn
Sīdī Ifnī
Wad Darʿah
A Z W Ā R
Hamāda du Darʿah (Draa)
Tn-Ḍfas (Tindouf?)
Maḥbes
Sāqiyah al-Hamrā'
Atlantic Ocean
Smārah
Wīn-Haylūn? (Barth's Wuín el Wán? or Wayn Silwān?)
M A S S Ū F A H
Tāzaggi?
Wayṭūnān?
G U D Ā L A H
Awkāzant (Turín?)
M A Q T A Y R
K A D Ā M
Wānzamīn (Inzimrān)
'The Gleaming Mountain'?
al-Jabal al-Lammāʿ?
Wādān
Āzuqqī
A d r a r
W Ā R Ā N
Chinguetti (Shinqīṭī)
Aguelt Nmadi
Agharf
L A M T Ū N A H
Tagānit
AZGŪNĀN
Ganeb
Aouker
Wārān
Awdaghust
Tamchaket
Senegal
N
0 200
km

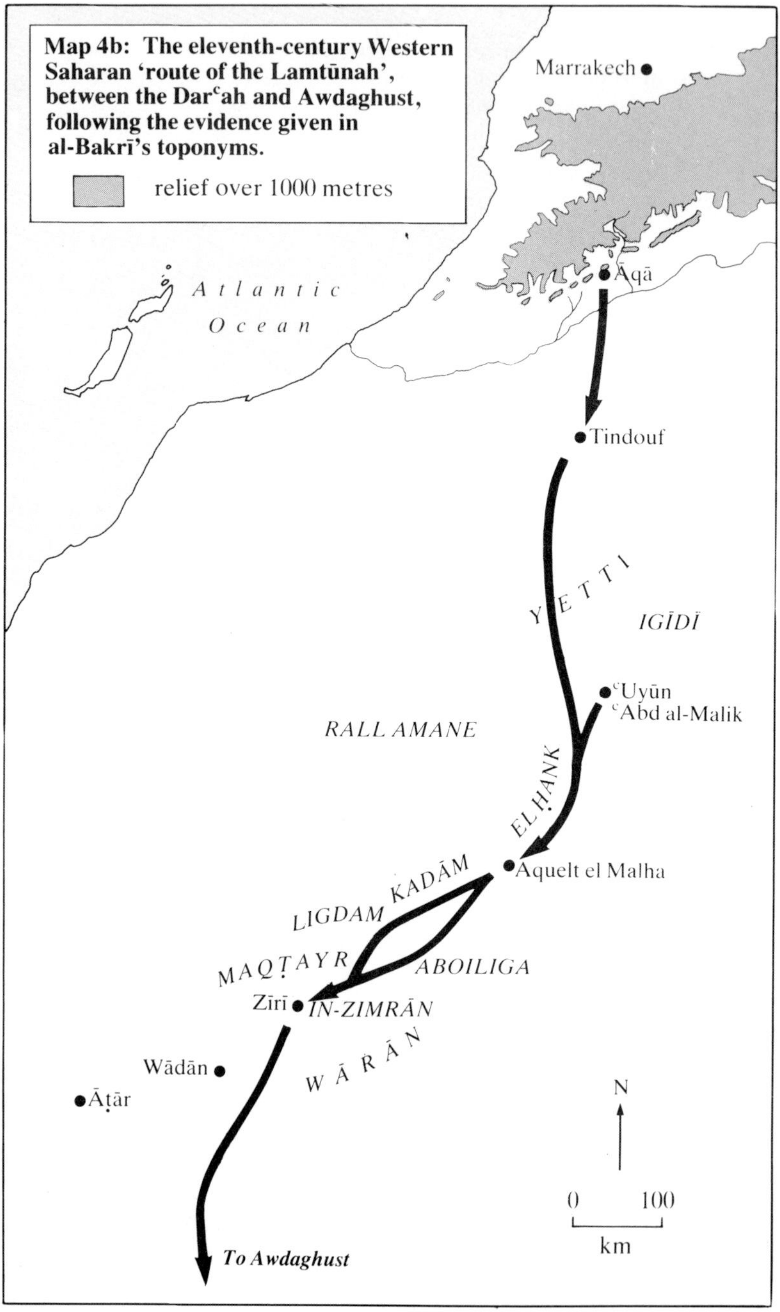

Map 4b: The eleventh-century Western Saharan 'route of the Lamtūnah', between the Darᶜah and Awdaghust, following the evidence given in al-Bakrī's toponyms.

ʿAtman ibn Menda, who was allegedly a "Caliph" of Ibn Yāsīn. The cameleers, the Ait Ejjmel, however, are Maʿqilian Tiknah. The Maʿqil did not enter Tiknah country until about 1252. The local accounts would seem to square with those of Ibn Khaldūn in regard to these details. Despite this latter-day dichotomy, it seems clear that al-Bakrī's Gazūlah cameleers were as nomadic as those Maʿqil Arab bedouin who later intermarried with the Gazūlah.

Whatever may be the historical accuracy of later Tiknah traditions, it is clear from al-Bakrī, and other Arab writers, that these raiders stemmed from the nomadic "wing" of the Gazūlah who lived in the region of the Nūn and the Darʿah (Draa). They were allies or relations of the Massūfah and the Lamṭah (possibly the Ilmaten referred to in local tradition and

Map 4b The eleventh-century Western Saharan 'route of the Lamtūnah', between the Darʿah and Awdaghust, following the evidence given in al-Bakrī's toponyms (based on discussion between Dr J. Bynon and author).

This route approaches the Mauritanian Adrār near its north-eastern tip at Wānzamīn, variant Wān Zmīran (al-Bakrī), which appears to be the pass of In-Zimrān, to the north-east of Wādān. In Morocco it commences at Tāmdūlt Āqā, crosses the Darʿah to the Ḥamādah of the Darʿah (Azwār) and passes by present day Tindouf. We site the route south of this point between the dunes of Erg Īgīdī to the east and the region called Rall (Ghall) Amane to the west. The latter means 'water is lacking' in Berber. Hence, the route could not have passed that way. Wīn Haylūn (unidentified) has parallels in the region of the Sāqiyah al-Ḥamrā', though the wells built at the command of the Arab commander, ʿAbd al-Raḥmān ibn Ḥabīb, in the days of the Caliph Hishām, suggest the ʿUyūn ʿAbd al-Malik in Yetti region. Hishām was the son of the Caliph ʿAbd al-Malik (685–705). The wells which follow, Tāzaqqā and Wīṭūnān (unidentified), could have been in the region of El Ḥank. Wīṭūnān was an extremely brackish well. It could be the well marked today as Aguelt el Malha. Awkāzant must lie near to Tiselrhatane, near the lip of Maqṭayr dunes at Aboiliga. Upon the edge of the dunes, at a narrow point, lies Ligdam or Kadām. The dunes which were so difficult to cross in al-Bakrī's day must be Maqṭayr. Once crossed, this would bring a caravan to Wānzamīn or In-Zimrān.

The route to Awdaghust (Mauritanian Hodh), south of this point, passed through Wārān, then Tagānit (al-Bakrī's Azgūnān). Wānzamīn was the key point on this route.

in the Chronicle of the *Zāwiyah* at Asā). Such long-distance raiding threatened the key point of Wānzamīn and Lamtūnah contacts with the Mauritanian Adrār, which was under threat from the Gudālah; and as these Gazūlah and Lamṭah were hardly loyal supporters of Ibn Yāsīn and his Lamtūnah lieutenants who had claimed to have subdued the Sūs and the Nūn, then they must have been foemen, and their activities suggest that Almoravid domination of the Western Sahara, as a whole, was very tenuous. This route may have been partially untenable, the north having absorbed all the Almoravid movement's military punch and martial activities.

There is no doubt that Wānzamīn was very close to al-Ghallāwiyyah, which is found today on the map of Mauritania. The latter point lies to the north-east of Wādān. The town of Wādān did not exist in al-Bakrī's time, though it is conceivable that the Massūfah settlement of Kawlān may have long predated it. The pass of al-Ghallawiyyah permits caravans to cross the barrier of the Mauritanian Adrār upland, the Ẓhar, which extends for some two hundred miles to the south-west. Muḥammad ibn al-Amīn al-Shinqīṭī alludes to Wānzamīn in his book, *al-Wasīṭ*.[11] Adjacent to al-Ghallāwiyyah he mentions In-Zimrān – no doubt the correct spelling of al-Bakrī's Wānzamīn. It is described as a black mountain containing a well. "It is a route where one ascends to the Ẓhar and where one descends to the Bāṭin of the Adrār." In-Zimrān is clearly distinguished from al-Ghallāwiyyah and from neighbouring al-Bayyiḍ, each one of these a crossing point. Wānzamīn and In-Zimrān, either names, were known to travellers well before the nineteenth century. The explorer, Barth, calls it Zwíri wen Zwemra and it appears in the histories of the Barābīsh as Zīr ibn (In-?) Zimrān. The varied continuity of this name for some eight hundred years illustrates the continuity of the cultural traditions of the Western Saharans, Berber and Arab alike. This remote region flanked by the dreadful dunes of Maqṭayr and Wārān has remained one of the most vital centres of communication in the whole Western Sahara.

The point of special interest in al-Bakrī's passage is this reference to the northerly Gazūlah and the Lamṭah coming as far south as this in order to waylay the caravans. Here is another example of the inter-relationship between the Nūl and Darʿah tribes and the Lamtūnah and Massūfah who acted as guardians and guides for the caravans. All these groups were to be caught up, as allies or as foes, in the religious movement which took them either to the north or into the Sūdān.

The desert and the town of Kākudam

Apart from the name, "the desert of the Anbiyah", which would seem to correspond to the regions near the "Empty Quarter" of the Western Sahara, *al-Majābah al-Kubrā*, or "the desert of Yasr or Nīsar", a large part of the mediaeval Western Sahara was known to the Arabs as the desert of Kākudam or Kawkadam.[12] On occasions it was vague in its limits, on other occasions bewilderingly specific. The name became attached to a tribe, or tribes, which dwelt in this tract, or, alternatively, the tract took the name of the tribe which sojourned within it. The following passages from the Arab geographers show how varied this locality appeared in the geography of the mediaeval world of Islam.

al-Idrīsī (1154):

> "As for the town of Āzukkī, it is in the country of the Masūfa and the Lamṭa. This is the first halting place in the desert. From there to Sijilmāsa is thirteen stages and to Nūl seven stages. Āzukkī is not a large town, but has a sedentary population. The inhabitants wear *muqandarāt*, which are woollen garments, called in their language *qadāwir*. A certain visitor to that town reported of the women who have no husbands, that when such a woman attains the age of 40, she offers herself to any man who desires her. She does not ward off nor hinder anyone who desires her. This town is called Āzuqqī [*sic*] in the Berber language, and in the Ganawiyya (Guinean) tongue Qūqadam. Whoever wants to go to the countries of Silā, Takrūr and Ghāna in the land of the Sūdān cannot avoid this town."[13]

Yāqūt (1224):

> "Kākudam [spelled out], a town in the Farthest West, to the south of the sea [*sic*] on the borders of the land of the Sūdān. This is where the veiled kings of the Gharb [West] who ruled before ʿAbd al-Mu'min [the Almohad] came from. There are merchants there and craftsmen who make arms such as lances and the *lamṭī* shields

and other things which the desert dwellers urgently need from craftsmen. For the veiled men, in their own country, did not need to resort to walled settlements, but were men of tents and desert dwellers [their tent ropes being made of white flax (*kattān*)], wandering in search of pasture.

"Their tribes are Lamtūna, Masūfa and Gudāla. Gudāla are the most numerous, Masūfa the most handsome, and Lamtūna the bravest. Authority resides in Lamtūna and of them was the emir of the veiled men Yūsuf ibn Tāshfīn, who ruled over the whole Gharb.

"In their land is an animal called the *lamṭ*, which is of the gazelle kind but of heavier build. It is white in colour. The *lamṭi* shields are made from its hide. The diameter of a shield is ten spans. Warriors have never fortified themselves with anything providing better protection. In the Maghrib, the price of a good one may be 30 *mu'minī* dinars. They are tanned in their country with milk and ostrich-egg shell."[14]

Ibn Saʿīd (1275):

"Connected with al-Jabal al-Lammāʿ, in this section, are the mountains of the Lamtūna, where the authority of the Mulaththamūn used to reside. These mountains extend from longitude 15°, latitude 3° and some minutes from the line of the Second Clime. To the west of these mountains is their capital Azuqqī, where the longitude is $14\frac{1}{2}$° and the latitude is 22°. From here one enters the desert of the *lamṭ*-antelope between this country and the land of the Sūdān. According to Bakrī this town is a fortress in the hills and has palms. They make from the skins of this creature the stout *lamṭ* shields which are tanned at the town of Kawkadam. This town, where they get their nourishment from camel's milk, is eight days' journey to the north-west of Azuqqī and 1° 30′ from the line from which the Third Clime is measured. It belongs to the Muslim Masūfa, whose mountains, to the east of it [*sic*], are connected with al-Jabal al-Lammāʿ and then tend to the north until they connect with the mountains of Gazūla. This is a long range, from the Atlantic Ocean to where the longitude is 12° and the latitude level with the Third Clime.

"The capital of Gazūla, to the south of this range, is the town of Tāghjīsht which is 1° from the line of the Third Clime and the same distance from the Atlantic Ocean."[15]

al-Qazwīnī (1275):

"Kākudam. A town in the Farthest West, to the south of the sea [*sic*], on the borders of the land of the Sūdān. There are artisans there who make arms such as lances and the *lamṭi* shields. These latter are made from the skin of an animal called the *lamṭ* which is to be found only there. It is white in colour, like a gazelle [*ẓaby*], but of heavier build. Its skin is tanned in their country with milk and the shell of ostriches' eggs for a whole year. Iron makes absolutely no impression upon it. If it is struck by swords the swords glance off. If it should happen to suffer a scratch or cut it is damped with water and rubbed with the hand and the mark disappears. Shields and cuirasses are made from it worth 30 [var 300] dinars apiece."[16]

al-Dimashqī (early fourteenth century):

"Let us begin with the west [and proceed towards the east]. So we say: the first desert region is that of Nūl Lamṭa, a town on the Ocean with a river flowing into the sea. Lamṭa is a Berber tribe. Then comes Awdaghusht, a sandy town with palms. It is a very unhealthy place. Its inhabitants eat sorghum [*dhura*] and meat. In the neighbourhood is a mine of excellent gold. The Berber tribes of the area are Lamtūna, Tāzakkāght,[17] Masūfa, Kākdam, and Juddāla. They are [commonly referred to as] *al-mulaththamūn* or *al-murābiṭūn*."[18]

Ibn Khaldūn (1374–8):

"They flourished and multiplied in these regions and formed numerous tribes such as Gudāla, Lamtūna, Masūfa, Watzīla, Targā, Zaghāwa, and Lamṭa, all brothers of the Ṣanhāja and inhabiting the area between the Ocean in the west and Ghadāmis to the south of Tripoli and Barqa.

"Lamtūna had many clans, such as B. Wartanṭaq, B. Niyāl, B. Mulān, and B. Nāsija. They used to live in that part of the desert called Kākadam and they were all pagans [*majūs*] like the Berbers of the Maghrib. They continued to occupy those territories [*majālāt*] until they adopted Islam after the conquest of Spain [by the Arabs]."[19]

Leo Africanus (d. after 1526):

"Of the desert inhabited by the people called Zuenziga. This desert beginneth westward from Tegaza, extending eastward to the desert of Hair which is inhabited by the people called Targa: northward it bordereth upon the deserts of Segelmesse, Tebelbelt, and Benigorai; and southward upon the desert of Ghir, which joineth unto the kingdom of Guber. It is a most barren and comfortless place: and yet merchants travell this way from Telensin to Tombuto: howbeit many are found lying dead upon the same way in regard of extreme thirst. Within this desert there is included another desert called Gogdem [*sic*], where for the space of nine daies journey not one drop of water is to be found, unless perhaps some raine falleth: wherefore the merchants use to carrye their water upon camel backes."[20]

It is obvious that if all the above accounts are compared several of them must be wrong in detail and some are incompatible. Al-Idrīsī, Ibn Saʿīd and Leo Africanus are obvious examples. On any geographical basis no way can be found to square the disparities of desert topography. One statement must be wrong and another correct, but it is almost impossible to say, with complete confidence, which writer was misinformed.

It is of more value to isolate some of the more unusual details in the above passages seeing whether these give any clues as to the tribal geography of the wastes of the Western Sahara in the Middle Ages. The following seem to me to be of special note:

(1) That there may well have been a tribe, or clan, of Saharans called Kākudam, who were part of the Massūfah or allied to the Massūfah, and, if al-Dimashqī is correct, they may well have been associated with the Tāzakkāght as well.[21] This would explain why "the Qūqadam" appear in Āzuqqī, with the Massūfah, in al-Idrīsī, in a northerly region of the Sahara in Ibn Saʿīd, in the town of Awdaghust in al-Dimashqī's account, and in the name of the Gogdem desert in the tribal heartland of the Zuenziga in the account of Leo Africanus.

(2) That common to almost every one of these accounts is the association of the name with the hunting of the oryx, the tanning of its skin and the manufacture of *Lamṭī* shields. The reference to milk and to ostrich eggs indicates that the manufacturing process was carried out in a desert region close to some major route along which these shields were carried to the north, and probably to the south.

(3) Leo's desert is similar in certain respects to a desert which was crossed by the traveller, Ibn Baṭṭūṭah, to the south of the great salt mine of Taghāzā. The latter wrote:

Map 5 The distribution of Ṣanhājah and non-Ṣanhājah Berber tribes in the north-west of the Sahara in the late medieval period (based on Antonio Rumeu de Armas).

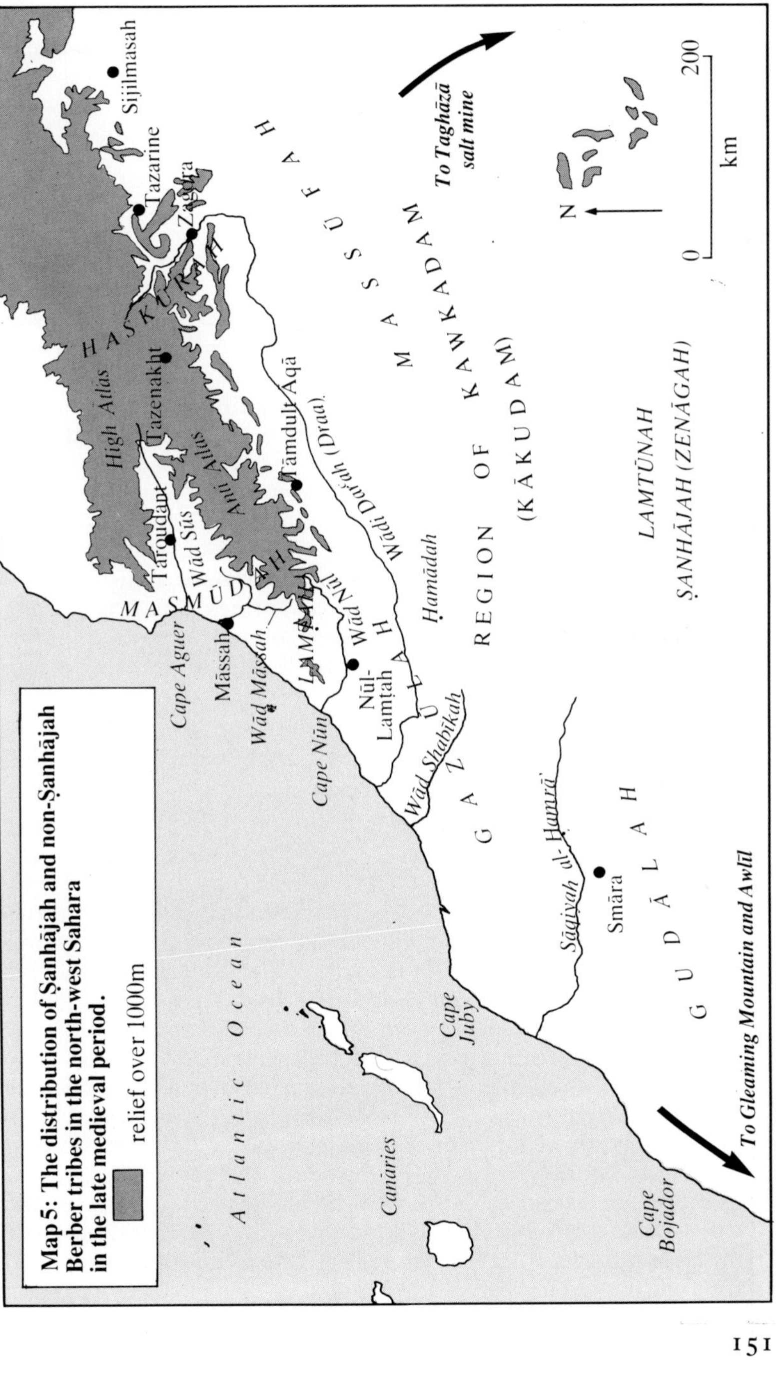

Map 5: The distribution of Ṣanhājah and non-Ṣanhājah Berber tribes in the north-west Sahara in the late medieval period.

> "Water is taken on there for entering the wilderness which comes after it. This is a distance of ten days without water except rarely. As for us, we found plenty of water there in pools left by the rain. On one day we found a pool between two rocky hillocks with sweet water in it, so we renewed our water supply and washed our clothes."[22]

He continued:

> "Then we arrived at Tāsarahlā. This consists of *aḥsā'* of water where caravans encamp. They stay there three days, resting and repairing their water skins, and filling them with water, and sewing palm leaf bags [*tillīs*] round them for fear of the wind. From here the *takshīf* is sent on. *Takshīf* is the name for any man of the Masūfa who is hired by the people of the caravan to go on ahead to Īwālātan with people's letters to their associates there, so that they may rent houses for them and come out to meet them with water for a distance of four days' travel . . . There are many demons [shayṭān] in this wilderness. If the *takshīf* is alone they play with him and seduce him so that he becomes diverted from his purpose and perishes since there is no clear road or track. There is nothing but sand blown about by the wind so that you see mountains of sand in one place then you see them transported to another."

These words of Ibn Baṭṭūṭah are matched, at a far later date, by Aḥmad ibn al-Amīn al-Shinqīṭī where he describes the desert of Limrayyah, likewise to the south of Taghāzā towards Bīr al-Ksaib (Tāsarahlā).

> "It is a land which lies midway between Shinqīṭ and Arawān. It is hard to cross and is without water and vegetation. It is dangerous for whosoever traverses it. If the wind blows in a storm there the caravan party there cannot continue in its march, for fear lest it loses its way, because the wind raises the sand so as to blur the distinction between the sky and the ground. Whenever they wished to carry salt from Shinqīṭ they used to jade the camels so that they became accustomed to drinking after some twenty days or thereabouts. Each man carries enough to drink in a stout provision container. Such is the case in the winter season. Sometimes water is exhausted for the whole party so they kill the camels and take what their bellies hold. They hang it up in their craws and beneath it they light a fire. When the water is purified they allow it to become cold and then they drink it. This was what

> was done by Khālid ibn al-Walīd, may Allāh be pleased with him, in the time of the *Riddah* wars. When he went in the direction of the Iraqi provinces after the battle of Yamāmah,[23] his guide was Rāfiʿ, who was one of the Companions, and who was famous for his ability to guide.
>
> The caravan party may stray and lose its way in Limrayyah and so utterly perish. They say that the guide there when he marches with the travellers goes in front of them. They follow after him and do not speak, for fear lest he be forgetful and that all would then perish. It is a distance of ten days."[24]

It seems fairly certain that the same desert is described in all three accounts. However, although some early maps call Leo's desert "the desert of Gogdem", in fact the name is spelt *Goeten* in the Latin version of Leo, dated 1559,[25] and in the French translation of 1556, "Il se trouve encore un autre désert appellé *Gogden*, auquel impossible est de trouver une seule goute d'eau."[26] The desert is shown eastward of Taghāzā in the direction of In Zīza in Algeria, so that one's eyes are drawn to such obvious names on the modern map as Tikkadouine, or toponyms just to the west of Timmisao – with its Koranic passages painted on a cave by the early Kel Es-Sūq[27] – toponyms like Ăġĕdĕm, and Ġoûdĕn,[28] valleys which vanish in the desert.

It is equally plausible to site Goeten/Gogden/Gogdem a little to the south of Taghāzā, and to place it around Taoudenni (Tawdannī),[29] the salt mine which took the place of Taghāzā, once it had been exhausted, some time after 1585. This change occurred after the time of Leo Africanus, and, of course, a very long time after Ibn Baṭṭūṭah's crossing of the Western Sahara.

One might likewise take into possible consideration the key point of Kadām (see pp. 97 and 274), eastward of Wādān, the nearest town of historic importance, and due west of Limrayyah, where Maqṭayr and Wārān meet. This is one contender for the water point en route to Wānzamīn (In-Zimrān), in Lamtūnah territory, which al-Bakrī names in his *routier* between Darʿah and Awdaghust. He spells it Awkāzant though it could be deformed. My colleague, Dr J. Bynon, has pointed out that the feminine suffix, *t*, could have become suppressed, but that its former presence would have turned an *n* into an *m*. This could have formed a toponym Awkāzam, which, if further shortened and with a possible *dh* instead of a *z*, left a name not far removed from Kadam or Kadām, hence Goeten/Gogden/Gogdem.

It can be seen that we are at a very great distance from the *Qūqadam* of al-Idrīsī. His description is wanting in a number of respects. His Āzuqqī is nothing like the fortress and date palms of al-Bakrī. No mention of them is made. The Lamṭah and Massūfah seem odd residents in the Lamtūnah "capital". The distances which he gives from Nūl and Sijilmāsah to Āzuqqī (near Āṭār) are absurdly short. Vincent Monteil has noted that, "Tindouf [ou surtout: Goulimine] Atar, par Bir-Mogrein: 40 jours en tout." The radial centre of routes he mentions seems to fit the Wānzamīn of al-Bakrī, and, elsewhere, al-Idrīsī confuses Awdaghust and Tādamakkat, comparing both of them to Mecca. One must respect his record, yet in it there is something of the *pot pourri* of much that was then known of the Western Sahara as a whole, in his days, in his sundry passages of description. One senses that other accounts are some way nearer the mark when one searches for the ancient homelands of the *Mulaththamūn*.[30]

The industry of the Darʿah region

One is deluded by *Shayāṭīn* if one attempts to find a centre for the tanning of oryx skins in the waterless deserts of Ibn Baṭṭūṭah and Leo Africanus. Yet having hit on this important Saharan axis of commerce one should perhaps stick to it and turn towards the north. The presence of the northerly Tāzakkāght, together with the Kākdam, in Awdaghust, the passing references to the Lamṭah and Massūfah, and the thriving industry in the manufacture and sale of *Lamṭī* shields all point in the general direction of the region of the Wādī Darʿah. It will be recalled that it was this region of the Massūfah and the Haskūrah – whose territory reached Darʿah – which knew the first of the Arab armies in the Western Sahara. The latter had begun to dig wells in the Jabal Banī and in the Ḥamādah of Tindouf.

Leo Africanus, in his *Description of Africa*, refers on several pages to the leather working which took place in the "Numidia region" on the southern slopes of the Atlas and down into Darʿah and towards Sijilmāsah.

He writes (*Of the citie of Elgiumuha* (al-Jumūʿah)):

"Neere unto the foresaid towne, within five miles, standeth Elgiumuha. It was in our time built upon the top of an high mountaine, and containeth to the number of five hundred families comprised in the villages of that mountaine. Here are innumerable springs and fountaines, and most pleasant and fruitfull gardens in all places. Here are likewise walnut-trees huge and tall. The little hils environing this mountaine doth yeeld barlie and olives in great abundance. In the said towne are great numbers of artizans, as smithes, leather dressers, and such like. And because they have here notable iron-mines, they make plentie of horse-shooes. And whatsoever commoditie proceedeth of their labour, they carrie it to forren regions where they thinke it is wanting: from whence they bring home slaves, woad, and the skins of certain beastes, whereof they make most defensive and warlike shields: these shields they transport unto Fez, exchanging them there for weapons, cloth, and other such things as they stand in neede of. This towne standeth so neere unto the high way, that the boyes will stand gazing and woondering at merchants as they come by, especially if they weare any strange attire."[31]

He writes (*Of the mountaine called Tensita*):

"Tensita is a part of Atlas, beginning westward from the mountaine last before mentioned [Tenueus], eastward extending to mount Dedes, and southward bordering upon the desert of Dara. This mountaine is well stored with inhabitants, having more than fiftie castles about it, the wals whereof are built of lime and rough stone: and by reason of the southerly situation it is ever almost destitute of rain. All the saide castles stand not far from the river of Dara, some being three, and some four miles distant there from. The greatest prince in all this region hath under his command well nigh fifteen hundreth horsemen, and about so many footemen as the prince of Tenueus before named. And albeit these two princes are most neerely conioined in blood, yet can neither of them refraine from most cruel wars against the other. It is a woonder to see, what plentie of dates this mountaine affoordeth: the inhabitants give themselves partly to husbandry, and partly to trafficke. Barly they have in great abundance: but of other graine and of flesh their scarcitie is incredible: for that region hath no flockes nor droves at all. The prince of this mountaine commonly receiveth for yeerly tribute twentie thousand peeces of golde; every of which peeces containeth not so much by one third part, as an Italian ducate. There hath alwaies beene so great amitie betweene the king of Fez and this prince, that either often sendeth rich gifts unto other. My selfe (I remember) once saw a most magnificent gift presented to the saide king in the name of this prince, to wit, fiftie men slaves, and fiftie women slaves brought out of the land of Negros, tenne eunuchs, twelve camels, one Giraffe, sixteene civet cats, one pound of civet, a pound of amber, and almost sixe hundreth skins of a certine beast called by them Elamt, whereof they make shieldes, everie skin being woorth at Fez, eight ducates, twentie of the men slaves cost twentie ducates a peece, and so did fifteene of the women slaves; every eunuch was valued at fortie, every camel at fiftie, and every civet-cat at two hundreth ducates: and a pound of civet and amber is solde at Fez for threescore ducates. Besides these were sent divers other particulars, which for brevities sake I omit."[32]

The Haskūrah and the Massūfah

The Haskūrah, who occupy a broad swathe of territory of the southern Atlas region to the east of Marrakech, and whose western homelands bordered upon the Gazūlah and whose southern marches stretched along the whole of the upper Darʿah to beyond Zagora, were, by descent, related to the Lamtūnah, the Massūfah and other Ṣanhājah. According to Ibn Khaldūn, the Lamṭah, the Gazūlah and the Haskūrah were matrilinealy descended from Tiṣgī "the lame", the daughter of Zaḥīk ibn Madghīs.[33]

These three "nations" (*umam*) occupied the Sūs and the adjacent areas of the Sahara and the Atlas regions, in the plains and on the mountains. The Lamṭah were chiefly nomadic, and so, likewise, were many of the Gazūlah. By the time of Ibn Khaldūn both were coming increasingly under the control of the Banū Maʿqil.

Ibn Khaldūn also adds that the Haskūrah, in his time, were reckoned among the Maṣmūdah and held to be Almohads in their religious loyalties. He corrects this impression pointing out that some did, in fact, embrace the Almohad cause, but that prior to the triumph of Ibn Tūmart, the founder of that *daʿwah*, the Haskūrah had been extremely hostile towards him and their preachers had cursed him in their pulpits. The Haskūrah had been the close allies of the Almoravids and had claimed a certain kinship with the Lamṭah and Lamtūnah.

Among the many clans of the Haskūrah, one, by the name of Ghujdāmah, undoubtedly recalls the Qūqadam of al-Idrīsī, though this may merely be coincidental. It is also to be noted that in the region of the Haskūrah, and also of the Gazūlah, there are several toponyms, which take the form of Ouagoudim, Ougoudim and Ūjadām[34] on the detailed maps of Morocco and in the gazeteers. This is especially true of the Anti Atlas, the Darʿah and the Jabal Banī. Among these examples the most northerly and the most impressive is Jabal Ouagoudim, which overlooks the valleys and passes leading into the Darʿah away to the north of Tazenacht and Ouazarzate. It is this mountain to which Leo Africanus referred when he wrote (*Of the mountain called Gogideme*):

> "Neare unto the foresaid mountain standeth another called Gogideme. This mountaine is inhabited only upon the north part thereof: but the south side is utterly destitute of inhabitants: the reason whereof they affirme to be, because that when *Abraham* king of Maroco was vanquished and expelled out of his kingdom by his disciple *Elmaheli*, he fled unto this mountaine. The inhabitants mooved with the kings distresse endevoured (though to small purpose) all that they could, to succour him: whereof his disciple *Elmaheli* was no sooner enformed, but comming with an huge armie and with great furie upon them, he destroyed all their mansions and villages, and the inhabitants he partly put to flight, and partly to the sword."[35]

This mountain fortress was a sort of "Masada of the Almoravids". It was one of their *ribāṭs* and the story of its seizure is partly told by Ibn Khaldūn.[36] After having compelled the Hazrajah to give him obedience, Ibn Tūmart had next turned on the Haskūrah, who were led by the Lamtūnī, Abū Daraqah, "possessor of the [*Lamṭī*] shield", and he conquered them. The town of the Ghujdāmah in this locality had at first shown him loyalty but had revolted. ʿAbd al-Mu'min ibn ʿAlī, Ibn Tūmart's future successor, punished them, declared their blood lawful and sacked the town of the Ghūjdamah, Ouagoudim. Many must have fled and have found a place of refuge in the Saharan provinces of the Almoravids.[37]

Ibn Tūmart and Kākudam

The earliest surviving reference to Kākudam in Arabic texts, spelt in this way, is in a passage where Ibn Tūmart bitterly attacked the Almoravids of the desert. He described them as having come from Kākudam region in order to impose their false anthropomorphic concept of the Deity upon the true believers of Islam.[38] On this page, in his book *Aʿazz mā yuṭlab*, Ibn Tūmart describes his enemies as uncouth shepherds, unshod, veiled like women, and aspiring to a settled way of life and a status of authority for which they were totally unfitted. All the contempt of the village dweller for the nomad herder is conveyed in this passage:

جميع علاماتهم ظاهرة منها ما ظهر قبل مجيئهم من كاكدم ومنها ما ظهر
بعد اخذهم البلاد ومنها ما ظهر من احوالهم وافعالهم فالذي ظهر منها
قبل مجيئهم خمس احداهن انهم الحفاة والثانية انهم العراة والثالثة انهم
العالة والرابعة انهم رعاء الشاء والبهم والخامسة انهم جاهلون بأمر الله

It would be very satisfactory confidently to identify Kākudam with the Qūqadam of al-Idrīsī, in short, with Āzuqqī the Lamtūnah capital in the Mauritanian Adrār. But it would be hard to do this with any conviction. Āzuqqī was a rearguard base, although threatened at Wānzamīn, in order to protect the Lamtūnah from their Gudālah enemies, it was *not* the main base for the Almoravid operations in the north, which were centred on Darʿah. When Ibn Tūmart wrote the above lines, the southern wing of the Almoravids had separated from the northern kingdom. Abū Bakr ibn ʿUmar, the Lamtūnī, had established a *Qāḍī* in office in Āzuqqī, a South Arabian Arab, the *Imām*, Abū Bakr Muḥammad ibn al-Ḥasan al-Murādī al-Ḥaḍramī. The latter died there in 1096. All the geographers, al-Bakrī, al-Zuhrī, Ibn Saʿīd, for example, call the Lamtūnah "capital", Āzuqqī, and al-Idrīsī is the only partial exception in this respect. It would have been bizarre of Ibn Tūmart, surely, to have chosen what al-Idrīsī calls a non-Berber "Guinean" name in order to convey some message to the Maṣmūdah readers of his *Risālah*?

The epistle is undated. It is a diatribe of propaganda with the purpose of undermining support for the Almoravid ruler, ʿAlī ibn Yūsuf, and his successors in Marrakech. It predated an operation against the main bases of the Western Saharans, the Lamṭah and Gazūlah in the southern Sūs.

The geographical scope of these operations are referred to by Ibn Tūmart himself, and also in the biography of him by al-Baydhaq. The *Mahdī* of the Almohads confidently predicted his own triumph in those southerly regions:

> "Woe unto those of the West, the most evil in their midst will bring about their final downfall. Woe unto those of the Sūs and to their neighbours, the Gazūlah of al-Kust,[39] and the Lamṭah, and to those of the South (*qiblah*), upon every one of them."[40]

As the *Mahdī* had predicted so it came about, at least in the record of al-Baydhaq:

> "In the year 521 [1127/1128], the *Mahdī* wrote to the Almohads the well-composed epistle [*al-risālah al-munaẓẓamah*] on the subject of certain of their expeditions. This is the same letter as the one sent later by the Caliph to the Gazūlah. In the same year the *Mahdī* conquered Tāsrīrt."[41]

These southerly operations are later described:

> "Then he pushed southwards. Before him the Ait Yīghaz fled towards al-Kust, where they joined al-Ṣaḥrāwī. Abū Ḥafṣ arrived in Sīrwān where he gathered together the Banū Wāwazgīt and he divided them into two halves: he gave one to the men of Tīnmallal and the other to the Hintātah. Shaykh Abū Ḥafṣ returned to Marrakech.
>
> "Then he sent in search of troops. When they had arrived, the Caliph divided them up into Ṭālibs and Ḥāfiẓs. He gave one army to Abū Ḥafṣ and another to Wasnār who left in the direction of al-Kust. He gave the commandership of the other armies to ʿAbdallāh ibn Abū Bakr ibn Wargī, to ʿAbdallāh ibn Fāṭimah and to ʿUmar ibn Maymūn, with the order to take Nūl Lamṭah. They left with the help of Allāh.
>
> "Shaykh Abū Ḥafṣ captured a fort called Kastūr. He did not kill its garrison so they could be converted to the Almohad cause. As for Wasnār, he reached Tāsrīrt and took booty from it. Then Abū Ḥafṣ turned to face the Hashtūkah, whom he defeated and from whom he took booty. Likewise Agg-u-Āngī challenged the Lamṭah, whom he defeated and from whom he took booty, and he attacked Āhukār, a Sulṭān of the Lamtūnah.[42] He compelled al-Ḥusain ibn Sulaymān, the lord of Tāʿgīzt,[43] to surrender and to join the Almohads. The booty reached Marrakech and it was put

on sale at Bāb al-Sharī'ah; the Gazūlah and Lamṭah women, the camels, the oxen and the sheep."[44]

These expeditions put an end to Almoravid support in the Sūs and the adjacent region of the western Dar'ah. It is clear that Kākudam, or any name like it, is not amongst those places attacked or captured. As for the Ghujdāmah amongst the Haskūrah, the first surrender of their base at Ouagoudim, to which reference has been made, had already occurred and the Almohads had installed their governer within it prior to this date.

However tempting it might be to see a connection between the Kākudam of Ibn Tūmart and the Almoravid *ribāṭ* at Ouagoudim, or with the tribe of the Ghujdāmah, in the last resort any such identification is very speculative. In the Almohad documents the Ghujdāmah are never found spelt with the form of Kākudam so, as in the case of Āzuqqī, it would have been most odd if Ibn Tūmart had spelt Ouagoudim in this way. Furthermore, no other writer of the Arabs, or the Berbers, thought of any possible connection between these two names. Clearly, the region of Kākudam, named by Ibn Tūmart, was situated away beyond the southernmost operations of the Almohads. It would seem to be situated beyond the Sūs, beyond Nūl Lamṭah, beyond the Gazūlah and beyond the Ghujdāmah and the Haskūrah. Since Ibn Tūmart would have used the term al-Bakrī uses for the capital of the Adrār, Āzuqqī, had he meant it, then he must have meant the northerly Saharan bases of his opponents, that is, the border regions of the Dar'ah, the Sāqiyah al-Ḥamrā', and the desert of Sijilmāsah, where local conditions and artisans permitted the tanning of *Lamṭ* skins, and possessed the equipment which Ibn Sa'īd, amongst others, has specifically described.

Some final clues as to the location of the pasturelands and the "industrial centre" of the northern Saharan Almoravids are to be found in the travelogue of 'Alī al-Janaḥānī al-Maghribī whose journey to West Africa may be discovered in the text of the *'Ajā'ib al-makhlūqāt wa āthār al-bilād* (1275) by Qazwīnī, a little before Ibn Sa'īd.[45] This traveller has described the "town of Zukundar" in the Sūs, with its silver mines and water wheels. It is clearly a reference to the capital of ʿAlī ibn Yiddir al-Zukundarī, lord of the Sūs, enemy of the Gazūlah and friend of the incoming Banū Maʿqil, about whom more will be said. Tāmdūlt Āqā with its silver mine may have been within his territory. This traveller mentions other Saharan places – Taghāzā and Kākudam (Āzuqqī is not mentioned) – either on the way to Takrūr, or on the way back. The territory is Massūfah territory, but is Kākudam between the Sūs and Taghāzā, or between Taghāzā and the Sūdān?

Qazwīnī cites his informant as follows: "The *faqīh* ʿAlī al-Janaḥānī relates that he passed by a high hill [*tall*] near Kākudam of which people say that whoever climbs it will be snatched away by the *jinn*. Nearby is the famed City of Copper [*Madīnat al-Nuḥās*], which will be mentioned in its place if God [who is exalted] wills."[46]

This reference to the wiles of the *jinn* recalls the hazards of the *Takshīf* of the Massūfah in Limrayyah, beset by *Shayāṭīn* and hemmed in by sand-hills which are so graphically described by Ibn Baṭṭūṭah. But this southerly desert, the desert of Leo Africanus, must be excluded, because of the details furnished by Ibn Saʿīd.

The latter mentions that Kawkadam is north-west or north of Āzuqqī. It is "eight days" from Āzuqqī, whereas Taghāzā is "seven days" from Āzuqqī.[47] Taghāzā (Ḥisn al-Milḥ) is 3°30′ from the line of the Second Clime, whereas Kawkadam is 1°30′ from the line from which the Third Clime is measured. Kawkadam is therefore near the mountains of the Gazūlah.

The evidence points to a desert region near the Sāqiyah al-Ḥamrā', possibly a small settlement linked to the Sūs, on the route to Taghāzā and on a route for the *Lamṭī* shields adjacent to those men – and here one means the Haskūrah and the Massūfah – who knew about tanning and the manufacture of these shields. This was the first major base of the Almoravids, although to make its location precise is now almost impossible.

One might hypothetically suggest the Asif Agoudim, to the north of Tazarine[48] and a little way to the east of Zagora, where an Almoravid fortress stands to this day. One might favour even more al-Bakrī's Tn-Ūdādn. In al-Bakrī's day this "well of the ibex" was on the route betwixt Darʿah and Sijilmāsah.[49] It then contained a copper mine, to which ʿAlī al-Janaḥānī could be alluding to in his reference to the Copper City legend.

There are some who will dispute that Leo's Guaden, which may well be Kākudam or Kawkadam, is Tin Ouadane (Wādān), namely, al-Bakrī's Tn-Ūdādn, or anywhere else in the Darʿah (Draa) region. They favour Marmól and others and see it as Wādān in Northern Mauritania, spelt variously, though often as Hodem or Audem. In fact, Raymond Mauny, in his "Notes d'Histoire et d'Archéologie sur Azougui, Chinguetti et Ouadane" (*Bull de l'I.F.A.N.* series B, vol. 17, nos. 1–2, 1955, pp. 142–63), not only regards Wādān as the likely spot for Ibn Saʿīd's Kawkadam, but would site Leo's Guaden in this more southerly location. According to Valentim Fernandes (1506–7) Wādān in Mauritania was a town of four hundred souls on the salt route. It had no walls and its inhabitants lived on barley, dates and camel's milk.

But the weighty arguments of Andrzej Dziubinski in favour of Leo's Tesset as Tissint, in the Jabal Banī, and Guaden in that same northerly region, are persuasive.[50]

There are pointers in favour of Guaden running from north to south at the head of the Wād al-Ḥamrā', to north and south of Tindouf, and near the meeting point of Morocco, Algeria, Mauritania and the Sāqiyah al-Ḥamrā' region of the former Spanish Sahara. The maps of the sixteenth and seventeenth centuries, for example, Forlani, 1562, and Pierre du Val of 1664, show Guaden and Goaden to the north of Taghāzā and due east of "Alhamara", while Wādān in Mauritania is far to the south and is spelt Hoden. Forlani shows Guaden to the west of Acca (Āqā), in the region of Tindouf. This sites it quite near the cliff of Kreb Akouadim, which is almost beside the strategic road across the Sahara from Morocco to Mauritania, close to Wād al-Ḥamrā', and the water points, seasonal or perennial, of Dāyat al-ʿĀm. This is a major region of nomadisation for the Rgaybāt. Akouadim seems to fit Kawkadam better than any other known Saharan locality.

On this assumption – rather, hypothesis – and on this unresolved question whether Guaden was in Morocco or in Mauritania – or in Algeria even – the last word must be left with the remarks of Ibn Saʿīd and of Leo Africanus. To the former the town of Kawkadam is in the north. It is a nomadic centre where men subsisted on camel's milk. It was poor in good water but it was a major centre for the tanning of *Lamṭ* skins for the making of *Lamṭī* shields. As for Leo Africanus, he says of the village of Guaden that it was situated in the "Numidian desert neere unto Libya [the Sahara]". It

> "is inhabited by most miserable and grosse people. Here groweth nothing but dates: and the inhabitants are at such enmitie with their neighbours, that it is dangerous for them to go abroad. Howbeit they give themselves to hunting, and take certain wilde beasts called Elamth, and ostriches, neither do they eat any other flesh. All their goates they reserve for milke. And these people also are blacke of colour."[51]

The Gazūlah and the Gudālah, the reconquest of Spain and the march to Byzantium

When ʿAbdallāh ibn Yāsīn al-Gazūlī, the founder of the *daʿwah* of the Almoravids, began his movement of reform amongst the Western Saharans, his mission was at first addressed to the Gudālah. They, it is recalled, were the Ṣanhājah people who lived as southern neighbours to the peoples of the Sūs. They occupied the desert along the shores of the Atlantic, through the Río de Oro, and they extended southwards almost to the mouth of the Senegal river. Their salt mine was at Awlīl in the Trārzah of Mauritania, which is first mentioned in Arabic accounts by Ibn Ḥawqal.[52] With Taghāzā it was the second of the great salt mines in the Sahara to the west of the Hoggar.

All the accounts tell of the welcome which Ibn Yāsīn received, at first, among the jurists of the Gudālah. If the report is true, then this can only mean some degree of Islamisation, if not Arabisation, among the circle of counsellors of the Ṣanhājah pilgrim chief, Yaḥyā ibn Ibrāhīm al-Gudālī, who, with a jurist, Jawhar ibn Sakkum, had beseeched Abū ʿImrān in Qayrawān to request Wajjāj the *murābiṭ* to send one of his neophytes to further their knowledge of the Islamic faith. The text of part of this letter of request by Abū ʿImrān has, allegedly, survived:

> "To proceed: when the bearer of this letter of mine reaches you, then send, with him, from amongst your students, him whom you trust in regard to his learning, his religion and his piety, and his

sound policy, in order that he may teach them [amongst the Ṣanhājah] to read and understand the Koran, and teach them the legally canonic rules of Islam, and to instruct them in the religion of Allāh. . ."[53]

وعبد اللّه بن ياسين هذا هو الذي وقع اختيار (وجاج بن زلو) عليه ، وانتدبه ليعمل على انبعاث الثقافة والدين بالمغرب الأقصى بدعوة من (أبي زكريا الكدالي) الذي شكا الأمر إلى (أبي عمران الفاسي) فكتب إلى (وجاج) :

« أما بعد : فإذا وصلك حامل كتابي هذا ، فابعث معه من طلبتك من تثق بعلمه ودينه وورعه ، وحسن سياسته ؛ ليقرئهم القرآن ، ويعلمهم شرائع الاسلام ، ويفقههم في دين اللّه .. »

ولما نزل عبد اللّه بالمغرب قام بأداء مهمّته وعندما قويت جموعه طلبهم للقتال فأستجابوا له ، وقاموا معه بغزو القبائل ، وقد أصيب في حروبه مع مجوس (برغواطة) وتوفي سنة ٤٥١ هـ .

After a stay of some time amongst the Gudālah, Ibn Yāsīn was rejected by them. This rejection was either on account of the severity of the legal measures, based on the *Muwaṭṭa'* of Mālik ibn Anas, which he enforced in a lax society, or else because the Gudālah jurists found a number of juridical errors and unorthodox practices in the Islamic doctrines which he taught. It should be noted that there is a paradox in this situation. Either the Gudālah were ignorant folk and were prepared to be led, or else they were better informed than first appears and, quite rightly, saw through the inconsistencies in the ideas of the Sūsī jurist, Ibn Yāsīn, however much they retained their respect for his master, Wajjāj, and his *murābiṭūn*.

Wajjāj rejected the Gudālah. Ibn Yāsīn switched his loyalties to the Lamtūnah who were chiefly centred to the south in the Mauritanian Adrār. Their relationship with the Gudālah, despite intermarriage, was far from amicable. It was the Lamtūnah and the Massūfah, and but a very few of the Gudālah, who moved north to seize Sijilmāsah and who raided the Sūs and crossed the Atlas mountains in order to found and expand the Almoravid Empire. Whilst they were engaged in this mighty project, the Gudālah tribe launched a major attack on the Lamtūnah near their palm-circled citadel at Āzuqqī. Yaḥyā ibn ʿUmar, the Lamtūnī, who was left in the Mauritanian south in order to defend it, was killed in bloody combat at an unidentified locality called Tabfarillā.[54]

Al-Bakrī, who records these happenings, then reports that the Gudālah withdrew "to the coast". By this act in fact they withdrew from history for some two hundred years. But in which direction did they withdraw? What part had they really played in the early days of the Almoravids? Was the colourful episode in some accounts, about a retreat by Yaḥyā and Ibn Yāsīn to an island on the Atlantic seaboard in Gudālah territory, a story which was invented later, or was it a seasonal sojourn, a trip to Awlīl for salt, or an oral tale which came to the notice of far later historians? Al-Bakrī knew nothing of it. Even if it be true, there is some evidence to suggest that it took place far to the north of the Bay of Arguin, let alone the mouth of the Senegal river or the islands in the Niger.

There is a passage in Ibn ʿIdhārī which states unequivocally that the sojourn of Ibn Yāsīn with the Gudālah was at no great distance from Gazūlah country and the Sūs, possibly as near as the Sāqiyah al-Ḥamrā'. This passage reads:

> "[On his return from al-Andalus Ibn Yāsīn passed by the Maṣmūdah in the Sūs and upbraided them] and he forsook them and he travelled from them to the country of the Gazūlah. *Then took place the affair between him and Yaḥyā ibn Ibrāhīm and the Gudālah*, referred to above. Then he journeyed from the Gudālah to the Lamtūnah. . .".[55]

فتركهم ورحل عنهم إلى بلاد جزولة فكان من أمره مع يحيى بن إبراهيم
وجدالة ما تقدّم ذكره . ثمّ رحل من جدالة الى لمتونة

The whole passage suggests a straight journey, the episode with the Gudālah centred on a northerly region bordering on, or within, the territory of the Gazūlah.

After al-Bakrī, it is the record of the Qāḍī ʿIyāḍ which furnishes the account which is chronologically nearest to the events.[56] But he was the laureate of the Lamtūnah, who had seized the reins of power. He could hardly be expected to say much good of the Gudālah, though he retained the roles of

Yaḥyā ibn Ibrāhīm and his jurist, Jawhar ibn Sakkum (who is called a Gazūlī) since they could hardly be expunged totally from the record. Noteworthy throughout all his writings is the glory attained by the Lamtūnah, and the backsliding and perfidy of the Gudālah. But in the account of Ibn al-Athīr (d. 630/1233) the tribes are more evenly judged, the story is more evenly balanced, and this trend continues in almost all the later historians and geographers. One technique they adopted was the introduction of a story of an island retreat in Gudālah country. This clever device turned the rebellious Gudālah into ascetic islanders, the backcloth of the drama being the Saharan coast near Tidra island, or else the Senegal's mouth near Awlīl. By the late Middle Ages far more had been learnt of this coast yet it still retained a remoteness of safety for story-tellers, like the story of some lost Atlantis.

One may suggest three reasons why the Gudālah were reinstated. First, the Lamtūnah dynasty of the Banū Tāshufīn had clearly been overthrown by the Almohads. The Banū Marīn had succeeded the latter. A reassessment and reappraisal of the Almoravids after 1250, if not before, became increasingly acceptable, although the Lamtūnah *per se* were not to be seen as the sole great force in that movement.

Secondly, much more was known about the Gudālah, their territories, mountains, rivers and settlements towards the end of the twelfth century than had been the case hitherto. However fanciful the accounts of a mountain which gleamed on the coast of the Río de Oro, or the town of Taghīrā, the "capital" of the Gudālah, at least shipwrecked seamen and adventurers had been there, and a few may even have touched the coast of the Canary Islands.[57] In fact, the reporting, however fantastic at times, quoted the garbled accounts taken first-hand from the mouths of Western Saharan Berbers who may have known some Arabic as well.

Al-Idrīsī has a very full account of the area of the Gudālah to the north of the Senegal. All kinds of places and deserts and towns may indicate borrowings from Classical sources, though there are certain coincidences which seem too remarkable to be nothing but chance or topographical *ameublement*.

One might select the mountain of Banbawān, located, most improbably, in the low-lying lands of south-west Mauritania. Al-Idrīsī says:

> "Next to the town of Naghīra [or Taghīrā, 'capital' of the Gudālah], slightly to the south of east of it, are the mountains of Banbawān, which is one of the highest ranges in the world. It is barren and of white earth; no plants grow there other than wormwood [*shīḥ*] and the saltwort [*ghāsūl*] called *ḥuruḍ*. The author of *Kitāb al-ʿAjāʾib* [al-Masʿūdī?], says of the height of this range in the air that the clouds shed their rain on the lower slopes without reaching the summit."[58]

This is sheer fantasy – or is it? The details in regard to desert plants and shrubs might suggest a first-hand report of a Gudālī who was familiar with the southern part of Mauritania near the salt-mine of Awlīl. What could Banbawān mean? According to Muḥammad ibn Aḥmad Yūra, in his book of *Zenāgah* toponyms of the Trārzah, *Kitāb Ikhbār al-Akhbār*,

> "*In-Banba*. It has been said that its origin is In-Banban. *Banban* are *high and lofty uplands* [*al-anjād al-murtafiʿah* in the *Zenāgah* language], and it was said that it was a name given to a village [*qaṣr*] in Fūta."[59]

In-Banba, or Banbawān, is either a coincidence or a metathesis, yet the report of a herder of the Gudālah might well be the explanation for this most unusual toponym in the dune country of the *Zenāgah*.[60]

Thirdly, and I believe the most significantly, by the thirteenth century, when the Spaniards were well on their way to achieving the *Reconquista*, a new Messianic idea was abroad in Islam. A new Saharan *Mahdī* was eagerly awaited. Something of this Messianic feeling is detectable in the account of the arrival of Ibn Yāsīn amongst the Gudālah (and the Lamtūnah) in the writings of Ibn al-Athīr.

> "In this year one of their men named al-Jawhar, of the tribe of Gudāla, went to Ifrīqiya seeking to perform the Pilgrimage. He was a lover of religion and men of religion and on his way through al-Qayrawān met a *faqīh* with whom a group were studying *fiqh* and who is generally reckoned to have been Abū ʿImrān al-Fāsī. Al-Jawhar lent ear to what he had to say and was pleased by their circumstances. So, on his way back from the Pilgrimage he said to the *faqīh*: 'We have nothing of this in the desert except the *shahādatayn* and the prayer, which is limited to a few of the upper class. So send with me someone who may teach them the laws of Islam.' So he sent with him a man by the name of ʿAbdallāh b. Yāsīn al-Gazūlī, an upright and astute *faqīh*. He travelled with

him until they came to the tribe of Lamtūna, when al-Jawhar got down from his camel and took the bridle of ʿAbdallāh b. Yāsīn's camel as a sign of reverence for the law of Islam."

After Ibn Yāsīn is described as "One who bears the *Sunnah* of the Prophet of God", the two men then depart on their way. As they did so,

> "an old man looked upon them saying: '*Something will inevitably happen to this camel in the desert which will be mentioned through the whole world.*' Al-Jawhar and the *faqīh* reached Gudāla, al-Jawhar's tribe, and ʿAbdallāh b. Yāsīn called them and the tribes in their neighbourhood to accept the judgement of the Law."[61]

But the history of this new *Mahdī* would differ considerably from that of Ibn Yāsīn, the builder of a desert town, a thaumaturge in the deserts of the Sūdān, and a divine law giver. If we are to believe al-Bakrī, Ibn Yāsīn, himself, was not averse to pressing his Messianic pretensions. But this new *Mahdī* in the Western Sahara would be followed devotedly by the Gudālah. He would also be followed by the Gazūlah of the Jabal Banī and the Sūs. It seems that the Lamtūnah no longer had any place whatsoever in this updated design to rescue Spain from the infidel, and then spearhead the triumph of the Muslim armies which would march to Byzantium and the Holy Land.

The Lamtūnah had earlier failed to put an end to the *Reconquista* and the dynasties which had followed had done no better. It was now the task of the "rejected" Gudālah, and the Gazūlah, led, it would seem by a Yemenite of Qaḥṭān, a herald of the end of time, conveniently at that very moment when the "Yemenite" Banū Maʿqil were mingling in the Sūs with the Gazūlah, Lamṭah and Gudālah.

Al-Qurṭubī in his *al-Tadhkirah* furnishes graphic details of these events:

> "The Chapter regarding the *Mahdī*, his description, his name, his gift, his stay and his going forth with Jesus to assist him to fight the Anti-Christ . . . Regarding the sign of his departure, the twice taking of the allegiance and how he will fight the Sufyānī[62] and will slay him.

> "The *ḥadīth* of Umm Salamah and Abū Hurayrah has already been mentioned, namely, that the *Mahdī* will take the oath of

allegiance betwixt al-Rukn and al-Maqām. This makes it clear that the oath of allegiance will not occur hitherto. The situation is otherwise, since, it is reported, from the *ḥadīth* of Ibn Masʿūd and others of the Companions, that he will come forth at the end of time from the Furthest Maghrib. Victorious succour will precede him for forty miles. His banners will be white and yellow and within them signs will be written with the name of Allāh Almighty. No banner of his will be defeated. The unfurling aloft of these banners and their being sent forth will be at the sea shore *at a place called Māssah* [var. *Jabal Māsinah*][63] in the direction wherein the sun sets. He will tightly knot these banners through a people whereunto Allāh has taken the covenant of succour and of victory."[64]

Further on he writes:

"It is reported from the *ḥadīth* of Muʿāwiyah ibn Abī Sufyān, in a long tradition on the authority of the Prophet, that the latter said, 'After my time a peninsula called al-Andalus will be conquered and the people of unbelief will conquer [the believers]. They will take their possessions and most of their country. They will take captive their women-folk and their offspring and they will ravage and rape and destroy the houses and most of the land will revert to desert and wilderness. Most of the people will evacuate their homes and forsake their possessions and they [that is, the enemy] will capture most of the peninsula. Nothing will remain save a very small part. In the Maghrib there shall be a tumult and fear and hunger will prevail there, and high price. Feuding will be widespread and some of mankind will devour others. At that time a man of the Furthest Maghrib of the family of Fāṭimah, the daughter of the Messenger of God, will go forth. He is the *Mahdī* who will arise at the end of time and he will be the first of the conditions of the Hour."[65]

"The chapter regarding the conquest of Byzantium, from whence it shall be conquered. Its conquest will be the sign of the *sortie* of the Anti-Christ and the descent of Jesus and his slaying of the former.

"Verily, the *Mahdī*, when he goes forth in the Maghrib, as has been reported already, will have the people of al-Andalus come to him and say, 'O Friend of God, give help to the peninsula of al-Andalus. It is ruined and its people have been ravished and the people of infidelity and polytheism of the sons of [the Franks and] Byzantium[66] have conquered it.' Then he will send his letters to all the tribes of the Maghrib, that is to say, *the Qazūlah and the*

Gudālah [*Khudhālah and Qudhālah*] and others besides them from among the people of the Maghrib. . . .

فيقولون يا ولى اللّه انصر جزيرة الأندلس فقد تلفتْ وتلف أهلها
وتغلب عليها أهل الكفر والشرك من أبناء الروم فيبعث كتبه إلى جميع
قبائل المغرب وهم قزولة وخذالة وقذالة وغيرهم من القبائل من أهل
المغرب أن انصروا دين اللّه وشريعة محمد ﷺ فيأتون إليه من كل مكان
ويجيبونه ويقفون عند أمره ويكون على مقدّمة صاحب الخرطوم وهو
صاحب الناقة الغرّاء وهو صاحب المهدىّ وناصر دين الاسلام وولى اللّه
حقّاً

. . . [saying], 'Help the religion of Allāh and the *Sharī'ah* of Muḥammad, Allāh's blessing be upon him.' So they will come to him from every place and they will respond to him. They will halt at his bidding and at their head shall be the Master of the Proboscis [*Ṣāḥib al-Khurṭūm*], namely, the Lord of the *She Camel with the Blaze*. He will be the Companion of the *Mahdī* and the *Helper of the Religion of Islam* [*Nāṣir al-Dīn*],[67] and the Friend of God in truth. At that time, thirty thousand warriors, some on horse and others on foot, will swear the oath of allegiance to him, may Allāh be pleased with them. Those are the Almighty's party. Such are they and they alone will be the ones who will prosper. As in a sale, they have pledged their souls to Allāh and He is the Possessor of such excellence as surpasses all others in might. They will cross the sea [from the Maghrib] and they will reach Homs, which is the city of Seville. There the *Mahdī* will ascend the pulpit in the Congregational Friday mosque and he will preach an eloquent sermon. The people of al-Andalus will come to him and all those who are Muslims will give him the oath of allegiance. Then he will depart with all the Muslims towards the country [of the Franks and] of the Byzantines. There he will conquer seventy cities [of the Franks and] of the Byzantines. He will forcibly remove them from the hands of the enemy.

"Then the *Mahdī*, and those with him, will arrive at the Church of Gold and in it they will find riches and wealth. These the *Mahdī* will take and he will divide them equitably amongst the people. Then within it he will find the Ark of the Covenant [*tābūt al-sakīnah*] and the head cover [cope? *ghaffārah*] of Jesus, and the staff of Moses – peace be upon them both – and this staff is the one which Adam brought down from the Paradise of Eden when he was expelled from thence. Caesar, the ruler of Byzantium [Rome] had taken it from Jerusalem amidst the total of the captives when he took Jerusalem. He took all of it to the Church of Gold and it is there to this day. And when the *Mahdī* will take it, and when the Muslims take the staff, they will dispute over it, and each one will desire to take the staff. When Allāh desires that the people of Islam will come to their end in al-Andalus then He will forsake their banner and He will rob the men of percipience of their reason. They will divide the staff into four parts and each troop of soldiers amongst them will take one part. At that time they will be four troops of soldiers. When they act thus, then Allāh will take away the succour and the victory from them and difference will be acute and grave between them on account of that.

"Kaʿb al-Aḥbār[68] has said, 'The people of polytheism will triumph over them until they come to the sea, and Allāh will send an angel in the form of a herd of camels [*ibil*]. With these he [the *Mahdī*] will cross the dam built by Dhū'l-Qarnayn[69] especially for this purpose. The people will follow him until they come to the City of Persia, and the Byzantine will be behind them, and thus they will continue. When the Muslims traverse a stage, then the polytheists will traverse it likewise, until they reach the land of Egypt with the Byzantine behind them.' According to the *ḥadīth* of Ḥudhayfah, 'They will possess Egypt as far as Fayyūm and then they will withdraw.' Allāh Almighty knows best."

It was believed that all these martial exploits of the *Mahdī*, with his army of Sūsī Gazūlah and Río de Oro Gudālah and Maghribī Muslims, would have the company of a Yemenite Arab.[70] Al-Qurṭubī also explained:[71]

"The Messenger of God said: 'The last hour will not come until a man from Qaḥṭān will come forth. He will guide men with his staff'. Al-Bukhārī and Muslim reported on Abū Hurayrah's authority that the Messenger of God said: 'The Hour will not befall until a fire comes from the land of the Ḥijāz which will illumine the necks of the camels in Bosra.'"[72]

As all the above passages show, by the end of the thirteenth century the Western Saharans had been given an eminent, if not unique, role in the Messianic vision of many. These latter believed that a new "Almoravid movement" was the only salvation for the Muslims in Spain. It can hardly be doubted – and the writings of Ibn Khaldūn in both his *Kitāb al-ʿIbar* and his *Muqaddimah* confirm it – that a far more prominent, and less uncomplimentary, role was, by that time, given to the Gudālah in the earlier, and historical, Lamtūnah Almoravid movement of the eleventh century. The writings of Ibn Saʿīd

(1286–7), Ibn Abī Zarʿ (d. 1315), Ibn ʿIdhārī (d. 1312), and especially Ibn Kathīr (d. 1372) seem to show some trace of the Messianic vision of such writers as al-Qurṭubī. All show far greater regard for the Gudālah than the *Qāḍī* ʿIyāḍ, who, as one would expect, gave all the credit for the victory of the Almoravids to the Lamtūnah, the enemies of the Gudālah. All the rest of the story follows: the Gudālah retreat upon an island, the magical Gleaming Mountain of the Gudālah, and their proximity to Māssah *Ribāṭ*, where the *Mahdī* would summon them and unfurl his banners.[73]

By chance perhaps, or there may have been a significance, towards 1300, the Yemenite Banū Maʿqil began to settle, control and dominate the Gazūlah and Gudālah tribes in the Sūs and on the northern border of the Western Sahara.

The Banū Maʿqil unite the Gazūlah and the Lamṭah

The *Ribāṭ* of Māssah had become a rallying centre for rebels at the very end of the Almoravid Empire, when the Lamtūnah kingdom was on the point of collapse beneath the assault of the Almohad forces led by ʿAbd al-Mu'min ibn ʿAlī. Following the capture of Marrakech in 1147 the Almohads extended their authority over the whole of the Maghrib but they were faced with revolt by Muḥammad ibn ʿAbdallāh ibn Hūd, a native of Salé, who, with the title of "the guide" (*al-Hādī*) took up arms in the Sūs. At Māssah *Ribāṭ* he assembled a band of criminals and vagabonds and he succeeded in preaching his doctrines to the Berber tribes to the north of Māssah and as far as the Wādī Darʿah and Sijilmāsah. He thwarted an Almohad attack, commanded at that time by a turn-coat Massūfī called Yaḥyā Angamar. This provoked a further Almohad assault on the *Ribāṭ* commanded by Shaykh Abū Ḥafṣ ʿUmar, who had earlier subdued the Gazūlah. Despite a force of sixty thousand infantrymen and seven hundred horsemen, al-Hādī, the rebel "guide", was deserted by his men and in Dhū'l-Ḥijjah 1147 his movement was crushed.

The expeditions of Abū Ḥafṣ against the Sūs, against the Haskūrah and against Sijilmāsah made a deep impact on the Western Sahara. Refugees found a safe haven there from the Maṣmūdah power which had destroyed the Almoravid Empire.

The sequence of events which led to the domination of the Sūs and Darʿah region by the Banū Maʿqil may have been heralded by events which took place around the city of Tilimsān in Algeria about 1360. When the Marīnid Sulṭān of Morocco, Abū ʿInān, died, Abū Ḥamū, the Sulṭan of the ʿAbd al-Wādites, occupied this city. The Marīnids counter-attacked and he sought asylum among the Banū Maʿqil in that region. From that time they supported Abū Ḥamū. In recompense they demanded from this prince one part of the plains which surrounded the city. When the Marīnid Sulṭān, Abū Sālim, died in 1361/2 there was tumult in the Maghrib and the Banū Maʿqil played no little part in it. Shortly after, their chief, Aḥmad ibn Raḥḥū, fell out with Abū Ḥamū and in order to satisfy his grievances invaded the territory of Tilimsān.

The Banū Maʿqil were now so powerful that the Marīnids were compelled to pay them a large amount from the taxes which were collected from the region of the Darʿah and they gave them the possession of the territories which depended on Tedla and al-Mādin. These controlled the southern passes which led into the interior of Morocco where they spent their springs and summers in order to gather corn. The city of Sijilmāsah passed into the hands of the *Aḥlāf* confederates,[74] the descendants of ʿImrān and Munabbāt, both of them brothers in the Dhawī Manṣūr branch of the Banū Maʿqil. Throughout the Darʿah region the Maʿqil imposed dues and taxes on the towns and the villages and this was over and above the land grant (*Iqṭāʿ*)[75] which had been bestowed on them by the Marīnid Sulṭānate there. Other members of the *Aḥlāf* roamed the deserts with their herds and, on occasions, they interrupted the Sūdān caravans, or made *sorties* against the towns and oases which were located deep in the Western Sahara.

As for the Sūs, the reduction of the Almohad bases in the far south-west and Anti Atlas had paved the way for the Maʿqil. When the Almohads had collapsed, a rebel, who claimed descent from the first Arab families which had settled there (*ʿArab al-Fatḥ*) ʿAlī ibn Yiddir al-Zukundarī, who has been mentioned on p. 161, became the *de facto* lord of the Sūs. But he soon became involved in a feud with the nomad Gazūlah. Finding the task of subduing them beyond his powers, he asked for the help of the Banū Mukhtār, who were Rqayṭāt Maʿqil. They entered from Algeria, bringing their families and herds.

The Banū Maʿqil found the Sūs to their liking. There was plenty of pasturage for grazing and the other nomads were relatively few. According to Ibn Khaldūn, they subdued the Gazūlah and they "assimilated" them (*wa-ghalabūhum wa-'aṣārūhum fī jumlatihim*). They also subdued the smaller towns along the valley of the Nūn which paid them tribute, and the dynasty of ʿAlī ibn Yiddir al-Zukundurī found it hard to curb them. Some of the Maʿqil opposed the Marīnids, others were their allies, and those who found favour with them were in receipt of the *Iqṭāʿ* as well as the local taxes which they collected.

Ibn Khaldūn provides a detailed description of the whole region.[76] He explains that the whole province was outside the control of the Marīnids. The Banū Maʿqil appropriated the taxes levied (*jibāyah*) and the subject people were divided up amongst them. The latter included the nomad Berbers. These were divided up amongst the Banū Maʿqil and formed an auxiliary force (*khawlan lil-ʿaskar*), furnishing the model for the later recruitment and service, bondage even, of the *Zenāgah* to the Awlād Ḥassān in Mauritania. These auxiliaries had to participate in Maʿqil military expeditions. The nomad Gazūlah marched with the Banū Ḥassān whilst the Shabbānāt Ḥassānīs were accompanied by the Zaqan and Lakhs, which were both branches of the Lamṭah.

It is clear that by 1400, and probably some while prior to this, the Gazūlah and the Lamṭah had become intermixed with the Banū Maʿqil. The same irreversible process involving the Gudālah and the Lamtūnah and the Ḥassānī groups of the Awlād Dulaym, the Awlād Bū Sbāʿ and others, had already begun a century later. The nomads increased in number, some Berber, some Arab, and most intermarried the one with the other. They took advantage of the commercial

Map 6 The route for the gold trade and the Spanish bases in the region of Wād Nūn and the Sāqiyah.

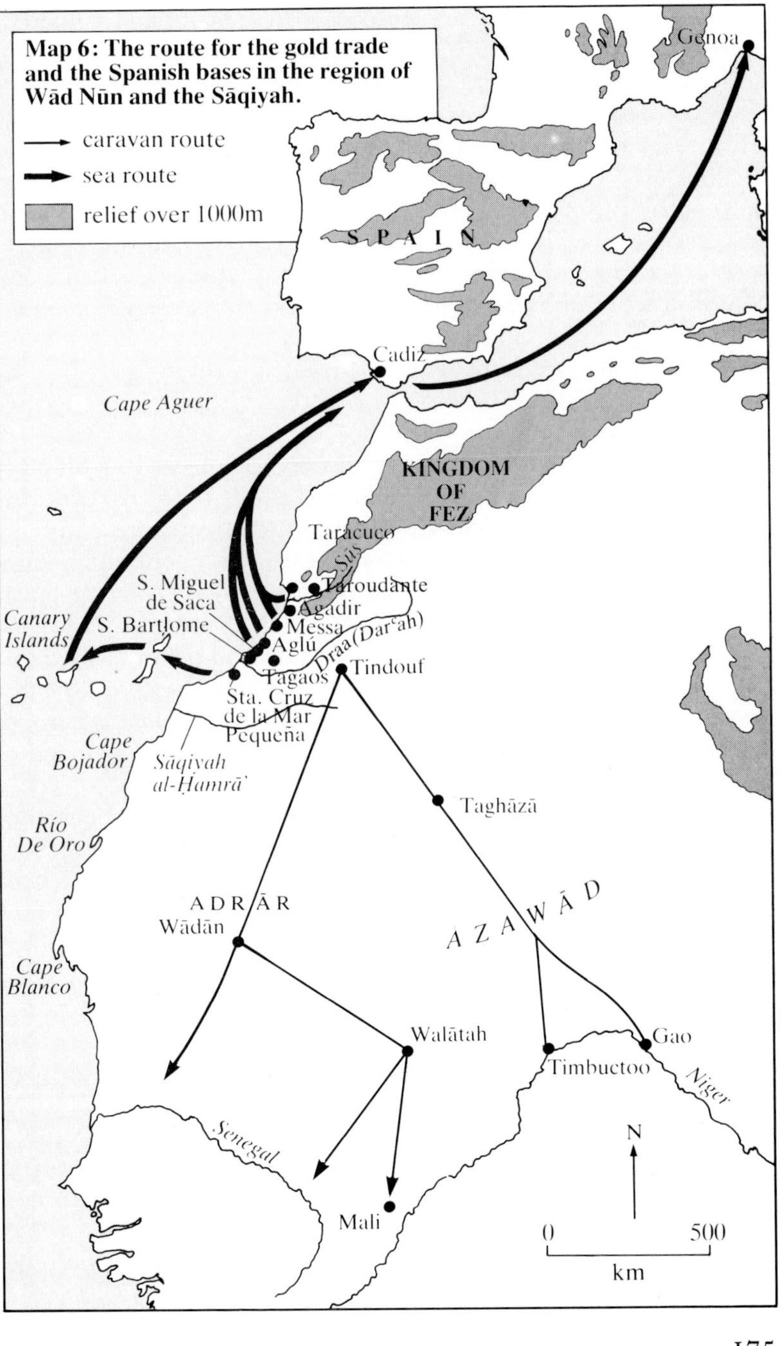
Map 6: The route for the gold trade and the Spanish bases in the region of Wād Nūn and the Sāqiyah.
caravan route
sea route
relief over 1000m
Genoa
SPAIN
Cadiz
Cape Aguer
KINGDOM OF FEZ
Taracuco
Sūs
S. Miguel de Saca
Taroudante
Agadir
Canary Islands
S. Bartlome
Messa
Aglú
Draa (Darʿah)
Tindouf
Tagaos
Sta. Cruz de la Mar Pequeña
Cape Bojador
Sāqiyah al-Ḥamrā'
Taghāzā
Río De Oro
ADRĀR
Wādān
AZAWĀD
Cape Blanco
Walātah
Gao
Timbuctoo
Niger
Senegal
N
Mali
0
500
km

routes which led southwards and northwards. They furnished their material needs from the leather workers and smiths and craftsmen in gold and silver whose families, many of them Jewish, had lived in the *quṣūr*, before the days of the Almoravids, in Nūl Lamṭah, Darʿah, Kawkadam and Sijilmāsah, and they supplied their sustenance from the date palms, the desert game, the herds of the pastoralists and the salt caravans. There was also the prospect of mercenary service and employment as caravan guides, since the Massūfah *takshīf* was now, sometimes, the Maʿqilī *ʿaqabah dalīl*, who, in the language of the *ḍād* in the *Klām Ḥassān*, lightened the boredom of his Saharan journeyings in verse which rephrased the love poetry of the ʿUdhrī poets, or the odes of Labīd.[77]

Islam and Christendom were shortly to engage in a bloody struggle on this coast from Māssah to the Río de Oro around the fortress of Santa Cruz de Mar Pequeña, and the Sāqiyah al-Ḥamrā' was to become a haven of refuge for scholars, some Arab and some Berber, who had been expelled from the land of al-Andalus which had seen no Gudālah and no *Mahdī* to rescue it for Islam. The sword of Islam was to be unleashed on the coast itself of the Western Sahara between 1434 and 1638. In the end the Spaniards were to relinquish their last territory in the Western Sahara, although its liberation would take many many centuries.

When this came about the Maʿqil Arabs had long been the masters of this Western Sahara. The intermarriage of Berber and Arab was, by then, a historical reality along this border of *Dār al-Islām*. On the eve of the *geste* of Santa Cruz, the north of the Western Sahara was advanced in its Arabisation. Further south, in the land of the *Zenāgah*, the coast was desolate, primitive and little touched, as yet, by the Arabic culture of Mauritanian towns, such as Walātah, far in the interior. It was fearful, just as Defoe described it in Robinson Crusoe, "Indeed, for near a hundred miles together upon this coast, we saw nothing but a waste uninhabited country by day, and heard nothing but howlings and roarings of wild beasts by night." In the north the social forces which were to transform the south had already taken shape. The Spanish historian, Antonio Rumeu de Armas, has succinctly referred to them in his *España en el Africa Atlantica* (Madrid, 1956):[78]

"From Māssah up to the river Sāqiyah al-Ḥamrā', there stretched the lands which were inhabited by the powerful Gazūlah confederation. As the transit region between the steppe and the desert that was a land which was multiple and varied, with sedentary agriculturalists in the small valleys and oases, transhumant shepherds in the pasturages and mountains, and, above all, nomads in the desolate plains of the desert. The agriculturalists dominated in Aglū, Tiznit, Ifnī and the oases of the Wād Nūn, the herders on the sloping buttresses of the Anti Atlas and the Jabal Banī, and the nomads in the desert zone of the present-day Tiknah, between the Wād Nūn and the Sāqiyah al-Ḥamrā'. In those lands, as we have said, there dwelt diverse tribes of Banū Gazūlah mixed with Lamṭah. The Arab Maʿqil deserve special mention. They were invaders, who, in the thirteenth century had introduced themselves there by force though without imposing their authority. Two centuries of co-habitation had established a certain fraternal relationship between Berbers and Arabs, in language, tradition and custom."

Clearly apparent from the gradual dominance of the Maʿqil over most of the Western Sahara, and the pressure of Christendom on the coast, was the evolution of a situation which made imperative the Saʿdian expedition across this same Sahara to the Western Sūdān, possibly the most important event of all which was to lead to the Arabisation of the Western Saharans: its impact wide, its axis eastward and its result a deeper and deeper penetration of the Awlād Ḥassān from the Darʿah region and the Southern Sūs towards Timbuctoo and towards the Adrār-n-Īfōghās.

This historical movement is well summarised by Zakari Dramani-Issifou in his study of the Moroccans and the Songhai in the sixteenth century:

"When at the beginning of the sixteenth century, the Saʿdians undertook to gain the mastery of Morocco, it was upon the branches of the Dhawī Manṣūr Maʿqil and the Shābbānāt that they put their reliance initially – both as Arabs, and secondly, because they were the uncontested masters of the caravan 'posts' between the Tāfilālt and the Darʿah. Thus, the Portuguese Christians and the Maʿqil Arabs and Muslims, constituted for the Saʿdians upon their accession powerful adversaries, both on the political and economic planes. Their conjugate actions, although in no way concerted, were an obstacle which disorganised, to the detriment of the Saʿdians, the happy flow of caravan commerce in

> the Western Sahara. The elimination of this obstacle and the control of the Saharan commerce, became imperative for the realisation of the Saʿdian undertaking."[79]

He concludes:

> "There is no doubt that the trans-Saharan traffic along its western axes in the direction of the furthest Maghrib was very seriously upset at the end of the fifteenth century and in the first half of the sixteenth, to the profit of the eastern axes. This situation is explained by the fact of the political and social troubles which prevailed in Morocco, on the one hand, and, on the other, by the conjugate action of the Portuguese on the Atlantic coasts between Santa Cruz of the Cap de Gue and the river Senegal, and by raiding bedouin of the Lamṭah and the Gazūlah to the north of the Ijjil salt mines. Finally, there were the Maʿqil Arab tribes between Sijilmāsah and Māssah. Having grasped, at an early stage, the economic importance of these trans-Saharan routes which escaped them, the Saʿdians, after consolidating their political power in Morocco, did not tarry in the undertaking of a series of actions, the ultimate goal of which was the undisputed control of the commercial axes which led to the land of gold and of slaves."[80]

Appendix I

A description of the Arabs of the Western Sahara by Wylde Clerke, an agent and a merchant at Santa Cruz (Ifni) which is included in a letter sent to John Aubrey (the author of Brief Lives*) dated 5 November 1678.*

For the Deserts, have informed my selfe of Severall Moores who have travelled hence to Guiny that there is a Certaine sandy deserte which affords nothing, of about 3 weekes Journey, over which they pass. They have Certaine Guides which goe by the Starrs, there being no tracke or path, & often many of them perish, being overwhelmed in the Sands, which with the wind is carride as the waves in the Sea. On the borders of which deserte, on this Side, abundance of Ostriches are there, which they runn downe with horses, choosing the Hottest day they can, at which time she Soonest tires by reason of Heate. And when they have killed them, the Flesh they Eate & Feathers sell to Jews, that goe amongst them heare, as commodity. The Arabs that live in those parts neither plowe or So; their food is cammells milke with the Flesh which they order in this manner. They take a young cammell & kill him, cutting all the Flesh into long thin peeces, & drie it in the Sunn, & when 'tis very dry They beate it to a powder & mixe it with cammells milke & have no other food. I have a man of Forty yeares of age, who told me <he> never Eate a piece of bread in his liffe; & further informed me that he very rarely had any Evacuation, but once in 3 or 4 days, & that it was so Generally with them, & tearming those peopell Stinkards, observing them go oute a daye. As for Elephants, never heard of any on this side Guiny. Sir, hope you will accept this at present, but for future shall note what may heare or come to hand worthy of observation, & think my selfe worthily recompensed by your correspondence, which is highly Esteemed of by,

Sir, your most humble Servant,

Wylde Clerke.

(I am grateful to Dr J. Bynon for this reference, which is taken from John Aubrey, *Three Prose Works*, Centaur Press, 1972, p. 483.)

Appendix II

Taysīr al-Fattāḥ fī'l-Dhabb ʿan Ahl al-Ṣalāḥ

A work by Shaykh Muḥammad Ignan Wa-n-Fadasen al-Sūqī al-Gunahānī al-ʿArabī, addressed to ʿAbd al-Kel Gefī, a scholar of the Kel Geres. Edited and abridged by Muḥammad Ḥabba ibn Muḥammad Aḥmad al-Sharīf al-Idrīsī al-Sūqī in the year 1970.

Reference has already been made to Shaykh Muḥammad Ignan Wa-n-Fadasen in Chapter 8, pages 126–7. This epistle of his is a late nineteenth-century composition in Classical Arabic. Some of it is in rhymed prose. It typifies the fluent Arabic style achieved by many of the scholars who lived amongst the Moors and the western Tuareg. Despite the loss of books and manuscripts on account of raiding, the author shows that he has such an encyclopedic knowledge of *fiqh* and *taṣawwuf*, and of the masters in these disciplines, that his own memory serves as his library. The composition demonstrates how Classical Arabic had become the only language which could be used for correspondence between scholars and some of the lettered princes in the south-western Sahara region before the arrival of the French. The quality and profundity of this work should be compared with the summary dismissal and tart remarks made by Mungo Park about these scholars, see page 71.

بسم الله الرحمان الرحيم وصلّى الله على طه محمّد الكريم وصلّى الله
على آله وصحبه أجْمعين وسلّم ، الحمد للّه الذي أحقّ الحقّ فأمر بتقديره
وتبيينه في الفضلاء وأبطل الباطل فاجتنبه العقلاء وهدى من وفّقه بفضله
وأضلّ من خذله بعدله والصّلاة والسّلام على من نزل عليه القرآن فبيّن
مجمله أي تبيين وعلى آله وأصحابه الذين فصّلوا ما أجمل في القرآن
والحديث وعيّنوا مدلولها أي تعيين ومن تبعهم من الأئمة الذين دوّنوا
مدلولها أي تدوين ومن تبعهم بإحسان وتحسين إلى يوم الجزاء والدّين
وبعد فيســـلّم الشيخ محمّد إكنن ونفدسن السوقىّ ثمّ الكنهانّى العربى
سلاما ما به غرار ويحاذيه توقير وإبرار سلاما يعمّ كلّ من ينتبه إذا نبه
ويتقطّر لتمويه المموّه اذا موّه .

In the name of Allāh, the Merciful and Compassionate. The blessing and peace of Allāh be upon Ṭāhā, Muḥammad the noble [Prophet]. The blessing of Allāh be upon his family and upon his Companions, one and all, and may He give them His peace. Praise be to Allāh who has established the reality of the Truth and who has commanded that its power and its clear statement should be imparted to those to whom preference has been shown. It is He who has invalidated the false and the untruthful so that men of reason and knowledge have avoided it. It is He who has rightly guided those upon whom He has bestowed the favour of His grace and He has caused to err those whom He has forsaken in His justice.

Blessing and peace be upon him to whom Allāh sent down the Koran and who made its content plain. How clearly and how wonderfully he did so. May blessings fall upon his household and upon his Companions who have comprehensively stated what had been succinctly expressed in the Koran and in the *Ḥadīth.* They meticulously marked and established fixedly their content with such a precision as to evoke marvel and astonishment. May blessings also descend upon those who followed after them, those amongst the *Imāms* of the faith who recorded their content upon parchment, a worthy record made by their hands. May blessings descend upon their successors likewise. May Allāh favour and grant them His charity until the Day of Recompense and of Religion.

Shaykh Muḥammad Ignan Wa-n-Fadasen al-Sūqī al-Gunahānī al-ʿArabī sends his greetings. In this, his greeting, no lack of regard or respect may be perceived. He expresses a greeting which encompasses everyone who is aroused if he is warned, a greeting which, so to speak, fumigates the air of him who falsifies.

This greeting is specifically addressed to ʿAbd al-Kel Gefī of the Kel Geres of Aïr, al-Yatāmī. I notify you, *O ʿAbd*, that I was compelled to write to you for two reasons. The first was on account of how [honourable] I imagined you to be. It was due to what I had heard about you, and due to what I had beheld of the sign of a true piety from you, observed at an earlier time when I had visited you. I had believed you to be a noble and orthodox *Sunnite*. Now the noble *Sunnite* is that man who is desirous of performing good works; yea who hurries to perform them. Because of that I am writing this letter to you. I have requested that my need should be fulfilled, by the despatch of the [pilfered] books of the Kel Es-Sūq to me. Acts which fulfil such needs are the good deeds which are demanded of the noble *Sunnite*, one [or more] of the good deeds by which blessing and prosperity are hoped for and sought for. As the Almighty has said [in His holy book], "Do that which is good, haply ye may prosper".[1]

In the Muḥammadan Covenants [*al-ʿUhūd al-Muḥammadiyyah*], by the Shaykh and knower of Allāh, 'Alī ʿAbd al-Wahhāb al-Shaʿrānī,[2] it is written,

> "We have been ordered to observe the general covenant from the Messenger of Allāh – His blessing and His peace be upon him – that, in truth, the performance of acts of obedience in principle stem from the belief that the human soul will be recompensed in the World to Come. None has attained the accomplishment of that save him, who, with a knowledge of Allāh, carries out the commands of the canonic *Sharīʿah* in obedience to the command of Allāh, and not merely out of the desire for some reward in the hereafter."

Shaʿrānī also said,

> "O my brother, carry out and fulfil the needs and the requirements of the Muslims for the sake of Allāh, the Almighty. If on account of it you look for a reward then ask the Almighty for it, as you make known your need. You cannot dispense with His grace, but be wary of accepting the gift on that account, more especially if it be from womenfolk and from the poor."[3]

Such, then, are his words. He goes on to say,

> "Shaykh Jalāl al-Dīn al-Maḥallī, the commentator of the *Minhāj*,[4] may Almighty Allāh show him His mercy, used to serve all the old men and all the old women of the quarter who were frail and helpless. He used to buy the requirements which they needed from the market. Sometimes a man who was in need would ask him and he would leave off teaching and arise in order to fulfil the need of that man. An old lady asked him to buy oil for her from the market, so he arose from his lesson. They said to him, 'Will you forsake the lesson on account of an old lady?' 'Yes', he replied, 'her

need takes preference over yours.' It was usual for him to go forth in order to fulfil the needs of the old ladies of his quarter with no shoes on his feet. He would say about that, 'Purity has its origin in the earth beneath.' He used to go out at night in the rain, with his belt tightly bound, and he would say, 'Whoever has need of a fire then I shall bring it from my oven.' He visited the old ladies of the quarter each in her turn, may Allāh Almighty be pleased with him. Shaykh Fakhr al-Dīn al-Nafīsī[5] remarked one day when they said to him, 'How is it that you give priority to the purchase of hot oil or to the bringing of a fire over and above the teaching of learning to us?' He answered, 'The essential factor is the offering of joy. When he who is in need is brought joy, through the fulfilment of his need, then it is of greater worth than what you receive by the teaching of academic knowledge.' "

It is reported by the two Shaykhs [Bukhārī and Muslim], and others besides these two, [in a tradition] with an unbroken chain of authorities [*marfūʿ*]. "Whoever has need of his brother, then Allāh is to be found in his need", and, "Whosoever relieves the worldly care of a Muslim, then Allāh Almighty will relieve him of a care in the after life." Al-Ḥāfiẓ al-ʿAbdarī has said, "Whosoever walks with one who is oppressed until he makes good his right, then Allāh will establish his feet firmly on the straight path on the day when other feet will slip." Al-Ḥafiẓ al-ʿAbdarī said, "I did not see this addition in any of its original [quotations]", and it has only been reported by Ibn Abī'l-Dunyā and al-Iṣbahānī[6]. In the readings of Muslim, Abū Dāwūd, al-Tirmidhī, al-Nasā'ī, Ibn Mājah and al-Ḥākim, with an unbroken chain of authority, are these words, "Whosoever relieves the affliction of a believer from one of the afflictions on the Day of Judgement, Allāh Almighty is the Helper of His servant, as long as that servant is the helper of his brother." Al-Ṭabarānī reported, together with Abū'l-Shaykh, in an unbroken chain of authorities, the following tradition, "Verily Allāh Almighty has a group of beings whom He has created. He created them to serve the needs of mankind. People in fear will come to them for a refuge in the hour of their needs and their necessities. Those beings will be the ones who will be safe from the afflictions of Allāh."[7]

The following tradition was reported by Abū'l-Shaykh ibn Ḥabbār,[8] and by others, in an unbroken chain of authority, "Whosoever goes forth to fulfil the need of his brother until he has made it easy for him, and he has accomplished it, [Allāh] will shade him with seventy-five thousand angels who will pray blessings upon his name, and they will pray for him, if it be the morning, until he enters upon the evening, and if it be in the evening until he goes forth on the following morning."

O ʿAbd, I had sent a letter to you in the first instance because of those things contained in these traditions and verses, urging and encouraging the performance of acts of bounty, kindness and welfare, and the fulfilment of a Muslim's needs. You have disappointed my belief in you and you have made me despair of any response to a favour which has been asked [of you]. I do not know whether that is due to the greed which you have to possess the books of the Kel Es-Sūq, or whether you envy them or have an enmity which you harbour against them on account of these books being your spoil. You have been accustomed to raiding the Kel Es-Sūq since time immemorial, and you have regarded their property as lawful, as you yourself declared it to be so in your letter. You addressed me in a manner which was unacceptable to the meanest among the Muslims, unworthy of the most ignorant amongst them. How then can it be accepted by the *ʿulamāʾ* who ply their trade in the two sciences, the canonic *Sharīʿah* and the mystic *Ḥaqīqah*; men who are the masters of the eight sciences of Literature and the sciences of the *Sharʿ* and the Canonic Sciences, those who discharge many of the arrows of Islam included in the [Koranic] verse, "The believers have prospered" . . . to the end of the verse,[9] together with the sharp barbs of Islam which are likewise to be found in these passages.

You have judged us to be guilty of infidelity. You have charged us with bearing the guilt of Fālij ibn Khallāwah,[10] although in matters concerning him we are quite innocent. Our innocence is like that of the wolf in regard to the blood of Joseph. In this matter you have stubbornly persisted in your error. You have disclosed to me knowledge of what lay on your conscience. All that you hide within you gets the better of your tongue. From every vessel oozes the [foul] liquid which it contains. The musk of iniquity cannot be rid of the odour of its evil, nor can a shoot from an *ʿIḍāh* tree be easily lopped.[11] Does any tree other than an ash-tree produce a *Khaṭṭī* spear?[12]

Then *O ʿAbd* you informed me of the evil within your innermost thoughts, by judging us to be infidels, us, and the likes of us from all those who have mixed with the Tuareg. All are likewise infidels. You single us out, we the company of the Kel Es-Sūq. However, between us and those others there is a clear distinction as we shall make clear to you if Allāh Almighty so wills it. It will be accomplished by that thing, the content of which you are unaware of. Nor have you any inkling of the intentions of the citers of it, nor of the intention of the citer towards the asker. Besides, you know not him who addressed the letter to the one who cites it. The likes of you have surrendered to a whim to distort its message and to interpret it wilfully and heretically within the faith. This fancy of yours, and of your colleagues, has gravely influenced you, so that you make and pass judgements by it, despite the fact that you, and the likes of you, are quite unfit and unqualified to pass judgement by anything, whatever it may be, since you have no cognisance of the nature of the evidence, nor the lack of it, neither have you distinguished between the general and the particular, nor between the loose and the tied, nor between the universal and the individual, nor between the substance of the text and its outward presentation. You have not learnt the conditions which apply to him who judges and who draws inferences, and so on and so forth . . . for it is unknown to all save to him who has a comprehensive knowledge of the science of the *Sharīʿah* and the Canonic Sciences. All of that which deceived you was due to your attachment to the branches [of the law], notwithstanding the fact that your obsessive attachment to them, unless it be from sheer necessity, is not permitted. Indeed, the *ʿulamāʾ* have declared that the attachment of him who has no true knowledge of the purport of learning is like the attachment of the ass's head to a nose-bag empty of barley.

Furthermore, they have declared that no reliance can be placed upon the understanding of him who masters the skill of the science of logic, and likewise in those sciences other than these two [aforementioned]. In truth all of them are closely tied together. None can know one unless he knows the others. *O ʿAbd*, I have despaired on account of what you faced me with in regard to the idea of the fulfilment of that [Muslim] need, "since the Muslim, no doubt, finds it hard to fulfil the need of the *unbeliever*", as it so alleged.

I was accordingly in some ignorance as to how to phrase my answer to you. I found myself in the middle betwixt two extremes. And then it became clear to me that a retort to what you had written to me would be of some kind as to help the Faith. *To help the Faith is something which is recommended, and to neglect that help and to forsake it is to be indifferent to its claims.* So then and there it was my appointed duty to undertake the defence of the Faith and the defence of the honour of the Muslims, their properties and their life-blood. If Allāh so wills, I shall furnish you with an answer which will convince and which will assuage the thirst of ignorance. It will be sufficient to satisfy that one who is attentive when he is awakened, and who follows his path backwards to the truth when it is established and explained, and who listens with both his ears when he is made to hear it, he who is chided, until the light of the day is made clear to him and he sees it with both his eyes. Then doubt will depart, similarly indifference, from the men of indifference to the Faith. Here I quote the words of ʿUmar ibn ʿAbd al-ʿAzīz, al-ʿAbbāsī,[13] "If the truth will not put them to right, then Allāh cannot do so either." A poet said, "It is my responsibility to scatter the pearls in their treasure houses, but it is not my responsibility if the cows show no understanding."

By this my retort and answer I do not seek to argue [with you]. Rather, its purpose is to be a help to the Faith. No indeed, for I had deemed an argument with you to be a vile pastime and I had judged it to be a wearisome task, in view of what has been said in Prophetic *Ḥadīth*, "Leave off argument and contention, for verily the disputer will end in total loss, such is his fate." In the Muḥammadan Covenants [*al-ʿUhūd al-Muḥammadiyyah*] we have been called upon to obey the general covenant from the Messenger of Allāh, the Almighty, the blessing and peace of Allāh be upon him, namely, that we should not enter into an argument over any of the learning of the *Sharīʿah* unless it be in order to assist the Faith, and it should be on the condition that it is done so with complete sincerity, guided by the presence of Allāh Almighty in that aim, which is based upon the discovery and the disclosure of proofs and witnesses and not on suspicion, hypocrisy, heedlessness and mere guesswork, or with an attempt to be better than one's opponents, from amongst the great men of our *Madhhab*, and others apart from them.

The two Shaykhs [Bukhārī and Muslim] have reported, and so also have others, by a chain of authorities, the following tradition, "The most detestable of men to Allāh Almighty is he who takes the most delight in defeating an opponent in an argument." O God, so be it, unless it be to correct the one who clings to a heresy [*bidʿah*] amongst us, one which has neither basis in the Book of God nor in the *Sunnah*. It is our duty to refute his case openly, and this for the sake of Allāh, His Messenger and for the believers. Nonetheless, your circumstance, and that of others who are like you, does *not* in fact justify attention. It does so only because of a necessity and because you have uttered [vile] words and you have blurted them out inconsiderately. You bring fables and delusions, you offer muddle and error; I have not experienced the like anywhere else, nor has the judge, nor the debater, nor one who follows an argument determinedly, nor by him who confirms, nor who denies, *the erroneous fact and information which will cause others to err in the religion*. All the above does not take into account the madness found in many stories which are reported, indeed, you totally lack knowledge of the case and its demands, what is necessary in it, what is called for, deemed of little worth, thought baseless, given preference, commended, pointed out, sought after, thanked for, fitting for being dealt with by humanity, and the like. These things which are found to be essential are connected with rulings and judgements. They determine whether matters which are false or base are in question. You know nothing about proofs, nor those matters which supply evidence or analogies, nor causes, nor points which are decisive, nor the difference between the evidence which is corroborative or concomitant as opposed to another which is disconnected. Nay, you totally lack knowledge of that thing which ensures the avoidance of error and the false step when comprehending the sought-for intention, or employing speech which is applicable to the dictate of the circumstances and the like. Neither are you aware of the distinction between the truth and the lie, nor the distinction between the actual basis of authority and that which is merely metaphorical. Indeed you have no idea as to how to cover one meaning and one content by varied turns of phrase. You do not know the difference between the proof which is palpably apt, and the proof which is implied, and the proof which is a necessary consequence, and so on and so forth, from those sundry sciences which are not to the liking of him who seeks for peace and who has not been disturbed in such matters, one who has not disdained to speak the Arabian tongue nor who has disdained to determine that its content is such and such after getting to know it well, grasping it correctly and knowing it thoroughly with a taste for its savour, albeit he may not have fully grasped its complexities.

I shall make clear to you, if Allāh Almighty so wills it, the substance of those things which you have cited and from which you have sought evidence against us. I shall do so, sentence by sentence, and word by word, until I shall draw out the scorpions of controversy and the vipers of error from their lairs. I shall do this by the "feline species" of sound identification, and the truth, so that the *Sunnah* of Muḥammad will last for ever while the heresy and *Bidʿah* of the Kel Gefī will die and will vanish for ever. Here then is a composition which contains my response to your letter and which exceeds the requirements of your misguidance. It is fitting that it should be titled:

The facilitation of the Divine in regard to the protection of the devout – although they have said that "Whosoever writes a book or recites a poem, opens his mind and heart thereby to the people. If it be sound then he will attain his goal, but if it is faulty then he will be charged for the committing of foul actions." They have also said, "A man will continue to enjoy comfort and ease in his affairs as long as he neither recites verse nor writes a book." Ḥasan,[14] may Allāh be pleased with him, said, "Poetry is nothing but the mind of a man which he presents to the assemblies, whether shrewdly or foolishly." I say, in Allāh Almighty lies success for what one hopes for and upon Him rests guidance to the straight path, by the high rank of him [Muḥammad] His Lord willed him to attain the aim of what he hoped for, by calling him, "O Prophet" and "O Messenger".

The replies of al-Maghīlī al-Tilimsānī

Regarding the saying of al-Maghīlī [in his answers to the Askiyā] as you allege, "As for the undertaking of a raid against those who commit acts of war [*al-muḥāribūn*], then this cannot be avoided";[15] this is a sentence [in Arabic] which is composed of a subject and a predicate and a protasis and an apodosis. The subject is "raid". Here it is a verbal noun, annexed to the object of a verbal sentence, the subject of which is unexpressed. The subject is in fact a vocative suffix, in the second person, namely "your" [that is, "your raid"], and the specific person who is addressed in this manner is specifically stated, namely, al-Ḥājj Askiyā, the *Imām* who was noted for his justice, whose *Imāmate* was wholly effectual and whose rule was widespread in the Maghrib. The *Imām* is the person who is addressed regarding the raid against the *muḥāribūn*. After it come conditions which I shall make clear to you, if Allāh permits. The word *al-muḥāribūn*, "those who commit acts of war", is the object of the action. The definite article, *al-*, [*muḥāribūn*] is used to indicate a precise indication of an individual, *al-lām lil-ʿahd*,[16] like the use of the definite article in the [Koranic] verse, "Lo they were both in *the* cave",[17] or the definite article in "*the* holy valley, *al-Wādī'l-Muqaddas*", and the definite article in "Lo they will give you the oath of allegiance beneath *the* tree", or, for the sake of yet another reminder, in these words of the Almighty in the Koran, "In it is the lamp of *the* lamp" . . . to the end of the verse.[18] Where the definite article of this type is employed it does *not* indicate a *general term*. Rather, it is employed specifically; while the meaning in the evidence and the judgement presented are of general application.

What is meant here, then by *al-muḥāribūn*, "those who commit acts of war", are *the infidels*. In the same way, al-Maghīlī used the expression "from those Muslims", in this statement, since *were they* [*the muḥāribūn*] *to be Muslims* and they had other Muslims, it would not be sound to specify these latter Muslims by their adherence to Islam, while those others [*the muḥāribūn*] were specified alone by their warlike activities. It would not be sound if Islam and Muslim were attributes which applied to them equally. Because immoral behaviour does not [alone] nullify the name of belief according to the *Ahl al-Sunnah*.

The evidence is further supported by that which was said by al-Burzulī,[19] as quoted by ʿAbd al-Ḥaqq, "As for the properties of Muslims when they reside under the rule of an infidel, then if the Muslims take them as booty" . . . and so on. There is also evidence in support if one reads what the Askiyā said in connection with his question, "What will your answer be in regard to the *muḥāribūn* from amongst the Fulani and others who are amongst them, the Massūfah and others, alleging that they are Muslims and that they dwell with them . . . and so on." Look closely at these words, thou scribe, and behold the meaning of the expression, *al-muḥāribūn*. In this context it means *the infidels*. This Askiyā was the *Imām* of *our land*. He was among the pupils of *our* forebears. We are qualified experts in regard to his history and the information regarding the novelty of his circumstances. He was an *Imām* in the most complete sense, and so too in the common and the general sense. He put this office into practice. The just *Imām* is the one to whom is assigned the task of raiding the *muḥāribūn* who are beneath his authority. The words of Khalīl "the just *Imām*" and "the raiding by the *Imām* for disobedience against Allāh" clearly show this. Raiding of the *muḥāribūn* is derived from the chapter which is concerned with changing the ways of the reprehensible by dealing him a blow and a punishment, by act of slaughter and by seizing his possessions.[20] This changing of the ways of the reprehensible is one of the tasks of the Sulṭān whose authority is spread abroad in the earth.

According to some of the commentators of the *Risālah*, the *jihād* is of four kinds: the *jihād* with the heart, which is the conflict against fancy and lust, the *jihād* with the tongue, which is the command to do that which is good and to eschew that which is evil, and the *jihād* with the arm, which is to smite the disobedient according to the limits and the penalties laid down. This latter is the entitlement of the *Amīrs*. None has authority to do this save a man amongst his own people, and this according to the manner allowed. Lastly, there is the *jihād* with the sword, to exalt the word of Allāh Almighty. Ibn Ḥajar al-Haythamī in his commentary to the *Arbaʿīn* of al-Nawawī, known as *Fatḥ Mubīn*,[21] said,

> "It is allowed for individual subjects to stop the committing of a major sin and crime if it is not prevented [in any other way], as long as the affair does not reach the point of open fighting and the unsheathing of weapons. If it reaches this stage then it will be silenced by the Sulṭān who is able to impose the penalties. It is he who has acquired the might in his family, justice in his person, the guardianship of his generation, the effective power of his word among his tribe and the concord of the word of the people of the four quarters over him, so that none during his time will be covetous and ambitious and he who is aggrieved will not despair of the protective shelter beneath his sway. If he does not combine these qualities, then there is no virtue in his holding onto that which he has no power to detain and to control, nay, rather, his holding a tight control upon it now is something which has become a duty which he has to fulfil, otherwise destruction will speedily come upon him because, either he seeks to impose a firm authority over a strong man like himself, hence he engages in a major trial of strength; that is the two of them fight together; or else he imposes its establishment upon him who is weak; but not on him who is strong, and so in the end he is destroyed. The Prophet said, the

blessing and peace of Allāh be upon him, 'Those who were before you simply perished, verily whenever a man of nobility stole amongst them they left him alone, but when he who was weak stole among them then they punished him.' Such is cited in the *Tanbīh* in regard to mistakes and faults."[22]

Some of the *'ulamā'* have made it their duty to refuse to take action in every circumstance, even if the reprehended had committed murder or if there were produced in his case some saying whch ran counter to this *Ḥadīth*. There is no valid argument to support them in a report which [tells of what] a man will say on Resurrection Day. When Allāh says to him, "What prevented you [from taking action] when you beheld such and such?", and he answers, "O my Lord I was afeared of the people." Allāh Almighty will then say to him, "I was that one who was most fitting to be feared." Why so? Because the meaning of being in fear of Him, that is to have the fear of Allāh, is to act as a shepherd of the people with power and with authority. If it were a duty to refuse to take action in a given situation then there would have been no point in this saying of the Prophet, the blessing and peace of Allāh be upon him, "If he [the *Sulṭān*] cannot fulfil this duty." Otherwise it is in order to use the term "infidelity" in the case of fear and compulsion as it is seen in the Koranic verse, "Let the relinquishing of the refusal to act be allowed in the first instance, since abandonment without taking action is amongst those deeds which are most abominable".[23]

Now the saying of al-Maghīlī, "then this [action] cannot be avoided" [namely it is a bounden duty to raid], this is the predicate of the subject in the sentence. It is an apodosis [if analysed grammatically]. As for the protasis, or the condition, which determines it, then it is this, "*O Imām, it has been appointed for you to raid the muḥāribūn, about whom you have asked, but on the condition that you have the power and the authority to do this, namely, that you have the power in canonic law as has been previously indicated with evidence of its application and its relevance.*"

Al-Nafrāwī said, "Lack of capability means lack of canonic authority to fulfil the command to do good and to eschew evil." Furthermore, the raiding of the *muḥāribūn* is an act of *jihād*. The *jihād* is not allowed unless it be to glorify the word of Allāh Almighty or to magnify the religion, not for the mere attainment of booty. So the meaning of this whole passage is this, "*Verily, you, O Imām, who asks, it has been appointed for you to magnify the religion, to raid the muḥāribūn, who are infidels, and others besides them, on the express condition that you have the capability to do this, that is, you have the power of canonic authority in the commanding of the good and in the eschewing of evil, as has recently taken place, that is, in respect of those who are under your authority but not those who are outside your authority.*"

As for your remark, already made about the statement, "No harm will be laid against you regarding those who fall [as booty] in your midst from among those Muslims", now this is a phrase which contains a remark, the substance of which, when [grammatically] parsed reveals a negation – "no" – which wholly denies the word "harm", followed by its noun, its predicate and its dependent parts; while the phrase, "from those Muslims" is a clear statement which indicates who they are among those who fall [as booty] in your midst from among the Muslims. Grammatically [phrased] it is a doubtful assertion.[24] The saying of his, "No harm will be laid against you", or will fall on you; here "no harm" is used because something else is better; namely, that it is to be preferred to it. For evidence, see the saying of Ashhab [and] Saḥnūn[25] that "this property is lawful due to the saying of the Prophet, the blessing and peace of Allāh be upon him, 'The property of a Muslim is only lawful if it be relinquished of his own free will.'" Hence, the remark of al-Maghīlī, 'from among *those* Muslims', is an indication that is clearly pointed towards the Muslims whom this question describes as having wronged themselves by living among those infidel *muḥāribūn*.

As for us, the Kel Es-Sūq, we do not live side by side with infidels, as you have alleged. I shall clearly explain to you what [proof] will clear us from all charge of infidelity, if Allāh Almighty so wills it. We have not wronged ourselves by living in the midst of those Tuareg, *because the land is our land and it is they who descended upon us, later*. We were in the jurisdiction of this *Imām*, and by him I mean Askiyā al-Ḥājj, who posed his questions to Shaykh al-Maghīlī. They [the Tuaregs] conquered our land in the eleventh/seventeenth century, three hundred years or more ago, and authority was fixed and attributed to their forebear [Karidenna] by the Amīr of Agades, al-Ghaddāl. He was the deputy appointed by the authority of the Commander of the Faithful at that time. Then the authority was made firm, was established and applied generally to the warrior class who had the power to "loose" and to "bind". The power was transmitted through his descendants up to the present time. This story is well known amongst us. I have omitted it since the purpose of this epistle has no connection with it. Regarding his saying, [that is, of al-Maghīlī] "because they have wronged themselves", and so on, the *lām*, that is, "because", is there for a reason, the cause of this ruling, that is to say, "*Your assignment to raid is* [due to the fact] *that they have wronged themselves by cohabiting with them* [the infidels]." The cause and the effect follow one another in succession, to prove and to refute.

Now this premise or cause is untrue in regard to us. The truth is applicable to the circumstance and the latter is [in our case], that our living as neighbours with them was perforce of dire necessity since we have seen none to whom we can go forth to live with, nor one whom we know, as we have no acquaintance with anybody from the remotest regions. Those whose neighbours we are, and whom we live with, are better for us than those others, they are more caring and kinder to us, and they show more mercy to us, since they do not raid and attack us, neither our persons, nor our properties, nor do they impose on us the duty to fight in battle with them against him whom they have gone forth to fight. We do not have to raid with them, nor have we to forsake the one whom they forsake, nor have we to hate the one they hate, nor should we augment the number of their host in anything which contravenes canonic law. On the contrary, they exalt us and they honour us with the highest honour and respect. They place their affairs in our hands amongst the peoples of the southlands. This circumstance, then, would assign them to the category of *other than infidelity*, until it be known for certain that infidelity is meant.

This is what the *Qāḍī* ʿIyāḍ wrote in his *Shifā*ʾ,[26] "The sin of neglecting one thousand infidels is of less consequence than expelling one Muslim believer from the *Millah*". The remark which he makes, "the thing which you have been told of, before it may lead to sin and iniquity avoid it and return it to its owner", you hearkened not unto it, because you did not avoid our herds and our possessions and you have not returned them to us, who, you so allege, are a company beneath the sway of an infidel king, despite the fact that you knew of them before their [alleged] wickedness, and despite the fact that we lived side by side with this king and became his neighbour out of dire necessity, for were we to flee to a land which is not his land then you would [still] rob us of our possessions. Besides, we have no knowledge of him to whom we can flee, since flight must only be from a land of injustice and wickedness to a land of security and piety. That is to be found nowhere in the regions of which we have knowledge.

Shall we flee to the Kel Geres, when they are more sinful, more oppressive and more unjust and more wicked than they [our rulers], are? They sell free men as slaves, and they seek to enslave them, and they take free women as concubines and slave women whom they have seized from among protected and inviolate properties. That is something which not one of the *ʿulamā*ʾ has spoken about, even one of them who was bizarre. Or shall we flee to the land of the Tuareg of the Kel Denneg? They resemble those others in their circumstance and they stem from the same stock, root and branch. Or shall we flee to the people of Aïr? We know that the distance between them and justice recalls the distance between this terrestrial earth and the far-off Pleiades. Or shall we flee to the remote desert tracts and be subjugated and humiliated just as the Igdalen[27] have been humiliated and debased, and the tribe of the Aghlāl[28] who went to such desert tracts and did not turn for support from anyone whatsoever. As a result they have attained nothing but humiliation and disgrace. You do not desire our emigration, in the sense you use it, except to win the contest and to get the better of us. As for the remark of al-Maghīlī, "As for him who dwells with them out of choice, and who used to raid with them, and who assisted them in the accomplishment of their wickedness, and thus is one of them, slay him and take his possessions as lawful booty and accept no repentence from him if Allāh gives you power over him", then this is a sentence which runs counter to the words of the Prophet, the blessing and peace of Allāh be upon him, "Whenever they say it, then they are protected from me. . ."

In the *Bidāyat al-Mujtahid*[29] are found these words, "The origin which legalises the property [of opponents] is infidelity [*kufr*]. That thing which safeguards it and protects it is the religion of Islam." The Prophet spoke thus, peace be upon him, and Ibn Rushd said, "Whosoever asserts that there is a person or a thing which makes property lawful other than infidelity, from the possessions of an enemy or from one who is not an enemy, then the burden rests with him to prove his claim and his assertion." And he also said, "And no evidence can stand against this *Ḥadīth*, 'Whenever they say it . . .'."

In the *Nawāzil* of Ibn al-Aʿmash[30] we read,

> "It is neither fitting nor seemly for the scholars [*ṭalabah*] to help in any way those who oppress and are iniquitous by proclaiming that which is taken as booty to be lawful property. As for those sayings which they cite as evidence of proof and which run counter to this, they are false and invalid. They are wicked views and opinions and show weak judgement. We say that they are alien opinions which derive no support from the root and the branch [of the canonic law], and the refuter cannot be cited as a valid argument of proof, neither in the remoter past, nor in the present. On the contrary this sound *Ḥadīth* is the fountain head of the claim."

As for raiding with the Tuareg, God forbid! No indeed, rather we keep ourselves completely aloof from this. We put them at a distance from us, attempting this course of action as far as we are able. We do not authorise Muslims to make such a raid. Rather, we, the company of the Kel Es-Sūq, give them counsel and tell them not to do so. Every day we chide them to our utmost. Were we the power in authority, then no goats would butt one another with their horns. Instead, we loan them mounts to ride, but we do not loan them weapons nor that thing which gives them power in their war making and their mischief. We in no way encourage them to do evil. The most that we do is to write amulets for them and charms to protect from limitless harm and injury. To do this is permitted; it is not unlawful – this [licence] may be found in ʿAbd al-Bāqī, at the saying of al-Khalīl[31] in regard to one who appears to be iniquitous, who sins against the *Imām* by writing for a tyrant, having been forced to write letters for an Amīr; and in them he treats men unjustly.

In our case, however, few of us wrote such things for them when the Kel Geres uprooted our family and they crushed us with their violence and their oppression. Let us repel them in any way we can. We have written amulets for them in order to thwart their oppression, not in order to destroy them. Our evidence is that the one whom you accused of having done that very thing, namely the noble *Sunnī* Shaykh, Muḥammad ibn Dāniyāl, the Ḥasanī *Sharīf*, said, regarding your accusation levelled against him for the use [of these things] for your destruction,

> "As for our use of them for these Tuareg, in order to defeat other Tuareg, then there is no basis [for such an accusation]. Whenever they ask us for that we make them despair of us raising our heads to oblige them, and this to such an extent that some of them are wrath on account of it. However, we adhere to our view. Our only wish is to preserve and to save the Muslims. Were we to make it our stubborn resolve to do this [at any time], then Allāh Almighty would give us success by His power and by His will.
>
> "Verily, we know the times which relate to the circumstances and their causes. We stipulate them and we know the signs wherein what we seek to accomplish is propitious. We know the names which are fitting for that, some of them are Arabic and some of them are Berber. We know the science of the squares whether they be numbered or lettered. We know the seals and the sign of the Zodiac of every human being at the very moment when the stars are in accordance. We know their rotation so that this will be of help to that person, or will work against him, and we know that thing, which, were we to divulge it, would deprive you of your reason. Your wildest dreams would become a reality. You could not understand it. By Allāh, Almighty, who knoweth all, if you had not left us alone, then we would have confronted you with the troops of Allāh Almighty. We would most certainly have sent you that which you could not have resisted or faced."

This is what he said to you. I also have told you that among us there are to be found those who can make the letters speak when they are examined. There are those who can cube them and draw forth the spiritual beings from them and who can empower the *ʿIfrīts* over you. So leave us alone as long as we leave you alone. As for those others amongst us from among the poor people of our country, they likewise are in the same state. They do not raid, nor do they busy themselves save in matters concerning their life in the hereafter and for their everyday living in this world. They earn their living and they engage in commerce and in hunting, not in raiding nor in thieving, except to a very small extent. In number they do not attain a tenth of a tenth of those who do not raid, some of them among the vagabond rascals and among the Īdawsḥāq and the Dabbākariyyīn, among those in the realm of Targhaytamat,[32] those whom you spoilt and uprooted unjustly and with such enmity a century ago or more and up to this very day. Despite that [inferior status] none raid from amongst them, save once or twice or thrice. It is a major event if the number reaches eight.

As for your remark, "Whosoever looks into this section, will know that the helpers of the infidels are to be found among the *ʿulamāʾ* and the scholars [*ṭalabah*], and the masses are infidels", up to your remark, "against *the armies of the Muslims* and what has happened has amounted to infidelity". This matter is not worthy of consideration. It is the casting of stones, conjecturally, in an empty space. It is an evil view of the Muslims. Now, an evil view of Muslims will not be compensated for, and atoned for, by the religious observances of seventy years. We do not help anyone against anyone else. Nor do we adulterate the true with the false, nor do we deem lawful that which is unlawful or taboo, and made so by Allāh Almighty. Neither do we declare to be inviolable and sacrosanct those things which Allāh Almighty has lawfully allowed, nor do we give any help against any particular army. If by "the Muslims" you mean the tribe of the Kel Geres, and you deem the Tuareg of our country to be "infidels", then you have erred in your desire. *O Saʿd, waterer of the camels, your path to the water-hole is not along this track*. You have conjectured like a blind man. You have acted without thinking because you have divided two things which look alike without criterion. You have judged of your own accord that the Kel Geres are Muslims. You are the most stubborn adherent to that which we have described, be it Anti-Christian Pharaonic tyranny, or in the way you live as protected clients of others, because *you yourself* live as the neighbours of the Kel Geres. You camp with them and journey forth with them. We are not like that at all. You go raiding with them and you speak to them about their raiding expeditions. We are not like that at all. You help them with your spear and with your sword and with your charms and amulets, and in many other ways. They are too many to be calculated. We are not like that at all. Now, if you mean by an army of Muslims the army of Muḥammad ibn al-Kumayt[33] [Măkhămmăd El-Kumati], who holds the office of the Drum of authority [*Ṭabl*] of the Iwillimmeden, then once again you err, because they are the enemies of the Kel Geres. The enmity [between them] is of long standing. Each one interprets as he so wishes and he believes that the property of the other is lawful booty for him, despite the fact that their interpretation and their case are without point since interpretation and exegesis can only be made by the scholars who have a right to *Ijtihād*.[34] It is stated to be so in the

Kitāb al-Kabīr by al-Khurashī. The two parties are alike, the one to the other, as two horses in a wager. Both look the same and both are as dark in their colour.

You have no means to discover [what knowledge] is to be found there. It is not your business, so follow your own course so that we may be spared from you. We have smelt the scent of ignorance from you, as you go your way producing text after text [supporting your case] yet they are not applicable to us in any way, though you maintain that they are, and at the same time you deny that they are applicable to yourself. You are more vociferous advocates than we are. You confuse your mind thereby. Were you sane when you did so? Or were you merely toying with your religion and paying no regard to it? Do you believe that we will not call you liars considering how the Kel Geres have been made to press hard upon us for upwards of forty years? This is by many degrees far worse than insanity. As for the fear that we may be given the victory over you, and that is a grave matter for Allāh Almighty, then be not deceived, *O ʿAbd*, by the circumstances of the present occasion. War is a matter of changes of fortune and varied chances. A poet once said, "We lose a battle and we win a battle, one day we are wretched but on another we are filled with joy."

As for what you have alleged when you have cited the book of *Bayān Wujūb al-Hijrah*,[35] namely, the answer given by al-Ujhūrī when he was asked about a party of Muslims with an infidel king, you did not understand its purport and you did not know its subject matter nor the whole point of the question. You feigned blindness so that by it you could consume the possessions of the Muslims. Rather, *we* were only raided by the *muḥāribūn* who were unbridled and evil oppressors. They were doers of wrong and injustice. They had no right to our possessions, no case before the eyes of Allāh Almighty in regard to what they did to us. By God, we shall most certainly detract from their virtues and load them with our vices on the day which they pay no heed to, despite your pride, your sword and your spear, and their swords and their spears. Those who have committed a wickedness will know what reverse they will suffer on that day.

We are not dwellers in the *Bilād al-Ḥarb*, woe to you, for verily among the *fuqahā'* the term *Bilād al-Ḥarb* is only applied to the land of the infidels, where war is a permanent state betwixt them and the Muslims. As for the case which you have presented, we shall poke out the eye of your proof, if Allāh Almighty so wills, by a retort which will rebuff. It will chide him who merits chiding and silence him who needs silencing. The case which you have argued from al-Burzulī will have its text displayed to you. You will see that it is not directed at us and that the evidence which you have cited in regard to the wealth and the possessions of the Companions of the Prophet, those items which they forsook and left behind in Mecca, they who fled to Medina, and ʿĀqil took their possessions,[36] is a matter of no relevance whatsoever in our circumstance.

In citing your proof you have combined two categories into one. Our circumstance is that we [in your view] have become neighbours and clients of evil-doers and we have followed them as accomplices. This is what you have alleged. You raided [the evil-doers] quite wrongfully since there was no feud between you and them, nor war in force, nor [need for] revenge, nor did you raid them in order to magnify the faith. Now the question of the Meccan people was that they had become Muslims in Mecca and they did not emigrate to Medina at a time when emigration was a bounden duty upon him who had no excuse not to do so. According to the most authentic of sayings, emigration has not been an obligation after the conquest of Mecca. The infidels took possession of their properties. In our case, none has taken possession of what we possess, rather we dispose of them in various ways. None has prevented us from emigrating if we choose to do so, nor do we know to whom we can emigrate since we are unaware of a country which is more just than our own. How can you find our analogy then in the people of Mecca? There is a vast difference between us and them. As for the dismissive summary which you have made, extemporising in regard to us and what we are, that is that we are content to dwell amongst the men of wickedness and evil living, then in this affair you have been stubborn and wilful to excess. You have flown in the face of the truth.

Truly, in our country one cannot find an [infidel] who claims divinity, nor one who shares this [claim] exclusively or in a limited way, neither did that affliction which befell us come about unintentionally, nor without deliberate choice. It all goes to prove that you, having left the Tuareg, returned [homeward] via our country. You know that it is our land from the [northern] bank of the Niger river and its islands, and you raided our herds and looted our possessions and you stole our [Arabic] books. In doing this you had in your mind the custom and the unruly nature of the Kel Geres in the past. *So you have followed after them at the time you declared our possessions to be lawful* [booty].

I have no idea whether what pressed you to do that was the piling up of sins. Verily the piling up of sins has, as its consequence, the committing of major and far greater sins, indicating that those who stray from Allāh's path will have a grave torment and punishment, due to their forgetfulness, on the Day of Reckoning . . . see the relevant Koranic verse. Or perchance you were driven to do that act due to lack of money, and due to cupidity, with a desire to get hold of worldly possessions and due to their high value? This, then, is what you have cited as evidence of proof! This is what you have relied upon, you and the likes of you, and this is what you have distorted and altered and have wrongly attributed and have made it an issue of dispute against the *ʿulamāʾ* of your time in regard to the legalising of Muslim possessions and their blood, quoting al-Maghīlī on the authority of Ibn ʿArafah on the authority of al-Burzulī.

Here is the text of the words actually said by al-Burzulī: "As for the properties of the Muslims who reside under the sway of an infidel, if the Muslims take it as booty, together with the possessions of the infidels, then it is *fay*ʾ[37] which belongs to the total of the possessions which are retained in the Public Treasury [*bayt al-māl*]." This is what was said by al-Burzulī, and also by Iṣbagh, and this was because its owner had no hand upon it, and the only hand upon it was that of the infidels. It was due to this that Ibn Rushd said, "It was upon this evidence that the properties of the Companions who left them behind in Mecca [were determined], and they had no right to them after the Conquest of Mecca." This remark is even more relevant to the case. Al-Riḍā said,[38] "These, by residing among the polytheists despite the consensus on the need to emigrate"; Ashhab and Saḥnūn said, "This is not allowed, and this due to the saying of the Prophet, the blessing and peace of Allāh be upon him, 'The taking of the possessions of a Muslim is not permissible, *unless it be of his own free will.*'" In the *Miʿyār* it is said,[39] "Regarding those who stay behind there is a difference of opinion regarding the lawfulness of the appropriating of their possessions. It is according to whether the ruling of *Dār al-Muḥtaramah* was of the *Ḥurmat al-Islam* or whether it was not."[40] The first saying is correct and this is what al-Burzulī said and not what you have imagined or alleged.

According to Ibn ʿArafah, quoted by al-Wansharīshī in the *Miʿyār*, he inclined to this same opinion. Abū ʿAbdallāh Ibn ʿArafah was quoted in regard to the actions of a Sulṭān, at a time when he should conquer a band of the bedouin of Ifrīqiyā, and all of them were *dhimmīs*.[41] He gave the answer that all of their possessions were to be deemed lawful booty as a body of spoils, until such time as the people who owned property which was licit [*ḥalāl*] could be ascertained. This was complicated by the fact that there were a large number of rebellious *muḥāribūn* and the total of the men was so many. Al-Burzulī said, "He did not lay down a ruling regarding the *ḥurmah* of him who left of his own free will and who did not mix in their number." See the rest of what he has said. Some of our *ʿulamāʾ* have also maintained that the Muslims did not attack the Muslim's attendants who resided amidst the polytheists. Some of them have applied this view to a matter which is to be read in the *Mudawwanah* of Saḥnūn, in the *Kitāb al-Jihād* and *al-Nikāḥ*. It is the question of the warrior who becomes a Muslim, who emigrates or who does not emigrate, and the man who leaves behind a widow, his property and his offspring. Al-Wansharīshī said, and the words which he chose were those of Ashhab and Saḥnūn, that there was a wide currency for this saying of the Prophet, the blessing and peace of Allāh be upon him, "The property of a Muslim man is not deemed to be *ḥalāl* unless he agrees to it of his own free will," and also his saying, "Everything of the Muslim is *ḥarām* for another Muslim." Where the point at issue occurs in the *Mudawwanah* [of Saḥnūn] it is weaker. The property of him who became a Muslim was *ḥalāl* before he embraced Islam. Nonetheless, the ruling was both transferred and changed by his adoption of the Islamic faith due to the saying, "Whosoever becomes a Muslim with his possessions then these latter are his own." Ibn al-Qāsim declared in favour of the *Ḥukm al-Dār*.[42] He said, "The hand of a Muslim in the first instance remains on his property, and in regard to it no good reason [*musawwigh*] has any priority [over it] nor preference." I have been informed that Iṣbagh, from amongst our companions, issued a *fatwā* in regard to its use as a subterfuge, that its owner had no hand upon it and that the only hand upon it was that of the infidel! Ibn Rushd has spoken in a similar way.

Al-Burzulī said,

> "Upon the basis of this ruling, proof was cited in regard to the disposal of the properties of the Companions which they left behind them in Mecca, due to the saying of the Prophet, the blessing and peace of Allāh be upon him, 'Has ʿUqayl left a house to us? . . . rather it is more fitting here that he should remain a resident among the polytheists.' So he imposed the *jizyah*[43] upon him. He and his property were beneath their sway, while the consensus was that he should emigrate if he could find some way in order to do so. We have an example like this in Africa among the people of Qawsarah [Cossyra]. They have remained beneath the rule of infidels by choice of some amongst their number whom the infidels subdued. As it was unavoidable it in no manner impairs their right, they were like one who was compelled, whereas he who has freedom of choice in the matter has his right impaired. A decision in regard to his property will be given depending on what has happened before. People like these in al-Andalus are called Mudejars."

This is what Ibn ʿArafah had to say. Al-Burzulī cited him as evidence for evidence of proof and he, in his turn, was cited by al-Maghīlī. He cited in his own text what was meant by the *muḥāribūn* and what they meant by infidels.

I maintain that the difference in regard to the property of a Muslim beneath the sway of an infidel, whether it be lawful to confiscate or whether its status be *ḥarām*, has come about due to the fact that each of those who differ in view regarding the matter can find evidence to support his case, more especially that one who says that it is inviolate [*ḥurmah*], because his evidence and proof is of a decisive kind, having been quoted from Ashhab and Saḥnūn. What is your view, then, regarding a Muslim who mixes with an impious wicked-living Muslim? The first matter related to the property of him [an infidel] who had Muslims beneath his sway *because he was an infidel*. An infidel's property is licit [*ḥalāl*] according to the consensus. Now this further question relates to him who declares licit booty that is the property of him who has a profound claim to it, because *both the parties* are Muslims, and the property of the Muslim is inviolate [*ḥarām*] according to the consensus.

In regard to the question of the presence of lawful booty (*fay'*) in the hands of *Muslim muḥāribūn*, among statements which have been made, then it has come about due to the co-existence of certain factors and consequences in the overall question. Otherwise, it can be viewed that the property was not theirs in its origin but that they looted it. A justifying factor, infidelity for example, did not make the property unsound. Evidence for this is that it is unquestionably maintained that this property which they claim as their own, and that nobody else has any claim to it, is inaccessible. This is what is said in the *Tabṣirah* by Ibn Farḥūn,[44] and in the commentary by ʿAbd al-Bāqī and by others, drawing upon *Ḥadīths* of the Prophet, verses of the Koran and the consensus [*ijmāʿ*].

Do you think, *O ʿAbd*, that Ibn ʿArafah has declared licit the property of a Muslim, deeming it to be "wicked property" by reason of the fact that he declares his person to be wicked? Or is it by reason of his mixing with those whom Allāh Almighty has declared it a duty to wage *jihād* against them? Allāh forbid that he should say such a thing! Ibn ʿArafah himself reported in his book, citing Saḥnūn, that ʿAlī, may Allāh Almighty be pleased with him, authorised the fighting of the Khārijites,[45] but he did not deem them to be infidels. He did not take them captive, nor did he declare their properties to be licit as booty. They were judged to be Muslims through the mothers of their offspring, through those who directed their affairs, in their slaves and in their wills and their bequests. The Khārijites were far graver and more harmful in their mischief than the *muḥāribūn*.

Ibn ʿArafah also said in his book,

> "If we were to fight the Khārijites together with those who make war and who assist them, then he who kills a Khārijite has no right whatsoever to rob him of his possessions unless it be the booty of a raider from a fighting group. If, on the other hand, it be from the booty of warriors from among the Khārijites, whose *amān*[46] the warriors had embraced after entering the Khārijite military camp, then I would not take it, for it is the property

of the man who has sought for protection. It is indivisible and it is an endowment for its people."

This is what Ibn ʿArafah wrote in his book and what al-Burzulī quoted in his book. Not one smallest item is misquoted or changed, quoted by or copied by an apostate who has been led from the right path, either because he is limited in his understanding of what is found therein, or because he is fully aware of what is to be found in it but has wilfully forsaken it unjustly and has misrepresented it in order to suit his fancies so as to permit the shedding of the blood of Muslims and to seize their possessions.

With the proviso that both of them say this, then it cannot be overlooked that what is said in these two books is partial, whereas what is said in the *Ṭurra*[47] is all embracing. There is no doubt about its comprehensiveness because it includes both the warriors of the infidels and the warriors of the Muslims. Here one is unrestricted, whereas with the former one is restricted. The former interprets and is construed with the latter. Action by that which has clearly proved a precise testimony and not a general statement which is a summary is one of the basic rules of the *Sharīʿah*. Either the one abrogates the other if its later date be known, or, alternatively, if its later date be unknown, then all that is left is to weigh up the two side by side. The word which is laid down in the text in the two books outweighs the other by the weight of the argument, supported by the Koranic text, by the *Sunnah* and the consensus; that is to say in support of the *ḥurmah* of the lives of Muslims and the *ḥurmah* of their possessions. As for Prophetic *Ḥadīth*, then we have already mentioned it; the words of the Prophet, the blessing and peace of Allāh be upon him, "One Muslim is *ḥarām* to another Muslim. . . .", and there are many other [similar] *ḥadīths*. As for the consensus [*ijmāʿ*], then this has been firmly fixed and has been believed from the time of Adam up to the present that the property of Muslims is inviolate [*ḥurmah*]. The above is quoted from the *Kitāb al-Tanbīh ʿan ghalaṭāt ṭalabat al-waqt*.

Be not deceived also by what is to be read in the *History of the Caliphs* by the Imām al-Suyūṭī. Here is his text:

"Al-Ma'mūn asked the *ʿulamā'* of Damascus, when he marched to Lower and Upper Egypt on a raid against the stubborn and abusive bedouin, saying, 'What have you to advise regarding this expedition of ours against these evil men who have set the land alight and who have oppressed men unjustly?' They agreed that the *jihād* against them was a *jihād*. Then he said, 'What say you regarding the possessions which are in their hands?' They said, 'He who has made lawful the shedding of their blood has made lawful the seizing of their possessions.' Then he said, 'What about the possessions of the Muslims which are in their hands, but their rightful owners have no power to take them away?' They said, 'Those who join forces with you and who increase the number of the Muslims are the most fitted to hold the possessions, as long as these latter are assembled in one collection. As for that item which you have assigned as an allotment, then it is not for anyone to take it, except by clear proof [of ownership]. As for him who possesses *dirhams* and who has joined forces with them [your opponents], but he is not one of them in their manner of living and their way of behaving, he will have nothing save what he holds in his hand. As for the remainder it is most fitting that it should be placed for safe keeping in the public treasury (*bayt al-māl*).' He said, 'Verily they pray and they fast.' They said to him, 'You will not fight them for their prayer, their alms giving and their fasting. You will only fight them on account of the evil which they do in the land.' Then he said, 'Allāh Almighty alone is the One who will recompense those who war against Him and against His Messenger and who work evil in the earth . . . [the Koranic verse[48]] . . .'' '

Be not deceived, *because this Ma'mūn was a Caliph and an Imām in his time*. He sought a *fatwā* from the *'ulamā'* of his time. They were either independent thinkers [*mujtahidūn*] or else they were traditionalists [*muqallidūn*].

You are neither a Caliph, nor have you made an expedition with a Caliph and a fatwā is not to be expected from you since you are neither a mujtahid nor have you attained any degree of competence in taqlīd, nor is it fitting that those who seek for a fatwā should ask you to give it. Verily, he who reads the *Ḥadīth* and who has no knowledge of Grammar is not to be trusted. He may lie against the Prophet, the blessing and peace of Allāh be upon him, who said, ''Whosoever lies against me, deliberately, will take his seat in the fire of Hell.'' This Ma'mūn was a *mujāhid*. He fought the *jihād* in that country in order to remove this harm from it; their burning, their arson, their rapine. Their harm came to an end *but you are not in that situation*. All you do is to augment the total of [unlawful] booties. Now booty, even though it be from infidels, if the *mujāhid* knows deep in his heart that he is not fighting the *jihād* except for that motive and to manifest his prowess, then it is illicit and prohibited [*ḥarām*] that he should take such booty. It is like the case of certain fruit which hangs so low on the tree that one is tempted to pluck it. What ails you, you who deem others to be infidels? Will you repeat and repeat and persist in your foolery? That we are beneath the rule of an infidel and you deem our king to be an infidel? You do this by a kind of soothsaying; is it intuition? You also deem *us* to be infidels, by the mere fact that we are beneath his sway, and you do so without paying attention to our circumstance, save by that which you have heard from the mob of villainy who go from you to us. Then they bring you lies which you repeat in order that you may devour what we possess on account of them, devouring them with greed, believing in the legality of what you do. In the *Iḥyā' 'Ulūm al-Dīn* [al-Ghazzālī says][49] that it is inadmissable to associate a Muslim with a major sin without verification. He also says in his book, ''Nu'mān drank wine. He did so repeatedly so one of the Companions [of the Prophet] said, 'Allāh curse him, how often he is brought drunk.' The Prophet, the blessing and peace of Allāh be upon him, said, 'Do not be an ally of Satan against your brother.' He told him not to behave in this way! Now this proves that a specific wicked abuse or curse is inadmissable."

In general, then, there is a risk involved in the uttering of a curse against another. Let it be avoided. But there is no risk in holding one's tongue and in refraining from cursing *Iblīs*, let alone another person. To utter a curse is not as heinous as pronouncing another to be an infidel, and the like. In the *Nawāzil* of Ibn al-Aʿmash [it is said] that the deed which makes infidelity a possibility among the people of the *giblah* [of the Southern Sahara] should be deemed to be non-infidelity until it be definitely determined. By this is meant infidelity as it is defined in the writings of the Qāḍī ʿIyāḍ in his *Shifā*' and in *Maʿūnat al-Ikhwān*, the Commentary of al-Sanūsī, where mention is made of the conditions which are applicable to him who utters the words of the confession of faith. Here is the passage: 'Whoever recites the confession of faith with belief but not with works is a lewd liver [*fāsiq*]. His testimony will benefit him in this world, because he is not killed, his blood will not be shed, nor will he be punished in the world to come except in accordance with his wickedness, then he will leave Hell Fire. He, by his belief and his works which are not in accord with the *Sunnah*, is a heretic. Such will benefit him in this world since he does not lose his life, nor is his property consumed and in the world to come he will benefit, only being punished to the degree of the gravity of his *bidʿah*.' This is what is said in the *Shifā*' of the *Qāḍī* ʿIyāḍ. As for the blameworthy state, it is to recite the creed [*shahādah*] with the tongue, but without belief in the heart. This is hypocrisy. Allāh Almighty has said, 'When the hypocrites come to you' . . . to his saying . . . 'Liars', that is, liars in what they say. That is on account of their belief in their hearts and the belief in their speech. They do not really believe and when their consciences do not speak the truth then it is no profit to them that they utter with their tongues what is absent from their hearts. They have departed from the name of the faith so its judgement does not apply to them in the world to come, since they do not possess faith and they will join the infidels in the lowest abyss of Hell fire.[50]

Islam's rule has not ceased to be the manifestation of the confession of the Faith with the tongue in the rulings of this world, which are to be associated with the *Imāms* and the judges of the Muslims, whose judgements are based upon the externals which they manifest of the marks of Islam; since it has not been appointed for man to find a way into the inner secrets, nor have they been ordered to seek them out. On the contrary, the Prophet, the blessing and peace of Allāh be upon him, forbade any judgement on that basis and he reproved it, saying, "Did you not take pity upon his heart?" After he had mentioned the qualities which one who is described by them should possess, if his love is to be perfect for the Messenger of Allāh, the blessing of Allāh be upon him, he said, "Whosoever is contrary to them in some matters, then he is deficient in his love, although he is not disqualified from the name." The proof of it may be observed in the sayings of the Prophet, peace be upon him, about the one whom he prescribed should suffer the penalty for wine-drinking. One among their number had cursed him and had said, "How often it is that this man is brought drunk", and the Messenger, the blessing and peace of Allāh be upon him, had said, "Do not curse him, for, verily, he loves Allāh and His Messenger."

Woe to you, O meddler in the pursuit of the whim of the heart, the pursuer of our stumbling steps, the intruder into the fancies of the discovery of our failings. Have you no fear and concern for being classed [among these] within his saying, the blessing and peace of Allāh be upon him, "He who seeks the stumbling of his brother will be asked about his own fault and his own dishonour." There is also another saying of his, "If Allāh turns aside from a servant he will inherit the disapprobation of the people of religion."

If you are amongst those who deem the people of the *giblah* [of the southern Sahara] to be infidels due to sin, then you have no notion whether their infidelity is less [grave] than another infidelity, or whether their infidelity has none worse nor greater than it. The former shows ingratitude for Allāh's favour, while the latter is disbelief in what was brought by the Prophet Muḥammad, the blessing and peace of Allāh be upon him. Yet again there is an infidelity which, because of it [and despite it], the name of the faith does not depart from him who is guilty of that infidelity. An example of it is a man who ceases to pray but who is not an apostate, or, on the other hand, it may be an infidelity which is so great that the name of the faith will depart from him who is guilty of it, for example, a man who ceases to pray and at the same time he is an apostate regarding the very necessity of having to pray to Allāh.

How do you assess the infidelity of him who says that Allāh is One and that Muḥammad, the blessing and peace of Allāh be upon him, is the Messenger of Allāh? Al-Ubbī[51] has said, "Neither denial, nor affirmation, nor the utterance, 'I testify', is a condition which is stipulated. Rather, if a man merely says, 'Allāh is One and Muḥammad is His Messenger', then his faith is sound." Like this are the words which were said by Abū ʿImrān al-Mālikī in the commentary to *Jamʿ al-Jawāmiʿ*. The texts state, "Amongst us what should suffice in regard to the faith, canonically, are all the reports which reveal the belief [of the believer] in that Allāh is One, and that Muḥammad is the Messenger of Allāh, whether that be the utterance of the two confessions, or by some other way."[52]

There are also the words of al-Nawawī, "Even though he says the two confessions in a non-Arabic tongue, and he knows the Arabic language perfectly, is he thereby made a Muslim? Here there are two aspects for our companions. The one that is sound is that he does indeed become a Muslim, due to the mere existence of the confession."[53] He then goes on to say, "As for the situation where a man is not proficient in Arabic, then it is sufficient that he should present what will indicate that he believes in the Divine Unity and the Messenger's mission with his tongue. There is unanimity in this, nay, some of them have reported that there was a consensus on it." Here ends the quotation from *Bughyat al-Ṭālibīn*. See what the Prophet, the blessing and peace of Allāh be upon, said to the one who cursed Nuʿmān, when he was brought to him and he commanded, "Be not a helper of Satan against your brother." There are other examples, such as the saying which he gave to the one who cursed that man whom the Prophet had given the penalty for wine-drinking, "Do not curse him, for verily he loves Allāh and His Messenger." There is also what was said by the *Qāḍī* ʿIyāḍ in his *Shifā'*,

> "Whosoever attributes to Allāh Almighty that thing which is inappropriate in the path of error and which is explained by a fanciful desire to anthropomorphise, or to portray offensively, or to deny a quality of perfection, then hereby the forebear differs from the successor in the determining of the infidelity in him who says it and in him who believes it. Mālik ibn Anas and his companions were not in accord over that."

The bulk of what was said by Mālik and his companions was that one should refrain from making remarks regarding their being infidels, one should abandon their slaughter or going to excess in their chastisement. Ibn al-Qāsim said, "They are Muslims and they should only be fought on account of their wicked opinion. In this view ʿUmar ibn ʿAbd al-ʿAzīz acted." Ibn Ḥabīb and others like him from amongst our companions were of the opinion that such men were infidels and that others like them were infidels. Amongst those men who transmitted on their authority the meaning contained in the other saying, namely, that an accusation of their infidelity should be relinquished, were ʿAlī ibn Abī Ṭālib, Ibn ʿUmar and al-Ḥasan al-Baṣrī. It is the opinion of a group among the *fuqahā'* when they had disagreed regarding the infidelity of "the men of fancies", the sectarians, despite the fact that their wickedness was worse than the *muḥāribūn*, since the greater part of their wickedness was directed against the religion, although it might intrude into the affairs of this world due to the enmity which they sowed amongst the Muslims. The evil of the *muḥāribūn* is only in regard to worldly possessions and the interests of this world. It may also enter into the realm of religion through the pilgrimage and the *jihād*.

Abū'l-Ḥasan al-Ashʿarī[54] was overwhelmingly in favour of giving up an accusation of infidelity, and that the latter was of only one kind and nature, namely, the ignorance of Allāh Almighty. He once said that whoever believed that Allāh Almighty was a corporeal being had no true knowledge of Him and he was an infidel on account of this. A similar view was adopted by Abū'l-Maʿālī,[55] may Allāh Almighty be pleased with him, in the answers which he gave to Abū Muḥammad ʿAbd al-Ḥaqq. He had asked him about this matter and had apologised to him that the error which had been made in it was hard to excuse because the entry of an infidel into the fold of Islam [*Millah*], or the expulsion of a Muslim from it, was a grave matter in religion. Others than these two men from among the verifiers said that the matter which needed to be guarded against was the pronouncement of infidelity upon those who interpreted or who commentated upon [holy writ]. For to declare that the lives of those who prayed could be lawfully slain was a grave matter, and that the error of sparing the lives of one thousand infidels was of less import in the eyes of Allāh Almighty than shedding, in error, a cupping-bowl full of the blood of one Muslim.

The Prophet, peace be upon him, said, "When they utter the *Shahādah* they guard their lives and their properties from me, save for the fulfilment of their due. Likewise, their account with Allāh Almighty for protection, all are determined by the confession of faith, and it will not be revoked." The difference of view over it [the confession] is allowable, save in a peremptory proof [of infidelity]. The canonic law is not to be curtailed nor is analogy to be permitted. Such of the traditions as appear in the chapter are open to interpretation, similarly those which declare that those who hold the belief of the school of the *Qadariyyah*[56] are guilty of infidelity and others. To them refers this *ḥadīth* of the Prophet, "They will have no share in the booty [*fay'*] of the Muslims." Similarly, the *Rāfiḍites*[57] are named as polytheists to be openly cursed, so too the *Khārijites* and others among the sectarians. This evidence is cited as proof by him who wishes to call them infidels, whereas the other view may maintain that there are those who say that there is a similar series of traditions which maintains the judgement of non-infidelity. The matter is difficult [with the] postulating of infidelity as less than disbelief and in the associating of Allāh with another less than outright polytheism.

An example of this may be seen in the parallel case of usury, in the rights of parents and of the husband, and in other sins and acts of disobedience. If an issue is open to two interpretations, then one of the two cannot be decisive unless it be by some decisive evidence of proof. An example may be found in the words said about the *Khārijites*, "They are the worst of humanity." This is a description of the infidels. There is also the saying, "The worst of those men slain beneath the sky, praised be the one who kills them, or that one whom they have slain." The Prophet, the blessing and peace of Allāh be upon him, said, "Wherever you find them then slay them just as the people of ʿĀd were slaughtered."

Now this infidelity is quite obvious and apparent, especially so in the likening of them to ʿĀd. He who is convinced of their infidelity cites such sayings as these as his proof. Another will say to him, "That order to slay them is only due to their withdrawing from the Muslims and their wickedness and their tyranny against them," proving thereby from the very tradition that they were slayers of the people of Islam. The slaying of them here was the penalty for their action, *not on account of infidelity*, and the reference to the people of ʿĀd is a simile or a colourful description of the act of slaying but not of the slain. So all who have determined that such a person should be slain did not determine that he was an infidel. This view may be countered by the saying of Khālid in the tradition, "Let me slay him, O Messenger of Allāh." The latter answered, "Perchance he is saying his prayers."

If you should say that such persons do not really pray, since they pray without ritual ablution, and he who prays without ritual ablution, by intention, is an infidel, then I can say that this is the view of the Ḥanafites [only]. Those who deem a man to be an infidel due to his prayer being said without ritual ablution is going to excess in exalting and in advocating ritual ablution and prayer. This is the case in *al-Fatḥ al-Mubīn* by Ibn Ḥajar al-Haythamī.

As for him who is ignorant of one of the attributes of Allāh Almighty then there is disagreement among the *ʿulamāʾ* in regard to him. Some of them deemed him to be an infidel. This was reported by Abū Jaʿfar al-Ṭabarī and by others.[58] Abūʾl-Ḥasan al-Ashʿarī said it once, while a party of others went so far as to say that it did not make that man an outsider to the faith in name. Al-Ashʿarī came back to this view himself and said that because this man did not believe that to be exactly so in his creed he deemed the matter to fall within the scope of religion and of canonic law. He would only call an infidel that person who unequivocally believed that what he said was an essential truth. These men found evident proof for their viewpoints in the tradition of Sawdah and the Prophet of Allāh, His blessing and peace be upon him, since he only asked her to believe in the unity of Allāh and not in anything else.[59]

O puny little scribe, look again at the words of the *Qāḍī* ʿIyāḍ in the *Shifāʾ*. He, unequivocally, supports the view that the one who says something whereby he leads the *Ummah* of Islam into error, is without question an infidel. Now *you* have said something which leads to the misguidance of the *Ummah*! Under heaven, there is not one godly man who is not the neighbour of one who is ungodly. Your judgement is therefore false. It is invalid in canonic law and in its manner of presentation. Canonically it is so, due to Allāh's word in the Koran, "If they repent and pray and pay the *Zakāh* then let them go their way" . . . to the end of the passage.[60] Likewise, the saying of the Prophet, the blessing and peace of Allāh be upon him, "When they regard it as little then they are protected from me" . . . As for its [invalidity in] manner of presentation, then this is because the form in which you have formulated your false proof shows that these Muslims are neighbours of evil-doers and oppressors. Hence [by this] everyone who is a neighbour of an evil-doer is an infidel. So these Muslims are all infidels!

O ʿAbd, you have indeed erred, in your citing of the evidence of your proof. You have ridden on the back of a blind mare. You have become one of those who pray on their hips. The true purport of your evidence is not neighbourliness, on the contrary, the real aim in [presenting] the causes which they have deduced and presented regarding the giving of aid and of the raiding with them [the Kel Geres] is to make lawful the unlawful and to remove protection from the sacrosanct and more besides. All these deductions and premises [which you cite] are contradictory. They are quite invalid in regard to us, the company of the Kel Es-Sūq and most of those who are poor and protected in our country. Are you not, you yourself, a neighbour of the oppressors who are more wicked and harsh than any tyrant? You have faults too and men have tongues. How can one who is far viler abuse the shameful?

I have only gone to great lengths to gather together and to quote [these things] because such circumstances had constrained me to do so, and to let you know that the act which you had committed was an audacity against Allāh and His Messenger. How fitting it would be that a proverb should be coined about you. "So and so is more brazen than the man who shaves the lion's mane." It is amazing that a man like you can make a judgement about us in a way which no other members of the *ʿulamāʾ* of your country have ever done before you. Those men were more learned than you are, men such as al-Mukhtār ibn Anāzel. They were more pious than you; a man such as Shaykh Sīdī Maḥmūd, for example.[61]

Perchance you have only done what you did due to your mixing with sinners from amongst the venal scholars of the district wherein you dwell and your nature borrowed its character from theirs. It has been said that one man's character steals from another's. Or is it because your stock is not that of the descendants of Ākall,[62] nor from the sons of ʿUthmān al-Mukkī,[63] nor from the sons of Aggāg Akhamma? The lineal tree of such men is that of many of the Kel Es-Sūq *and many of the Kel Geres*, and men are to be trusted and believed in their lineages which they claim. The tongues of men are the pens of the truth. You should hold them before you as your ideal example. The *ʿulamāʾ* of the Tagaraygarayt[64] are those who have taught you this. They have erred. In order to do what they do they have depended upon a commentary to this paltry collection of passages [which you have cited] which touch upon the most trivial of matters, namely those things which you have cited to support your case and your proof from the sayings of al-Maghīlī [in response to] Askiyā al-Ḥājj. *Khalīl* has said, "Once you interpret, then all is to no avail and purpose." They rested their belief in an interpretation. Such is not the case. The commentary of the [competent] *mujtahidūn* is meant. The *Kabīr* of al-Khurashī states, "What is meant by the commentary of the *mujtahidūn* means using the analogy of the action of the Companions [of the Prophet]."[65] According to ʿAbd al-Bāqī, "If a group . . . have thought . . .", likewise in the commentary of Ibn ʿAbd al-Salām[66], "The unjust are of two kinds, those who interpret and those who are stubborn." He goes on to say that this judgement, that is one which is null and void, is confined to men who interpret from amongst the unjust. He does not go futher to the second category, that is to those men who are stubborn. Where the verb "think" and "suppose" [*ẓann*] is introduced, then it refers to the *mujtāhid* since it is only he who has done the thinking and the supposing.

An ancient enmity exists between the Tagaraygarayt and the Tuareg of our country. Feuding has attained a degree which exceeds that of what is justified and right. Its people have not paid heed to the *Sharīʿah*, the canonic law. In fact they have shattered the canonic law into fragments. Were they to pay attention to the canonic law and turn to it for guidance, then they would follow as their custom what the canonic law permits to them [to know of] the way of the example which is to be followed among the community in accordance with the Almighty's words in the Koran, "Sacred things are to be avenged . . ." "Retribution for an evil is an evil like it" . . . to "without the truth" . . . and His saying, "He who attacks you should be attacked by you in return *in the manner and to the degree he did so*." The verse where He says, "Sacred things are to be avenged" [is especially relevant].[67] It is said in the *Fatḥ al-Bayān fī maqāṣid al-Qur'ān*,[68] where there is a commentary to this verse and to its meaning, that every sacred and inviolate thing which is outraged justifies punishment and retribution. "He who desecrates a sacred thing amongst you, it is up to you to desecrate a sacred thing of his in retaliation." "Care not" was mentioned. *Now this was at the time when Islam had its beginning*. It was abrogated by the command to fight. It was said that it was fixed among the *Ummah* of Muḥammad, the blessing and peace of Allāh be upon him, and whoever was assaulted, whether it be in property or in body, then he, in his turn, should make an assault to the same degree as he was assaulted. Al-Shāfiʿī and others spoke on this basis.[69] However, others said that matters which were concerned with retaliation should be restricted to judges, likewise properties. This is due to the saying of the Prophet, the blessing and peace of Allāh be upon him, "Observe and fulfil the *amānah* to him who entrusts it to you, or who has put his faith in you, and do not betray him who betrays you, rather expel him from the community." This is quoted by al-Qurṭubī and by others.

Abū Ḥanīfah said this and most of the Mālikis and ʿAṭā' al-Khurāsānī. The first saying is the predominant one. It was cited by Ibn al-Mundhir, and it was chosen by Ibn al-ʿArabī and al-Qurṭubī, and it was also cited by al-Dāwūdī. Its case is supported by the permission which was given by the Prophet, the blessing and peace of Allāh be upon him, to the wife of Abū Sufyān,[70] that he should take from his property the wherewithal to support her and her offspring. It is in the *Ṣaḥīḥ* [of al-Bukhārī]. I shall not elaborate, nor clarify the words of the Almighty when he said, "He who uses aggression against you, then you act likewise by destroying his aggressiveness."[71] This statement is included within the ruling which supports the first which I have mentioned, namely, "Avenge the desecration of sacred things." Aggression of a like nature and force has been called a requital, as stated earlier. Ibn Abī ʿAbbās has said in regard to this verse and the saying of the Almighty, "The requital of an evil is by an evil like unto it," and His saying, "For him who is victorious after having been wronged . . .",[72] and His saying, "If you punish them in the way you have been punished . . .",[73] he said, "This and the likes of it were revealed in Mecca." The Muslims at that time were very few. They had no authority with those who could subdue the polytheists. The latter used to abuse them and to injure them, so Allāh ordered the Muslims to requite them in the same manner and degree as they had been afflicted.[74] Otherwise they should be steadfast or else they should forgive.

When the Messenger of Allāh, His blessing and peace be upon him, emigrated to Medina, and when Allāh had made his authority to be great, he ordered the Muslims to bring their complaints and injustices to the Sulṭān, and that none should assault one another like the people of the Age of Ignorance [*Jāhiliyyah*]. He said, "He who is wrongfully slain has been given a Sulṭān as his protector and his helper."[75] His word says that the Sulṭān will assist the aggrieved until he assures him justice against that one who has oppressed him. He who therefore avenges himself *without the Sulṭān* is a sinner. He is most exceedingly disobedient, he has behaved in the manner of the tribal fanaticism of the *Jāhiliyyah*. He has not accepted the law of Allāh Almighty. I maintain that this verse, which Ibn ʿAbbās alleged was one which abrogated another, supports the verses, which he had deemed to be abrogated, and they confirm them in fact. He said,

"The external meaning of the words of Allāh Almighty are these, 'We have established as his benefactor [or guardian] a Sulṭān. A Sulṭān has been appointed for him.' That is to say, 'He has appointed for him a power in authority whereby he will exercise power and might over the slayer and the murderer.' "

Because of this He said, "Do not go to excess in [your] killing." If, therefore, we are content that the meaning of the verse is as he said it, that is, that it *specifically applied to killing and to manslaughter*, throughout the whole corpus of variant verses and passages, mentioned above, it is therefore no abrogation. It has only been established in the text in the verses in regard to murder alone. Those verses cover it comprehensively, and other matters as well. Such is well known in [the use] of the Arabic language, which is the source of the Word of Allāh Almighty itself.

When the Almighty allowed them lawfully to exact retaliation in like fashion, and it is a habit of the heart to love excess in matters of revenge against an enemy, He cautioned them against this and He said, "Fear Allāh in the circumstance where you are made triumphant over him who has committed an aggression against you. Do not do the same to him *save to the extent lawful to you* and to requite an evil, with an evil like it." He, may He be glorified, made it quite clear that *equity* in retaliation rests on an *equality*, hence, the literal meaning is of general application. Al-Muqātil and al-Shāfʿi and Abū Ḥanīfah and Sufyān [*sic*] all said that this is of particular reference to the wounded man who takes his revenge against the one who wounded him. It does not apply to another. Mujāhid and al-Sāʿdī said that it is the response to the wicked when he says to you, "May Allāh disgrace you", and then you should say, "May Allāh disgrace you", in turn, but *without physical hostility*. When one is triumphant, then the fulfilment of an act [instigated] by another's injustice is completed and accomplished. The instigator is freed of any right [in the matter] which he may have had, whilst the sin of having begun the conflict rests upon him, and so does the sin against the due right of Allāh Almighty. Requital is therefore given the name of "an evil", either because of the affliction suffered by him upon whom it happens to fall, or else it is used to show a comparison, in order to compare like with like, the one with the other.

Know, *O ʿAbd*, that I am not litigating on behalf of the Tuareg, in view of what has been said by Almighty Allāh, "Be not a litigator for those who betray."[76] Neither am I one likewise for all those who resemble the Tuareg [in their behaviour]. It has been said in *Fatḥ al-Bayān fī maqāṣid al-Qur'ān*, regarding the Koranic verse, that here is the proof that it is not allowable for anybody to act as a litigant for another unless one is certain of the rightness and justice of his case. Ibn Shaʿbān used to treat the Berber tribes as infidels, holding firmly to the words of the Prophet, the blessing and peace of Allāh be upon him, "He is not one of us if he bears weapons against us," and also his saying, "Abuse of the true believer is wickedness, and to fight him is infidelity." He went to excess in this respect to the extent that he declared the enslavement of these Berbers to be lawful. He said, "Verily, they are not free of two things, either they became Muslims in ancient times and then they apostatised, or else they became heretics and were godless. They are therefore like the Carmathians and the Banū 'Ubayd."[77] The *'ulamā'* at this time concurred that [the latter] should be slain and that it was lawful to enslave them. This was due to their heresy and the way they desecrated holy and inviolate things and abused judgements and laws during their conquests. In their circumstance they could hardly have been worse than these [Tuareg] tribes which are solely devoted to the stealing of possessions, the shedding of blood and the destruction of duties and obligations. They refuse to obey canonic rules, and in themselves bear witness to their infidelity. They say to the Muslims in their vicinity, "You will do this and that", and saying, "We shall not help the Muslims." If they get hold of a Muslim they will sell him to the Christians. Yet despite all that they pronounce the two confessions.

The Muslim traveller in the land of the European Christian is safer in regard to his life and his property than he is in the country of those [Tuareg] tribes which tyrannise and reject Islam. Nay more so, the travelling to this land is [canonically] prohibited [*ḥarām*] due to the rash exposure of one's life and property without advantage, and due to what one will see upon them [the Tuareg] of those abominations which demand to be changed. If one should confess that one has no power to bring this about, then at least one should not expose oneself to the displeasure of Allāh Almighty in the commencing and undertaking of such a journey. For one must know that at that moment one will behold such things. Hence one would be a disobedent sinner if one set forth on such a journey. If such a traveller were to enter their tents pitched amidst the unlawful [*ḥarām*], then he would eat their food and see their number. He would arrive at a great door of wickedness and be in fear of the blinding of his vision. Because, to look at them with an approving eye will lead to hardness of the heart, and the latter will result in [*spiritual*] blindness. If he who sees and he who eats is in their power then what attitude can one have of that one amongst them who takes the properties of the Muslims from their hands? No friend or protector can be found for this individual who is preoccupied by his selfishness and by his desire to lay his hands upon the benefits of the Muslims. The course of his action is clear from the path which he follows. What he cannot get hold of he leaves, since Allāh Almighty will not enable him to obtain what is beyond the limit of the power decreed. In that, the Lawgiver has offered guidance in His words, "Your souls are yours to keep. He who errs will not hurt you if you are rightly guided."[78] The Messenger, the blessing and peace of Allāh be upon him, interpreted that when he said, "If you behold avarice obeyed and fancy followed, and one is dictated by one's vision, then it is time for one to be concerned with matters of the soul." What is meant here, is that one should forego being exposed to the vanities of the masses [*ʿāmmah*], because they have departed far from the truth, and have adopted [evil] paths and ways and customs. On that basis they have built structures from evil fancies. Such is the sense of the Prophet's words, peace be upon him, when he said, "I do not fear that you will be confused as to the way so that you will become lost, rather my fear for you is that you may follow your fancy and fall into heresy." That in no way conflicted with the saying of the Prophet, the blessing and peace of Allāh be upon him, "He is not one of us, he who has no interest in the Muslims, because concern and interest is a duty laid upon the Muslims. It is that which does not lead into harm and injury in your religion, nor does it in any wise destroy manly virtues. Such virtues exist side by side with the thought of helping and in offering provision and the furthering of devotion of the mass of mankind to the truth". All of these qualities and virtues are absent in this our day and age. It was only the prevailing situation when this *Ummah* first came into being.

Shall I be an advocate for these [Tuareg] when Allāh Almighty has said, "Do not litigate for those who deceive themselves," that is, they deceive through disobedience; nay, rather, I am only an advocate for our *Amīr* [Muḥammad ibn al-Kumayt], due to the close attention and the deep concern which he pays to us in respect of our being within his realm, for you have shown your attention O embarker in the private affairs of the most exalted office! Indeed our *Amīr*, whom you deem to be an infidel, us likewise infidels due to our being within his realm, when he became the *Amīr*, and when the office of *Imārah* was fixed in his person by those who were men empowered to "loose" and to "bind", through conquering his foes, then his sister came to us, she called Takarsadat, and she said, "You were those who established as ruler that one who was marked with the stamp and marks of [the house of] Targhaytāmut.[79] It was not their wont to frequent the teachers, and they paid scant regard to matters of their religion; teach him, therefore, the legal basis of the faith and its creeds." So we obeyed her command and he submitted to it. He appointed one of us called Saʿīd to tutor him. He was happy with his teaching and Saʿīd continues to repeat to him what is needful and dutiful for him, be it religious or be it worldly matters. We do likewise. We repeat it to him whenever we visit him. But the sons of Karidenna[80] are too proud and exalted to speak words of infidelity or to pronounce and utter those things which are deemed to be heathenish and ungodly. Among them [the chiefs of the Iwillimeden] are those who perform the ritual ablutions, and there are also amongst them those who memorise much of the Koran. Amongst them are those who have learnt the laws and the creeds, nay, rather *all of them* believe in Allāh's unity. We have examined them and we have searched thoroughly into what they believe, by Allāh, in Allāh and for Allāh. We have not found a single one of them, but one and all is a believer in the Divine Unity. We have not heard a single one of them speak to anyone [with hostility] unless the latter has grieved them in their country and has done them an injustice. On the contrary they stay aloof from taking men's lives, Allāh Almighty be praised. If they commit an unjust act, then it is only in respect of possessions and of properties, that is to say the possessions of their subjects, although it has to be conceded that their case and excuse rests on dubious grounds in this respect.

Their scholars base their case on two rules. The first is: "Whosoever transfers another's benefit, be it in money and wealth or be it in some other kind, either with that person's permission or without his permission, then the restitution of it will be demanded from him." Now this rule arises out of the saying of the Prophet, "From money, or possessions other than money, is [demanded] the price of the sacred intention [*ḥarām*]." The answer [which they give] is that the value of the sacred intention [*ḥarām*] is fixed by that [evaluation], although he personally may not have contributed anything which he himself possesses, be it a provision of his or his beast of burden.

The second is the law of him who restitutes property from an illegal seizure. He is entitled to a half of it. It has also been said that he is entitled to a third of it, if it entails him in some burden in respect of it, so too from an enemy who is outside the country. Shaykh Sīdī'l-Mukhtār al-Kuntī said in one of his writings,[81]

> "As for the enemy who normally resides outside the country, who is a law unto himself, whose habitation is remotely located, who is in a state of rebellion, there is nothing for the master of the property in regard to what they have seized from him, whether the recoverer does so by purchase, or whether it be as a gift, or whether warriors from those lone wolves of his land come upon it in a raid. Under the force of necessity its owner will be obliged to despair of [the recovery of] the property, and it will become part of that which is subject to loss."

He then went on to say,

> "What about the situation where they have conquered a tribe, and they have launched a raid upon it, and after they have withdrawn into isolation

with the possessions they pass by another tribe, and the latter try to recover it from their hands after a great exertion and effort and fierce fighting?''

He said,

''I consider that they should divide those properties between themselves after the paying of the blood money of those who had been slain and the inheritance of the wounded, unless there be some cooperation between the parties before that. That will be an impediment, and if the one who recovers the property from their hands be one of the tyrants of their country, then he will either be one who takes the tax [*maks*],[82] or one of those who do not take anything of it. If he be one of those who take the tax [*maks*] from it, then they will have no claim to it [here], because [the *Ineslemen*] only gave them [the right to such a] tax in order to debar them from [oppressing] those who gave it to them. They acted in that manner [to determine the affair] since they are the mantle of Islam and the guardians of learning, and those who are competent and efficient in it in all their land.''

The [Iwillimmeden] Tuareg in their country have risen up [to act] on behalf of the scholars in the face of their enemy. They, the latter, have established and furthered the practice of the true faith. They have built mosques and they have inculcated learning among the ignorant until some of them have become saints and they have guided men who hitherto had been fools. So the poor have become rich and the rich have become nobles. Such then is the consequence of Islam [amongst them]. This does not come to pass save through him who, in his heart, has the fear of Hell Fire, or who earnestly desires to enter the Paradise of the Pardoner, or who seeks after caring and showing his concern for the rights of Allāh and His due, and also that of His Messenger. That point was made by Ibn Shaʿbān and Ibn Bashīr. It was either in regard to a tribe more dissolute than the Tuareg, or else it was a warning to keep a watch against the imposition of hard conditions and of harsh treatment. Had they both known of the circumstances of the people of our country, and the company of those [poor Muslims] who are the protected neighbours of the Tuareg, then they would know that [submission to this protection] was unavoidable for us, that is the protection of the Tuareg [ruled by Măkhămmăd ''El-Kumati'']. Were it not for them [and their protection] all the others would have perished in a massacre, since everyone who can achieve the benefit for himself and for his tribe by dominating his brother, weakens the latter or weakens his tribe or terrifies his kinsmen. He takes the property of the tribe by force, or he conquers him, or he fights him, and the two of them die together. If one of them dies, and the other takes away his wealth, then neither will gain anything They will evoke nothing but terror, causing earthquakes and the extermination of tribes, since there is not one who will stand in the way of this amongst them, save for the Tuareg [who protect them]. They will not find a portion of order and tranquility except with them. None will then venture to impose on them, whether he be [another] evil client, or else a marauder in the night.

I litigate for those who are the clients of the Tuareg, but who are not like them at all. I likewise defend them, making use of what I can find in regard to the defence of the Muslims, and about the Muḥammadan Covenants [*al-ʿUhūd al-Muḥammadiyyah*] written by the Shaykh who is spiritually aware of the Almighty, ʿAbd al-Wahhāb al-Shaʿrānī.[83] This is what he writes,

> "A general covenant has been imposed on us by the Messenger of Allāh, may His peace and blessing rest upon him, namely that we should defend the honour of a brother Muslim when one amongst us tries to slander and discredit him, that is, if we consider that we have the power at our command to do so. The bulk of mankind have begun to infringe this covenant, even among some of the *Mashāyikh* of this age, among the pious and the godly and the scholarly. You behold how they vent their wrath. How they back-bite against their brother, and sometimes they show their spite in this manner between themselves. This is one of the strongest indications of their lack of being weaned away from love of this fleeting world, through the guidance of a wise counselling Shaykh. Verily, the lover of this world loves to enjoy a unique and unrivalled status within it. He loves a reputation and an unrivalled renown and he hates anyone else overshadowing him in that respect. He thinks that through the slandering of men against one who is superior to him that the people, once their esteem in which they hold him diminishes, will lose their belief in him and will then transfer their belief to him. What he fails to see is that he who intends something, or effects it, then the like of it will be done to him, too, in his turn. If he were to show his disdain for those who slander his brother Muslim, then Allāh Almighty would raise him in a status above all his peers because protection only comes from Allāh Almighty and not from men. Vows and covenants have been imposed on us by the *Mashāyikh* that we should strengthen the light of our brothers with all our might so that the like of that will return to us. Verily he who strives to put out the light of his brother, Allāh Almighty will extinguish his own light."

In this matter, also, Aḥmad ibn Ḥanbal[84] reported by a sound chain of authority and transmitted [this *Ḥadīth* of the Prophet], "He who protects the honour of his brother, Allāh will turn aside Hell Fire from his countenance on the Day of Resurrection." Then the Messenger of Allāh, the blessing and peace of Allāh rest upon him, recited, when in a state of unconsciousness, "It is right for Allāh Almighty that he should release him from Hell Fire." Al-Tirmidhī has reported with a transmitted chain of authority, the following [*Ḥadīth*], "He who defends the honour of his brother, Allāh will turn aside from his countenance Hell Fire on the Day of Resurrection." Then the Messenger of Allāh, His blessing and peace be upon him, said, "It is a duty imposed upon us to assist the true believers." There is another tradition reported, by a transmitted chain of authority, by Abū Dāwūd[85] and by others, that, "He who protects a true believer from a hypocrite who has done him an injury, then Allāh will send His angel to him and he will guard his flesh from Hell Fire." Ibn Abī'l-Dunyā[86] reported this tradition transmitted by a chain of authority, "He who assists his brother Muslim against slander, Allāh Almighty will assist him in this world and the next." Abū Dāwūd also reported this transmitted saying of the Prophet,

> "There is no Muslim who helps another in a place wherein the honour of the latter is denigrated, and he is subjected to the violation of honour and privacy, but Allāh will aid him in a land where His help must be given to him when he is in need."

My heart has been burdened to speak about two matters, matters which I was obliged to speak of, due to their direct relevance to the matter which concerns us with regard to the protection of the weak Muslims, and to give aid and support to the religion [of Islam].

One of these two is that you find fault with us, the company of the Kel Es-Sūq. You call us heretics because we do not carry weapons and because we do not fight the *muḥāribūn* in a *jihad*. This is due to your ignorance of what is involved in that matter, and because you are misguided in the literal meaning of the words of Allāh Almighty, "Be on your guard . . .",[87] and the saying of some of the *'ulamā'*, "the *jihād* of the *muḥāribūn* is a *jihād*", and in some copies this reads, "the war of *jihād* against the *muḥāribūn* is more pertinent and more momentous than the war against the infidels", and in others, "it is of greater consequence than against the Byzantines".

Our case and our excuse in giving up the carrying of weapons is due to our adherence to the letter of the words of the Prophet, peace be upon him, "He who carries weapons against us is not one amongst our number." By this *Ḥadīth* the trustworthy Ibn Sha'bān determined the infidelity of some of the Berber tribes. Our plea for the abandonment of the *jihād* against the *muḥāribūn* is the *Ḥadīth* reported by Abū Dharr, which the *'ulamā'* interpreted as the giving up of [force] and the holding back of the hand in the event of uncertainty. Here is the *Ḥadīth* of Abū Dharr, in Muslim and al-Nasā'ī,

> "The Prophet, the blessing and peace of Allāh be upon him, said, 'O Abū Dharr, have you pondered how you would behave if men were to [unjustly] impose their will on another?' He answered, 'Allāh and His

Messenger know better than I do.' He said, 'Sit quietly in your house and shut your door to the outside world.' He said 'What then, if I am not left alone?' He said, 'Then comply with the wishes of those whom you live with and be with them.' He said, 'Shall I take my weapon?' He said, 'You will associate with them in their business, but if you are fearful that the flash of the sword will fill you with alarm then throw the hem of your mantle over your face so as to acknowledge his fault and your own.'"

All this is quoted from the *Fatḥ al-Bayān*. Among the authorities in the Tradition of the Prophet [*ḥashwiyyah*] there are a people who do not permit the obtaining of weapons for defence, because the Prophet, the blessing and peace of Allāh be upon him, warned against feuding and told men to beware of them. He ordered that bows should be broken and also other weapons. Maysarah said, "If the Muslims find themselves powerless and incapable, then to rise up against the wicked is not allowed due to their powerlessness and incapacity." Powerlessness, incapacity and impotence is a true summing up of our condition in necessity. The rule which we have mentioned has been discussed. It is for us to abide by it. The rule is this: that in the greater and the lesser of two evils it is wiser and more fitting to desist. This was the view expressed by ʿAbd al-Bāqī in the Chapter on Warfare [*al-ḥirābah*] in his Commentary to the *Mukhtaṣar* of Khalīl. There, instead of the need to slay the *muḥārib*, to cite the words mentioned by the author [*muṣannif*] "As long as the common good lies in sparing him, that is, that one fears a far greater evil and wickedness in the slaying of him than in the sparing of his life, *then in this case it is not permitted to slay him*. Thereby one commits the lesser evil of the two."

THE QUESTION OF THE *IMGHĀD*[88]

The second of the two matters is your effort to enslave the class which is called *Imghād*, whether their members be amongst those who moved away from us to your country, or whether they be others. You find your evidence and proof for their status as slaves by the inheritance system of the Tuareg in regard to their properties. You do this at one time, although at another time you allege that this is the ruling of tribal law [*ʿurf*] and custom [*ʿādah*]. So you cover up by this means your evil practice, despite your ignorance of what is clear evidence of proof, or how to set about the discovering of proof in this matter. It would have been the wisest course for you if you had sought the security of your faith and the state of guiltlessness which is to be found therein. Then you would have questioned us about the history of those who moved away from us, or who were captured from us. Indeed, *we are the experts* in regard to their report and their history and the facts told in regard to their affairs. Their tale is that they are a substantial group of people who dwelt in a country called Ibdaqan Kannār.[89] They were fought by an army of the Companions, who had at their head, ʿAmr ibn al-ʿĀṣ ibn Wāʾil, ʿUqbah al-Mustajāb and Abū Maḥdhūrah, the *muezzin* of the Prophet, the blessing and peace of Allāh be upon him, and they became Muslims at their hands and they appointed to be their *Amīr* over them one of their tribes who was called Kusaylah and some of the army dwelt there.[90] Their tombs are there with their names engraved on them save for Abū Maḥdhūrah. He died in Umm Raḥīm. They taught them the religion and the needful branches of learning and they taught them to meditate and practise the faith. The situation continued in this wise for a long while. Then the times changed with new events and happenings.

Next, there arrived amongst them the tribe called Iwillimmeden, with a Shaykh of ours called Muḥammad Aḥmad al-Gunahānī.[91] The latter used cunning against them and they fought them. Fate's vicissitudes were to the detriment of those former people and, they [the Iwillimmeden], conquered them and they appropriated the districts which belonged to them and their territories and they became, by Allāh's might, the Giant and Mighty Lord, beneath their sway. They ruled them severely and they crushed them. They tried to carry out mischief amongst them and they imposed dues and taxes upon them. This has continued up to the present day. The pursuit of their whim and fancy has gone so far that they now inherit their possessions, and they dispose of them as the lord disposes of his slaves. Some of them take their property [from them] by virtue of their [assumed] status as guardians and custodians of it, for him who is inherited. Some of them give them property as a means of absorbing the property which they own either during their lifetime or after they die. This then is a kind of consuming of a man's own property, quite falsely, and wholly illegally. You have followed their example, you have cited their deeds as your evidence, despite your knowledge that the *Imghād* claimed free status for themselves, and that he who claims his status to be that of a free man is in the position of the defendant in his case to maintain the firmness of his origin, for the latter is rooted amongst those who are free. Whosoever is in the position of a defendant, where his status as a slave is called into question, he, that is the defendant, is in the position of a plaintiff by his mere pretension to a [free man's] origin. Customary law witnesses to his truth. The onus is upon him to offer some clear proof, or else to confess his lack of it. You, however, have turned away from his judgement and have followed the customary behaviour of those Tuareg.

Now they [the *Mujtahidūn*], have said that the adherence to a tradition *in deeds and actions* is unlawful. Indeed, al-Maḥallī has said, according to the *Jam' al-Jawamī'*, "It is not to be called adherence to tradition (*taqlīd*)." Ibn 'Arafah said, quoting Ibn Bishr, in regard to the citing of proof by the deed and act of the learned, "the doing of any action does not indicate that it is permissable or to the contrary. Nor that it is a necessity, unless it be the deed of one who has been inspired by the infallibility of the Prophet, the blessing and peace of Allāh be upon him." This is quoted from the *Kitāb al-Tanbīh 'an al-ghalaṭāt*. It has been established in the *Uṣūl* of Jurisprudence that adherence to tradition *is not permissable in actions, but it is only so in sayings and in words.* Reference was made to this by the Imām al-Ḥaramayn in his book where he said, "Adherence to tradition of the *Muftī* is only allowable in the *fatwā* which he gives." His commentator has remarked,

> "Here he pointed out that only in the *fatwā* is *taqlīd* permitted. It is not allowed in deeds and in actions. When the ignorant sees the knowledgeable doing an action, then it is not permissible for him to imitate his example [*taqlīd*] in what he does by the mere fact that he has done that deed."

Now if this be valid in regard to the *Mujtahid*, then what view have you then of him who abides by a tradition with mere imitation [*muqallid*] since he may not know whether what he does is permitted or not? This man spoke correctly when he said,

> "Due to the lack of care in preserving the purity of the *Sunnah* and the *Sharī'ah*, today, evil is to be seen in many of the circumstances of some of the people of this time. You will find one of them is guilty of heresy [*bid'ah*], but if you tell him to desist he will argue to prove that it is the *Sunnah* in fact, because it is the opinion of his Shaykh or the one whom he esteems to be superior acts thus. He says, 'my lord so and so acts in this way'."

So the action of his Shaykh has become an excuse for that thing [allegedly] in the *Sharī'ah*, which [in fact] has been established by the hands of men. His Shaykh is not among the infallible, nor amongst the men of the [first] three centuries of Islam. If we concede that practice then error will mar the *Sharī'ah*. Anyone who thinks well of something which he has done, or who hates something which he has omitted, and his example is [slavishly] followed by others, he is [in fact] an abrogator of the *Sharī'ah* or Muḥammad. May Allāh Almighty forbid such a thing. He has protected this *Millah* from being cut off. Anyone who introduces a thing which is contrary to the custom of the first and foremost of the *Millah*, then he is one who has the worm [of death and destruction] upon him. Similar to this is the *Sharī'ah* of Jesus [son of Mary], peace be upon him. It was altered and modified, and by that I mean the system of practice [*taqlīd*] of the rabbis and the monks.

Al-Shaykh al-Sanūsī said,[92] may Allāh Almighty have mercy upon him, "The sources of infidelity [*kufr*] and innovation [*bidʿah*] are seven in their number." He numbered them as follows: *Evil taqlīd*, and he interpreted and explained this to be the owing of allegiance to another on account of tribal partisanship and fanatical loyalty without seeking the Truth. He counted amongst them *ignorance which is abyssmal and compounded*. Here he was intending one who is ignorant of the Truth and who is totally unaware of his ignorance. Al-Bayḍāwī said,[93] "*Taqlīd* in actions, where it is permissible, is only so in the main for him who knows that he is correct and true."

The evil of your *taqlīd* of these ignorant men will be clear to you. If he denies the permissibility of *taqlīd* of the man of learning in deeds [which he does], then how [can it be permitted] to the ignorant? Nay, further to this, you have no permission to judge by the sayings of the scholars, sayings which are proper to *taqlīd*, since you enjoy no share in the knowledge of the nature of *taqlīd*. In the rules which are gathered together there is to be found the true nature of that which should be initiated by the *muqallid*, be he a Mālikī, or a Shāfiʿī, or a Ḥanafī, or a Ḥanbalī, that is, if he comprehensively grasps the meaning of the indications and proofs of the person who is initiated [in it], its analogies, its pretexts, its general applications, its particular and peculiar applications, and its qualifications. If such are not applicable [in his case], then he is *no* kinsman of an *Imām* who is appointed to the task, nay rather, for *you* it is not permissible to cite proof and evidence at the source, neither in the Koran, nor in the *Ḥadīth*, nor in the words of the scholars. As for the Koran, there it has been made a condition that he who cites proof should be knowledgeable in preferable opinion, and that he should know the many categories of the Koranic science. You have no knowledge of one single category amongst them!

As for the *Ḥadīth*, then it is because he who recites it, but who has no knowledge of grammar, cannot be relied upon to have escaped lying against the Prophet, the blessing and peace of Allāh be upon him, who said, "Whosoever lies against me, intentionally, will occupy his seat in Hell Fire." As for the words and the sayings of the scholars, then it is due to what has been said already about the nature of knowing what *taqlīd* is all about, the thorough knowledge of the initiator in the proofs of evidence which are to be found with the one who is to be imitated, his analogies, his pretexts and also about what is rigidly adhered to by him who cites proof in a legal judgement in matters of jurisprudence, restricted in category, a proof in itself, a container of proof. The premise, namely the evidence of proof, is a basis itself and is incumbent for a basis. Now the basis is either rational or else it is traditional. The latter is made conditional by it being sound in support [*sanad*] back to him who is its initiator, that is to say to him [the Prophet] upon whom rest the blessings of Allāh Almighty. [Secondly] it should be clear and explicit in its indication of the ruling which is sought after. [Thirdly] it should be of lasting authority for the judges who decide. [Fourthly] it should outweigh everything which opposes it. These, then, are four conditions. You have no knowledge of them!

Furthermore, the custom in which you are proficient is only to be applied in respect of that which is based upon it. It is not relevant to anything other than this. ʿAbd al-Bāqī said, citing al-Tunadī[?],[94]

> "It is unlawful for a *Muftī* to issue a *fatwā* of divorce until he knows the customary law [*ʿurf*] in that country, and that he know all the rulings which are built upon codes of legal practice which are the customary law, that is currencies, coins, dies used in dealings, transactions and in benefits and lettings on lease, oaths, wills and vows."

So pay heed to what he says, "built upon . . . [*mabniyyah*] and so on". Built upon established practice, and not simply upon textual authority, for that which is regarded as a text-book ruling in such things as these, lacks the renewal of a customary law which contradicts it.

Your judgement in regard to the class called *Imghād*, in the light of the way you have judged in this case, namely that their status is that of slaves, the sanctioning of their properties, and making the Tuareg their inheritors by custom, is a case of an intellectual gloss. To pass judgement and determine by such embellishment is both false and worthless. Such is the case in the books of the first principles of Jurisprudence and in the books of the science of Dogmatics, so too judgement by intellectual disparagement, as is also the case in these books. As for the *Imāmate*, al-Māwardī says,

> "The *Imāmate* has been laid down for the Prophetic Caliphate and the guarding of the Faith, and for the political management of worldy affairs. Its binding compact for him who undertakes it is a duty and an obligation, even if the nations and the communities turn aside from it. As for the *Imām*, he is the Caliph, the protector of the Faith. The conditions in regard to him are that he should be a lord in might and judgement, effective in executing his command, great in awe and esteem, chaste in his outward behavior, covetous in little and of much piety."

Such is lacking in your land.

Woe to you, what is the matter with you, *O ʿAbd*, you who make sport with the honours of those whose circumstance you have no knowledge? Your cheek and your arrogance in what you say has reached such lengths that you have deemed to be infidels those Muslims who have made the confession, which is to testify that Allāh is the Sole God and that Muḥammad is the Messenger of

Allāh, may His blessing and peace rest upon him. They have performed the Muslim religious duties, namely the statutory prayers, they have performed the act of assistance which is to pay alms [*zakāh*], and the act of shield and protection [*junnah*], which is the fast, and the act of pilgrimage [*ḥijjah*], which is the annual pilgrimage to Mecca, and the act of triumph and success, which is the greater Holy War, namely the *jihād* of the soul, and the act of loyalty which is the command to do good and to accomplish charitable acts, and also to forbid and eschew acts which are reprehensible, and the acts of union with believers, and of personal care [*ulfah*], which is the meeting together in the assembly [*jamāʿah*] and the act of atonement and expiation which is the diligent search for knowledge. They live according to, and they follow, the canonic laws of Islam [*Sharāʾiʿ*] which is to speak the truth with the tongue and to act with obedience, and to fulfil the covenant and to follow the *Sunnah* of the Prophet.

As for the decisive answer which I promised to give you in regard to the six matters, then I leave the following counsel to do it for me, "Empty your heart of that which fills it of those things which it covets after." The first of these matters is the gap which divides the company of the Kel Es-Sūq from others who are not of their kin. It is this, that those who are not amongst the Kel Es-Sūq are eager to join with the Tuareg in their pursuit of those acts which they commit. They are acts of evil and wickedness and acts which encourage others to commit them and so set men at variance, the one with the other. Now the Kel Es-Sūq, Allāh Almighty be praised, are not like that despite the disdain of every man who is envious of them, nay, rather, in the *jihād* with the heart they avoid the contrary impulse of its fancy and the desire of the heart and the tongue. They act to fulfil the command to do good and to forbid and to eschew that act which is evil. The second of these matters is to keep a promise, and the third of them is that which I have already mentioned to you in regard to the conditions of the *Imām* and the *Imāmate* in the words which have already been expressed. The fourth of them is the answer concerning our being within the province of an infidel prince, whereas he is, as we have already made quite clear, one upon whom we have fixed and established the rules of the Faith and its dogmas. We have explained that he has submitted to that. The fifth of them is that which removes the eye of your proof. As I have mentioned to you it is that wherein there are decisive answers from the Koran and the *Ḥadīth* and the fundamental laws and root principles. The sixth of them is that [evidence] which banishes any status of infidelity [*kufr*] from us, from our prince and from our subjects one and all. It is as I have mentioned to you, and I have quoted from the *Kitāb al-Shifāʾ* by the *Qāḍī* ʿIyāḍ, and from *Maʿūnat al-Ikhwān*, the commentary of al-Sanūsī, and *Bughyat al-Ṭālibīn*,[95] likewise his commentary, and so too, in a nutshell, the claim that the utterance of the words of the confession of the Faith even though it be in a language other than Arabic, nay, even if he make no mention of a denial or affirmation, even if he only say that Allāh is One and Muḥammad is His Messenger, *then he is a Muslim*. Indeed many of the people of our land have adopted much which the Prophet has bestowed upon them, and they have eschewed much which he has commanded them to avoid; such things which have become offshoots and branches from the Faith and which are embraced by the books of Dogmatic Theology, and, on the other hand, those things which have branched forth from Islam itself, and which are embraced by the Science of Jurisprudence, and those things which have come out of good works and from godliness and which are embraced by the books of Ṣūfism, and those of the seven obstacles, the plagues and their treatment, the categories of morality, the states [*maqāmāt*] and spiritual degrees [*aḥwāl*] and such, and many and renowned are those things which indicate to us that they are truly Muslims.

How well spoke Muḥammad al-Amīn ibn Hammahamma,[96] who said, "Islam has abolished infidelity [*kufr*] since Zayd [the personification of Arabic language and grammar] came with enlightenment in his countenance." How blessed a youth he is! *O brother* in the religion of Allāh, of Allāh, of Allāh, I repeat, among the *servants* of Allāh, of Allāh, of Allāh, I repeat, in His ways and His rulings, be on your guard over your hearts in those matters amongst yourselves, and in that matter between yourselves and your Lord. One consequence will be followed by another. Death brings what indeed it must, but let it not give you cause for concern. Each one of you is concerned with some matter which is not his business. Repent to your Lord over those sins which you have committed. Free yourselves from the pollution of those crimes which you have committed and convert them into the whiteness of clarity and into spotlessness. Subject them to the curbs of true self-guidance, by that true guidance of the pious, and force them to follow the *Sunnah* most glorious, the *Sunnah* of the Prophet Muḥammad, the blessing and peace of Allāh be upon him.

He is the lord of the Prophets, for verily, he who makes the *Sunnah* the lord of his soul will utter words of wisdom, whereas he who makes fancy the master of his soul will utter heresy (*bidʿah*). Be humble, be not pompous and proud, be meek and be not self-satisfied. Know that the judgement is with Allāh, and that the labour of love for Allāh Almighty is the search for knowledge for His sake, according to the *Sunnah* of the Messenger of Allāh, His blessing and peace be upon him. Consume not your possessions amongst yourselves falsely and let not your doubt master you and oppress you, verily you are men of learning. In the tradition it is said that learning has an all demanding mastery, like the mastery and domination of a man by riches. This title, the name given to one as a scholar, a man of learning, is not fitting save for that man who is able to search to the depths and to draw forth branches from their stems and to join branches to their stems and their roots, as it is said in the book, *Kitāb Mīzān al-Sharī'ah* by 'Abd al-Wahhāb al-Sha'rānī.

Verily your Lord is watchful. He will know those who have acted unjustly, in the way of all flesh and its changing circumstances. The blessing and peace of Allāh be upon him who has condemned wickedness and injustice, and also upon his family and his Companions, all of whom have been raised above that thing which causes blame and reproof. Blessing be upon those Messengers who were sent, and praise be to Allāh, the Lord of the Worlds.

Here ends what is written by the hand of the sinful Shaykh who makes many slips and errors, in the morning and in the evening, Muḥammad Ḥabba ibn Muḥammad Aḥmad *al-Sharīf* al-Sūqī, then al-Idrīsī, completed on Friday the twenty fifth of the month of Rabī' II, 1389 of the *Hijrah*. Upon the lord of it be Allāh's blessing and peace. He wrote it for his brother in Allāh, Muḥammad Ibrāhīm ibn Muḥammad al-Mu'min ibn 'Abd al-Karīm. He did so as a service to knowledge and to its people.

Appendix III

The Golden Chain of the Shaykhs of the Kuntah

The Golden Chain is based on an incomplete manuscript which is preserved in Walātah and which was written by a Kuntah or Maḥājīb scholar there.

This text appears to be an abridgement of a famous Kuntah work entitled, "The book of uncommon and precious things, both acquired and inherited, as were displayed in the miracles and godly deeds accomplished by the two leading elders, the mother and the father, Shaykh Sīdī'l-Mukhtār al-Kuntī and his wife." This summarises the biographies of the earliest scholars of the Kuntah in the Western Sahara. It is a compendium of hagiographical folktales, tribal history and cherished miracles. It typifies this *genre* amongst the Mauritanian *Zwāya* and the Malian Kel Es-Sūq. However, the latter seem to have been less interested in the hagiographical biographies than many of their Moorish counterparts. Their greatest aim was to master Arabic grammar and their lives were dedicated to unravelling the complexities of Arabic text-books and commentaries on legal issues, so that they could transform the social habits of the nominally Muslim peoples around them from within. The Kuntah scholars combined the Ṣūfī piety of the Moors of *Zenāgah* origin with the juridicial speculation of the later Kel Es-Sūq. Their administrative and diplomatic skill was unmatched and the political influence of the Kuntah on the history of the Western Sahara was crucial.

The [Ṣūfī] Golden Chain from the Banū'l-Raqqādi was [linked to] Sīdī'l-Mukhtār al-Kuntī[1] who was a saint, a scholar, a devout man and a poet of eloquence. His father was Sīdī'l-Amīn, and he, too, was a pious saint and an active scholar. His father, Sīdī'l-Mukhtār, who was called ʿAntarah,[2] was a scholar in sundry branches of learning, devout and ascetic and credited with numerous miracles. His father, Sīdī ʿUmar (al-Shaykh), attained a degree unsurpassed in religious science and in devotion and asceticism. This was also true of his father, Sīdī Aḥmad, for it was he who built the retreat for devotion [*Zāwiyah*] in response to Allāh's [command] and was a worker of miracles. Such, likewise, were his father, Sīdī Muḥammad al-Raqqādi, and the father of the latter, Sīdī Aḥmad of the split lower molars and the latter's father, Sīdī ʿUmar [al-Shaykh the Elder]. Even more so did (such piety) characterise his father, Sīdī Aḥmad al-Bakkāy (the Elder). It has been handed down, in a tradition related by consecutive testimonies, and it is the truth and authenticated, that he lived for one hundred years. No tear which he shed was ever dried, and that was on account of one single prayer which he missed in the Friday gathering. He lived, may Allāh show him His pleasure, in the year 911/1505–6. Sīdī Aḥmad ibn al-Ḥājj ʿAbdallāh ibn Sīdī Aḥmad al-Raqqādi reported that he had seen a document in his handwriting which he had written amidst the date groves which he had purchased in the town of Shinqīṭī in the year aforementioned. The Shaykh, Allāh's pleasure be bestowed upon him, said, and I was also told by the *faqīh* Muḥammad And ʿAbdallāh al-Walātī, who said that his father, *al-faqīh* Muḥammad ibn *al-faqīh* Aḥmad had told him, on the authority of his father the *faqīh* Aḥmad, on the authority of his forbear Sīdī ʿAbd al-Raḥmān al-Maḥjūbī, who reached the pole of mystic attainment [*Quṭb*], that he had received learning and sanctity from the perfect *Quṭb*, Sīdī Aḥmad al-Bakkāy [the Elder], and that when the negroes left Walātah for Ghānah the site of the former town became a course for the flood waters and the tomb of Sīdī Aḥmad al-Bakkāy was on the very lip of the *wādī* so that, if the flood water flowed there, it would dislodge it and carry it away. The flood water ceased to flow in that *wādī* so that the wells in the sandy bottom lost their water in the earth and the people of the town

Sīdī Aḥmad al-Bakkāy

were on the point of evacuating it. But, in a dream, [the deceased] Sīdī Aḥmad al-Bakkāy came to one [of three saints] of the offspring of ʿAbd al-Raḥmān al-Maḥjūbī. He said to him, "Verily, if thou wishest that your *wādī* flow with flood water then remove me from the path of the flood water for the flood ought not to flow by my tomb." Then, in a dream, he came to a second saint and said these same words, and then to a third to whom he said the same. The latter told the people what he had seen. The second said, "I have seen the like of what you saw," and the third said, "I have seen the like of what you both have seen."

The chief men of the town assembled, and Walātah at that time had seventy scholars, and they were of one mind on the counsel of the saints that the earth would not encroach on saintly bodies, and so they went to his tomb, they disinterred him, and lo, he was as one in a trance-like sleep. Nothing of his shroud had altered, aside from the body itself. One of their number put his hand between his face and his shroud and, lo, the eyes of the saint were shedding tears just as he had shed such tears in his lifetime. So they moved him to the place where his body now rests.

It is also reported, in a tradition related by consecutive testimonies, that when he came to Walātah he camped in one of its mountain trails, outside the precincts of the town. At that time it was infested with wild beasts: lions and panthers. Not an animal crept outside Walātah after nightfall but it was devoured by them. The townsfolk came to him though they knew not who he was. They said, "O Shaykh, if you sleep in this spot the lions will devour you. They snatch people up from between the houses in the town quite brazenly and openly." He answered, "Allāh will not give them power over me." When night descended the lions gathered together, every one of them, before him, in order to be blessed by him. When the people left the town the next morning they were quite sure that he had been eaten. They went to him and, lo, the lions were gathered around him rubbing against his clothes. They beheld a sight which they had not envisaged. They said, "This is only a saint amongst Allāh's saints." They were in awe of approaching him due to the great number of lions round about him. But he indicated to them that they might approach since they had nothing to fear. They came to him, walking between the tamed lions. He said to them "What do you want of these lions, they are at my command?" They said, "We want you to order them to leave this town of ours." He commanded them to do so and they left for the land of Ghānah just like departing cattle, some following others.

Then he decided to travel away from them. Their chief scholar said to them,

> "You have not brought resolution into your affair [relating to this saint]. There comes a saint of Allāh, like this very one, and then you simply let him depart from your town. You know into what evil and mischief it has fallen and how it has forsaken the *Sunnah* of the Prophet."

They said, "Who is the man among us to speak in regard to his staying amongst us? Who can persuade a man whom the lions obey?" They said, "You can persuade him." Others said "How can this be accomplished!" He [that scholar] said, "By the call of the return to the *Sharīʿah*. He will not disobey the precious and mighty *Sharīʿah*." So they accepted and followed his advice. They caught him up just as he was about to begin a journey of wandering as a desert ascetic. They said, "By Allāh, and by the *Sharīʿah* we are your men." When he heard them speak thus he fell on his face and he clenched his hands tightly behind his back. He said, "To hear is to obey." He did this for the sake of Allāh and His Messenger, and for the *Sharīʿah*. He returned to the town in their company. They said, "We shall bring you before our [chief] scholar." "I am content to do so," was his reply. He said, "The situation is clear for the eye to see. This is a wicked town. So sinful has it become that a husband cannot prevent his wife from sinning to excess."[3] He made two conditions in his answer. "Do not disobey what I command you to do from Allāh Almighty and that brought by His Messenger." They agreed to his demand. He also commanded them to observe a strict observance of the veil and seclusion. They complied, and he commanded that no woman should enter, or be visited in, a house unless the visitor or the visited was in a degree of consanguinity precluding marriage. They became strict adherents of the *Sunnah*, they studied at his feet, until he died, may Allāh be pleased with him. Such was his story and his mission. Allāh honoured them from that time. Learning abounded and understanding was made sharp, up to and including our very day. None of the bedouin Arabs [*Aʿrāb*] harmed them, for if one did so then Allāh decreed the power which he had to be worthless and He banished him from their land. He [the reporter] said, "At his tomb I have seen a lion and a lioness. When they came near me the lioness stood opposite and away from me. The lion came to me and said, 'No lion remains of those blessed by this your grandfather save this lioness and myself.' I know not whether either were descended from them or were both frequenters who came to me. Allāh Almighty is able to accomplish all things."

Sīdī Aḥmad ibn Muḥammad al-Raqqādi

The mother of Sīdī Aḥmad ibn Muḥammad al-Raqqādi was a Jakāniyyah and he grew up amongst the Tājakānt. The mother of his son, Sīdī ʿUmar [al-Shaykh], was a daughter of Sīdī'l-Mukhtār al-Kuntī [the Elder]. When he [Sīdī Aḥmad] achieved fame by his miracles, it is told that he, having come from the lord of Karzāz[4] to whom he had been sent by his father Sīdī Aḥmad of the split lower molars, arrived in Tuwāt and he stayed with Sīdī ʿAbd al-Qādir, the Master of the retreat [*Zāwiyat* Kuntah]. He was a visionary who disclosed his innermost thoughts. He said,

> "O Ibn al-Raqqādi, build a retreat [*Zāwiyah*] where your mule passes water; betwixt the two strongholds of the Banū Quṭbī,[5] men who are unjust tyrants; do this so that Allāh may grant relief and freedom from them [to me] through you. Allāh Almighty has appointed that the retribution of the unjust will take place at your hands. They have done much wickedness in the land and they have declared their mischief. I have beheld it written on the inscribed tablet [*al-lawḥ al-maḥfūẓ*] that the [Kel] Ahaggar Tuareg will become by your hands in awe of the image of a dog."

The [Kuntah] Shaykh said to him, "My men and myself are not ones who are wont to take the forms of dogs, nonetheless, if you should wish it so, then you yourself shall assume the shape of a dog to face them." "It shall be so ordered." A huge army [*ʿarim*] of the sons of their [Kel Ahaggar] prince launched a raid against the [centre of] Tuwāt, and when they reached the middle stage of their journey on that way they came upon a great glade adorned with fragrant flowers and extraordinary streams and they were made careless [of their purpose] by the [sight of] gazelles. Their leader said, "Would that we had a dog to help us hunt these gazelles." Lo, at that instant, there leaped a red dog before them and the sons of the chief hastened towards it. It halted, and one of them took it by the neck and another by its rear and they disputed over the possession of it. Each one unsheathed his dagger and slaughtered his companion. The people were divided and resisted to a man. They all died and neither caller nor responder amongst them returned to his tribe. The tribe having lost all news of them, and their absence having been prolonged, at length believed that the people of Tuwāt had exterminated them. Those [left] in the tribe mounted and rode forth; none remained save Ṣāliḥ Abū Muḥammad al-Khayr, whom they left behind.

When they reached the border of that bower they were startled by the playfulness of the gazelles. The dog rose up before them. The two chiefs made towards it and it waited for them both until they had mastered it, as it had done previously with their two sons, and they disputed over it and they fought, and the people fought, and they all perished. Thus Allāh safely rid His servants and their land of the wickedness of these men and their evil deeds. The orphans [left by them] were collected together by the [pious] Ṣāliḥ, [the *Amenukal* of the Kel Ahaggar].[6] He was under the control of Shaykh Sīdī Muḥammad ibn ʿAbd al-Raḥmān ibn Abī Naʿāmah.[7] Ṣāliḥ was succeeded by his son, [the *Amenukal*] Muḥammad al-Khayr.[8] He met Shaykh al-Wālid [Sīdī Mukhtār al-Kuntī], Allāh be pleased with him, and he was honourably received in all awe and solemnity and he returned to him [Shaykh al-Wālid] what property had been looted or stolen from the Kuntah. He said to him [Shaykh al-Wālid], "Sire, the Kuntah are foolish, they avoid us and our tracks. You never see them joining with us. We have returned to them all that we have ever seized and it is an insult to us not to combat them." Shaykh al-Wālid said to him, "If you come upon them then make them stay. But if they refuse, resist, and turn their backs on you then you may fight whom you wish and leave unharmed those whom you wish." Then the Shaykh [al-Wālid] returned, and when he reached al-Mabrūk,[9] lo the Kuntah had begun to sound the alarm for battle. He intercepted them and said,

> "Do not show hostility, and stay where you are. Verily, the enemy have returned to you all that they held and they have requested me [to inform you] that none should shun their path. I have given them a promise and I have taken the responsiblity in regard to them that should you so refuse then they will triumph over you. You must not shun them."

The rest of the Kuntah stayed, but the Dirimshāka[10] Kuntah withdrew, together with the Yaddāsen[11] and the Awlād Mullūk. Seven or eight of the Banū'l-Wāfī went with them, amongst them Sīdī Muḥammad ibn al-Ḥājj Ḥabīb Allāh and Sayyid al-Mukhtār ibn Sīdī ʿAlī. The two paternal uncles of Sīdī Muḥammad [aforementioned] were amongst men, he being in authority and old in years. They were ʿAlī ibn ʿAbdallāh ibn Aḥmad al-Dirimshākī and ʿAlī ibn al-Ṭālib Yāsīn. They came upon the [Kel] Ahaggar at Tantagārt. They fought together and the Kuntah were defeated. Over seventy men were killed; twenty of the Dirimshāka, twenty of the Yaddāsen, among them ʿAlī ibn al-Ṭālib Yāsīn, twenty of the Awlād Mullūk and twenty of the Aʿlā'iq [clients?] of the Awlād al-Wāfī and two of the Ṣamīm ibn Ben Sīdī and Ibn Ṣā'im al-Shams and [the Kel Ahaggar] showed favour to many of them, on that day, and they fled. The Shaykh [of the Kuntah] resolved what [feud] there was between the Kuntah and the [Kel] Ahaggar through the tactful and discreet mediation [*mudārāh*] which entailed as recompense the payment of eight young camels distributed between the tribes. He sent them to them every year. Thus bloodshed was stopped and it pacified the senseless feuding between them. To Allāh is due all praise and all grace.

Sīdī Muḥammad al-Raqqādi

We have learnt on the authority of his Shaykh and his father, Sīdī Muḥammad al-Raqqādi, who, may Allāh show him mercy, was a scholar of diverse ability, a man of piety and prestige. He died, may Allāh be pleased with him, in the year 994/1585/6. His mother was the daughter of Sīdī Aḥmad ibn Sīdī Abī Bakr ibn Sīdī Aḥmad al-Bakkāy. The Shaykh [who reported] said, making known the name of Shaykh Sīdī Muḥammad al-Raqqādi, the reason for his nick-name, *Raqqād* "the somniloquist", was that people once came to him having gathered to resolve a difficult problem.

They found him asleep and he judged between them as he was sleeping. Then his novices gathered around them and he explained and commented to them about his sleep. It was on account of this that he was called *al-Raqqādi*. It is reported, on his authority, that he safely guarded a volume which he possessed. From it he drew all the sciences which were traced back to his grandfather, Sīdī ʿUmar al-Shaykh. It has been handed down in a tradition related by consecutive testimonies that, when he slept, light came forth from his nostrils and his mouth, so that the close friend and the common populace beheld it. No blame in matters godly fell upon him from a blamer and no wicked act was done, save by a hand other than his. The unjust began to avoid involvement in sins and injustices lest he know. Sometimes he cursed the doer [of such] and he suffered affliction at that very hour.

An insolent tyrant of the bedouin Arabs [*ṭāghiyah min al-ʿArab*] afflicted one of the towns of Tuwāt. He [the Shaykh] cursed him on account of a matter which reached his ears. Allāh responded to his prayer and he perished and his progeny and his stronghold were torn asunder. Until this moment it is a ruin. When he travelled he was amply supplied with provisions. He was asked about that, and he answered, "He who does not count his maintenance for his family should not be meagre in provisions." It is mentioned that a delegation came to him. He brought food to them. It was not very much and they found it too little for themselves. He said, "Eat of it, and if it is insufficient then I shall give you more." They ate of it until they were satisfied, while it was in the situation it had been before. They said, "Did you recite anything over it?" He said, "There is no God but Allāh. He has blessed it in order to show you His grace and His favour and so that you may know that He is the satisfier and that it is He who pours forth and supplies your drink and your food." Some became repentant at his hands and they stuck close to him. They became his novices from that time onwards and he shared his benefits with them.

Sīdī Aḥmad al-Fayram

The following report is on the authority of his Shaykh and his father, Sīdī Aḥmad, nicknamed "the man with the split lower molars" [*al-Fayram*]. He was an active scholar and a perfect saint. He died in the year 950/1543/4. Our Shaykh said, may Allāh be pleased with him and with us through him, it has been handed down by consecutive testimonies in regard to him that he used to teach his pupils which were not only humans but the *jinn*. Among his famous miracles was one which took place while he was in a large caravan and they were heading for Tuwāt. Lo, they beheld an army and it was followed by another army. When this occurred he ordered the detaining of that caravan and it halted. Then he pointed with his finger in the direction of the enemy and he said "You are sufficient against them,[12] halt," and thus they did. The enemy came and, behold, the caravan was turned to stone, or so it seemed to them.[13] One of the enemy shook his spear and said, "By Allāh, this stone was a man on a white camel and he was wearing white clothes." He cast a stone and it struck the teeth of the [petrified] Shaykh and it broke them. So ever after that he was called "the toothless", the one with split lower molars. The chief of the enemy said,

> "Oh men [of stone], if you are human people then remove the charm which divides us. Yours is the oath and the covenant of Allāh and of His Prophet. We shall do you no harm as long as you protect us, and our offspring will not harm your offspring, as long as the world lasts."

The Shaykh gave a sign with his sleeve and the spell was broken. They beheld the caravan and, lo, the cooks were cooking and the camels and all the baggage were as they had been. Kādim[14] and a party of the enemy repented at the hands [of the Shaykh] and the offspring of Kādim up to today have remained amongst the Kuntah. The others returned to their kinsfolk having obtained nothing.

The Shaykh was a devoted servant of God, an ascetic, a recluse and an eschewer of wordly things. He did not turn aside from his recitation of the Koran, save when teaching preoccupied him. His mother stemmed from the Īdayshalli, and she was called Tmqdst, the daughter of the *faqīh*, Yallab.

Sīdī ʿUmar al-Shaykh (the Elder)

It has been reported on the authority of the Shaykh, his father, the universal mystic pole [*Quṭb*], the succourer with gently flowing rain, Sīdī ʿUmar al-Shaykh [the Elder]. Our Shaykh [reporting] said, intending to guide aright, making known his story, that he [Sīdī ʿUmar al-Shaykh the Elder] was amongst the saints renowned for their learning and their sanctity. He bore the nickname of the Shaykh. It is handed down by consecutive testimonies that before he attained full vigour in his puberty he knew by heart one thousand volumes in various branches of the Islamic sciences [ʿ*ilm*]. He went to the western lands of Islam encharged with gaining profitable learning after his father and his Shaykh, Sidi Aḥmad al-Bakkāy [the Elder] had given him supplies. He went about all the land of the Maghrib and found none who would benefit him, or from whom he could profit, in matters of learning in the branches of the Islamic sciences. So he loaded his mount and saddled it and he journeyed to the land of Syria. It was there, too, that he encountered none from whom he could profit, none under whom he could study. Rather, those whom he met took their learning from him.

Then he went on the pilgrimage [*ḥajj*] and returned to the Maghrib. He explored the land of Takrūr[15] and while he was there he met the great Shaykh and perfect pole [*Quṭb*], Sīdī Muḥammad ibn ʿAbd al-Karīm al-Maghīlī.[16] He had come from Hausaland[17] and was making for Takrūr and for Morocco, by reason of the call of the people there for [true] Islam and for true guidance, and for the [practice] of the command given to do that which is good and to eschew evil. The public observance of the *Sunnah* and the public observance of modesty and veiling [was his mission]. They discussed in depth all branches of Islamic science. He [Maghīlī] said to him [Shaykh ʿUmar], "From what land and people came ye?" He said, "From the extreme Maghrib where I was born. It is the place where I reside and where I was brought up." Maghīlī said, "Verily a [brilliant] young man like you has no need of me." Then their discussion deepened into matters relating to the secret meaning of revealed texts [ʿ*ilm al-bāṭin*] and in this matter, he [Shaykh ʿUmar] was trained by Shaykh ʿAbd al-Karīm [al-Maghīlī]. He opened his heart and mind to him in all the knowledge which he had and the two were joined in a close friendship for some thirty years. During that period they went to the East. When they reached Cyrenaica [Barqah], lo, the chief amongst its bedouin had married his step-daughter. The Shaykh [Sīdī ʿUmar] learnt of that and went to see him. When he faced him, he rebuked him and said, "You accursed one, you have disobeyed the Book and the *Sunnah* and the consensus of the *Ummah* in this act which you committed." The other attacked him with his spear intent upon thrusting him through with it, but the Shaykh pointed his fingers towards him and his head flew from his corpse by the mere sign made by the Shaykh. Both the latter and al-Maghīlī pursued their goal and they reached the town of Assiut [in Egypt], which is on the shore of the sea [*sic*] of Byzantium facing towards Cyrenaica. There they met the perfect Shaykh Sayyid ʿAbd al-Raḥmān al-Suyūṭī.[18] He asked them both regarding their master who was authorised to teach the Ṣūfī litany [*wird*] and grant an *ijāzah* of affiliation to their Ṣūfī *ṭarīqah*, namely their *muqaddam*, and what view they held of him. The Shaykh reported to him [Suyūṭī] the event which had taken place between him and the head of the bedouin of Cyrenaica and about his death at his hands, granted by Allāh Almighty.

It was not long before they saw the claimants [for retribution] in pursuit of them. All that alarmed al-Suyūṭī, who said, "Verily we are from Allāh and verily to Him we are returning." The Shaykh said to him, "O ʿAbd al-Raḥmān al-Suyūṭī, do you think that we have come here to seek your help and your succour? Have we come as fugitives to you? Were I so to wish it then I could cast this town of yours into the surrounding ocean." Then they went forth to meet the claimants. He [the Shaykh] pointed to the ground and the earth was cloven asunder before them and behind them by the will of Allāh until they beheld with their eyes the furthest limits and crevasses. When they did this they asked the Shaykh and al-Maghīlī for pardon. Both declared, "There is no pardon unless you seek repentance and you must show your repentance for the act of your chief. You must not waylay the pilgrims as long as you live." So a covenant and an agreement was made between them. Then he [the Shaykh] pointed to the ground and it returned to its former state. The people [amongst the claimants] retraced their steps to their people.

The two men [the Shaykh and Maghīlī] visited al-Suyūṭī in his mosque and the Shaykh ʿAbd al-Karīm al-Maghīlī said, "What sciences have you, O ʿAbd al-Raḥmān al-Suyūṭī?" He answered, "Verily, I am counting up the *ḥadīths* of the Prophet, the blessing and peace of Allāh be upon him, from the first one to the last." He [a Maghīlī] said, "It may be that you should not do this. If what you say is correct then I shall disclose to you the *ḥadīths* of sound report on the authority of the Messenger of Allāh, His blessing be upon him." So he began to dictate them to him. He (Suyūṭī) said to him, "This I have not heard." Then he would go round one of the pillars in his mosque and come back to him and say to him, "What you said was absolutely true." He told him some five hundred *ḥadīths*. Sīdī ʿUmar al-Shaykh said, "Why [O Maghīlī] does he not believe your word in regard to a *ḥadīth* unless he circumambulates the pillar?" He said,

> "He is unable to see the Prophet in a vision until the pillar conceals him. Then he sees him and asks him about the *ḥadīth*. The latter says, 'It is a sound one on my authority.' But if he, the blessing of Allāh be upon him, were absent from me for the twinkling of an eye, then I would not regard myself as one amongst the true believers."

It was at that time that al-Suyūṭī acknowledged the pre-eminence of Ibn ʿAbd al-Karīm [al-Maghīlī] both in the Islamic sciences and in sanctity. Each Divine took the *wird* [of the *Shādhiliyyah?*] from the other. Ibn ʿAbd al-Karīm al-Maghīlī only used to call him "the little servant of the Merciful", ʿUbayd al-Raḥmān. When he composed the book entitled, *The Proof* [*al-Burhān*] he said [about Suyūṭī], "The learner scholar, ʿAbd al-Raḥmān, has become a man of learning" [*ʿālim*] and when he composed the *Excellent Perfection* [*al-Itqān*], "al-Sayyid ʿAbd al-Raḥmān has become a 'merchant' in the Islamic sciences."[19] Then both men [Maghīlī and Sīdī ʿUmar al-Shaykh the Elder] went on the Meccan pilgrimage.

Then both men turned aside to visit Medina, intent on fulfilling the duty of visiting [the Prophet], the blessing and peace of Allāh be upon him. When both men overlooked the city and its dweller, the most exalted blessing and peace of Allāh be upon him, [the Shaykh] composed his wonderful ode which has as its opening verse:

> Be joyful, O heart, this is the lord of the nations
> and this is the presence of the Chosen One in the sanctuary.[20]

When he came to the noble tomb and its chapel in order to enter it, the guards took steps to prevent him doing so. He then said:

> O my lord, O Messenger, take my hand,
> the servant [of God] is a guest, and the guest of Allāh is not wronged.[21]

At that moment the noble tomb shook, its door was opened and the guardians fled due to the might which they beheld. He entered the noble mosque surrounding the tomb [*rawḍah*]. He stayed an hour there. The people came to him and he began to say,

> "I am not here for you, I do not desire my business to be disturbed by you. He, within, is the one to give his *barakah* and blessing to him amongst you who seeks it. His sepulchre is the right hand of mercy and the fountain-head of wisdom and the source of divine guidance."

When the two men returned from the pilgrimage, that coincided with the hostile attack by one of the towns of Tuwāt upon the son of Shaykh Ibn ʿAbd al-Karīm al-Maghīlī. They killed him. The [Songhai] Askiyā Isḥāq used to honour and extol the Shaykh Ibn ʿAbd al-Karīm [al-Maghīlī]. He reported to the Askiyā the killing of his son by the people of that town. He said to him, "Slay his killer." "No," he answered, "they were all implicated in his murder." Ibn ʿAbd al-Karīm [al-Maghīlī] said,

> "If you do not do so, then I shall pray to Allāh who will certainly ruin this town of yours [Gao], and he will take away this [Songhai] kingdom from you, and I shall pray to Allāh to curse the people of the town where the slain was resident. They will perish and the town will be destroyed. Its properties and incomes will be vitiated."

That [demand] angered the Askiyā. So the Shaykh [al-Maghīlī] and his novice, Sīdī ʿUmar al-Shaykh [the Elder], departed and they reached a town called Katsina.[22] Its people met them and showed them respect and honour and they studied the faith and Islamic learning. When both men saw this, he [Maghīlī?] sent one of his companions to Gao, the city of the Askiyā, and [al-Maghīlī] said to him before he departed,

> "If he should ask you about me, then say that the Shaykh [al-Maghīlī] has died. If he is sorrowful and he seeks [my] return, then leave him and his kingdom, and [Gao] his city will remain inhabited until the end of time. But if you see that he cares not a whit then I shall transfer his state and authority to Katsina and his city will become a ruin field until the end of time."[23]

When the companion of the Shaykh [al-Maghīlī] came to him [the Askiyā], he asked the companion about him [Maghīlī]. He said that he had died, may Allāh have mercy upon him. He [the Askiyā] said, "I care not." When the companion returned to the Shaykh and told him about that, he made a sign with his sleeve and said,

> "His city of Gao is a ruin-field, the state of the Songhai is lost and has perished [*madīnat Gūgū kharāb wa dawlat Sughay tabāb*]. We have transferred its structure to Katsina and the latter will be the capital [of Takrūr] until the command of Allāh comes. Then Tuwāt will be smitten and He will ruin that town and He will wipe out its people and it is now as good as ruined."

When he was about to die, may Allāh be pleased with him, he assembled those people who were there and said to them, "He who desires my *barakah* and to profit, then let him seek them from Sīdī ʿUmar al-Shaykh [the Elder]."[24] The latter took charge of the washing of his body and preparing him [for burial]. When he had fulfilled what he commanded him to do, he [Sīdī ʿUmar] returned to his people and he became old, calling the people [to respond] to Allāh Almighty.

He guided the wanderer from the path, he educated the ignorant, he commanded the furtherance of the good and the avoidance of the evil. He encouraged the holding of the festivals, caring for the weak and the poor, the chiding of tyrants and oppressors and the confiscation of what their hands possessed. He told his sons to act the same, he urged them to do so, and he used them to bring it to pass. When the end of his life came, and his sons undertook the rectification of the masses, he devoted himself exclusively to adoration and contemplation. He died when he was upon the spur [?] of one of the mountains of the [Moroccan] Sūs. It so happened that he was in prayer when some Berber robbers passed by him and they shot him with a fire arm [*bunduqah*, cross bow?]. When he was wounded and his blood flowed, his light was mixed with the clouds [ʿ*anān*] and they were frightened to behold it. They came to a town called Āqā[25] and they said to them [there], "We have seen a wonder tonight. We found a man praying on the mountain and we shot him with the *bunduqah* and when his blood poured forth there came forth a light which mixed with the sky. We have fled to tell you of it."

The people of the town went to where he was. They prepared him for burial and carried him. When they laid him down to pray over him, lo, many birds, like a flood, covered him. They found an odour of musk. When they said "Allāh is great" over him, they heard this *takbīr* proclaimed between heaven and earth and voices accompanied it high above to the clouds. Over his body they constructed a shrine [*qubbah*]. He rests there to this day, visited to this very day. They bestow alms upon his tomb, be it in *dīnārs* and *dirhams* and various kinds of properties and grain. That is taken by him who is needy from the weak and the poor and those who visit the shrine eat of it. The report is handed down in a consecutive testimony among the pious of the people of the Sūs. None comes to his tomb in need which is acute but that need is fulfilled [by him]. He died within the year 960/1552/3[?]. He did not die until he had attained the supreme status of mystical polarity [*quṭbāniyyah*]. It is also reported, by a consecutive testimony, that he used to behold what lay betwixt the throne [of God] and the beds of the believers in Paradise. He did so as clearly as he saw the *dirham* in his hand, may Allāh be pleased with him, and be generous to us from His manifold mercies.[26]

Glossary

Adrār of the Lamtūnah This is the name given by the mediaeval Arab geographers to the northern Mauritanian province of the Adrār. Its present capital is Āṭār, though in the mediaeval period its principal towns were Āzuqqī (Azougui), which, for a while, was the "capital" of the southern wing of the Almoravid movement, and Wādān, which was an important halting place between the salt mine at Ijjil (Afdayrak) and the region of Timbuctoo. The Adrār is a sandstone massif. In it are found numerous palm-groves which contain, in all, over 400,000 date palms.

Adrār-n-Īfōghās Not to be confused with the above, although in the mediaeval period elements of the Lamtūnah Berbers were also to be found there. This massif is situated in Mali, to the north of the Niger buckle. It is to the east of the route which joins Gao to the southernmost oases of the Algerian Sahara. The mediaeval city of Tādamakkat is probably to be located at al-Sūq, although there are other archaeological sites in the Mali Adrār. It is inhabited by the Īfōghās Tuareg, elements of the Kuntah Moors and the Kel Es-Sūq who are a pacific group devoted to learning, teaching and the breeding of cattle and herds of sheep, goats and camels.

Aïr (Abzen) An important massif to the east of the Mali Adrār and situated in the Niger Republic. Its peaks rise to 6,000 feet or more. To the north of Agades, capital of Aïr, there are gardens of wheat, onions and tomatoes. At one time the massif was able to support a semi-nomadic Tuareg, and sedentary negro population of between 10,000 and 20,000 people.

Almohads The dynasty of the *al-Muwaḥḥidūn* began in the political and religious movement of Muḥammad ibn Tūmart (1078–1130). He preached the doctrine of the oneness and non-anthropomorphic nature of the deity among the Maṣmūdah Berbers of Morocco. The Almohad dynasty was founded in 1130 by ʿAbd al-Mu'min ibn ʿAlī who defeated the Almoravids. The dynasty lasted until 1269 when it fell to the Banū Marīn (the Marīnids).

Almoravids The name of *al-Murābiṭūn*, which is the source of the name which distinguished the dynasty of Ṣanhājah Berbers, mostly Lamtūnah, who ruled the Maghreb and Spain between 1061 and 1106, is the subject of much controversy. None dispute that the Gazūlah ʿAbdallāh ibn Yāsīn, at the behest of the orthodox saint and scholar, Wajjāj ibn Zalwī, gave his Saharan adepts this name; but whether it was on account of their affiliation to the fraternity of Wajjāj in the Moroccan Sūs, or on account of the establishment of a base (*ribāṭ*) in Gudālah territory in southern Mauritania, or because of their prowess, unity and close bond in the faith, is unclear from the Arabic sources. The Moors of Mauritania maintain that many of the *Zwāya* and all the Īdaw ʿĪsh of Tagānit are the descendants of the Almoravids.

Anbiyah One of the names given by the early Arab geographers to the Ṣanhājah tribes of the Western Sahara, prior to the name *al-Murābiṭūn*. It may denote the "first Ṣanhājah kingdom" under the leadership of the Lamtūnah in the desert.

Anṣār The Medinan followers of the Prophet. Certain Saharan tribes claim descent from these personalities. Often the Anṣār are confused with the Yemenites with whom certain Saharan groups claim blood relationship.

Arawān The capital of the region of Azawād in Mali to the north of Timbuctoo. It was founded by elements of the Ṣanhājah, the Ḥassānī Barābish, and scholars from the Mali Adrār.

Azelay (Azalay/Azalai etc.) The *Azelay* or *Taghalam* caravan set out from Aïr every autumn to bring salt from Bilma, the chief town of the Kawar oasis. There was also an *Azelay* caravan which carried salt from Tawdannī to Timbuctoo, and it is this caravan which is referred to in the Timbuctoo manuscript in the text of this book. The word itself is derived from a Tamasheq Tuareg word, which Sir Francis Rennell Rodd translates as "parting" or "separation". On the economic, historical and geographical importance of these Saharan salt caravans the reader is referred to Knut S. Vikør, *The Oasis of Salt, the History of Kawar, a Saharan Centre of Salt Production*, University of Bergen, 1979.

Barābīsh The Barābīsh, who occupy the Azawād region of the Sahara of Mali, are, in part, one of the most ancient branches of the Awlād Ḥassān. They were amongst the most powerful of them and they dominated the eastern marches of the Moorish Western Sahara. Leo Africanus described them as a branch of the Dhawī Ḥassān, and he says that they possessed the Sūs of Morocco in his day. "They are a huge multitude, neither have they any riches beside camels. Unto them is subject the city of Tesset, which scarce sufficeth them for the maintenance of their horses, being but a few."

Bīḍān The name used by the Saharan Moors, both Arab and Berber speakers in order to distinguish themselves from the negroes. The term, meaning "the whites", is found in quite early writings. According to La Courbe (1685), "The *Senegal* separates the *Azoaghes* [*Zenāgah*], *Moors* or *Bazanez* [*Bīḍān*], from the *Blacks*; so that on one side of the river are *Moors*, rather white than black; and on the other, men perfectly black."

Chaamba Arabs The Chaamba Arabs (al-Shaʿānibah) live in the Sahara to the east of the Rgaybāt. Their territory extends from the M'zab in the north as far as the Tidikelt and the Tuareg districts of southern Algeria. Their two principal centres are, the Wād Matlīlī, which is situated close to Ghardaia, and, on the other hand, El Golea and Ouargla, which were conquered and settled in the sixteenth and seventeenth centuries. In 1871 the Chaamba seized Touggourt. The Chaamba claim to be descendants of a legendary maiden and her two brothers who were members of the Awlād Mahdī, one of the tribes of the Banū Hilāl. Their tribe had been wiped out on a raiding expedition and the few who escaped alive wandered in the region of the Wād Matlīlī. They were later joined by sundry vagabonds. They were organised into a group by the saint, Sīdī'l-Bū Ḥafṣ of the Arab Awlād Shaykh. In the sixteenth century they were too many in number to remain in the Wād Matlīlī and they broke up into three branches, the Chaamba Berezga who stayed in their homeland, the Chaamba Monadhi who conquered the region of El Golea and the Chaamba Ben Rouba who seized Ouargla. At a later date the Chaamba penetrated further south into the Sahara. See Cabot Briggs, *Tribes of the Sahara*, pp. 190–210. For a recent history of the Chaamba (Shaʿānibah) much information may be gleaned from Jean Lethielleux, *Ouargla Cité Saharienne, des origines au début du XX siècle*, Librairie Orientaliste Paul Geuthner, S.A., Paris, 1983.

Dulaym Today, the Awlād Dulaym (Dalīm) are an important group among the population of the former Spanish Sahara. In the days of Leo they were very poor, ill clad and inclined to rob. They exchanged cattle for dates and could field 10,000 fighting men.

Fiqh The name given to jurisprudence in Islam. In its widest sense it covers all aspects of religious, political and civil life. A man expert in *fiqh* is called a *faqīh*.

Gazūlah A mountain and desert people who inhabit the region between the Wād Nūn and the Anti Atlas in Morocco. ʿAbdallāh ibn Yāsīn, the founder of the Almoravid movement, was a Gazūlī. The Gazūlah and the Gudālah are sometimes confused in the Arabic texts.

Ghāna The title of the king who ruled the region of Awkār in the Mauritanian Hodh. At the height of the kingdom, in the tenth century, it ruled the entire region between Tagānit in Mauritania and the Niger. Ghāna became a Muslim state, although it was not destroyed, during the rule of the Almoravids in the Maghrib in the eleventh century or early twelfth.

Gudālah The most westerly and southerly of the Ṣanhājah *mulaththamūn* in the Western Sahara. They were the first group to be approached by ʿAbdallāh ibn Yāsīn when he preached his *daʿwah* but they were rapidly disillusioned, and later became the bitter enemies of the Lamtūnah who formed the core of the Almoravids. According to F. Nicolas, their name is derived from *Zenāgah gudağén*, denoting "les Maures qui ne sont pas de nègres". Mukhtār wuld Ḥāmidun suggests the very opposite, that the root of the name indicates the colour "black Moor" and that Gadūl is an eponym. The name has been corrupted to *Igatig* which means "slave chief". The Igdalen of Niger may be a branch of this group. They are a pacific maraboutic group who live near In Gall.

Ḥadīth A record of actions or sayings of the Prophet which has been transmitted. It has come to mean the whole corpus of Muslim tradition.

Ḥarāṭīn The coloured tributaries or the manumitted slaves of the Sahara and their descendants. They work as share-croppers and they are in a legal category distinct from the slaves. While it has to be conceded that in fact the status of these people, so too the **Imghād** among the Tuareg, has been unlawfully abused and that many are little better than slaves, the text of al-Gunahānī, like many others amongst the Moors and the Kel Es-Sūq, argues that this treatment is wholly contrary to the *Sharīʿah* law of Islam.

Ḥassān A Western Saharan Arab extended family who claim descent from the Banū Maʿqil of the Yemen. They are also called Banū Maghfar, and, loosely used, this term is used to indicate the Arabic-speaking aristocracy, of non-*Zwāya* character, in Mauritania.

Ḥassāniyyah The colloquial Arabic which is spoken by the Moors in the entire Western Sahara. It is also spoken by the Kel Intasar of Azawād, the Kuntah of Mali and Niger, and certain Arab groups in Morocco and Algeria.

Hilāl A collective term for the Banū Hilāl who entered the Tunisia region from Egypt and Libya in the eleventh century and thence spread throughout the Maghrib. According to Leo Africanus, "The Arabians which inhabit Africa are divided into three parts: one part whereof are called Cachin [Jusham], the second Hillel [Hilāl], and the third Machill [Maʿqil]."

Ḥimyarites A collective name for the pre-Islamic peoples of South Arabia. It sometimes is applied to Yemenite Arabs without distinction and in the Maghrib is often used to describe the ancestors of certain "Berbers", more especially the Western Saharan Lamtūnah and Massūfah who, allegedly, entered Africa from Arabia in pre-Islamic times.

Hodh The most easterly province of Mauritania, bordering on Mali. It is derived from the Arabic *al-Ḥawḍ*, "the basin". The old pre-Arab names of this region were Awkār and Wagadu.

Hoggar The massif in the Central Sahara, inhabited by the Tuareg and called by them the Ahaggar. It is now part of Southern Algeria.

Ibāḍiyyah One of the main branches of the unorthodox Khārijites, who broke with the Caliph ʿAlī over his decision to put the succession of the Caliphate to arbitration. Their chief centres are in ʿUmān, East Africa, Tripolitania and Southern Algeria. Formerly they had a wide following in the Western Sahara, more especially in Sijilmāsah and in Awdaghust.

Īdaw ʿĪsh A formerly powerful, once Berber-speaking, group who are centred in the Tagānit region of Mauritania. They claim Ḥassānī status despite their different origin.

Idnān The Idnān (or Idenan) are, by repute, one of the two Lamtūnah or Massūfah or Tuareg groups which founded Timbuctoo about 1100.

Imām In the Western Sahara this term may mean "leader in prayer", or a Sulṭān appointed by the Caliph, or a leader or chief of a tribal group when his office entails religious obligations, whether temporary or permanent.

Imghād A Tuareg word (sing. *amghid*) indicating vassals rather than serfs. This class exists in all Tuareg groups save the Kel Geres. Hence the entry on this subject in the epistle of al-Gunahānī who tries to show that their view is contrary to the laws of Islam.

Ineslemen The religious class among the Tuareg corresponding to the *Zwāya* among the Moors.

Iwillimmeden The name of a Tuareg confederation which came into being in the region of the Niger buckle about 1600. According to the Tuareg of that region its members formed a part of the Tuareg groups which had arrived from the region of Libya. They incorporated groups of the Tādamakkat and Imagsharen and Kel Es-Sūq, together with some of the Kuntah as their spiritual advisors, and subordinate Arab groups. The Iwillimmeden split into the Kel Aṭarām of the West and the Kel Denneg of the East. The organisation of society was akin to that of the Moors of Mauritania, with patrilineal succession and a comparable class division of labour and activities.

Kel Es-Sūq A protected, weaponless, group of maraboutic tribes who were once centred in the Adrār-n-Īfōghās, but who are to be found today in many parts of Mali, Niger, and Burkina Faso. Foremost among them are the Daghūghiyyīn and other families who claim descent from the Prophet. The scholars are masters in the Arabic language and they are in a sense both allies and competitors of the Kuntah. They excel in language, Islamic law and in Ṣūfī commentaries.

The contribution of the Kel Es-Sūq to the "Arabisation" of the south-western Tuareg may be summarised as:

1. The composition of a corpus of Classical Arabic poetry which, in its excellence, compares favourably with the masterpieces of the Mauritanian poets.
2. The legacy of a corpus of works of jurisprudence (*fiqh*) in Classical Arabic which probably outstrips their attainments in writing on mystical subjects. These legal works – and in some respects the *Risālah* of al-Gunahānī exemplifies such works – were often centred on the subject of the legality or illegality of slavery, or the oppression of lower classes, in those tribes and groups which dwelt on the border of the Southern Sahara and the Western Sūdān. The evolution of a highly stratified class society, was *not* the outcome, *per se*, of the entry of the Maʿqilian Arabs and their allies and clients into the Sahara. Its evolution transcended those tracts which had become the territories of the Ḥassānīs.

   In fact, future evidence from Saharan texts may yet confirm that the fundamental factor which brought about the stratified social system in the entire Western Sahara, and much of the Central Sahara, and the Western Sahel, was due to the necessity of a local *Sulṭān* or *Amīr*, be he Almoravid, Songhai, Tuareg or Ḥassānī, to establish a "college" of legal and spiritual counsellors, well versed in all branches of the *Sharīʿah*, who were able to furnish a ruling on such matters as the status and lawful ownership of slaves, the claim to booty and spoils, the rights of those who transported salt, or who were engaged in Saharan trade, and the resolution of divergences between the *Sharīʿah* and the customary law of the bedouin. The crisis had come about due to the raiding and capture of herds and persons and their distribution amongst the chiefs without regard to the strict rules laid down in canonic law. It was the contention of the scholars of the Kel Es-Sūq that the great mass of "subjects" of the Iwillimmeden, or for that matter, the Kel Geres and other Tuareg tribes, and also some of the Ḥassānīs, were to be classed as *Mustaghriq al-Dhimmah*, this term denoting that their masters possessed properties, inanimate and animate, of a legal category which was either illicit booty, or of ambiguous legal validity, or was subject to controversy and was indefensible in law.

Kuntah Arabic-speaking Moors who claim descent from ʿUqbah ibn Nāfiʿ, one of the Prophet's Companions, through Sīdī Muḥammad al-Kuntī who died in the fifteenth century. They are to be found throughout the Western Sahara and they propogated the Qādiriyyah Ṣūfī fraternity in that region.

Lamṭah An ancient branch of Saharan *mulaththamūn* who were separate from the principal tribes of the Almoravids. They inhabited the Wād Nūn and the Central Sahara rather than Mauritania. They were famous for their massive oryx-skin shields made from the skin of the *lamṭ* which they hunted.

Lamtūnah The most powerful of the Sanhājah *mulaththamūn* in the Western Sahara during the tenth and eleventh centuries, amongst whom were born the leaders of the Almoravids. The Lamtūnah were more especially centred in the Adrār of Mauritania, and there were families in the Adrār-n-Īfōghās and in Aïr, particularly in the later mediaeval period when many scholars moved east. Small groups of the Lamtūnah survive in Southern Mauritania apart from the Īdaw ʿĪsh of Tagānit who claim to be descended from the Lamtūnah.

Maghīlī Muḥammad ʿAbd al-Karīm al-Maghīlī (d. *circa* 1504) was a key figure in the formulation of Islamic belief and political policy in the Sahara and West Africa. He firmly believed in strict *Mālikī* orthodoxy, strict application of the *Sharīʿah*, the nature of unbelief in a semi-pagan environment and the obligation of the Muslim ruler to combat those who make war against Islam (*al-muḥāribūn*).

Maʿqil The eponym of the vast majority of the Arab nomadic tribes in the Western Sahara. They are descended through the Dhawī or Banū Ḥassān, subdivided into Dulaym, Barbūsh, Ūday Raḥmān and Ḥamrun.

Marīnids The Banū Marīn succeeded the Almohads in Morocco and they began the settling of Maʿqil groups in the region of the Sūs and using them as caravan guides and as military units in the Sahara and elsewhere in North Africa.

Massūfah An important branch of the *mulaththamūn* who were centred in the region of the Draa, the Hodh and in Mali, particularly at Walātah and Timbuctoo, and in Niger around Tageddā and south-west Aïr. The Mashḍūf of Mauritania claim to be Massūfah.

Nīsar desert A tract which al-Idrīsī says had no water supply for a traveller over a period of some fourteen days. The desert appears to correspond to the *Majābah al-Kubrā*, to the north-east of the Hodh and north of Azawād, in al-Bakrī's account. The latter says that the first water-point is in the territory of the Banū Yantasir (probably the Kel Intasar of today). It is difficult not to see some connection between Nīsar or Ysr and the name of this tribe or people.

Rgaybāt The Rgaybāt are amongst the most powerful *Ḥassāniyyah*-speaking peoples of the north-west Sahara, bordering on Morocco, Algeria and Mauritania. They are great warriors and they once raided over vast distances of the Sahara; they were also great caravan guides in the desert between Morocco and Timbuctoo, either in co-operation with, or in conflict with, the Barābīsh and the Kuntah. They are a relatively recent group to have become united, possibly within the last two hundred years. They claim descent from the scholar-saint, the Ṣūfī Mawlay ʿAbd al-Salām Ibn Mashīsh, or else from Sīdī Aḥmad al-Rgaybī, a *Sharīf*, who, by repute, came to the Draa region of Morocco as a missionary about 1503 and married an Arab woman. He is buried at al-Aḥbāsh, a burial ground for several holy men to the north of the Sāqiyah al-Ḥamrā'. The Rgaybāt are principally subdivided into the *Sāhel* Rgaybāt and the Rgaybāt *al-Guwāsim*, the former bordering the Atlantic and the latter towards Tindouf in Algeria.

Ribāṭ A fortified post, where horse were sometimes stabled, and the garrison of which combined military duties with agriculture and pious and ascetic practices, geographically located on, or near, the frontier of *Dār al-Islām*. At times, however, this word had a metaphorical meaning and indicated a frame of mind, a spiritual resolve, or that which combined deep devotion to Islām, self-sacrifice and the courage to face alone, or with a like group, those enemies which threatened the faith.

Sahel Nowadays, it indicates the belt of savannah and encroaching desert between the Sahara proper, and the high grasslands and the tropical rain forests of West Africa. Mauritania, Mali, Niger and Chad must be included. To the people of the Hodh and Azawād it denotes the North and the North-West as a point of the compass.

Ṣanhājah One of the principal divisions of the Berbers. The three major Saharan tribes prior to the entry of the Maʿqil Arabs into the Western Sahara were the Gudālah, the Lamtūnah and the Massūfah. The first European visitors to this region called them Aznagues and Zenagas, with variants, an approximation to the form Aznāg, Ṣinhāj, and Zenāgah, again with variants, in Arabic records.

Sharīʿah The canonic law of Islām. The term *Sharʿ* is also used.

Sharīf In its strictest sense, a descendant of the Prophet in the male line through his daughter Fāṭimah. Amongst the Kel Es-Sūq the Esh-Sherifen claim to be Shurafā', plural of Sharīf, but elsewhere in the Tuareg world the title may mean little more than "holy man".

Sijilmāsah A very important commercial town and terminus for caravans situated in the oasis of Tafilalt in the south-east of Morocco. It was founded in AD 757 and was destroyed in 1362. Major ruins survive.

Songhai Gao in Mali was an important meeting point on the Niger for the Saharan salt routes and also the trans-continental trade route. Early in the eleventh century it became the capital of the Songhai, who had earlier spread there from the south-west. It was converted to Islam at this time. The Songhai kingdom was annexed to Mali by Mansa Musa in 1325. In 1335 the dynasty was re-established, though nominally subject to Mali until the reign of Sonni ʿAlī (1465–92) who was an enemy of the Ṣanhājah. He was succeeded by the pious Soninke general Muḥammad (1493–1529), the founder of the Askiyā dynasty. He brought Songhai to the height of its power; however, the empire collapsed under the attack of the Moroccans who captured Gao and Timbuctoo in 1591.

Ṣūfism Islamic mysticism (*Taṣawwuf* or *Ṣūfiyyah*) in the Western Sahara has rarely taken the private and personal form which once characterised the way of life of Muslim mystics in the early days of Islam. Private retreat may have been a feature of one phase in the Almoravid movement, it may also have been a way of life among the Kel Es-Sūq and the Kel Intasar. The bulk of the Western Saharan mystics have been affiliated to the great orders of the later mediaeval period, the *Shādhiliyyah* and the *Qādiriyyah*, the latter having branches peculiar to certain holy men of the region. An order like the *Khalwatiyyah* characterises the centre rather than the west of the great desert and its borders. Both the Kuntah and the Kel Es-Sūq are amongst the most fervent devotees of the *Qādiriyyah*. Their scholars have insisted, as al-Gunahānī does, upon a perfect balance between *Taṣawwuf* and *Fiqh*. Neither takes preference over the other. The mystic orders are housed in a *Zāwiyah* (pl. *Zawāyā*), and it is noteworthy that the Moors have dubbed the class of their scholars and religious teachers, *Zwāya*, the *Ḥassāniyyah* equivalent.

Sulaym The Banū Sulaym were paired with the Banū Hilāl, but played a subordinate role during their entry into the Maghreb. Ibn Khaldūn describes them as rebellious and prone to brigandage.

Sunnah Originally this term indicated local custom. Among the early schools of Muslim law (*Madhāhib*), of which the Mālikī was supreme in the Maghreb, it indicated the accepted doctrines of these schools. After al-Shāfiʿī (d. AD 820) it indicated the practices of the Prophet and the precedents which he set.

Tafsīr Any form of explanation, exposition, elucidation, interpretation and commentary in Arabic, but more particularly of Prophetic *Ḥadīth* and, most important of all, the Koran itself.

Tamasheq (Tamahaq) The Berber language of the Tuareg peoples who live in the Central and part of the Western Sahara and in the Sahelian states.

Takrūr A vague term which began as the name of a town on the Senegal river but in time came to be used to denote all the negroes between the Sudan Nile and the mouth of the Senegal. See ʿUmar al-Naqar, "Takrūr, the history of a name", *Journal of African History*, vol. 10, 1969, pp. 365–74.

Uṣūl al-Fiqh The sources of law and the principles of jurisprudence.

Yantasir The name of a Saharan people on the border of the Hodh and Azawād. Their name is variously spelt and they probably represent the original stock of the Kel Intasar of today near Goundam and Tegharost in Mali, who claim to be part *Anṣār* and part Lamtūnah.

Zenāgah The name of a Berber language in south-west Mauritania now nearly extinct but probably close to that of the Almoravids. This term is also applied to non-negro tributaries in Mauritania.

Zenziga An individual but unidentified Berber people, related to the Ṣanhājah and mentioned by Leo Africanus, who are associated with the route between the Adrār of Algeria and Gao, especially around In-Ziza well which may explain their name and its presence on some early African maps.

Zwāya The scholar class amongst the Moors of Mauritania. This is the *Ḥassāniyyah* form. In Classical Arabic it is *Zawāyā*, short for *Ahl al-Zawāyā*, inmates of Ṣūfī lodges, retreats and semi-monastic communities.

Notes and References

Notes and References to Chapter One

1. John Damis, "The Moroccan–Algerian Conflict over the Western Sahara", *Maghreb Review*, vol. 3, no. 2, March–April 1979, pp. 49–57.
2. John Mercer, *Spanish Sahara*, George Allen and Unwin, 1976, pp. 77–8.
3. The date of the workings at Ijjil is still not known with any certainty. It is called "West Taghaza" in later writings. The history of Wādān is most conveniently summarised in "Notes d'histoire et d'archéologie sur Azougui, Chinguetti et Oudane", *Bulletin de l'Institut Français d'Afrique Noire*, vol. 17, series B, nos. 1–2, 1955, pp. 142–63.
4. N. Levtzion and J. F. P. Hopkins, *Corpus of Early Arabic Sources for West African History*, Cambridge University Press, 1981, p. 73.
5. Johannes Leo, *A Geographical Historie of Africa*, London, 1600, Da Capo Press, Amsterdam and New York 1969, pp. 266–7. This identification is now disputed.
6. Johannes Leo, *ibid.*, p. 17. Guaden is either Wādān or in the Darʿah, see p. 162 in this book.
7. Regarding Ibn Baṭṭūṭah's route, see Levtzion and Hopkins, *op. cit.*, pp. 282–6.
8. J. G. Jackson, *An Account of the Empire of Marocco and the Districts of Suse and Tafilelt*, 3rd edn, London, 1814 (reprint Frank Cass and Company Ltd), pp. 285–7.
9. The desert described is Zemmour and its guelta in the extreme north of Mauritania to the south of the Sāqiyah al-Ḥamrā'.
10. The White Mountains are near the Adrar Sotuf in the southernmost part of the Río de Oro.

11. The Ḥassānī Banū Maghfar, those branches of the Banū Ḥassān who claim descent from Ḥassān ibn Maʿqil.
12. The Awlād Bū Sbāʿ, "the first to attempt to make a settlement in the coastal desert", see the useful summary in Mercer, *op. cit.*, pp. 133–4, and Julio Baroja, *Estudios Saharianos*, Instituto de Estudios Africanos, Madrid, 1955.
13. According to Jackson, *op. cit.*, this place is Arguin despite the way that it is spelt.
14. Maurice Cortier, *D'une rive à l'autre du Sahara*, Paris, 1908, part 2, p. 271.
15. Henri Lhote, *Les Touaregs du Hoggar*, Payot, Paris, 1944, p. 124.
16. On the historical significance of this passage from Leo, see P. Marty, "Les Berabich", in *Etudes sur l'Islam et les tribus du Soudan*, Paris, 1918–19, vol. 1, pp. 179–81, and on matters relating to the diet and subsistence of these Ṣanhājah, see T. Lewicki, *West African Food in the Middle Ages*, Cambridge University Press, 1974, pp. 48, 94, 103, 122, 160
17. Leo Africanus, *op. cit.*, p. 281.
18. The exact point to the west of Taghāzā is not specifically stated. This place is also mentioned within Ṣanhājah territory. Nor is there any mention of West Taghāzā.
19. The name is probably mis-spelt. It relates, it seems, to a specific locality in the Algerian Sahara. As to the alternatives, the whole subject forms part of my last chapter, see pp. 147–63.
20. On this practice, see al-Sharīshī's commentary to the *Maqāmāt* of al-Ḥarīrī (d. 516/1122). See Levtzion and Hopkins, *op. cit.*, pp. 152–3. It might be noted that according to Ghoubeïd Alojaly, see his *Lexique Touareg-Français*, Copenhagen, 1980, p. 23, the Tuareg word, *uddam*, denotes *bu jusqu'à la dernière goutte*. Such is the fitting description for this desert passage.
21. A spelling of unknown origin but presumably based on Guanziga rather than Zuenziga, hence closer to one possible reading of Ibn Khaldūn's Watrīkah or Watzīlah as Wanzīkah.

Notes and References to Chapter Two

1. Ibn al-Kalbī's *Kitāb al-Aṣnām*, The Book of Idols, has been described as "perhaps the most important source book on the religious practices of pagan Arabia". Aḥmad ibn Abī Zarʿ of Fez (d. *circa* 726/1326), the historian, maintained that Ibn al-Kalbī also reported, quoted by Abū ʿUbaydah, that the Yemenite king, Ifrīqush, or Ifrīqish, settled the Berber Ṣanhājah and Kutāmah in the Maghrib. This story was attacked by the scholar, Ibn Ḥazm, and was criticised severly by Ibn Khaldūn,

likewise views of a similar kind attributed to another Yemenite, Muḥammad ibn al-Ḥasan ibn Aḥmad ibn Yaʿqūb al-Hamdānī (d. 334/945), the author of the *Kitāb al-Iklīl*. Much of the latter has now been edited and published but the text sheds little, if any, light on these assertions and refutations of a later era.

2. Literally "the poets" of Ḥaṣīn or Ḥuṣayn.
3. Abī Ṭālib was uncle to the Prophet and Jaʿfar was the spokesman of the Muslim emigrants to Abyssinia.
4. See the discussion on this point in *al-Ḥilf al-Hilālī* in Aḥmad ibn ʿAli al-Maqrīzī, *al-Bayān wa'l-Iʿrāb ʿammā bi arḍ Miṣr min al-Aʿrāb*, edited by ʿAbd al-Majīd ʿĀbidīn, Cairo, 1961, pp. 125–8.
5. See the *Encyclopedia of Islam* under "*Ḳarmaṭians*".
6. Ibn Saʿīd was born in Granada in 610/1214 and died in Tunis in 685/1286–7. His works were used by al-ʿUmarī and Abū'l-Fidā', as well as by Ibn Khaldūn.
7. See De Slane's translation of Ibn Khaldūn, *Histoire des Berbères*, Paris, 1982, vol. 1, pp. 115–34, more especially the earlier pages.
8. René Basset, *Mission au Sénégal*, Paris, 1909, vol. 1, pp. 455–6. Nowadays Dalīm is almost always spelt Dulaym.
9. This theme is discussed in my *The Adventures of Antar*, Aris and Phillips, Warminster, 1980, pp. 28–30.
10. The Barābīsh are discussed at length on pp. 77–100.
11. This Arabic work, *The Ascent of Jupiter*, is printed in Fez although I have not seen a copy. The author's most famous work is his *Kitāb al-Istiqṣā'*, Casablanca edn, 1954. In vol. 2 the author discusses the origins of the Maʿqil (pp. 159–62). The author's full name is al-Shaykh Abū'l-ʿAbbās Aḥmad ibn Khālid al-Nāṣirī.
12. Muḥammad al-Mukhtār al-Sūsī, *al-Maʿsūl*, vol. 18, 1962, pp. 166–7.

Notes and References to Chapter Three

It should be pointed out that the Moors themselves are by no means certain, or even know, why the *Zwāya* came to bear this name. According to the unpublished Mauritanian work, *Dhāt Alwāḥ wa Dusur*, "perhaps the naming of the *Zwāya* [*Zawāyā*], by this, their name, is due to the fact that they adopted places of retreat, that is to say buildings specially assigned to learning and devout adoration, hence this name they bear. Perhaps the reason for their being called 'student scholars or schoolmen', *Ṭulbah*, is that they were those who went forth in the pursuit of learning [*Ṭalabat al-ʿilm*], and perhaps the reason for them being called *Mrābiṭ* [*Murābiṭ*] is on account of the expression *Ribāṭ fī sabīl Allāh*, that is to say being in a post of alertness and preparedness against the foes of Islam [*Murābaṭat al-ʿAdūw*]. It is possible, however, that it is related to the Almoravid state [*Dawlat al-Murābiṭīn*], famous in the (Arab) West, just as the Zenāgah (*Aznāg*) are related to the Ṣanhāgah [*sic*] which is one of the tribes of the Berbers, and that it is related to the language of the Zenāgah, namely the Īdaw ʿĪsh in their entirety. . ."

However, the expression and term of *Zwāya* is not exclusive to *Ḥassāniyyah* society in the Western Sahara. It is also to be found amongst the Kel Es-Sūq who are subordinate to the Iwillimmeden. The Kel Es-Sūq, in their later documents, refer to themselves as members of a *Zāwiyah* (singular of *Zawāyā/Zwāya*), a religious community in a special geographical region near the Niger basin set apart from the rest of the Iwillimmeden. No evidence exists which shows when this term became current amongst the Kel Es-Sūq. It was either known prior to the so-called "War of Shurbubba" in Mauritania, or else the Kel Es-Sūq adopted the expression from the Kuntah, either prior to Shurbubba or some time afterwards and perhaps during the lifetime of Shaykh Sīdī'l-Mukhtār al-Kuntī (d. 1226/1811).

The very fact that the term *Zāwiyah/Zwāya* spans the whole Western Sahara – both Moor and Tuareg – is sufficient to disclose a flaw in the historical theories of many Moorish scholars in south-west Mauritania, namely, that the whole *Zwāya* class in their country was to a large extent created by the "War of Shurbubba" and a status imposed upon them by the victorious Ḥassānīs. It is more likely that the scholar class as a whole coined the expression themselves under the influence of the spread of Ṣūfism and its orders, with the most tenuous connection, historically, with those events which gave rise to the Amīrates of the Banū Maʿqil in these Saharan regions.

1. This precise summary about the Awlād Ḥassān is taken from the short Arabic work, published in Morocco, by Dār al-ʿIlm lil-ta'līf wa'l-tarjamah wa'l-nashr, with the title, *al-Ja'sh al-Rabīṭ fī Maghribiyyat Shinqīṭ wa ʿArabiyyat man bihā min murakkab wa basīṭ*, by Shaykh Muḥammad al-Imām ibn al-Shaykh Mā' al-ʿAynayn. This chapter is to be found between pp. 27 and 31 in that work, in the section which is called *al-Kalām ʿalā ʿArab Maʿqil al-Shinqīṭiyyah wa man inḍamma ilayhim wa-mā yataʿallaqu bi-dhālika min khabar al-jamīʿ bi-khtiṣār*, "Discourse on the Maʿqil Arabs of Shinqīṭ, about those who were joined to them and what is connected with that from the report of the people entirely, though abridged and summarised".

2. This whole passage is clearly a summary of Ibn Khaldūn who in his *History of the Berbers* has a section specifically about the Banū Maʿqil and their wanderings in North Africa. The theory about the three Maʿqils and other related topics is to be found in Ibn Khaldūn, *Histoire des Berbères*, trans. by De Slane, Paris 1982, vol. 1, pp. 118–19.
3. At the beginning of the tenth century the Carmathians became the dominant power in the province of Baḥrain. On 12 January 930, they seized Mecca and carried off the Black Stone from the Kaʿbah to al-Aḥsā, where it remained for thirty years.
4. See Ibn Khaldūn, *op. cit.*, vol. 1, pp. 8, 9, 38, 118 and 137.
5. *Ibid.*, pp. 127–31, and vol. 2, pp. 104–5.
6. See the important article of Julio Baroja, "El Grupo de Cabilas 'Hasania' del Sahara Occidental", *Estudios Mogrebíes*, Instituto de Estudios Africanos, Madrid, 1957, pp. 111–21. This supplements his *Estudios Saharianos*, Madrid, 1955. The plural *Dhawū* is more correct.
7. Between 1269 and 1465. Their apogee was between 1331 and 1398.
8. According to De Slane, *op. cit.*, vol. 1, p. 117, "une taxe appelée *port de bagage*" and, in fn. 1, "*droit de transit*".
9. De Slane, *op. cit.*, p. 117, renders this passage by, "Jamais ces Arabes ne commirent de brigandages sur les limites du Maghreb ni sur les plateaux; jamais ils n'interceptèrent les caravanes qui se rendaient au Soudan de Sidjilmessa et d'autres lieux . . ."
10. *Ibid*, "En recompense de leur conduite paisible, les Makil obtinrent quelques concessions; mais ces *ictā* étaient considérés moins comme un droit que comme une faveur."
11. *Yusr al-nāẓirīn ʿalā manẓūmatihi rawḍ al-nisrīn*. Sīdī ʿAbdallāh ibn al-Ḥājj Ibrāhīm of Tījikjah (d. 1233/1818) was one of the most important Moorish scholars of the late eighteenth century. Regarding this historical poem and its commentary, see my *Saharan Myth and Saga*, Oxford Library of African Literature, 1972, pp. 163–4.
12. See p. 39. The author was advocating Moroccan claims to the Western Sahara when he wrote his work, and this no doubt added extra point to his statement. On relations between Mauritanians and the Sulṭān of Morocco about 1830, see my *The Pilgrimage of Aḥmad, Son of the Little Bird of Paradise*, Aris and Phillips, 1977.

Notes and References to Chapter Four

1. *The Voyages of Cadamosto and other documents on Western Africa in the Second Half of the Fifteenth Century*, translated and edited by G. R. Crone, Hakluyt Society, 1937, pp. 86–7. Also Cadamosto, *ibid.*, pp. 16–19.
2. T. Whitcomb, "New Evidence on the Origins of the Kunta – 1", *Bulletin of the School of Oriental and African Studies*, vol. 38, part 1, 1975, p. 115. H. Barth in his *Travels in North and Central Africa*, Appendix III, p. 562, refers to the Ibidúkelen as an *Ineslemen* group amongst the Tuareg of the Niger buckle and around Tādamakkat. They were associated with the Isakkamaren.
3. Idnān. According to Sir Francis Rennell Rodd, *The People of the Veil*, Macmillan, London, 1926, p. 407, the Idenan were among the Berber groups which founded the city of Timbuctoo. See also p. 89.
4. For all these references see the edition of *Kitāb al-Ansāb* by Wālid ibn Khālunā in *Chroniques de la Mauritanie Sénégalaise, Nacer Eddine*, by Ismaël Hamet, Paris, 1911, p. 91 (Arabic text), p. 262 (French text), and René Basset, *Mission au Sénégal*, Paris 1909, vol. 1, p. 447.
5. This name is also spelt Zenzīgah and Genzīgah. Levtzion and Hopkins spell the name as Watrīka, see *Corpus of early Arabic sources for West African History*, Cambridge University Press, 1981, p. 331.
6. The plural of *najīb*. It is translated by Levtzion and Hopkins *op. cit.*, as "thoroughbred".
7. Ibn Khaldūn, *Histoire des Berbères*, pp. 331–2.
8. This plural form of *Ṣanāhijah* is a Saharan form and it is not given in the lexicons.
9. The text is one in the private collection of Shaykh Muḥammad Ibrāhīm al-Aghlālī, citing the seventeenth-century Tuareg scholar, Muḥammad ibn Taghin (Tighna?), author of *Talfīq al-Fawā'id*. It remains likely that the term *Imām*, which is used in this passage, is the same as *Imanen* in the Tuareg tongue, this latter denoting the chiefs who ruled the Central Saharan Massifs, who had sworn some kind of *bay'ah* to a Caliph, who also sometimes prided themselves on the title of Sulṭān and whose high rank was partly religious. They were all allegedly descendants of the Prophet and their authority was symbolised by a large drum (*eṭṭebel*). The reader is referred for further details and a bibliography to Jeremy Keenan, *The Tuareg*, Allen Lane, 1977, Chapter 1. It is difficult to determine how ancient this tradition might be. Connected with patrilineal descent it

seems to go hand in hand with a strong movement of Islamisation, possibly of Arabisation, and of a marked "caste" character. Al-Bakrī refers to a group in the Sahara called the Banū Wārith, which, if accurately reported, suggests an Arab group in the Mauritanian Hodh in the eleventh century, or else a social class which bore an Arab title. Both *Imām* and *Wārith* appear side by side in Koran 28 verses 1–6, where Pharaoh's division of the people into sects or castes (*shiya*ʿ) is contrasted with the Almighty's division of the "weakened" in the earth into "models" (*A'immah*, plural of *Imām*) and "heirs" (*Wārithīn*, plural of *Wārith*). Could this have foreshadowed the warrior, Zwāya/Ineslemen, Zenāgah/Imghād division?

10. Rodd, *op. cit.*, pp. 128–30.
11. The name of the desert of the Lamtūnah and Massūfah is variously spelt, Kākudam, Kākadam, Kawkadam and Qūqadam.

    There are several explanations for the inconsistency of Arabic orthography. It may originally have been a tribal name, hence its peripatetic character in the accounts. The name of the tribe may have been given to localities where it stayed at various times. Ptolemy mentions a Libyan people called the Ogdaemi, who lived in the vicinity of Mt Ogdaemum which was sited by him in the eastern parts of Libya rather than in the Western Sahara. There is to this day a Berber group which is centred in the Atlas near Dilā' who are called the Ait Ouaggoudim.

    Despite this obscure geographical information, and despite the total ignorance of this name amongst Mauritanians today, I hope in my last chapter to show that it is possible to offer some resolution of these inconsistencies.
12. See Levtzion and Hopkins, *op. cit.*, pp. 121–2.
13. *Ibid.*, p. 341.
14. See n. 2 above, also "The Kunta, Sīdī al-Mukhtār al-Kuntī and the office of *Shaykh al-Ṭarīq al-Qādiriyya*" by A. A. Batran in *Studies in West African Islamic History*, vol. 1, *The Cultivators of Islam*, ed. J. R. Willis, Frank Cass, 1979, pp. 113–47, more especially pp. 118–19.
15. Levtzion and Hopkins, *op. cit.*, p. 337.
16. This is the accepted Saharan view of the class system in the Western Sahara; see my *The Berbers in Arabic Literature*, Longman, 1982, pp. 111–31.
17. Compare this account with Batran, *op. cit.*, pp. 118–19.

    The Egyptian historian, al-Qalqashandī (d. 1418), writing in his work on the Arab tribes, entitled, *Qalā'id al-Jumān fī'l-Ta*ʿ*rīf bi Qabā'il* ʿ*Arab al-Zamān*, specifically makes mention of the remnants of the Lamtūnah, in any number, being nomads in the north-western Sahara, presumably near the Sāqiyah al-Ḥamrā', and this at a time when the Maʿqil Arabs were well established in the districts of the Sūs and the Darʿah (Draa). The text reads:

وبقايا لمتونة على حد الكثرة موجودون بصحراء المغرب وبلاده ، لا يأخذهم حضر إلى الآن .

The impression given in Kuntah accounts that a close alliance was established between the Kuntah families and the Ḥassānīs is not confirmed from other statements in their archives. The wives of the greatest Kuntah Shaykhs came from a variety of Saharan groups, some Ḥassānī, others Ṣanhājah, including the Awlād Bū Sbāʿ, Awlād ʿUqbah, Īdayshallī and especially Tājakānt. The mother of Sīdī Muḥammad al-Kuntī was an Ibdūkaliyyah, a Lamtūnah woman from the same group whom the Ḥassānīs were supposed to have conquered and subdued. All this suggests that any sort of alliance with the Awlād al-Nāṣir could only have been short-lived. Much of the historicity of the account of the conquest by the Maʿqil of the region of the Sāqiyah al-Ḥamrā' has to be regarded with the utmost scepticism.

18. See Whitcomb, *op. cit.*, part 2, 1975, pp. 407ff.
19. See Th. Monod's notes for *Description de la Côte d'Afrique de Ceuta au Sénégal (Valentim Fernandes, 1506–7)*, Paris, 1938, p. 77.
20. See my "Znaga Islam during the Seventeenth and Eighteenth Centuries", *Bulletin of the School of Oriental and African Studies*, vol. 32, part 3, 1969, pp. 509–22.
21. Basset, *op. cit.*, pp. 451–3.
22. This passage is taken from my manuscript copy of the commentary of al-Yādalī to his poem *Ṣalātu Rabbī*.
23. See my article "The Legacy of the Banū Ḥassān", *Maghreb Review*, vol. 2, no. 2, March–April, 1977, pp. 21–5.
24. Michel Abitbol, *Tombouctou et les Arma*, Paris, 1979, pp. 144–5.
25. *Ibid.*, p. 186.
26. Abitbol exaggerates the Moroccan case at this point, nor was Smara founded until the commencement of this century.
27. See *Esmeraldo de Situ Orbis*, ed. Epifiano de Silva Dias, Lisbon, 1905, bk 1, Chapter 25, pp. 75–7.
28. *The History and Description of Africa*, trans. by John Pory, Hakluyt Society, 1896, pp. 142, 145, 146, 150, 156. Andrzej Dziubinski, in his "L'Identification de Tesset et Guaden, Localités de Numidie, d'après la Déscription de Jean-Léo

l'Africain", *Africana Bulletin*, vol. 13, Warsaw, 1970, pp. 31–41, makes a powerful case for Tesset as Tissînt in the Jabal Banī of Morocco and not in Mauritania at all. His argument for an identification of Wādān (Guaden) with Tin Oudane, also in the Sahara north, is a little less convincing, but still persuasive. If he is ever proved correct, then this will inevitably mean a major re-examination of the southward penetration of the Banū Ḥassān before the seventeenth century. Personally, I have accepted his arguments.

Some descriptions of the Mauritanian Adrār are very detailed for this period. One example is the following extract from a letter sent by Melchior Petoney to Miguel de Moura at Lisbon.

> A relation sent by Melchior Petoney to Miguel de Moura at Lisbon, from the Iland and Castle of Arguin, standing a little to the Southward of Cape Blanco, in the Northerly latitude of 19 degrees, concerning the rich and secret trade from the inland of Africa thither: Anno 1591.
>
> As concerning the trade to this Castle and Iland of Arguin, your worship is to understand, that if it would please the kings majesty to send hither two or three caravels once in a yeere with Flanders and Spanish commodities, as Bracelets of glasse, Knives, Belles, Linnencloth, Looking-glasses, with other kinds of small wares, his highnesse might do great good here. For 50 leagues up into the land the Moores have many exceeding rich golde mines; insomuch that they bring downe their golde to this Castle to traffique with us: and for a small trifle they will give us a great wedge of gold. And because here is no trade, the sayd Moores cary their golde to Fez being 250 leagues distant from hence, and there doe exchange the same for the foresayd kindes of commodities. By this meanes also his majesty might stop that passage, and keepe the king of Fez from so huge a masse of golde. Scarlet-clothes, and fine Purples are greatly accepted of in these parts. It is a most fertile countrey within the land, and yeeldeth great store of Wheat, flesh of all kindes, and abundance of fruits. Therefore, if it were possible, you should do well to deale with his majesty, either himselfe to send a couple of caravels, or to give your worship leave to traffique here: for here is a very good harbour where ships may ride at ancre hard by the Castle. The countrey where all the golde mines are is called The kingdome of Darha. In this kingdome are great store of cities and townes; and in every city and towne a Captaine with certaine souldiers; which Captaines are lords and owners of the sayd townes. One city there is called Couton, another Xanigeton, as also the cities of Tubguer, Azegue, Amader, Quaherque, and the towne of Faroo. The which townes and cities are very great and fairely built, being inhabited by rich Moores, and abounding with all kinde of cattell, Barley and Dates. And here is such plenty of golde found upon the sands by the rivers side, that the sayd

Moores usually carry the same Northward to Marocco, and Southward to the city of Tombuto in the land of Negros, which city standeth about 300 leagues from the kingdome of Darha; and this kingdome is but 60 leagues from this Iland and Castle of Arguin. Wherefore I beseech your worship to put his majesty in remembrance hereof; for the sayd cities and townes are but ten dayes journey from hence. I heartily wish that his majesty would send two or three marchants to see the state of the Countrey, who might travell to the aforesayd cities, to understand of their rich trade. For any man may go safe and come safe from those places. And thus without troubling of your worship any further, I humbly take my leave. From the Iland and Castle of Arguin the 20 of January 1591.

Your worships servant
Melchior Petoney.

The following tentative identifications may be made: Darha is the Mauritanian Adrār, rather than Darʿa or Draa; Couton is Wādān; Xanigeton is Shinqīṭī; Tubguer is (T)abbʷayr – if correct this suggests that this town or village still existed in the sixteenth century, side by side with its neighbour Shinqīṭī; Azegue is Āzuqqī to the west of Āṭār; Amader is Āmdayr al-Kabīr and Āmdayr al-Ṣaghīr, both of them a journey of a day and a half from Shinqīṭī in the direction of Āṭār. Quaherque is possibly Asharayrīg in the Adrār; it is a spring which adjoins the mountain where the tomb of the scholar Aḥmad ibn al-Bashīr al-Ḥanshī al-Ghallāwī is located. Faroo suggests no obvious locality. It might just possibly be a deformation of Biru, which was the ancient Soninke name for Walātah.

29. Abū'l-ʿAbbās Aḥmad ibn Khalīl al-Nāṣirī al-Salāwī (d. 1897), *Kitāb al-Istiqṣā' li-akhbār dawlat Maghrib al-Aqṣā*, published in Cairo in four volumes, 1894.
30. The Arabic text is in Basset, *op. cit.*, pp. 561–3.
31. Basset, *op. cit.*, pp. 544 and 548.

Notes and References to Chapter Five

1. *L'Afrique de Marmol*, Paris, 1573, vol. 1, chapter 32, "Life and customs of the Arabs". See also Marmol y Carvajal, *Descripción General de Africa*, Granada, 1573, folio 41 (Cap. XXXII); Leo Africanus, *Description of Africa*, 1, page 75, lib 1; and Baroja, *Estudios Saharianos*, Madrid, 1955, p. 41, note 1.
2. See René Basset, *Mission au Sénégal*, Paris, 1909, vol. 1, p. 361.
3. See notes of J. Dupuis to *The narrative of Richard Adams, a Sailor*, John Murray, London, 1816, p. 132, and *Nouveau Voyage dans l'Interieur d'Afrique, 1810–14*, trans. by Frasans, 1817, pp. 177–8.
4. J. G. Jackson, *The Empire of Marocco*, London, 1814, p. 289.

5. N. Levtzion and J. F. P. Hopkins, *Corpus of Early Arabic Sources for West African History*, Cambridge University Press, 1981, p. 190. See p. 166.
6. *The Chronicle of the Discovery and Conquest of Guinea by Gomes Eannes de Azurara*, trans. by C. R. Beazly and C. Prestage, Hakluyt Society, 1896, vol. 1, pp. 45 and 48.
7. Levtzion and Hopkins, *op. cit.*, p. 286.
8. See my *Shinqīṭī Folk Literature and Song*, Oxford Library of African Literature, 1968, pp. 34–50, 77–8.
9. See Mohamd el Moktâr ould Bah, "Introduction à la Poésie Mauritanienne (1650–1900)", *Arabica*, vol. 18, Brill, 1971, pp. 35–6.
10. Norris, *op. cit.*, p. 49.
11. See Ibn Khaldūn, *Histoire des Berbères*, trans. by De Slane, Paris, 1968/9, vol. 1, pp. 37–41 and 51.
12. Muḥammad al-Fāsī, "La Littérature Populaire, Malḥūn", *La Pensée*, Rabat, no. 1, 1962, pp. 67–70.
13. See G. S. Colin, *Initiation au Maroc*, Rabat, 1932, pp. 146–9.
14. Norris, *op. cit.*, pp. 40–9.
15. *Ibid.*, pp. 69–74.
16. *Ibid.*, pp. 78–92, and Mohamd el Moktâr ould Bah, *op. cit.*, p. 14.
17. *Ibid.*, pp. 56–7 and 82–3.
18. Mohamd el Moktâr ould Bah, *op. cit.*, p. 42.
19. *Ibid.*, p. 43, and *al-Wasīṭ*, Cairo, 1960, p. 94.
20. *Dīwān Imri'il-Qays*, Dār Ṣādir, Beirut, 1377/1958, p. 126. Likewise similar is a poem of Labīd ibn Rabī'ah al-'Āmirī in Th. Noeldeke's *Delectus Veterum Carminum Arabicorum*, 1890, pp. 104–5.
21. Basset, *op. cit.*, p. 625.
22. Mohamd el Moktâr ould Bah, *op. cit.*, pp. 1–48.
23. *Ibid.*, p. 12.
24. Cited from an unfinished article by Muḥammad wuld Mawlūd wuld Dāddāh on the subject of popular literature in the newspaper, *Mūrītāniyā*, undated but published in Nouakchott in 1961 or 1962.
25. Mohamd el Moktâr ould Bah, *op. cit.*, p. 38.
26. Norris, *op. cit.*, pp. 36–9.
27. See L. Massignon, "Un poète saharien: la qasida d'el Yedali", *Revue du Monde Musulman*, vol. 8, 1909, pp. 199–205.
28. I quote here part of a folio in the manuscript of *Fatḥ al-Murabbī fī Sharḥ Ṣalāti Rabbī*, by Shaykh Muḥammad al-Yadālī. Varied reasons are given in al-Yadālī's commentary for this ode's composition. Since they are seemingly incompatible one cannot exclude the hand of another in the final shaping of this text. In

one place al-Yadālī says that he was about to set out on a journey and that he heard a group of musicians playing on stringed instruments, probably the *tīdinīt* or *ardīn*. They were singing a very beautiful Arabic song to a melodious air (*malḥūn*), and the words of the song were in Classical Arabic. This made him make up his mind to compose an ode in praise of the Prophet, employing the same metre. Elsewhere in the commentary there are at least two different reasons given, although they entail Mauritanian musicians and their singing (*leghna*).

"*Thirdly*," he writes, "I thought well of this pleasing *Ḥassāniyyah* verse. Men have said that one of those things which evoke the love of the Prophet, the blessing and peace of Allāh be upon him, in the heart, is the sweet sound which the singer makes when he sings and he lauds the qualities of the Prophet. When, by chance, they are stirring to the heart they bring a restful joy and delight to him who listens to the sweet sound, because the sound of voices is a powerful way of drowning heart and mind in delight. At the same time, the soul is stirred, so that it journeys in the direction of the beloved. The portrait of that loved one is brought into one's presence within the inner eye of the mind. . .

"*Fourthly*, the metre of this ode is not one of the sixteen metres [of Khalīl] plus that known as *Mutadārik*. The [Classical] metre which it resembles the most is luxated *Basīṭ*, expressed in hemistichs each of which forms its own verse. This ode is measured in feet on the pattern *mustafʿalātun* [– – v – –], repeated singly. Now this is *not* one of the regular feet [of *Basīṭ*]. Some shortening may effect the feet [when scanned], curtailing the second so that it may become *mufāʿalātun* [v – v – –]. Such is pleasing because it is lighter. The foot may also be subject to the curtailing of a letter [*ṭayy*]. Here there is an ellipsis of the fourth so that it may become *muftaʿalātun* [– – – – or – v v – –]. Among the *Ḥassāniyyah* verse upon which this ode is measured is this one [addressed to the Amīr of the Brāknah, Muḥammad wuld Hayba, who died in *Rajab* 1762].

> *Sawlaan iblaʿjab: Yaad daayr limṣayb(a).*
> *Minhu(u) Ṭifl-aʿrab: Kuun Awlad Hayb(a).*
> An unsurprising question, O Thou who seekest a reward.
> Who is an Arab gallant, other than Wuld Hayba?

If you ponder on this verse, on the one hand, and my ode on the other, you will find both of them to be upon one measure, be it Classical verse (*baḥr*), or be it *Ḥassāniyyah* verse (*batt* = *taqṭīʿ*). The difference is that one is *Ḥassāniyyah* and the other is Arabic."

In fact, the variation of feet (*tafāʿīl*), referred to above is to be observed scattered throughout the ode (see *Kitāb al-Wasīṭ*, pp. 223–6), with examples of (v – v – –) in second place, and sometimes not, likewise (– v v – –). This ode is discussed in my *Shinqīṭī Folk Literature and Song*, pp. 37–9. On the relevence of forms of *Basīṭ* to popular verse, and more especially Yemenite *Qūmā*, and Mawāliyā, found in all the Arab East and Maghrib, as well as in *Muwashshaḥ*, see J. D. Latham, "New Light on the Scansion of an Old Andalusian *Muwaššaḥ*", *Journal of Semitic Studies*, vol. 27, no. 1, Spring 1982, pp. 61–75, and more especially pp. 70–1.

Reference might also be drawn to the contribution of Professor Latham to the *Festschrift* to mark the retirement of Professor R. B. Serjeant, *Arabian and Islamic Studies*, Longman, 1983, "Prosody of an Andalusian *Muwashshaḥ* re-examined", pp. 86–99. This poem dates from the eleventh century when the city of the poet, al-Jazzār, namely the city of Saragossa, was under the rule of the Almoravids, one of whom, Ibn Tāfilwīt, "the son of the twin", bore the same name as the Berber word *tāfilwīt* which is employed in *Ḥassāniyyah* verse to indicate a hemistich. It is most curious that these Berber words should appear as technical terms in this verse if Zenāgah verse is later in date.

29. Norris, *op. cit.*, pp. 70–4.
30. *Ibid.*, pp. 36–7.
31. *al-Wasīṭ*, Cairo, 1958, pp. 277–84.
32. See n. 24. Since reference is made to the "dune of a woman minstrel", *kathīb tīggigt*, in one of Wālid ibn Khālunā's works, in a locality where the Ḥassānīs were recent arrivals in the south-west, it would seem that Muḥammad wuld Mawlūd wuld Dāddāh is correct in his assumptions. The lady minstrel would have been unwelcome in the puritan camps of the Zenāgah *Zwāya*, who are described by Wālid, but presumably she was in the camp of some other Berber chief, or negro chief, or else one of the earliest Ḥassānī groups. Awlād Rizq or Awlād Mubārak, in southern Mauritania. Minstrels are less well known among the *Ḥassāniyyah* speakers of Azawād in Western Mali. The verse, which seems to lack the elaborated metrical forms of Mauritania, is either recited unaccompanied, or it is accompanied on the *tam tam*. In some ways it is closer to the verse forms and the improvisation described by Adams and Jackson? On the *Ḥassāniyyah* of Azawād, see H. Ben Alhousseini, "Aperçu sur la poésie Maure de l'Azaouad", *Etudes Maliennes*, no. 9, March 1974 (published by the Institut des Sciences Humaines), pp. 19–43.

BIBLIOGRAPHY

MICHEL GUIGNARD, *Musique, Honneur et Plaisir au Sahara*, Librarie Geuthner, Paris, 1975.

ALBERT LERICHE, "Poésie et musique maure", *Bulletin de l'Institut Français de l'Afrique Noire*, vol. 13, Dakar, 1950, pp. 710–43.

AHMED-BÂBA MISKÉ, *Al-Wasîṭ, Tableau de la Mauritanie au début du XXe siècle*, Klincksieck, Paris, 1970.

ALINE TAUZIN, "Autour de la poésie amoureuse maure de la Mauritanie et du Mali", *Littérature Orale Arabe-Berbère*, Bull. 13, Paris, 1982, pp. 129–46.

Notes and References to Chapter Six

1. Ismaël Hamet, *Chroniques de la Mauritanie Sénégalaise, Nacer Eddine*, Paris, 1911, pp. 230–1 (French text), pp. 61–2 (Arabic text).
2. A Ḥassānī group much mixed with the Berbers. The name al-Zenāgiyyah was adopted by this group either because of some matrilineal survival in their lineal system, or else simply out of ignorance as to their true lineage.
3. Hamet, *op. cit.*, p. 232 (French text), p. 62 (Arabic text). *Tishitayit* is *balanites aegyptica.*
4. The version of their lineage furnished by Paul Marty, "Les Maures du Sahel et du Hodh", *Etudes sur l'Islam et les tribus du Soudan*, Paris, 1921, vol. 3, p. 399, establishes the descent as follows:

Ḥassān
Ūday
Maghfar
ʿUthmān

ʿUmrān — Yaḥyā

[line of ʿUmrān:]
Muḥammad
Dhīb
Faḥfāḥ
Mubārak
Hamūk?
ʿUmar
Banyūg
Hannūn

[sons of Hannūn:]
Muḥammad Zanāgī | Ghuwayz, the Awlād Ghuwayzī | ʿUmar al-ʿAbaydī, ancestor of the ʿAbaydāt and Awlād Aḥmad ibn ʿUmar

5. Aḥmad ibn al-Amīn al-Shinqīṭī, *al-Wasīṭ fī tarājim udabāʾ Shinqīṭ*, Cairo, 1958, pp. 486–7.
6. Marty, *op. cit.*, pp. 381–8.
7. I can find no references to this in my copies of the Walātah Chronicle.
8. Mungo Park's *Travels in the Interior of Africa*, Everyman Edition, pp. 118–19. His remarks hardly square with the aristocratic habits portrayed by al-Shinqīṭī, *op. cit*, pp. 486–7, and the French translation by Mourad Teffahi, *El Wasit, Etudes Mauritaniennes*, no. 5, Centre IFAN, Saint Louis, 1953, pp. 71–3.
9. *Ibid.*, p. 119.
10. *Ibid.*, p. 120.
11. *Ibid.*, p. 114.
12. According to Paul Marty, *op. cit.*, p. 397, the Awlād Mubārak had no religious *Zwāya* or scholars of their own but depended

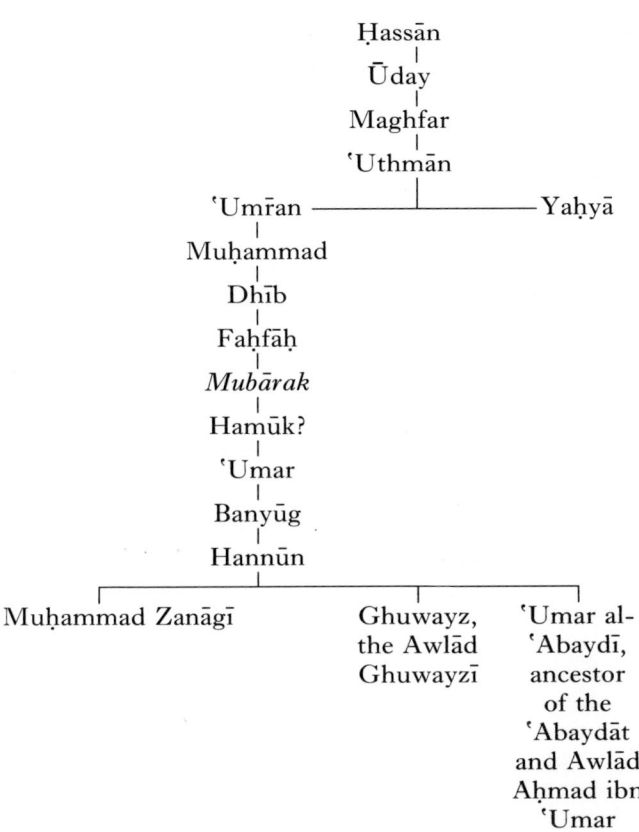

heavily on the Tinwājiyū for religious services and instruction. Mungo Park's description of the Moors whom he met as fanatics and strict observers of the fast is dismissed by Paul Marty as an exaggeration.

13. Literally, "The draught of Bayshān regarding the lineages of the Banū Ḥassān." As the author was an amateur Moorish geographer he may have come across references to the Biblical Bashan in what he read. Muslims held that the saints who preserved the cosmic order (*abdāl*) resided in Bashan. See *Badal* in the *Encyclopedia of Islam*. Here, however, the choice was no doubt simply a literary ploy.

    The eight works of importance attributed to Shaykh Ṣāliḥ ibn ʿAbd al-Wahhāb are:
    (1) The *Ḥaswah*, which was composed at the request of Shaykh Muḥammad al-Mukhtār ibn Sayyid ʿAbdallāh al-ʿAlawī, one of his teachers.
    (2) *Al-Iʿlām fī ʿulūm al-ādāb*, in two volumes.
    (3) *Fatḥ al-alqāb l'ibn ʿAbd al-Wahḥāb fī'l-ta'rīkh.*
    (4) *Zakhārif al-sulūk fī maʿārif al-mulūk.*
    (5) *Al-Awwaliyyāt.*
    (6) *Kitāb Qurrat al-ʿayn fī sharḥ waraqāt Imām al-Ḥaramayn fī'l-uṣūl.*
    (7) *Kitāb al-Durar.*
    (8) *Asmā' al-buldān.*

    To the above may be added a *dīwān* of Arabic verse.

14. See endpapers.
15. At this time the Inbāṭ Znāga (Īdaw ʿĪsh) were under the sway of the Awlād Mubārak. It was under Aʿmar ibn Muḥammad Khūna, and his son Bakkār (d. 1175/1761/2), that they gained their independence.
16. A couplet (*gāf*) in septisyllabic *Bu ʿUmraan* or *Tayduum* metres.
17. An octosyllabic *gāf* of unknown metre.
18. *ʿArabī* is used in the Hodh in preference to Ḥassānī.

Notes and References to Chapter Seven

1. Sīdī al-Mukhtār al-Kuntī was born in 1729 and died in 1811. He was born to the north-east of Arawān at Kathīb Ughalu, and he was taught at Tawdannī, amongst other localites, one of the most wretched and hottest localities in the Sahara. As a boy, one of his earliest teachers was a member of the Kel Inallbush, a saintly family of the Kel Es-Sūq. He had a considerable following among the Barābīsh, especially among the Awlād Bū Khaṣīb of the Awlād Ghaylān. He was a major influence on the Barābīsh Amīr, Muḥammad ibn Raḥḥāl, and on his son, ʿAlī.

The Shaykh, on occasions, employed contingents of the Barābīsh to fight his enemies among the Awlād Dalīm. His role was that of a mediator, conciliator and counsellor between the Barābīsh and the Tuareg, the Awlād ʿAllūsh, the Īdaw ʿĪsh and other tribes.

2. See Paul Marty, *Etudes sur l'Islam et les tribus du Soudan*, Paris, 1920, vol. 1, pp. 75–127.
3. *Ibid.* pp. 117–22 and H. T. Norris, *The Tuaregs*, Aris and Phillips, Warminster, 1975, pp. 168–71.
4. *al-Wasīṭ*, Cairo, 1958, p. 458, Azawād and Arawān.
5. Quoted by Muḥammad wuld Muḥammad wuld Dāddāh al-Chennafi in "Sur les traces d'Awdaghust", in Denis Robert, Serge Robert and Jean Devisse, *Tegdaoust 1*, Paris, 1970, vol. 1, p. 104.
6. Cited by T. Lewicki in his *West African Food in the Middle Ages*, Cambridge University Press, 1974, p. 94, and Marty, *op. cit.*, pp. 179–80.
7. Marty *op. cit.*, pp. 177–80.
8. Michel Abitbol, *Tombouctou et les Arma*, Paris, 1979, p. 112. An early penetration of Azawād by the Kuntah should not be overlooked, although we rely entirely on translated missing Arabic source material for the evidence. One source refers to the arrival of the Kuntah in Tuwāt in 1460, another in 1551. It is also reported in these sources that in 1469 some of the Awlād Ibn Dāwūd and Ḥassānī Awlād Dulaym or Dalīm left for Azawād because of a drought. See *Kunta Settlement in Azawad*, in A. A. Batran, "The Kunta, Sīdī'l-Mukhtār al-Kuntī, and the office of *Shaykh al-Ṭarīqa'l-Qādiriyya*", contributed to J. R. Willis (ed.), *Studies in West African Islamic History, vol. 1, The Cultivators of Islam*, Frank Cass, 1979, pp. 124–7.
9. Marty, *op. cit.*, pp. 238–40. On the Islamisation of Tādamakkat, see T. Lewicki, "Les Origines et l'Islamisation de la ville de Tādmakka d'après les sources Arabes", in *Le Sol, la Parole et l'Ecrit, mélanges en hommage à Raymond Mauny*, Paris, 1981, vol. 1, pp. 439–44. For details consult V. Monteil, "Sur quelques textes arabes provenant du Soudan (Région de Tombouctou)", *Bulletin du Comité d'Etudes Historiques et Scientifiques de l'A.O.F.*, 1938, pp. 499–517.
10. Marty, *op. cit.*, pp. 186–7 and 239, and Monteil *op. cit.*
11. Marty, *op. cit.*, p. 240. On the Igellād, that is the Kel Intasar, see pp. 251–327.
12. *Ibid.*, p. 240.
13. In ʿAbdallāh Agg Ādda, *Ta'rīkh al-Sūqiyyīn*, Timbuctoo manuscript, B.R.I. 176, written originally by ʿAbdallāh ibn al-Shaykh ibn al-Ḥājj Muḥammad ibn Ādda, although the copy is

dated from about 1944/5. The text in parts adumbrates the foundation legend to be found in almost all Sūqī texts.

14. The salt mining is described by Ibn Baṭṭūṭah in the fourteenth century. In his days the village had a number of houses and mosques which were built of blocks of salt and roofed with camel skins. None lived there save for the slaves of the Massūfah Berbers of Taghāzā who worked the salt mine. According to Cadamosto, who was writing about 1507, the annual caravans for salt, the *azelay*, were owned by Azanaghi Berbers, but also Arabs, Maʿqil ancestors of the Barābīsh. The salt was carried to Timbuctoo and then to Mali where it was sold for gold. See, *The Voyages of Cadamosto*, Hakluyt Society, Series II, vol. lxxx, 1937, p. 21. See also Knut S. Vikør, *The Oasis of Salt, the History of Kawar, a Saharan Centre of Salt Production*, Bergen, 1979, pp. 39–41, and R. Mauny, *Tableau géographique de l'Ouest Africain au Moyen Age*, IFAN (L'Institut Français d'Afrique Noire), Dakar, 1961, pp. 328–32.
15. About 1450 to 1480 during the period of Tuareg rule in the city.
16. The whole passage is discussed in context in my "A summary of the History of the Eastern Kel Intasar attributed to Ibn al-Najīb (*circa* 1710–1720)", *Maghreb Review*, vol. 3, no. 2, March–April 1979, pp. 36–40.
17. I am grateful to Mamoud Zoubeir for a microfilm copy of the text. Its author is undoubtedly one of the Kel Es-Sūq, probably of Arawān, and the copy appears to be in the hand of the late scholar of Timbuctoo, Muḥammad Bū Laʿrāf.
18. Imaghsharen is the name given by the writers of the histories of the Western Sudan to the pre-Arab, Berber peoples of the region of Azawād. The spelling is close to the Tuareg *Imajaghen*, the name given to their military aristocracy. This is a class name, not a tribe, so we have no idea from the sources as to the true tribal affiliation of these people, whether they were Massūfah or Lamtūnah or Lamṭah or a distinct group. Some sources refer to them as "Arabs", meaning warriors.
19. This is an interesting explanation for the name of Tuareg although hardly definitive and one which is rivalled by more plausible alternatives, see my *The Tuaregs, op. cit.*, pp. 9–12 and 32.
20. They are in fact a branch of the Kel Intasar, see Marty, *op. cit.*, pp. 305–6.
21. The expulsion referred to is an indication of the constant problem of the Moroccan dynasties, Marīnids, Saʿdians and ʿAlawites, in having to control the Maʿqilian bedouin. See Marty, *op. cit.*, p. 188. The Raḥāminah were one of the tribes which were employed by the Moroccan Sulṭān in the province

of Marakkech (al-Ḥawz). Ramon Lourido Diaz, in his *Marruecos en la Segunda Mitad del Siglo XVIII*, Madrid, 1978, remarks, in regard to the reign of Sulṭān Sīdī Muḥammad ibn ʿAbdallāh 1757–90, on p. 119, that "reinstalled in Marrakech, the Raḥāminah Arabs, imitating those of Safi, also pressed their sons into the Caliph's service. With them, and with the one thousand five hundred former soldiers, Sīdī Muḥammad formed the first corps of a permanent army, which was completed, in case of dire need, and on occasions, with units of the Ḥawz region."

The relation which developed between the Imaghsharen, the townsfolk of Timbuctoo and the chiefs of the Barābīsh is not outlined at all in this text. However, Ismäel Hamet, in his "Villes Sahariennes", *Revue du Monde Musulman*, vol. 19, 1912, pp. 276–7, citing local sources, informs us that the founders of Timbuctoo were *Zwāya* called Irma Niyāl. These constituted the sedentary population of the city. According to his source "their nomads" were Tuareg nobles of the Iwillimmeden, who, of course, entered this region far later than the Imagsharen. These "nomads" who imposed protection money on others in exchange for their protection, were themselves subject, in some manner, to the Barābīsh, whose chiefs from the Banū Raḥḥāl (Awlād Sulaymān) acted as mediators and advisors. Whether this distinction, if true, has any early validity is very doubtful. Elias N. Saad in his important book, *Social History of Timbuctoo*, Cambridge, 1983, writes, "Historically, both Tamashagh and Ḥassānī speakers owe their origin to the Berbers of the southern Sahara who are first known as Masūfa, Lamtūna and Judāla and who later make their appearance as Magsharen, Kel Aghlāl, Kel Antasar, Kel al-Suq, Barābīsh, Kel Tadmekkat *etc.* In the chronicles, these groups are identified by their clan and confederation names, rather than by any linguistic, ethnic or cultural criteria."

22. The Askiyā in question was Isḥāq II who assumed power in 1588. The Moroccan expedition to Taghāzā in 1584–5 ended in disaster.
23. The text, which gives the meaningless *ḥarīsh*, is possibly corrupt. Perhaps the word should be *ḥarbah*. A javelin, or two javelins, and two horse-shoes are apparently intended. See Dahiru Yahya, *Morocco in the Sixteenth Century*, Longman, 1981, pp. 156–6 and 166.
24. *Ibid.*, p. 154. Certain details from the Walātah chronicle relate events which took place further to the east at this time. Mention is made of the stay of the Askiyā *Amīr* Dā'ūd in the town at the end of *Muḥarram* in 1551. Towards 1583/4, he sent his Berber

Tuareg and half-Tuareg squadrons of *Msg* (probably *Mzīg/Mzāzga*) and Tadʿamrt towards the Walātah district where they punished Arab tribes on the rampage up to a place called Kishall (?) and Walātah and Tinmal, these localities being in that area of the Niger buckle. The date given in the Chronicle for the arrival of Jawdar and the Armas in Timbuctoo is 1590/1.

25. The Kel Intasar claim that it was they who dug the well at Telek/In Talak which became a Kuntah centre in Azawād.
26. Muḥammad ibn Infa is also credited with the digging of this well. See the previous passage quoted on the Kel Intasar.
27. Paul Marty described this episode as legendary, *op. cit.*, pp. 187–8.
28. A brief life of Shaykh Sīdī Aḥmad al-Khalīf al-Raqqādi, founder of the Tuwāt *Zāwiyah* of the Kuntah, who died in 1652, is given by Marty, *op. cit.*, pp. 130–3.
29. *Ibid.*, p. 188. The Kel Tintahoun are a subdivision of the Kel Intasar. According to the map published with Barth's travels, 1850–5, Sheet no. 14, Tintahón is marked as lying east of the route between Arawān and Timbuctoo.
30. Rather than "the fasters", those presumably meant here are the Ṣiyām who are a branch of the Īdaw al-Ḥājj of the Mauritanian Adrār.
31. Saḥḥār means "magician" and is hard to explain. However, Anīs is described as a great "marabout" by Marty, *op. cit.*, p. 188, so this may refer to his abilities to use supernatural forces.

    Mukhtār wuld Ḥāmidun has kindly furnished me with the following note regarding the chieftainship of the Barābīsh: (a) among the clan of the Awlād ʿAbd al-Raḥmān (the Raḥāminah), ʿĪsā ibn Sulaymān, and his son Filālī, in the seventeenth century; (b) among the clan of Awlād Sulaymān, Muḥammad ibn Yūsuf (d. 1168/1755), then Muḥammad ibn Raḥḥāl and his sons, ʿAlī (d. 1215/1802), Mahammad (d. 1222/1818), then Aḥmad ibn Aʿbayda (d. 1269/1851), then Mahammad ibn Aḥmad (d. 1293/1846), then his son Sīdī Muḥammad, when France entered, then his son Maḥmūd ibn Daḥmān, who was still living in 1960.
32. The *Gibla* must refer to the Hodh, the region to the south-west of Arawān. The Bū Fāyid have been referred to, together with the Awlād Mubārak, in Chapter 6. For a far fuller account of events at this period involving the Awlād ʿĀmir and other elements of the Barābīsh see the translation by Houdas of *Tadhkirat al-Nisyān*, Paris, 1901, pp. 105–6, 156–9.
33. Ḥām wuld Budal. This is a very Tuareg name. Ḥām must refer to a Berber or a negro, while Budal is found among the Awlād Mubārak and Iwillimmeden.

34. The Rgaybāt are a powerful tribe in the north-western Sahara. They are to be found in the former Spanish Sahara, Mauritania, near Tindouf in Algeria, and in the adjacent deserts of Mali. See A. Cauneille, "Les Nomades reguibat", *Travaux de l'Institut de Recherches Sahariennes*, no. 6, Algiers, 1950, pp. 83–100; J. Dubief, "Les Reguibat Lgouacem, chronologie et nomadisme", *Bull. de l'IFAN*, series B, vol. 17, nos. 3–4, pp. 528–50.
35. The ʿArab al-Giblah are to be connected with the Ḥassānī elements to be found in the region of the Hodh. According to Barth, *Travels in North and Central Africa*, Appendix II, this is the name given by the Tuareg to Ūday Ḥassānīs (Udayen in Tamasheq).
36. Marty, *op. cit.*, p. 195.
37. This must refer to a delegation to the Kuntah, Marty, *op. cit.*, p. 196 may refer.
38. On this holy man, see pp. 85–6.
39. See p. 86, and Marty, *op. cit.*, pp. 244–5. The passage regarding the visit of Ṭālib Sīdī Aḥmad to Sīdī Aḥmad al-Hoggārī is almost a direct quotation from the text called *Fatḥ al-Shakūr fi Maʿrifat Aʿyān Ulamā' al-Takrūr*.
40. The family of the great Kuntah Shaykh, Sīdī'l-Mukhtār al-Kabīr.
41. Literally "the camel's belly", the name of one of two sub-tribes of the Barābīsh, see Marty, *op. cit.*, p. 229. They are Awlād Aʿysh, Ghannām, Ghaylān, and Bū Khaṣīb.
42. The *Azelay*, French *azalai*, is the at least annual, and sometimes twice annual, in winter and summer, salt caravan which journeys between Taoudenni (Arabic Tawdannī) and Timbuctoo. Prior to 1585 or perhaps before 1506/7 this caravan journeyed between Taghāzā and Timbuctoo. See Marty, *ibid.*, pp. 246–9.
43. This strange Arabic expression was either his personal name, referring to himself alone, or, as seems far more likely, was a name based on an oath made to God for whom "neither slumber seizeth Him, nor sleep", E. W. Lane's translation of *Sūrah* 11, verse 254, in the Koran.
44. The Sahel here is *not* the West African Savannah lands but the desert areas to the north, north-north-west of Azawād. *Sahel (sāḥil)* is a northerly point of the compass for the dwellers in the Hodh and Azawād.
45. For a detailed description of Taoudenni (Tawdannī), see Marty, *op. cit.*, pp. 245–9, and Barth, *op. cit.*, Appendix II.
46. The Awlād ʿAllūsh are a division of the Awlād Dāwūd, see G. Poulet, *Les Maures de l'Afrique Occidentale Française*, Paris, 1904, pp. 123–6. See also Barth, *op. cit.*, Appendix II.

47. Kadām. According to Barth, *ibid.*, Appendix II, vol. IV, "Moorish tribes in Áderér", "It is encircled towards the north by the awful zone of immense sandhills, called 'Maghtér', and towards the south by another similar, but less sterile girdle, called 'Warán', both these districts joining towards the east of Áderér, at a point called 'El Gedám', at a distance of six days from Wadān, in going from east to west." One of these points, reached on the fourth day, is called Zwíri wén Zwemra which is probably that mentioned earlier in this text, p. 95, as Zīr ibn Zimrān.

It would seem that El Gedám (Ligdam on the map), corresponds to the Guedam desert and the so-called "lake of Guedam", away to the east of Wādān on the map of Ortelius, called *Barbariae et Biledulgerid*, printed in Antwerp in 1570, and based on Gostaldi's Africa map of 1564. In fact, this lake may be indicating the Mares de Tiselrhatane (Tiselghaten), shown to the north-east of the area of El Gedám on some maps.

Whether Kadām, in the manuscript, refers without doubt to this place is by no means certain. It could be in Azawād or it may refer to the locality called Kādām lying between Tīshīt and Walātah in Mauritania. Nevertheless, the northerly direction of the operation favours El Gedám.

It should also be noted that the name in the text in Arabic is spelt Kadām, with a long vowel and without the definite article. This would suggest that the root of the name is either Berber or Azayr and that it has nothing to do with the Arabic *al-qadam*, meaning "the foot".

48. *Gīr* is a name found in several Saharan regions. A well marked Guir on some maps is to be found due east of Arawān.

49. *al-Aʿlāb* may refer to a locality called Ellib el Hejar on Barth's map. Ellib el Aghebe is shown north of Timbuctoo. The term refers to dead and very elongated and rounded dunes.

50. That is of the Kuntah.

51. Al-Ḥank. According to Barth *op. cit.*, Appendix II, "Érgshésh is a long and narrow girdle of sandhills, which stretches out in the direction from Tawát to Warán, and passing at no great distance to the west of Taödénni, joins Magh-tér, or rather Warán, at the S.W. end. This district which is similar in its nature to Gídi, and not destitute of water between the high sandhills, although not adorned by nature with the equally graceful and useful palm-tree, is only from twenty to thirty miles broad, and is bordered towards the north by the smaller district called *El-Ḥank*, consisting of black vegetable soil, rich in trees, and intersected by rocky hills or kódia. There is in this district a famous spot called Lemezarráb, with a large group of

palm trees, the fruit of which is gathered by the Kunta, who, however, leave these trees without any cultivation whatsoever."

52. A *nafga* is one kilogram weight in grain according to Pierret.
53. Submission of the Barābīsh to the Hoggar Tuareg is discussed by Marty, *op. cit.*, pp. 201, 208, 209. According to Mohammed Ben Said, in his valuable "Les tribus arabes de la région de Tombouctou", *Revue Tunisienne*, Tunis, 1904, p. 487, "Les Berabich sont continuellement pillés par les Hoggar et les Aouallimeden ou par leurs tribus serves". He wrote this in 1896.
54. Literally "herders" according to the text but perhaps "Rayahs", that is *raʿāyā*, subject tribes, is meant. In that case subject tribes which are not of Raḥāminah stock must be meant. See Marty, *op. cit.*, p. 229.
55. Among the edible grasses mentioned by R. Pierret in his *Etude du Dialecte Maure*, 1940, p. 134, is *tādrīṣ*, singular *tādrīṣāyyah*. It is described as a "petite plante rampante à baies garnies de piquants".
56. See Jeremy Keenan, *The Tuareg*, Allen Lane, 1977, p. 42.
57. Inlāḥi is spelt Eneláhi by Barth. It is situated due east of Arawān.
58. Probably *Hīb*, a well known Mauritanian game. Mauritanian games are described by Mukhtār wuld Ḥāmidun in his *Précis sur la Mauritanie*, Etudes Mauritaniennes No. 4, Saint Louis, Senegal, 1952.
59. Perhaps the tribe of the chief of the Mashḍūf of the Hodh is meant.
60. According to Barth it lies to the north-west of Gundam. He spells it Geléb-el-gheném.
61. The port of Timbuctoo.

Notes and References to Chapter Eight

1. Henry Barth, *Travels in North and Central Africa*, 5 vols, London, 1857–8. See vol. 5, Appendix III, which is specifically devoted to the Iwillimmeden and their branches, especially p. 552.
2. This matter is discussed in my chapter on the Iwillimmeden in *The Tuaregs*, Aris and Phillips, Warminster, 1975, Chapter 7, pp. 98–108.
3. Taken from a manuscript copy written by a member of the Kel Es-Sūq, Ḥammād ibn Muḥammad al-Kel Sūqī. The copy is a personal one. According to Mohammad Ougenett, a former chief of the Kel Es-Sūq, the Tuareg chief, Karidenna, brought

the differences with his brother, Karoza, before the Sulṭān of Agades for his arbitration. The latter invested Karidenna at that time. If this is historical fact, and not merely a folk story, then it would follow that the investiture was prompted by circumstances which were entirely different from those surrounding the investiture of Karidenna in Timbuctoo by the Moroccans. See M. Cortier, *D'une rive à l'autre du Sahara*, Paris, 1908, part 2, "L'Adrar, moeurs et coutumes des Touareg Ifor'as", pp. 394–6.

The Sulṭān al-Ghuddālā, variants al-ʿAddāla/al-ʿĀdil, appears to have ended his reign about 1003–4/1594–6, see J. Hunwick, "The Dynastic Chronologies in the Central Sudan in the Sixteenth Century: Some Reinterpretations", *Kano Studies*, new series, vol. 1, no. 1, 1973, pp. 38–9.

4. See T. Whitcomb, "New evidence on the Origins of the Kunta - l", *Bulletin of the School of Oriental and African Studies*, vol. 38, part 1, 1975, and part 2, 1975, especially pp. 407ff. Also the whole of the chapter by A. A. Batran on the Kuntah in *Studies in West African Islamic History, vol. 1, The Cultivators of Islam*, ed. J. R. Willis, Frank Cass, 1979, pp. 113–47.
5. Batran, *op. cit.*, especially pp. 126–7.
6. See C. C. Stewart, *Islam and Social Order in Mauritania*, Oxford Studies in African Affairs, 1973, pp. 10–33, and on the Kuntah tradition in general, pp. 34–53.
7. On the life and *jihād* of al-Jaylānī, see my *The Tuaregs*, Aris and Phillips, Warminster, 1975, pp. 145–610.
8. This passage has been translated from a copy of the page of *Kashf al-Ghummah* which is to be found, I believe, in the *Institut Aḥmad Bābā* in Timbuctoo. The copy was made for me by the late Muḥammad Bū Laʿrāf.
9. J. Nicolaisen, *Ecology and Culture of the Pastoral Tuareg*, Copenhagen, 1963, pp. 456–7. Also see pp. 438–9.
10. F. Nicolas, "Coutumes et traditions chez les Twareg. Matriarcat et patriarcat", *Review de l'Institut de Belles Lettres Arabes*, vol. 4, 1946, pp. 403–11.
11. De Foucauld in his *Dictionnaire abrégé de noms propres*, Paris, 1940, spells this place Ġouñhân, *mont; vallée; point d'eau*, (p. 77). The Kel Geres were once centred in the Tādamakkat region, since the Arab geographer, al-ʿUmarī, in his *Masālik al-Abṣār fī Mamālik al-Amṣār, circa* 1337/8, refers to the Tin Gharās, who are almost certainly the same people. Whether another tribe of al-ʿUmarī's, the Madūsah, also called Maddāsah, have some connection with the name Wa-n-Fadasen is far less certain.

Notes and References to Chapter Nine

1. Dr Sabah Ibrahim Said al-Sheikhly of the University of Baghdad who is now translating her thesis into Arabic.
2. Unpublished thesis submitted to the University of Manchester, 1980, pp. 97 and 104–115 in particular.
3. Andrzej Dziubinski, "L'Identification de Tesset et Guaden, localités de Numidie, d'après la Déscription de Jean-Léo l'Africain", *Africana Bulletin*, vol. 13, Warsaw, 1970, p. 36 in particular.
4. See N. Levtzion and J. F. P. Hopkins, *Corpus of Early Arabic Sources for West African History*, Cambridge University Press, 1981, pp. 50, 67, 70, 219 and 237. Ibn Abī Zarʿ spells this town as Tātaklāsīn (var. Tātaklātīn). Both Levtzion and Hopkins opt for Bānklābīn. However, I am sure that Ibn Abī Zarʿ is nearer the mark. H. Barth, on his map in *Travels in North and Central Africa*, shows a locality on the route between the Adrār of Mauritania and Walātah, on the Ẓhar to the north of Tīshīt, which he spells *Akáratín é sbot* and *Akáratín el had*, in the area described by al-Bakrī. The falling away of the feminine prefix *Ta-* and the change of a *rā'* to *lām* would be quite regular.
5. See Levtzion and Hopkins, *ibid.*, p. 129. The site of Nūl is either at Asrīr of the Azwafid or at Tagaost (Ksabi).
6. Cited in the thesis of Dr al-Sheikhly who, on pp. 6–7, reproduces part of the text of Abū ʿAlī Ṣāliḥ ibn Abī Ṣāliḥ ibn ʿAbd al-Ḥalīm al-Ḥilānī al-Maṣmūdī, *Kitab al-Ansāb*, Manuscript Kar (Qarawiyyīn), no. K, 1275, Morocco. It is by no means impossible that Īghirān Yaṭṭūf was in the region to the south of present-day Tindouf. Īghirān might indicate the *Zenāgah* word *igerjān*, meaning terrains covered with *panicum turgidum*, and Yaṭṭūf either Tindouf itself, or Yetti, which is situated directly to the south of it.
7. Levtzion and Hopkins, *op. cit.*, p. 22.
8. *Ibid.*, pp. 66–7. Apart from these routes and wells one should also note the spread of the use of water channels and conduits constructed underground, as in Persia and the Yemen, the *qanawāt* (sing. *qanāh*) and *khaṭṭārāt*, which are to be found in the Wādī Darʿah and in Tuwāt, of no certain date, but possibly very early. It is known that the Almoravids encouraged their construction and that the *Amīr*, ʿAlī ibn Yūsuf, commanded the Andalusian engineer, ʿAbdallāh ibn Yūnus, to design a hydraulic network for the zone (*ḥawz*) of Marrakech.
9. *Ibid.*, p. 67.
10. *Ibid.* p. 67. In *al-Wasīṭ*, Cairo, 1958, p. 438, regarding al-Maqṭayr, the author refers to a well discovered by Ṭālib ibn

Khalīl in which were found ancient spears and bows.

11. *al-Wasīṭ, ibid.*, p. 428.
12. The initial Kā/Kaw in this name may simply be a feature found in the Arabic spelling of many African names, for example Aïr is sometimes spelt Kāhīr and there are other toponyms spelt in this way.
13. Levtzion and Hopkins, *op. cit.*, pp. 127–8. "The language of Guinea" (*Janāwiyyah*) may simply indicate the language of the Ignāwen Ḥarāṭīn of the Saharan oases. Tisgui al-Haratin lies west of Akka.
14. *Ibid.*, p. 173.
15. Probably Tarhjijt, some thirty to forty miles east of Goulimine. Levtzion and Hopkins, *ibid.*, pp. 190–1.
16. *Āthār al-Bilād*, see Levtzion and Hopkins, *ibid.*, p. 180.
17. The toponym, or tribe, Tāzakkāght, bears a resemblance to Tazarharht or Tazaghart, to the north-east of Jabal al-Kust in Gazūlah country. It is near the town of Tafraout.
18. Levtzion and Hopkins, *ibid.*, p. 209.
19. *Ibid.*, p. 327.
20. Johannes Leo, *A Geographical Historie of Africa*, London, 1600, Amsterdam and New York, 1969, p. 281. On most maps of the sixteenth and seventeenth centuries this place is shown as Gogdem or Gogden. The Latin edition of 1559 reads *Includitur in hoc deserto aliud quoddam Goeten appellant.*
21. See al-Maqrīzī, *al-Bayān wa'l-I'rāb 'ammā bi Arḍ Miṣr min al-A'rāb*, Cairo, 1961, p. 57. "It is said that the offspring of Ṣanhāj are Yaktūn [*sic*], who are the *Mulaththamūn*, and Tazkīk/Tazgīg and Massūfah and Masṭūfah, who are the manufacturers of the Lamṭ shields." It is possible that Tazkīk and Tāzakkāght are the same, and also the Tayzgah of the Mauritanian Adrār.

    The form of these names, Tazgīg, Tāzakkāght, may have a connection with Mzk, the Mazīg or Mzāzga, and the Arabic form of Imagsharen. It is also by no means unlikely that the name of one of the earliest kings of the Western Saharan Ṣanhājah, Zāghī ibn Zāghī, is an Arabised form of one or other of these names. According to Ibn al-Faqīh (*circa* 290/903) the territory of this kingdom lay to the south of the Idrīsids of Morocco.
22. See Levtzion and Hopkins, *op. cit.*, pp. 282–3.
23. Following the revolt of the false prophet Musaylimah, see Philip Hitti, *History of the Arabs*, London, 1946, pp. 141, 148 and 149.
24. *al-Wasīṭ, op. cit.*, pp. 458–9.
25. See note 21.

26. Leo, *op. cit.*, Lyon, 1556, vol. 1, p. 317.
27. See page 132.
28. The Kūfic-type inscriptions contain verse 131 from Sūrah 11 of the Koran. My colleague, Dr D. Bivar thinks that they could date back to the third century of the *hijrah*, although they are difficult to date. Timmissao is a mosque in the desert, a shrine even, for the Kel Es-Sūq "Companions of the Prophet". Al-ʿUmarī refers to an independent Sulṭān between Aïr and Tādamakkat about 749/1349, in a locality spelt Dmwshh and it is possible that this is the place. Caravans seek water and shelter here from the Tanezrouft. See Th. Monod, "Sur les inscriptions peintes de Tim-missao, Sahara Central", *Journal. Soc. Africainists*, 1938, pp. 83–95.
29. See De Foucauld, *Dictionnaire Abrégé, Touareg-Français*, Paris, 1940, p. 62. The root of the toponym of Taoudenni, according to De Foucauld, p. 192, are the radicals WDN. This, or In-Wallan, could be at the basis of Leo's spelling of Goeten, or rather its lost Arabic original.
30. Al-Idrīsī may have been misinterpreted, and the error may lie with his editors and translators, as a variant, Azqan or Azqanī, is found for Āzuqqī.
31. See Leo, *op. cit.*, p. 94.
32. *Ibid.* pp. 97–8.
33. Madghīs al-Abtar, or Mādghīs, was the ancestor of the Berbers according to the Arab genealogists and historians.
34. Toponyms of this kind are found in the region of Tazenacht; for example, Adrar-n-Ouaougdim. Ait-Ouguiddem is located to the north-east of Tiznit, near the barrage of Yousuf Ben Tachfine. A scholar named Abū Muḥammad Jaldāsun ibn Isḥaq al-Rakūnī, "the crippled handed", who lived in Ribāṭ Ūjadām in southern Morocco, is mentioned in Abū Yaʿqūb Yūsuf ibn Yaḥyā al-Tādilī's *Kitāb al-Tashawwuf*, ed. A. Faure, Rabat, 1958, p. 210:

٨٠ ـ ومنهم أبو محمد جَلْداسُن بن إِسحاق الرَّكوني

صَحب عبدَ الخالق بن ياسين وكان من الافراد . توفّي ببلده برباط او جدام
من بلد ركونة عام سبعين وخمسمائة . سمعت أبا إبراهِيم بن عبد العزيز
يقول : كان أبو محمد جلداسن أقطع اليدين من الكفين

35. Leo, 1600, *op. cit.*, p. 98. In the French translation it is spelt Gogideme and Mons Gogidema in the Latin.

36. In his *History of the Berbers*, see De Slane's translation, *L'Histoire des Berbères*, Paris, 1982, vol. 2, p. 172.
37. See the interesting comment of W.D. Cooley in his *The Negroland of the Arabs*, Frank Cass, 1966, pp. 19 and 20. As a tribal group, "the Kākudam or Qūqadam" may possibly have been itinerant, or resettled Haskūrah Berbers. Miquel Barcelo, in his article, "Els de Marraqush. Una Immigracio d'Epoca Almoravit o Almohad", *Estudis de Prehistòria, d'Història de Mayûrqa i d'Història de Mallorca*, Mallorca, 1982, pp. 141–2, has argued the case for a settlement of Haskūrah (Xocora) in Majorca from about 1203, although an earlier date is not impossible. Thus a village of Ghujdāmah Haskūrah in the Darʿah, or in Āzuqqī, would seem plausible; likewise another group at Awdaghust.
38. *Le Livre de Mohamed ibn Toumart, Mahdi des Almohades*, I. Goldziher, Alger, 1903, p. 258.
39. Spelt Jebel Lkest, in the region of Tafraout in the Anti Atlas.
40. E. Lévi Provençal, *Documents Inédits d'Histoire Almohade*, Paris, 1928, p. 20 (p. 12 Arabic text).
41. Marked on the maps as Souk-Tleta de Tasserirt, south of Tafraoute.
42. The name Āhukār is remarkably close to that of the Hoggar or Ahaggar Tuareg.
43. Probably the same as the Gazūlah capital of Tāghjīsht, which is spelt sometimes as Tāʿjst.
44. Lévi Provençal, *op. cit.*, p. 194 (p. 118 Arabic text).
45. See M. Kowalska, "Zwei wenigbekannte muslimische Reisende in West-Sudan im 13 Jh", *Folia Orientalia*, vol. 3, pp. 231–41.
46. The legend of the Copper City, located in the desert of Sijilmāsah, a story derided by Ibn Khaldūn, was widespread in the Islamic East and West. Copper deposits in this whole region may have given rise to the legend.
47. Levtzion and Hopkins, *op. cit.*, p. 191. Lewicki does not now identify the Fortress of Salt (*Ḥisn al-Milḥ*) with Taghāzā. Because of the distance in days given by Ibn Saʿīd from Āzuqqī, and because of its generally north-western direction, he makes the interesting suggestion that Sabkhat Ijjil must be meant, the salt mine mountain and deposits near Fort Gouraud and F'Derick, in Mauritania. The weakness in his case is that almost all Mauritanian sources, oral and written, maintain that this was once the salt mine of the late mediaeval Kuntah and that the discovery of the salt there was made relatively late, certainly long after the writings of the mediaeval Arab geographers, Ibn Saʿīd amongst them. Ibn Saʿīd's Kawkadam was a day further

to the north so this would site it in the region of the Guelta Zammour, somewhere along the border of Mauritania and the disputed territory of the Western Sahara. It would be south of the Sāqiyah al-Ḥamrā' and not to the east of it. A point in favour of this hypothesis is that a town for the making of Lamṭī shields would be located within easy reach of a good source for salt, used in their manufacture. It would also lie on a Saharan route. See T. Lewicki, *Etudes Maghrebines et Soudanaises*, Editions Scientifiques de Pologne, Warsaw, 1976, vol. 1, p. 46.

48. Tazarine on the maps; compare Idrīsī's variant Azqan. Asif Agoudim vanishes in the desert near the Dar'ah (Draa).
49. See V. Monteil, al-Bakrī (Cordoue 1068), "Routier de l'Afrique blanche et noire du Nord-Ouest," *Bull. de l'IFAN*, series B, vol. 30, no. 1, Dakar, Jan. 1968, p. 50.
50. See my *Saharan Myth and Saga*, Oxford Library of African Literature, 1972, pp. 86 and 87. Ibn Khaldūn mentions that the date-grove-lined Dar'ah pours into the sea betwixt Nūn and Wādān. He can hardly mean Wādān in Mauritania. This must be another Wādān, either in Jebel Ouarkziz, or in the Sāqiyah, or else a very badly misplaced Tn Ūdādn.
51. Leo, 1600, *op. cit.*, p. 267.
52. In his *Ṣūrat al-Arḍ*, see Levtzion and Hopkins, pp. 46–7.
53. *Al-Adab al-Maghribī*, ed. Muḥammad ibn Tawayt and Muḥammad al-Ṣādiq 'Afīfī, Beirut, p. 146.

    The powerful personality of Abū 'Imrān shaped many of the characteristic ideas and beliefs of the Almoravids. One *Sūrah* of the Koran in particular, *Sūrah* III, Al-'Imrān, had a particular influence on their doctrinal position. It is, presumably, quite incidental that the name of Abū 'Imrān and the name of the *Sūrah* are one and the same.

    Hanna E. Kassis has made the important point in his article, "Qāḍī 'Iyāḍ's Rebellion against the Almohads in Sabtah (A.H. 542–3/A.D. 1147–1148), New numismatic evidence", *Journal of the American Oriental Society*, vol. 103, no. 3, 1983, p. 507, fn. 11: "Surah 3:85(79). This sūrah as a whole seems to have been favoured by the Almoravids who, in my opinion, derived their name from verse 200 rather than the much discussed *ribāṭ*." This ultimate verse reads: "O ye who believe! be patient and vie in being patient, and be on the alert (*rābiṭū*), and fear God, that haply ye may prosper." (Palmer's translation.)

54. Levtzion and Hopkins, *op. cit.*, p. 73, and note in their Index–Glossary.
55. *Ibid.*, p. 219. The impression is given that the story of Ibn Yāsīn and Yaḥyā ibn Ibrāhīm took place in Gazūlah country.
56. *Ibid.*, pp. 101–3.

57. *Ibid.*, pp. 130–1.
58. *Ibid.*, p. 117.
59. Futa Toro or Senegalese Futa.
60. René Basset, *Mission au Sénégal*, Paris, 1909, vol. 1, pp. 567–8.
61. Levtzion and Hopkins, *op. cit.*, p. 159.
62. The lost cause of the "hidden Imāms" of the Marwānid "Sufyānī house" and its Mahdist hopes and counter hopes are explained in full detail in the *Encyclopedia of Islam* under *al-Mahdī*. This false *Mahdī* was expected to come forth at the Dry Wādī in the Maghrib.
63. The region of Tamesna lies between Azemmour and Buragrag in Morocco and Jabal Māsinah is adjacent to the Sabou river towards Tangier. The *Ribaṭ* at Māssah, to the south of Agadir, is meant since Ibn Khaldūn writes: "There are many people of weak intelligence who journey to a monastery [*ribāṭ*] at Māssa near al-Sūs. They assume that they [will be able] to meet him there, thinking that he will appear at that monastery and that the oath of allegiance will be rendered to him there. Also, that monastery is close to the veiled Gudāla, and they believe that [the Mahdī] will be one of them, or that they will be in charge of his propaganda. This is a conjecture that has no basis except the fact that these nations are strange ones and too remote [for others] to have a definite knowledge of their numbers and their weakness or strength." See *Kitāb al-ʿIbar*, p. 583, and F. Rosenthal's translation of the *Muqaddimah*, London, 1958, Chapter 3, Section 51, "Sufi Opinions about the Mahdi", pp. 196–7.

    A very early reference to the prophecies to which both al-Qurṭubī and Ibn Khaldūn refer is to be found in the text of the *Kitāb al-Tījān*, by Wahb ibn Munabbih (d. 732)/Ibn Hishām (d. 833), Hyderabad edition, 1347, more precisely in the supplement which is the *Akhbār* ʿUbayd ibn Sharyah, which could be as early as the reign of Muʿāwiyah (661–80). On p. 323 it is reported, "I was told in the *ḥadīth* which was carried back in a report direct to the Prophet, the Blessing of Allāh be upon him and his family, that [he said], 'Beauty and desire have been divested from the Children of Israel and have been appointed for the womenfolk of the Berbers.' I have heard also that the sons of Barbar ibn Kanʿān ibn Kūsh ibn Ḥām are those who will march to meet a man from the offspring of Fāṭimah and they will send him back to Mecca. He is the master of Justice and Equity at the end of the age and his companions will be called the Strangers [*Ghurabā*']." There is clearly a play on the sense of Strangers and "Maghribīs" (*Maghāribah*) in this passage.

64. Al-Qurṭubī (d. 671/1272), *al-Tadhkirah fī Aḥwāl al-Mawtā wa-Umūr al-Ākhirah*, ed. Dr Aḥmad Ḥijāzī al-Saqqā, Cairo, p. 723.
65. *Ibid.*, pp. 734–5.
66. "Rūm" may also denote Spaniards as well as Byzantines.
67. Many of these signs and models were applied to Nāṣir al-Dīn, the leader of the Zwāya in the War of Shurbubba, see pp. 35–43.
68. On this seventh-century converted Yemenite Jew, the source of much fascinating folk lore of ancient Arabia see Hitti, *op. cit.*, page 244.
69. By tradition, the *Qanṭarah*, dam, weir or dyke at the Straits of Gibraltar was built by Alexander the Great to protect the people of Spain from Berber excursions from the Sūs.
70. A Yemenite warrior is featured in the Maghrib located legend of the City of Brass (*Qiṣṣat Madīnat al-Nuḥās*).
71. *Op. cit.*, p. 742.
72. Buṣrā is in the Syrian Hauran.
73. The Gleaming Mountain of the Gudālah (*al-Jabal al-Lammāʿ*), with its serpents and precious stones, may have been sited near Cape Bojador, see Levtzion and Hopkins, *op. cit.*, p. 190. I would in fact favour this, rather than locating it further south near Arguin, as Lewicki and others are tempted to do. This Gleaming Mountain of the Gudālah was given its name because of the shiny snakes which infested it. In fact, al-Bakrī already referred to the Azwār mountains, ten days' journey from Sijilmāsah to the Atlantic, and nearly as far as eastern Algeria and beyond, as being a mountainous region (Daran) wherein innumerable serpents were to be found. The whole Ḥamādah of the Darʿah could form part of the Gleaming Mountain. Near to the coast and towards the mouth of the Sāqiyah al-Ḥamrā' it was Gudālah territory and Taghīrā, their "capital", might lie between the Sāqiyah and the Darʿah. The mountains of the Lamtūnah are without question the Adrār of Mauritania. The mountains of the Massūfah lay in the Ḥamādah to the east of Tindouf and the eastern end of the Sāqiyah al-Ḥamrā'. The mountains of the Gazūlah were the Jabal Banī in Morocco. The five rivers which descended from the Gleaming Mountain could, as Mukhtār wuld Ḥāmidun has suggested, have been a reference to tributaries which flow into the end of the Sāqiyah al-Ḥamrā' from the Ḥamādah of the Darʿah in the region of Kreb Akwadim.
74. The *Aḥlāf* was an alliance between two clans of the Maʿqil Dhawī Manṣūr.

75. *Iqṭāʿ*. On the history of this see M. A. Shaban, *Islamic History, a New Interpretation*, Cambridge, 1976, pp. 71–88.
76. Levtzion and Hopkins, *op. cit.*, p. 324. In this connection, Ibn Khaldūn makes several other observations regarding the geography of the region to the north and to the south of the Wād Nūn. In vol. 2 of De Slane's translation of the *History of the Berbers*, pp. 279–80, Ibn Khaldūn says that beyond *Ribāṭ* Māssah, where the "Fatimid" *Mahdī* is awaited, two days' journey brings the traveller to the *Zāwiyah* of the Awlād Abū Nuʿmān. Beyond that region lay the course of the Sāqiyah al-Ḥamrā', which was the "limit" of the Maʿqil in their winter camping places. When he wrote, the Shābbānāt Maʿqil were the allies of the Lamṭah in the Atlas foothills, while the Dhawī Hassān had an alliance with the Gazūlah.
77. See p. 49.
78. See de Armas, *op. cit.*, p. 24.
79. Zakari Dramani-Issifou, *L'Afrique Noire dans les relations internationales au XVIe siècle*, Paris, 1982, p. 101.
80. *Ibid.*, p. 105.

Notes and References to Appendix I

1. Koran, *Sūrah* XXII, *The Chapter of the Pilgrimage*, verse 77.
2. The famous Ṣūfī scholar, (d. 1565), the author of *Lawāqiḥ al-anwār al-qudsiyyah fī bayān al-ʿuhūd al-Muḥammadiyyah*, the full title of this work.
3. The source of this quotation is unidentified.
4. About this scholar see Brockelmann, *G.A.L.* Vol. 1, p. 267.
5. Unidentified.
6. The authors of the *Ṣaḥīḥān*, the two most honoured collections of authoritative Prophetic tradition, were the two *Shaykhs*, al-Bukhārī, d. 256/870, and Muslim, d. 261/875.
7. Abū Dāwūd, d. 275/888, al-Tirmidhī, d. 279/892, al-Nasā'ī, d. 303/915 and Ibn Mājah, d. 273/886. These latter collections are not held in the same esteem as the collections of al-Bukhārī and Muslim.
8. Ibn Ḥabbār, born at the beginning of the eleventh century, was a poet of the Saljūq period although he was also known as the reporter of traditions, *al-muḥaddith*.
9. Koran, *Sūrah* XXIII, *The Chapter of Believers*, verse 1.
10. Unidentified. I am uncertain of this passage.
11. According to Lane, an *ʿIḍāh* tree is a name applied to any large desert tree which has thorns.

12. A *Khaṭṭī* spear takes its name from al-Khaṭṭ, the coast of Bahrayn in eastern Arabia. These spears were later imported from India.
13. Here the author is citing, surely, ʿUmar II (717–20) the Umayyad Caliph.
14. Presumably al-Ḥasan ibn ʿAlī ibn Abī Ṭālib, the eldest son of ʿAlī and Fāṭimah, the daughter of the Prophet.
15. The passage in the text of al-Maghīlī is as follows:

وأما المحاربون فلا بد من غزوهم ولا بأس عليكم فيمن أصيب بينهم من أولئك المسلمين لانهم ظلموا أنفسهم بالنزول معهم .

16. See Wright's *Arabic Grammar*, Cambridge, 1955, Vol. 1, p. 269.
17. Koran, *Sūrah* IX, *The Chapter of Repentance*, verse 40.
18. Regarding the use of the definite article in these latter passages, see Koran, *Sūrah* XX, *The Chapter of Ṭāhā*, verse 12, *Sūrah* XLVIII, *The Chapter of Victory*, verse 18, and *Sūrah* XXIV, *The Chapter of Light*, verse 35.
19. Abū'l-Qāsim al-Burzulī was a Mālikite jurist who was famous for his collection of *fatwās*. He was one of the sources of the *Miʿyār* of al-Wansharīshī. He died in Tunis in 841/1438.
20. In reference to the replies of al-Maghīlī and the status of the *muḥāribūn* see Père Cuoq, *Recueil*, Paris, 1975, pp. 422–6 and J. O. Hunwick, *Sharīʿa in Songhay*, OUP, 1985, pp. 79n, 87–8, 127–8, 131.
21. Muḥyī'l-Dīn Abū Zakariyyā' Yaḥyā al-Nawawī was a Shāfiʿi jurist, who died in 676/1277, whose *Kitāb al-Arbaʿīn* was frequently annotated. He had an exceptional knowledge of Tradition and was a highly regarded jurist. See *Encyclopedia of Islam*, under *al-Nawawī*.
22. Ibn Ḥajar's commentary on his works is known as *al-Tuḥfah*. Al-Nawawī wrote several biographical and grammatical studies including his *al-Taḥrīr fī alfāẓ al-tanbīh*.
23. Certain references to the passage in the Koran have not been possible due to uncertain readings in the text at this point. This is only an approximate meaning.
24. The Arabic is unclear but appears to read *Ṣīghat al-tamrīḍ*.
25. ʿAbd al-Salām ibn Saʿīd ibn Ḥabīb al-Tanūkhī, usually referred to as Saḥnūn, died in 854. He was one of the founding fathers of the Mālikī school in Qayrawān and his *Mudawannah* is a major work of jurisprudence.
26. Abū'l-Faḍl ʿIyāḍ ibn Mūsā ibn ʿIyāḍ al-Yaḥṣubī of Ceuta, generally referred to as the Qāḍī ʿIyāḍ, died in Marrakech in

544/1149. His work, *al-Shifā' bi-ta'rīf ḥuqūq al-Muṣṭafā*, about the virtues of the Prophet, is widely revered and expounded in North Africa.

27. The Igdalen are a pacific maraboutic group who now live in the region of In Gall in the Niger Republic. They are described by the explorer Barth in several passages in his famous *Travels*. The most recent comprehensive description is to be found in Edmund and Suzanne Bernus, *Du Sel et des Dattes*, Etudes Nigeriennes, no 31, Niamey, 1972.
28. The Aghlāl are a maraboutic group among the Iwillimmeden. They are possibly of Mauritanian origin, see my *The Tuaregs*, pp. 119–20.
29. The handbook of Mālikī branches of jurisprudence, *furū' al-fiqh, Bidāyat al-Mujtahid wa-Nihāyat al-Muqtaṣid*.
30. Regarding the *Nawązil* of Ibn al-A'mash, see *al-Wasīṭ*, page 578. Al-Ṭālib Muḥammad ibn al-A'mash al-'Alawī is by repute the first Mauritanian scholar to have composed legal rulings in the form of *Nawāzil*. Other works by him include a commentary on the text of the *Iḍā'at al-Dujunnah* by al-Maqqarī. The author of *al-Wasīṭ* has stressed that the Tājakānt scholars are in error when they attribute this honour to Ibn al-A'mash al-Jakanī, the lord of Tindouf. None of these *Nawāzil* have been edited as yet so it has proved impossible to check the accuracy of this text.
31. Abū'l-Ṣafā' Khalīl ibn Isḥāq ibn Mūsā al-Jundī, d. 1365/1374, the author of *al-Mukhtaṣar*, the principal Mālikī legal text book.
32. Some of these names require further explanation. Muḥammad ibn Dāniyāl was a noted scholar of the Kel Es-Sūq who wrote a commentary on the Koran. He was likewise a jurist. The Īdaw Isḥāq, or Iswaghen, are a group of part Arab, part Berber, part Songhay people who are assimilated to the Tuareg near Menaka in Mali but who speak their own dialect or language. Targhaytamat would seem to refer to the name of one of the matrilineal *Amīrates* which were to be found among the Iwillimmeden in earlier times.
33. Muḥammad ibn al-Kumayt, Măkhămmăd ăg-Ghăbdessălam "El Kumati" of the Kel Nan, was the chief of the eastern Iwillimmeden between 1875 and 1905.
34. *Ijtihād*, the ability to exercise independent and individual judgement on legal questions, in earliest Muslim usage was equated with analogy (*qiyās*), exerting oneself in order to form an opinion in a case or in regard to a rule of law. This was done by the application of analogy by a *mujtahid* – as opposed to a *muqallid*, a traditionalist – to both the Koran and the *Sunnah* of the Prophet. See *Encyclopedia of Islam, Idjtihād*.

35. One of the famous works of the Sokoto Caliph ʿUthmān ibn Fūdī, d. 1232/1817. The full title of it is *Bayān wujūb al-hijrah ʿalāʾl-ʿibād.* It has now been edited and translated by Dr F. H. Elmasri (Department of Arabic, University of Khartoum), published jointly by the Khartoum University Press and Oxford University Press, 1978.
36. On the topics under discussion in this extended passage, see *Encyclopedia of Islam* under *Dār al-Ḥarb* and *Dār al-Ṣulḥ.*
37. *fayʾ*. See under *Faiʾ* in *Encyclopedia of Islam* for a full discussion of this term. It is applied to all possessions which are taken from unbelievers without fighting, and, by extension, to land in the conquered territories.
38. Any identification is not certain, possibly Riḍā ibn ʿAbd al-Raḥmān ibn ʿĪsā al-Maʿlamī.
39. *Kitāb al-Miʿyār al-Mughrib* by Aḥmad ibn Yaḥyā al-Wansharishī who died in 1508.
40. The law of the inviolable within Islam.
41. See *Encyclopedia of Islam* under *Dhimmah.* According to Muslim canonic law consequent to the conquest of a non-Muslim country by Muslims, the population which does not embrace Islam, and which is not enslaved, is guaranteed life, liberty, and in a modified sense, property.
42. An ordinance or decree. Here it may refer to the rule that a locality cannot be deemed *Dār al-Ḥarb* as long as a single legal decision of Islam (*ḥukm*) is observed within it.
43. *jizyah.* See under *Djizya* in the *Encyclopedia of Islam.* This is the name given to the indulgence taxes levied on the *Ahl al-Dhimmah*: Jews, Christians and sometimes Zoroastrians.
44. The Mālikī Ibn Farḥūn, died 1395, is one of the outstanding authors on public law.
45. Khārijites, See under *Khawārij* in *Encyclopedia of Islam.* They are the earliest sectarians in Islam and they opposed the claim of ʿAlī to the Caliphate. Many of them were slain by him in the battle of Nahrawan in 658.
46. *amān* is variously rendered as peace, clemency and the assurance of protection.
47. Unidentified.
48. Koran, *Sūrah* V, *The Chapter of the Table,* verse 33.
49. The masterpiece of the great theologian and mystic of Islam, al-Ghazzālī of Ṭūs, who died in 505/1111.
50. Koran, *Sūrah* LXIII, *The Chapter of the Hypocrites,* verse 1 ff.
51. A scholar who died 828/1425.
52. Possibly Abū ʿImrān Mūsā ibn Abī Ḥajjāj al-Fāsī, prominent Mālikī *faqīh* of Qayrawān, d. 430/1048.
53. The *Shahādah*, or profession of faith in the unity of God and the

Prophethood of Muḥammad, is not to be found in a composite form in the Koran. The closest approximation to a creed is to be found in *Sūrah* IV, *The Chapter of Woman*, verse 135.

54. Abū'l-Ḥasan al-Ash'arī, the famous theologian who was born in Basra in 260/873/4 and who died in Baghdad in 324/935. He is the founder of orthodox scholasticism (*kalām*) in Islam.
55. Al-Juwaynī, Abū'l-Ma'ālī 'Abd al-Malik, known as the Imām al-Ḥaramayn, was a famous author on the principles of jurisprudence according to the Shāfi'ī school. He was born in 419/1028 and died in 478/1085. His greatest work was *Kitāb al-Waraqāt fī uṣūl al-fiqh.*
56. *Qadariyyah*, see *Encyclopedia of Islam* under *Ḳadariyya*. This name was sometimes applied in the early days of Islam to the much better known sect of the *Mu'tazilites*. The *Qadarites* were accused of heresy by making man a partner in the act of Creation.
57. *Rāfiḍites* is the name applied to the *Rāfiḍah* or *Rawāfiḍ* who were an exrtreme group of *Shī'ites*, one of a group of three. See *Encyclopedia of Islam* under *Rāfiḍites.*
58. The famous historian and Koran commentator Abū Ja'far Muḥammad ibn Jarīr al-Ṭabarī was born about 225/839 and died in 310/923. His greatest work is his World History, *Ta'rīkh al-rusul wa'l-mulūk*, and close to it comes his commentary on the Koran, *Jāmi' al-bayān fī tafsīr al-Qur'ān.*
59. Regarding Sawdah bint Zam'a, see *Encyclopedia of Islam* under her name.
60. Koran, *Sūrah* IX, *The Chapter of Repentance*, verse 5.
61. The two scholars mentioned, al-Mukhtār ibn Anāzel and Sīdī Maḥmūd, are both from Aïr. I can find no mention of the former who may have been a jurist of the Kel Geres. The latter is probably Sīdī Maḥmūd al-Baghdādī, the Iraqi or Persian mystic who, in the sixteenth century, founded lodges in the Massif of Aïr. These were frequented by the learned of the Kel Es-Sūq. Sīdī Maḥmūd was "martyred" by the *Sulṭān* of Agadez in the sixteenth century, or in the early seventeenth century.

    Pierre Bonte and Nicole Echard, in their studies of the Kel Geres, who were the protectors of 'Abd al-Kel Gefī the addressee of this epistle, have pointed out that the Kel Geres have some Arab books, though the number is not many. None appear to be detailed histories (*tawārīkh*). Portions of chronicles may be found, together with correspondence on legal topics.
62. Ākall was an ancestress of many scholar families of the Kel Es-Sūq.
63. An unknown scholar although possibly the *faqīh* 'Uthmān,

who was the husband of Ākall. He was nicknamed Iddantamazgadda.

64. Tagaraygarayt are the Tuareg of the Centre of the Iwillimmeden. They are now resident between Abalagh and Tahoua in the Niger Republic.
65. Al-Khurashī, or al-Khirshī, who died in 1101/1689/90, wrote an important commentary on the *Mukhtaṣar* of Khalīl (who died in 776/1374).
66. This passage is uncertain in the text. ʿAbd al-Bāqī ibn Yūsuf al-Zurqānī?
67. Koran, *Sūrah* II, *The Chapter of the Heifer*, verse 194.
68. I am uncertain as to the author of this work.
69. On al-Shāfiʿī, the founder of the school of law which bears his name, who died in 204/820, see the entry under his name in *Encyclopedia of Islam.*
70. See A. Guillaume, *The Life of Muhammad*, Oxford University Press, 1955, p. 553.
71. Koran, *Sūrah* II, *The Chapter of the Heifer*, verse 194.
72. Koran, *Sūrah* XLII, *The Chapter of Counsel*, verse 40 and verse 41.
73. Koran, *Sūrah* XVI, *The Chapter of the Bee*, verse 126.
74. This whole passage is amplified in detail in the *E of I* under *Ḳiṣāṣ*.
75. Maḥmūd of Ghaznah is credited with being the first in Islam to be designated *Sulṭān*. It was known earlier amongst the Saljūqs.
76. Koran, *Sūrah* IV, *The Chapter of Women*, verse 105.
77. See *Encyclopedia of Islam* under *Ḳarmaṭians.*
78. Koran, *Sūrah* V, *The Chapter of the Table*, verse 105.
79. The name of one of the Tuareg princesses of the Iwillimmeden who encouraged the Islamisation of the Iwillimmeden.
80. The sons of Karidenna means both the western and eastern branches of the Iwillimmeden. See the diagram of relationship in Ghubăyd ăgg Ălăwejeli, *Ăttarikh en Kel Denneg*, *Histoire des Kel Denneg*, Akademisk Forlag, Copenhagen, 1975, pp. 30–31.
81. None of the texts of Shaykh Sīdī'l-Mukhtār al-Kuntī are available in text or translation. It has not proved possible to check this text. For some comment, however, reference should be made to The Kunta, Sīdī'l-Mukhtār al-Kuntī, and the Office of *Shaykh al-Ṭarīqa'l-Qādiriyya*, by A. A. Batran, in J. R. Willis, *Studies in West African Islamic History*, *Vol 1*, *The Cultivators of Islam*, Frank Cass, 1979, pages 113–46; see also Batran: "The Qadiriyya-Mukhtaryya Brotherhood in West Africa: The concept of Tasawwuf in the writings of Sidi al-Mukhtar al-Kunti (1729–1811)", in *Transafrican Journal of History*. Vol. 4, nos 1 and 2, 1974, pp. 41–70.

82. *Maks*, toll or custom duty, see *Encyclopedia of Islam* under *Maks*.
83. ʿAbd al-Wahhāb al-Shaʿrānī, who died in 973/1565, is described by R. A. Nicholson as "the last great Muḥammadan theosophist". He regarded theology as the first step towards Ṣūfism and he sought to harmonise the four great schools of law.
84. Aḥmad ibn Muḥammad ibn Ḥanbal, who was born in 164/780 and who died in 241/855, was the author of the great encyclopaedia of tradition, the *Musnad* and the founder of the fourth great legal school or *madhhab*.
85. Al-Tirmidhī and Abū Dāwūd lived in the ninth century and were the authors of *muṣannaf* works of tradition.
86. The traditionist Abū Bakr ʿAbdallāh ibn Muḥammad ibn ʿUbayd Abī'l-Dunyā died in 280/892 or 281/894.
87. Koran, *Sūrah* IV, *The Chapter of Women*, verse 71.
88. The vassal class in Tuareg society, corresponding to the *talāmīdh*, the *znāga* and the *laḥmah* amongst the Moors. These tributaries vary greatly as to the dues imposed on them and the freedom which they enjoy. For a detailed examination of their status see Francis Rennell Rodd, *People of the Veil*, London, 1926, and C. C. and E. K. Stewart, *Islam and Social Order in Mauritania*, Oxford, 1973.
89. Ibdaqan Kannār cannot be identified with any certainty. The names of Muddūkan, variant Mddūgen, is a Saharan toponym found in the region of Timbuctoo and elsewhere. The pagan peoples of the Western Sahara are located by some of the mediaeval Arab geographers in a vague region which they call Qamnūriyyah. Mukhtār wuld Ḥāmidun would like to identify this with Gannār district in Mauritania. The statements of the Sūqī scholar here seem to echo the early Arab geographers, see for example al-Idrīsī in Levtzion and Hopkins, *Corpus of early Arabic sources for West Africa*, Cambridge University Press, 1981, pp. 116–17.
90. According to Barth, Kusaylah, the Berber slayer of the Arab commander ʿUqbah ibn Nāfiʿ, is believed by Saharans to have been a member of the Imedidderen *Imghād*. These were degraded tribes of ancient stock who later came under the rule of Iwillimmeden princes. In all likelihood this tradition was extant in the region of Tādamakkat as early as the tenth century, since Ibn Ḥawqal in his *Ṣūrat al-Arḍ* mentions that amongst the Ṣanhājah, some in that district were the Banū Kasīla.

    The *Tadhkirat al-Nisyān*, see the translation by Houdas, page 100, refers to an expedition made by the *Armas* against Tondibi near Gao. The Tuareg were raided together with the jurists of the Kel Es-Sūq who are specifically mentioned as distinct from them and who by 1695 were already a religious class amongst the Iwillimmeden.

91. This scholar is not identified for certain. Clearly one of the Kel Gunahān of the Kel Es-Sūq, he was resident in the Adrār-n-Īfōghās when the descendants of Karidenna first entered the district. The story of the domination of the *Imghād* by a combined army of warrior Iwillimmeden advised by a holy man is not a historical record but a folk epic common in the whole Western Sahara.

92. Sīdī Muḥammad ibn ʿAlī al-Sanūsī was born in 1206/1791 and died in 1276/1791 at Jaghbūb, the founder of the brotherhood of the Sanūsiyyah. Among his works was one which argued that there was a harmony between the Koran and *Ḥadīth*. This could be established without taking account of the *taqlīd* of any of the four rites. He postulated *Ijtihād*. The latter claim was rejected by the Mālikīs in Cairo.

93. ʿAbdallāh ibn ʿUmar al-Bayḍāwī, one of the most famous commentators on the Koran, in his *Anwār al-tanzīl wa-asrār al-ta'wīl* (died either in 685/1282 or in 716/1316).

94. This name is unidentified, perhaps it should read al-Tirmidhī?

95. See note 92 and "La Confrérie Musulmane de Sīdī Muḥammad Ben ʿAlī Es-Senousī et son Domaine Géographique", *Bulletin of the Geographical Society of Paris*, V, 1884, pp. 145–226.

96. One of the greatest *Qāḍīs* of the Kel Es-Sūq, Muḥammad al-Amīn ibn Hammahamma ibn Salahu al-Sūqī.

Notes and References to Appendix II

1. The following are the most important sources of reference in regard to the history of the Kuntah: *The Kuntah* by J. Hunwick in the *Encyclopedia of Islam*; A. A. Batran, "The Kunta, Sīdī'l-Mukhtār al-Kuntī, and the Office of *Shaykh al-Ṭarīqa'l-Qādiriyya*", in *Studies in Western African Islamic History*, vol. 1, *The Cultivators of Islam*, ed. J. R. Willis, Frank Cass, 1979, pp. 113–47; T. Whitcomb, "New Evidence on the Origins of the Kunta, I and II, in *The Bulletin of the School of Oriental and African Studies*, vol. 38, part 1, 1975, pp. 103–23, and part 2, 1975, pp. 403–17; and Paul Marty, *Etudes sur l'Islam et les tribus du Soudan*, Paris, 1920, vol. 1, pp. 1–175. The short and incomplete document translated here is clearly an abbreviation of one of the *Tawārīkh Kuntah*, to which Marty refers on pp. 1–26. The great Shaykhs of the early Kuntah who are referred to in the half legendary account were related as follows:

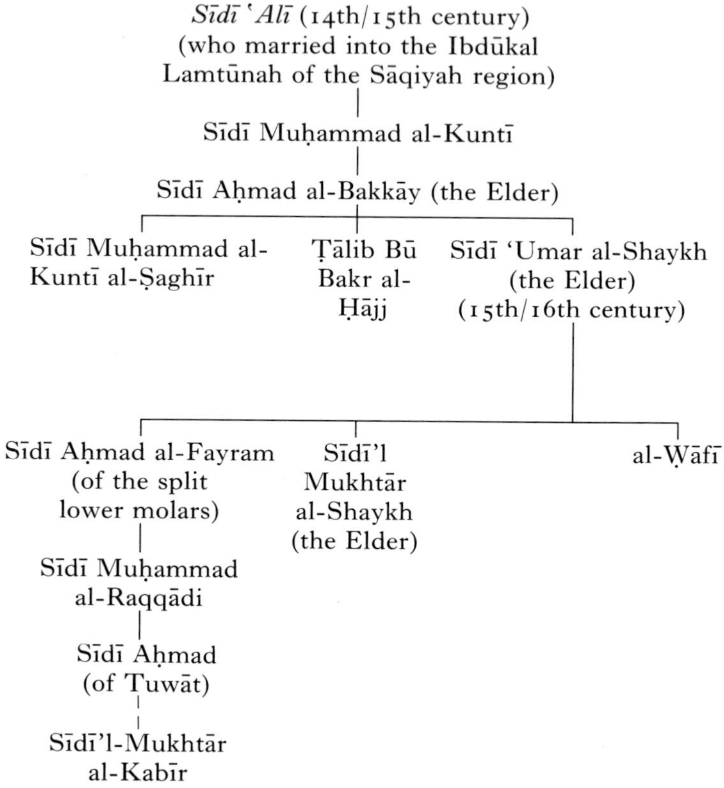

2. Marty shows these Shaykhs who came between Sīdī'l-Mukhtār al-Kabīr and Sīdī ʿUmar al-Shaykh on a family tree on p. 159 of his work. He spells them, Mohammad Lamin and Sidi-l-Mokhtar. ʿAntarah is not a common name amongst "maraboutic" elements. The name was an ancestral one among the Awlād al-Nāṣir of the Ḥassānīs.
3. This description of immorality in Walātah, especially the freedom of its women, is very similar to the remarks made by Ibn Baṭṭūṭah, see p. 52.
4. Karzāz is located in the Algerian Sahara between Beni-Abbès and Timimoun, to the north of the Oued Saoura. It was an important centre for Ṣūfism in the whole Western Sahara and was much frequented by Kuntah on their way to Zāwiyat Kuntah in the Algerian Adrār to the south. The religious order of the Karzāziyyah or Aḥmadiyyīn was founded by the Sharīf Aḥmad ibn Mūsā al-Ḥasanī Mawlāy Karzāz (b. 1502). The order was almost identical with the Shādhiliyyah order. See

Louis Rinn, *Marabouts et Khouan, étude sur l'Islam en Algérie*, Algiers, 1884, Chapter 23.

5. Banū Quṭbī. At this point the manuscript is barely legible and I am basing my reading upon Marty *op. cit.*, p. 130, who, unfortunately, gives no information from his sources as to their tribal identity. The name here reads approximately *Abnā'* al-Makkī(?)/Qaqbī in the Walātah text.
6. For information about Ṣāliḥ, the first *Amenukal* of the Kel Ahaggar, and his relations with the Kuntah, see Jeremy Keenan, *The Tuareg*, Allen Lane, 1977, pp. 25–6. He lived about 1650.
7. Keenan, *ibid.*, p. 25, and Marty, *op. cit.*, pp. 131–3.
8. Keenan, *ibid.*, p. 26, and Marty, *ibid.*, p. 131.
9. Al-Mabrūk in Azawād was founded about 1720/1 in conjunction with the Barābīsh, see Marty, *ibid.*, pp. 113–14.
10. A branch of the Kuntah, of part-Tuareg origin, from Timbuctoo region, see Marty, *ibid.*, p. 170. They would appear to have had very early links with the family of Sīdī 'Umar al-Shaykh if a letter from the Sulṭān of Bornu dated about 883/1478 is genuine; see J. Cuoq, *Recueil des sources arabes*, Paris, 1975, pp. 437–8.
11. The Yaddāsen are a Tuareg group. Their name is spelt in various ways, see Marty, *ibid.*, p. 170. See also pp. 74, 76, 276 note 11 in this book.
12. A talismanic citation of the Koran, *Sūrah* 11, verse 131, also used by the Kel Es-Sūq and painted in the Saharan grotto at Tim-missao in the Algerian Western Sahara of the Tassili-n-Adrār; see my *The Tuaregs*, Aris and Phillips, Warminster, 1975, p. 28.
13. A story in the tradition of Arabian Romance (e.g. *The City of Brass*) and also inspired by fantastic Saharan rock formations.
14. Marty spells the name as Kadi, not Kādim, see *op. cit.*, p. 25, the former a name well known amongst the Tuareg. On Kādim and the Western Saharan tribal name of Kākudam, etc., in this book, see pp. 147–63.
15. Here the Songhai empire is meant, together with Agades region and Hausaland.
16. His major role in the Arabisation and Islamisation of the Western Sahara is discussed throughout this book. For a translation of his short biography by the Timbuctoo scholar, Aḥmad Bābā, see Cuoq, *op. cit.*, pp. 433–6. The passage on him is chiefly missing in the Walātah text.
17. An important detail which is confirmed in Aḥmad Bābā's biography. His stay in Hausaland, *prior* to his journey to the Askiyā, may reflect a deliberate policy on the part of al-Maghīlī

in his plans to further Islam in the Sahara and on its borders. This subject will be closely examined in a future study I am about to commence on Islam in the region of Aïr.

18. Al-Suyūṭī has also been discussed. The texts reveal the rivalry between Maghīlī and Suyūṭī, though phrased in a fanciful manner. For the biography of Suyūṭī, see E. M. Sartain, *Jalāl al-Dīn al-Suyūṭī*, Cambridge, 1975, vol. 1. Assiut is on the Nile.
19. *al-Burhān* is not the title of a work listed amongst those in Dr E. M. Sartain's book, *ibid.*, pp. 218–20. The *Itqān*, though, is given. Its full title is, *al-Itqān fī ʿulūm al-Qurʾān*.
20. If this poetry is genuine then these verses (late fifteenth century) are amongst the oldest examples of Classical Arabic verse composed by Western Saharans. The Arabic text reads:

    (a) بُشراك يا قلب هذا سيّد الأمم

    (b) وهذه حضرة المختار في الحرم
21. The Arabic text reads:

    (a) يا سيّدي يا رسول خذ بيدي

    (b) فالعبد ضيف وضيف الله لم يضم
22. Nowhere does Aḥmad Bābā mention that Sīdī ʿUmar accompanied Maghīlī.
23. Maghīlī appears to have planned to make Katsina in Hausaland the main base for his movement after his split with the Askiyā.
24. See Marty, *op. cit.*, p. 21. It is far from clear whether the order is Shādhiliyyah or Qādiriyyah, or indeed if the story is factual.
25. In the Moroccan Sahara. On Āqā see pp. 15–16.
26. These miracles recall the description of the preserved body of the Gazūlah saint, Muḥammad ibn Sulaymān al-Jazūlī, the author of *Dalāʾil al-Khayrāt*, who was believed by some to be "*Mahdī* of the Gazūlah".

Bibliography

MICHEL ABITBOL, *Tombouctou et les Arma: de la conquête marocaine du Soudan Nigerien en 1591 à l'hégémonie de l'Empire peulh du Macina en 1833*, Maisonneuve et Larode, Paris, 1979

JULIO BAROJA, *Estudios Saharianos*, Instituto de Estudios Africanos, Madrid, 1955

"El Grupo de Cabilas 'Hasania' del Sahara Occidental", *Estudios Mogrebíes*, Instituto de Estudios Africanos, Madrid, 1957, pp. 111–21

RENÉ BASSET, "Etude sur le dialecte Zenaga", *Mission au Sénégal, Notes sur le Hassania*, Recherches historiques sur les Maures, vol. 1, Paris, 1909

C. BROCKELMANN, *Geschichte der arabischen Literatur*, 2nd edn., Leyden, 1943–9

W. D. COOLEY, *The Negroland of the Arabs*, Frank Cass, London, 1966

M. CORTIER, *D'une rive à l'autre du Sahara*, Paris, 1908

J. M. CUOQ, *Recueil des sources arabes concernant l'Afrique occidentale du 8e au 16e siècle*, Editions du Centre National de la Recherche Scientifique, Paris, 1975

J. DEVISSE, "Le question d'Awdaghust", in Robert, D.S. and Devisse, J., *Tegdaoust: Recherches sur Awdaghust*, vol. 1, Paris, 1970

"Routes de commerce et échanges en Afrique Occidentale", *Revue d'histoire economique et sociale*, vol. 50, pp. 42–73

PAULO FERNANDO DE MORAES FARIAS, "The Almoravids", *Bull. IFAN* (Institut Français d'Afrique Noire), series B, vol. 29, nos. 3–4, 1967

M. GUIGNARD, *Musique, honneur et plaisir au Sahara*, Paris, 1975

ISMAËL HAMET, *Chronique de la Mauritanie Sénégalaise*, Nacer Eddine, Ernest Leroux, Paris, 1911

IBN BAṬṬUṬAH, *Textes et documents relatifs à l'histoire de l'Afrique*, (extracts drawn from the journey of Ibn Baṭṭuṭah, annotated translation by R. Mauny, V. Monteil, A. Djenedi, S. Robert, J. Devisse), Université de Dakar, Publications de la Faculté des Lettres et Sciences Humaines, Dakar, 1966

JOHN O. HUNWICK, *Sharīʿa in Songhay: The replies of al-Maghīlī to the questions of Askia al-Ḥājj Muḥammad*, Oxford University Press, 1985

IBN KHALDŪN, *Histoire des Berbères*, trans. by De Slane, Librairie Orientaliste, Paul Geuthner, Paris, 1968/9

The Muqaddimah, trans. by F. Rosenthal, 3 vols., New York and London, 1958

F. DE LA CHAPELLE, "Esquisse d'une histoire du Sahara occidental", *Hespéris*, vol. 11, 1930

LEO AFRICANUS, *Description de l'Afrique*, trans. by Alexis Epaulard, and annotated by A. Epaulard, Th. Monod, H. Lhote and R. Mauny, Paris Maisonneuve, 1956

A. H. A. LEUPEN, *Bibliographie des Populations Touarègues*, Afrika-Studiecentrum, Leyden, 1978

N. LEVTZION and J. F. P. HOPKINS, *Corpus of Early Arabic sources for West African History*, Cambridge University Press, 1981

T. LEWICKI, "A propos d'une liste de tribus berbères d'Ibn Hawḳal", *Folio Orientalia*, vol. 1, 1959, pp. 128–34

"Du nouveau sur la liste des tribus berbères d'Ibn Hawḳal", *Folio Orientalia*, vol. 13, 1971, pp. 171–200

"Les origines de l'Islam dans les tribus berbères du Sahara Occidental", *Studia Islamica*, vol. 22, 1970, pp. 203–14

"Les Origines et l'Islamisation de la ville de Tádmakka d'après les sources arabes", in *Le Sol, La Parole et L'Ecrit*, mèlanges en hommage à Raymond Mauny, Paris, 1981, vol. 1, pp. 439–44

H. LHOTE, *Les Touaregs du Hoggar*, Payot, Paris, 1955

MUḤAMMAD IBN ʿABD AL-KARĪM AL-MAGHĪLĪ, "Replies to the Seven Questions of the Askiyā al-Ḥājj Muḥammad" in Cuoq, *op. cit.*, pp. 398–432

G. MARÇAIS, *Les Arabes en Berbérie*, E. Leroux, Paris, 1913

La Berbérie musulmane et l'Orient au moyen-âge, Paris, 1946

RAYMOND MAUNY, *Tableau géographique de l'Ouest Africain au Moyen Age, d'après les sources écrites, la tradition, l'archéologie*, Mem?, *IFAN*, no. 61, Dakar, 1961

A. H. MIRANDA, "La salida de los Almoravides del desierto y el reinado de Yûsuf b. Tâshfîn", *Hespéris*, 3e–4e, 1959, pp. 155–82

H. T. NORRIS, *Saharan Myth and Saga*, Oxford Library of African Literature, 1972

The Tuaregs, Aris and Phillips, Warminster, 1975

The Berbers in Arabic Literature, Longman/Librairie du Liban, 1982

FRANCIS RENNELL RODD, *The People of the Veil*, Macmillan, London, 1926

ELIAS N. SAAD, *Social History of Timbuktu*, the role of Muslim scholars and notables 1400–1900, Cambridge Studies in Islamic Civilization, Cambridge University Press, 1983

C. C. STEWART, *Islam and Social Order in Mauritania*, Oxford, 1973. "Southern Saharan Scholarship and the Bilād al-Sūdān", *Journal of African History*, vol. 17, no. 1, 1976, pp. 73–93

J. S. TRIMINGHAM and T. WHITCOMB, *A History of Islam in West Africa*, Oxford, 1962
"New evidence on the origins of the Kunta", I and II in *Bulletin of the School of Oriental and African Studies*, vol. 38, part 1, 1975, pp. 103–23, and part 2, 1975, pp. 403–17

DAHIRU YAHYA, *Morocco in the Sixteenth Century: Problems and Patterns in African Foreign Policy*, Longman, 1981

JEAN-CLAUDE ZELTNER, "L'installation des Arabes au sud du lac Tchad", *Abbia*, 16 March 1967, pp. 129–53

Index of Qur'ānic references

Index

Arāk, battle of 93
Arawān vii, 8–9, 77–9, 112, 244
  development of x, 81–4, 87–100, 104
  scholars of xvii, 84–6
al-Arawānī, Sīdī'l-Wāfī ibn Ṭālibinā 86
al-Ash'arī, Abū'l-Ḥasan 207 & n., 208
Ashhab 192, 199–201
Askiyā, Muḥammad 79, 89–90, 122, 124–5, 127, 189–90, 192, 210
Attafrīj 108, 115
Awdaghust ix, 5
  and Saharan routes vii, 8, 135–6, 141, 144–5, 149–50, 153–4, 157n.
Awlīl, salt mine xvii, 167
al-'Aynayn, Mā' 18, 50, 136
A'ysh, Awlād 92–4, 98
Azanaghi Berbers 82n.
Azawād region:
  and Arabisation xvi, 30, 33, 103–4, 127–8, 141
  and Awlād Ḥassān 77–100
  early history 3, 6, 9, 22, 78–80, 86–100
  scholarship, culture v, 65n., 77, 84–6, 111
Azawān (sung poetry) 56–7
Azayr language 50
azelay (caravan) 78, 82n., 95, 97, 244; *see also* caravan
Aznages 26–7, 35, 250
Āzuqqī 39, 42, 139, 165, 243
  and Saharan routes 5, 135–6, 141, 147–8, 150, 154, 157n., 158, 160–1
Azurara, Gomes Eannes de 51

Bābā, Aḥmad 79, 129, 236n.
al-Bakkā'ī, Sīdī Aḥmad 3
Bakkār ibn Aswayd Aḥmad, Banū 22
al-Bakkāy, Sīdī Aḥmad 128, 130–1, 228–30, 233, 236
al-Bakrī, Abū 'Ubayd 5, 7, 32n., 44, 136–9, 172n.
  and Ibn Yāsīn 165, 168
  and Kākudam/Kawkadam desert 153–4, 158, 160–2
  and Saharan routes 141–7, 148, 250
al-Balādhurī 73, 140
Banū, *see under individual tribes*
al-Bāqī, 'Abd 195, 201, 210, 219, 223
Barābīsh tribe xix, 22, 31, 44, 78–84, 86, 87, 89n., 106–8, 112, 115, 146, 249–50
  in Azawād region 92–100, 103–4, 244
  lineages 15
  origins of 92–3
  scholars vii, x, 77, 111
  see also Abū Makhlūf
Barbier, Maurice vi
Barcelo, Miquel 157n.
Bard, Awlād 97
al-Barkannī, Aḥmad ibn Hayba 45, 47
Baroja, Julio Caro x, 19n., 31
Barth, Henry 108–9, 119, 126, 139n., 142, 146, 194n., 220n.
al-Bartīlī, Muḥammad 85
Basset, René 14, 47, 59
Baṭn al-Jamal 94–5
Bāy, Shaykh 78, 128
al-Bayḍāwī, 'Abdallāh ibn 'Umar 222
al-Baydhaq 159–60
Ben Alhousseini, Hamid v–vi
Berbers:
  Arabisation 11, 105–8, 120, 128, 149
  and Awlād Ḥassān 35–8, 44, 61, 76, 77
  and Azawād 77, 78–80, 82n., 88
  and Banū Ma'qil xiv–xv, xvii, xviii, 11, 20, 28, 33, 172, 174–6
  definition xx
  early history 9, 17, 22, 27, 103, 135, 142, 156n.
  folklore 132
  and Islam 213, 218
  language xii–xiii, xx, 50, 63n., 87, 121, 123, 142, 252
  in Morocco 138
  movement of 32, 150–1
  see also Lamtūnah; Maṣmūdah; Massūfah; Ṣanhājah
Bernus, Edmund *and* Suzanne 194n.
Bīḍān 245
Bivar, D. 153n.
booty 29, 92, 121, 159–60, 191, 194, 196, 198–201, 207, 248–9; *see also* tribute
Brāknah xix, 22, 37, 39, 46–7, 68, 80
  culture 61, 63, 65
Briggs, Cabot 245
Bū 'Ali, Awlād 37
Bū Fāyid, Awlād 74, 92
Bū Jbayha, town vii, 77, 85–6, 94–6, 112
Bū Khaṣīb, Awlād 78n., 92, 94n.
Bū Sbā', Awlād 8n., 174
al-Bukhārī 85–6, 171, 184, 187, 211
Burkina Faso 105, 248
al-Burzulī, Abū'l-Qāsim 189, 197, 199–200, 202
Bynon, J. 145, 153–4, 179

Cadamosto, Portuguese traveller 26–7, 82n.
Caillié, René 119
camels, use of 29, 81, 91–2, 118–19, 179
caravans:
  guides (*takshīf*) 6, 33, 152–3, 176, 249–50
  and siting of towns vii–viii

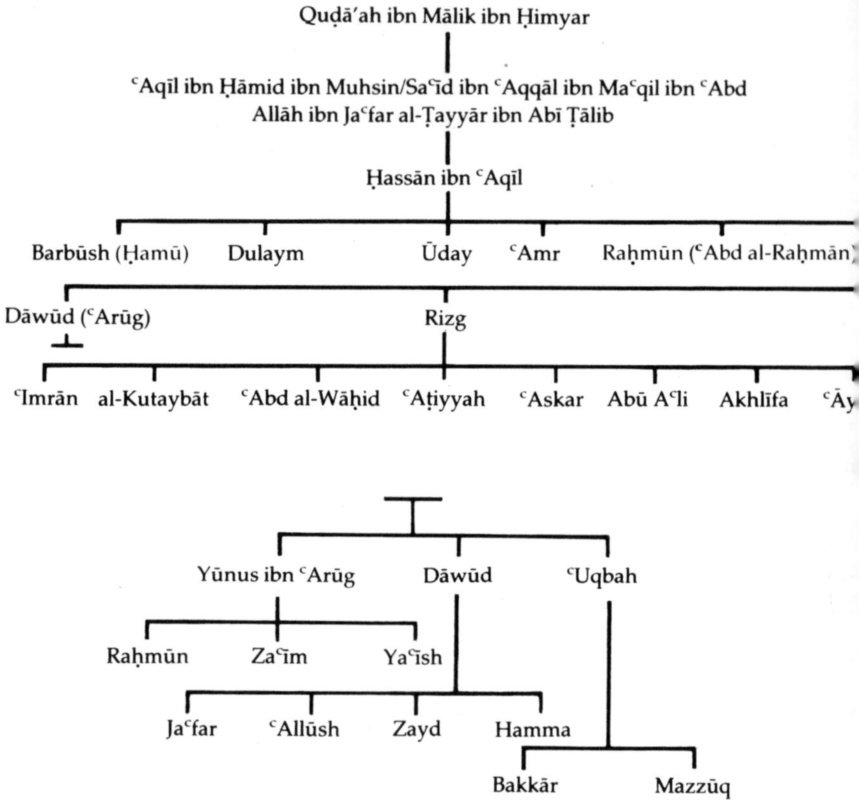

Lineages of the Awlād Ḥassān

These lineages are not definitive and are to a large extent based on the information furnished in *al-Ḥaswah al-Baysāniyyah fi'l-Ansāb al-Ḥassāniyyah* written by Shaykh Muḥammad Ṣāliḥ ibn ʿAbd al-Wahhāb al-Nāṣirī, who lived in the Mauritanian Hodh in the last century.